MORE SCRAMBLES IN THE CANADIAN ROCKIES

3RD EDITION

ANDREW NUGARA

RMB

RMB | Rocky Mountain Books Ltd.
rmbooks.com
@rmbooks
facebook.com/rmbooks

Cataloguing data available from Library and Archives
Canada
ISBN 978-1-77160-200-6 (softcover)
ISBN 978-1-77160-201-3 (electronic)

Front cover: Nicole Lisafeld makes her way up Little
Lougheed.

Back cover: Marko Stavric beautifully captures the extraordinary environs of James Walker Lake, while Amelie explores
the lakeshore.

All photographs are by Andrew Nugara unless otherwise
noted.

Printed and bound in Canada by Friesens

Distributed in Canada by Heritage Group Distribution and in
the U.S. by Publishers Group West

For information on purchasing bulk quantities of this book,
or to obtain media excerpts or invite the author to speak at
an event, please visit rmbooks.com and select the "Contact
Us" tab.

RMB | Rocky Mountain Books is dedicated to the environ-
ment and committed to reducing the destruction of old-
growth forests. Our books are produced with respect for the
future and consideration for the past.

We acknowledge the financial support of the Government
of Canada through the Canada Book Fund and the Canada
Council for the Arts, and of the province of British Columbia
through the British Columbia Arts Council and the Book
Publishing Tax Credit.

Disclaimer

The actions described in this book may be considered inher-
ently dangerous activities. Individuals undertake these activities at their own risk. The information put forth in this guide
has been collected from a variety of sources and is not guaranteed to be completely accurate or reliable. Many conditions
and some information may change owing to weather and
numerous other factors beyond the control of the authors
and publishers. Individuals or groups must determine the
risks, use their own judgment, and take full responsibility for
their actions. Do not depend on any information found in
this book for your own personal safety. Your safety depends
on your own good judgment based on your skills, education,
and experience.

It is up to the users of this guidebook to acquire the necessary skills for safe experiences and to exercise caution in
potentially hazardous areas. The authors and publishers of
this guide accept no responsibility for your actions or the
results that occur from another's actions, choices, or judg-
ments. If you have any doubt as to your safety or your ability to attempt anything described in this guidebook, do not
attempt it.

Internet resources such as the Dafferns' Kananaskis Trails
blog, kananaskisblog.com, describe many recent updates and
changes. It may be wise to do some web research on the mountain you intend to ascend, before you go.

In memory of Rick Collier,
a Canadian climbing legend, humanitarian, and inspirational leader –
a true role model for us all.

The spectacular view of Mount Birdwood and the Birdwood lakes as seen from the summit of "Smutwood Peak."
Photo: Zeljko Kozomara

From the Odlum/Loomis col, watching the sun set over a blanket of clouds.

THE FLOODS OF JUNE 2013

As many know or will remember, the Canadian Rockies, generally most places in and around Canmore and downstream of Canmore, were dealt a serious blow by nature starting on June 20, 2013. Heavy rain caused many creeks and rivers to flood their banks, destroying roads and property, wiping out trails and changing the landscape in significant ways.

Every effort has been made to describe specific changes where the environment has been altered by the floods to the point where route descriptions may have to be drastically altered or revised.

Unfortunately it is an extremely difficult task to retrace every route in the book and many areas remained closed to the public long after the floods, making it impossible to assess any damage and/or changes. Therefore, there may be situations where sections of the routes described in this book will no longer work. Be prepared to improvise if necessary. This really emphasizes the need for all mountain travellers to develop their route-finding skills, map-reading and GPS use and to be self-sufficient in the mountains.

CONTENTS

PREFACE

Thanks in large part to Alan Kane and his outstanding guidebook *Scrambles in the Canadian Rockies*, my life changed in a way I least expected, in July of 2001. That was when my brother Mark dragged me up Grizzly Peak via the route described in Kane's book. Though the experience initially left me wanting nothing more than to sit at home with a good book instead of repeating the ordeal, I did return to try another scramble, and another, and in short order Mark and I were both completely hooked. From then on, a trip to the beautiful mountains of the Canadian Rockies became a weekly ritual. We later took an avalanche safety course, a snow-and-ice weekend and an introductory rock-climbing course to better prepare ourselves for more challenging objectives. Through it all, though, scrambling, or unroped climbing, remained the primary focus of our trips.

By the time we had completed about half the scrambles in Alan's book, we started to become more and more interested in ascending mountains that were not in the book, and thus there often was no route description available. We found the experiences to be challenging and enormously gratifying (especially if we were able to make it to the top!). In time, we had built up a small collection of ascents and Mark suggested that I compile the information into a sequel to Kane's book. Once started, the book pretty much wrote itself – after all, the mountains are always there; all we had to do was find an interesting route up each one. I was also lucky enough to receive invaluable route information and advice from other scramblers, which made the task of ascending each mountain that much easier.

If you are new to the hobby of scrambling, it is strongly recommended that you pick up a copy of Alan Kane's *Scrambles in the Canadian Rockies* and complete a number of the easy and moderate ascents described there before tackling trips in this book. This is not at all to suggest that the ascents described here are of greater difficulty than the ones in Kane's book. In fact, I would say that, in general, the scrambling in this volume is easier. I would also say, however, that the ascents in this book involve longer approaches and perhaps require a little more physical stamina. In addition, many of these scrambles take you far from the road and have a remote feel to them. More than likely, you or your party will be alone throughout the ascent, with help a long way off.

Opposite: Fun scrambling up the main ascent gully on Vimy Peak.

PREFACE TO THE THIRD EDITION

The first edition of *More Scrambles in the Canadian Rockies* was focused on areas around Canmore and everything south of there. For the second edition my goal was to fill in as many blanks in those regions as possible and to start to explore north of Canmore. This third edition is a continuation of the second, with an emphasis on what many describe as "one of the most scenic drives in the world," Highway 93 North, the Icefields Parkway, between Lake Louise and Jasper. I concentrated on the south section of the highway, between Lake Louise and Saskatchewan River Crossing, but also included several new trips near the world-famous Columbia Icefield.

There are 41 new scrambles in this edition, of which a few of my favourites include "Carthew Minor," "Noseeum Peak," "Molarstone Mountain," Mount Jimmy Simpson, "Jimmy Junior," "Chimper Peak," "The Onion," Silverhorn Mountain and the "North Towers of Mount Saskatchewan." Here is the complete list of all the new trips in this volume:

- "Carthew Minor"
- "Big Bend Peak"
- "Boundary Peak"
- Bow Peak
- "Buffalo (Bison) Peak"
- "Buller Creek Peak"
- "Chimper Peak"
- Chinook Peak
- "Cloudy Ridge Junior"
- Crowfoot Mountain
- "Deadman Peak"
- "Devil's Thumb"
- "Dundy Peak"
- Emerald Peak
- "Headwall Peak"
- Hillcrest Mountain
- Isola Peak
- "Jimmy Junior"
- "Little Lougheed"
- "Little Temple"
- Lys Ridge (north ridge route)
- Lys Ridge (Ruby Lake route)
- "Molarstone Mountain"
- Mount Jimmy Simpson
- Mount Lillian (via Buller Pass)
- Mount Lillian (via Upper Galatea Lake)
- "Mount Racehorse"
- Mount Richards (north face route)
- "Mount Roberta"
- "Mount Saskatchewan Junior I"
- "North Towers of Mount Saskatchewan"
- "Noseeum Peak"
- "Ochre Spring Peak"
- "Packenham Junior"
- Pulpit Peak
- Pyriform Mountain
- "Racehorse Peak"
- "Rawson Lake Ridge"
- Silverhorn Mountain
- "The Onion"
- "Top Hat"
- Wasatch Mountain

ACKNOWLEDGEMENTS

Of course, I am once again indebted to Alan Kane, whose outstanding guidebook *Scrambles in the Canadian Rockies* (now in its third edition) provided the primary inspiration for the original sequel and both new editions of *More Scrambles*. Kane's book is the scrambler's bible, and everyone who aspires to ascend peaks of the Canadian Rockies should have a copy.

Gillean Daffern's current five-volume fourth edition of her *Kananaskis Country Trail Guide* is another extremely well written and invaluable resource. The ragged edges of both volumes of the third edition in my possession attest to how much I have used them over the years. My new-edition copies are likewise starting to show considerable wear.

Destined to be a classic set of guidebooks is David P. Jones's *The Climber's Guide to the Rocky Mountains of Canada* (four volumes projected). I salivated over the first instalment, *Rockies Central*, for months and have done several great routes described therein. Thank you, Mr. Jones.

In addition to those who provided ideas, route information and photos for the first two editions, my sincerest thanks to Bob Spirko, Dinah Kruze, Rafal Kazmierczak, Vern Dewit, Graeme Pole, Rick Collier, Marko Stavric, Amélie Doucet, Sonny Bou, Gillean and Tony Daffern, Zeljko Kozomara, Dave McMurray, Eric Coulthard, Dr. Ben Nearingburg, Steven Song, Mike Potter, Geoff Hardy, Josée Ménard, Fabrice Carrara, Wietse Bijlsma, Matthew Hobbs, Matthew Clay, Doug Lutz, Geoff Hardy, Allan Truedino, Calvin Damen, John Martin, So Nakagawa, Marta Wojnarowska, Kerry Vizbar, Kevin Barton and Nicole Lisafeld for their invaluable contributions to this new edition.

The folks at Rocky Mountain Books have all been nothing but delightful to work with, as usual. A huge thank you to publisher Don Gorman, art director Chyla Cardinal and editor Joe Wilderson for all their hard work.

Eternal thanks to my family: Mum, Larry, Johnny, Mark, Keri, Rogan, Kian, Skye, Dad and Lori for always supporting and encouraging me.

As with the first two *More Scrambles*, this new edition would not have been possible were it not for my brother Mark, who introduced me to scrambling, encouraged me to author all three editions and accompanied me on the majority of the ascents. As well as a terrific scrambling partner, Mark has been an incredible source of inspiration to me. Not for a single second has he ever allowed his condition (he is legally blind) to deter him from his enjoyment of the mountains. I will always be his #1 fan. Thanks, bro!

INTRODUCTION

It's been 15 years since I completed my first scramble, and the Canadian Rockies have yet to lose a single ounce (gram, I guess, since we are beautifully metric up here) of their power over me. I continue to be captivated and mesmerized by the awe-inspiring beauty of their craggy peaks, serene and hypnotically colourful lakes, flowery meadows, dense forests, powerful rivers, stunning glaciers and incredible variety of wildlife. There is something new and different and intriguing at every turn in our mountains and it is a true privilege to have access to that on our very doorstep.

The Canadian Rockies still enjoy an isolated and untouched feeling that is woefully absent in other major mountainous areas around the globe, while at the same time being easily accessible to anyone.

Our national and provincial parks, appreciating the importance of conserving this environment, have done an excellent job in limiting human development in the mountains. Of course, they can do little to control the number of people visiting the mountains and thus it becomes increasingly important for all who venture into this terrain to be stewards of that environment.

Enjoy the mountains, appreciate them, cherish them, be thankful for the opportunities we are afforded in having access to them, and above all take care of them. How we treat the environment defines us as a species as much as how we treat each other does. Throughout history we've failed consistently on the latter; let's not do so on the former as well.

The fantastic view of Mount Hector and "Noseeum Lake" from the ridge of "Noseeum Peak." Photo: Zeljko Kozomara

SCRAMBLING IN THE CANADIAN ROCKIES

Scrambling basically means getting to the top a mountain without technical gear (i.e., without ropes, climbing protection etc.) or technical climbing techniques, though the occasional use of climbing moves may be required for particularly difficult sections or manoeuvres. In the strictest sense of the term, scrambling involves the use of the hands to ascend or descend terrain. That is what distinguishes it from steep hiking. However, anyone who has completed a number of scrambles in the Canadian Rockies knows full well that the overwhelming majority of scrambles involve a significant amount of hiking and many never require use of hands. Thus, some of the scrambles that earn an "easy" rating could probably be more accurately described as steep hikes. Regardless of the terminology you use, though, scrambling can be one of the most rewarding ways to enjoy the beauty of the natural world that surrounds us, and you get a physical workout that is second to none at the same time.

Scrambling has a few advantages over other forms of mountain recreation. Since the sport is non-technical and doesn't require the use of rope, scramblers can move very fast, covering considerable horizontal and vertical distances in a short amount of time. A quick perusal of the estimated round-trip times of the scrambles in this book will immediately reveal why this is important.

Though all human activity in the mountains has negative impacts on the environment and wildlife, scramblers and hikers can keep those impacts to a bare minimum. More so than most other groups of mountain users, scramblers leave the environment in exactly the same condition they found it in – no pitons, bolts, tattered webbing or slings, rappel stations or other climbing paraphernalia. No one will ever clear-cut a large section of land for scramblers as the ski resorts see fit to do for their customers. On the downside, the above-mentioned ability of scramblers to move fast also enables them to venture into remote areas that would otherwise be spared the detriments of human intrusion. This means scramblers and hikers simply have to be that much more cognizant of their responsibilities and obligations to leave these remote areas exactly the way they found them and make as little impact as possible while they are there.

There is no question that nine times out of ten the best view is from the top. The visual rewards of making it to the top of a mountain are often unequalled. There are few things better in life than the unobstructed view from a mountaintop on a cloudless day, be it summer, spring, autumn or winter. More than likely you will also encounter innumerable wondrous scenes and views on the way up. And every mountain is a completely unique experience, even when two trips are located very close to each other geographically.

As well, the emotional rewards of scrambling can be an end unto themselves. I don't think saying scrambling can be addictive is a misrepresentation of that word at all. I'm sure every scrambler can relive, in vivid detail, the elation of taking the final few steps to the summit of a particularly challenging or interesting mountain.

Back to reality for the final word! It cannot be stressed enough that scrambling can be extremely dangerous. If you have not done so already, please read the sections **Scrambling grades** and **Scrambling v. climbing**, on pages 13 and 21 respectively. It could save your life.

THE SCRAMBLING SEASON

The length of the true scrambling season in the Canadian Rockies can be described easily in a couple of words: "too short!" That may be a little dramatic, but out of the 12 months of the year, two will generally guarantee good scrambling (July and August), while the two months on either side of that (May/June and September/October) can be fairly reliable but hit-and-miss in some years. The "Try from (insert given month) on" labels in most of the trip introductions are general guidelines and certainly not written in stone. A long winter can push those suggestions even later into the year, and an early spring may move them forward. As well, a good period of chinook weather may render some of the peaks in the front ranges ascendable in any month of the year. I distinctly recall an early January ascent of Wendell Mountain in which I didn't have to step on a single flake of snow.

Late September in the Castle offers a surreal palette of colours, such as here on the magnificent Victoria Peak to Ridge traverse. (Photo: Vern Dewit)

In addition to weather, the scrambling season is also heavily dictated by location. As mentioned, front range peaks will come into scrambling condition much earlier than main range mountains and are more likely to benefit from chinook clearing. Highway 40 South is often the best bet for off-season ascents, whereas peaks around Lake Louise and along Highway 93 North are unlikely to become snow-free until mid-June or July.

Personally, September is my favourite month for snow-free scrambling. The days are long enough to get in a reasonably long trip; forest fire smoke is usually gone; extended periods of stable weather are common; the extraordinary fall colours come out, including yellowing larches in the latter part of the month; and there are no insects to bother you.

If you do choose to scramble as a year-round activity, here are some of the advantages and disadvantages for each season.

Summer

ADVANTAGES	DISADVANTAGES
long days	bears
warm temperatures	afternoon thunderstorms
no ticks	high water for river/creek crossings
snow-free ascents (no avalanche danger)	smoke from forest fires (depends on the year)
bike approaches are possible	

Autumn

ADVANTAGES	DISADVANTAGES
early snow enhances scenery	bears (berry season)
fantastic lighting for early-morning photos	
low water for river/creek crossings	
comfortable hiking temperatures (not too hot or too cold)	

ADVANTAGES	DISADVANTAGES
typically good weather and very few thundershowers	
no ticks	
bike approaches are still possible	
larches changing colour	

Winter

ADVANTAGES	DISADVANTAGES
gorgeous winter scenery	avalanche danger
use of snowshoes or skis is possible	travel can be more strenuous/difficult
alpenglow	cold temperatures and high wind chill
no ticks	area closures, limited access
no bears (no yelling to warn them)	short days
glissading	

Spring

ADVANTAGES	DISADVANTAGES
less snow, making for easier ascents and great scenery (late spring)	bears come out of hibernation
	ticks
	high water for river/creek crossings
	area closures, limited access
	high season for avalanches (February, March, April)

Don't let the number of (or lack of) items in either column deter you from going out in any given season (specifically spring). In my opinion the single best advantage from all these lists is the stunning scenery of winter – it's simply unbeatable!

PARK PASSES AND PERMITS

It is necessary to purchase a day pass, multi-day pass or yearly pass when entering and stopping in any national park in Canada. Specifically for this book, that means all ascents in:

- Waterton (except for Lakeview Ridge, "Rogan Peak," "Cloudy Ridge Junior", Vimy Peak and Sofa Mountain)
- Banff and Highway 93 South
- Lake Louise and Yoho
- Highway 93 North

A park pass in not needed for ascents in:

- The Castle
- Crowsnest
- All quadrants of Kananaskis

In addition, if you intend to backcountry camp within a national park, a permit ($10 per person/per night) is also required. Stop in at or call a Visitor Centre to inquire. Roadside campgrounds are available on a first come, first serve basis.

SCRAMBLING GRADES

The three scrambling grades in this book and Alan Kane's do not conform to a standardized system such as YDS (Yosemite Decimal System). Trying to draw parallels between scrambling grades and other systems is often confusing and self-defeating. However, scrambling grades in this book are quite simple and after doing a few trips of varying grades, most scramblers will get a feel for what

Examples from Mount Dungarvan of the three grades of scrambling, starring Mark Nugara, James Wright, Dan Cote and Andrew Nugara! Left: Easy; middle: Moderate; right: Difficult.

constitutes an Easy, Moderate and Difficult scramble. Note that all the grades are only applicable when conditions are DRY.

- **Easy:** mostly hiking, with potentially long, steep sections but requiring little to no use of hands; little exposure; and often not on maintained trails. Not surprisingly, most easy scrambles are not scrambles at all but are mostly steep off-trail hikes. "Big Bend Peak" and the north side of Loaf Mountain are prime examples.
- **Moderate:** frequent use of handholds required; possible exposure but not usually enough to be a "death fall." Some route-finding involved. Examples would be Anderson Peak and Silverhorn Mountain.
- **Difficult:** much use of handholds required; sections may be steep, loose and exposed, or rock could be smooth and downsloping. Fall distance may be significant enough to be fatal. Route-finding skills are generally necessary to determine the most practical and feasible way for specific sections. Less experienced parties may prefer the security of a climbing rope for short sections, and being off-route may well require technical climbing. Anyone with vertigo or a fear of heights should avoid scrambles rated difficult. Examples are Mount Dungarvan and Pulpit Peak via Margaret Lake.

Some difficult scrambles earn the qualifier "a climber's scramble." These are for experienced scramblers who are comfortable with extended sections of very exposed scrambling and the occasional lower 5th class climbing move. Examples are the north ridge of Mount Richards and the west ridge of Mount Baldy's west peak.

Always remember that regardless of the scrambling grade, scramble routes become much more difficult when they are wet, snowy or icy. Many scrambles are then climbs and mountaineering ascents that require technical climbing gear and the use of anchors and belay techniques. **These scramble ratings are applicable only in optimal conditions: dry and free of snow.** Some years, dry conditions may not even occur on some routes.

TRIP DURATIONS

The suggested round-trip times are based on personal experience. They assume a certain level of fitness. Adverse or snowy conditions may lengthen the times needed to complete a trip beyond the suggested maximum. Although it is possible to gain up to 600 vertical metres an hour on some slopes (the start of Mount Ogden comes to mind), 300 m is an average amount of vertical progress for one hour. Also, as a very general rule, the descent time for most trips will usually be one-half to three-quarters of the ascent time (I typically budget for two-thirds, e.g., 6 hours up equates to 4 hours down). It is always a good idea to monitor your ascent time and choose a turnaround time if necessary.

FOOTWEAR

Boots

The best footwear for scrambling is still a pair of sturdy leather boots with a lugged Vibram sole and a half or three-quarter shank for rigidity. This type of footwear offers the best level of comfort, support, protection and durability that will be required for the enormous amount of scree bashing you will undertake as a scrambler in the Canadian Rockies. Running shoes and ultra-light hiking boots are unsuitable, giving too little ankle support and protection on talus slopes. They also wear out quickly. Some scramblers are more comfortable wearing full-shank (completely rigid) mountaineering or ice-climbing boots.

Approach/climbing shoes

This type of footwear is becoming increasingly popular with scramblers and climbers. Though there are many advantages to scrambling in approach shoes, there are also a couple of major drawbacks. And of course, approach shoes come in many styles and varieties, each with their own set of pros and cons. Note that these are *not* rock shoes, which are intended for technical rock climbing and fit the foot very tightly.

Obviously, low-cut shoes offer no ankle support at all. Many people note that even high-cut ones offer only negligible support, though high-cut shoes will at least offer some protection (if only minimal) from rocks striking your ankle bones. More important than ankle support to most people, though, is the thickness and material of the soles. High-end approach shoes often have thin, sticky soles that are extremely "grippy" on all kinds of surfaces. These are the closest things to rock shoes. Scramblers can often feel very confident on high-angle, exposed terrain with these types of shoes. This is especially noticeable on steep limestone slabs such as are common in the Canadian Rockies. Often, handholds on limestone slabs are very small, if you can find any at all, and thin-soled approach shoes allow the scrambler solid

and reliable foot placement when handholds are less than bomber. You will note that there are many routes in this edition for which approach shoes are recommended, and in my opinion these thin-soled shoes will serve you best. Personally, I bring my approach shoes for anything in the Crowsnest, where steep slabs are common.

The downside to these types of shoes is the lack of support and protection they offer. If you do not have strong ankles, wearing approach shoes may increase your chance of ankle-related injuries. Of course, it may also improve your ankle strength and therefore make you less prone to ankle injury – roll the dice!

Approach shoes can also wear out very quickly, especially if you use them on scree and rubble slopes. Generally, the thicker the soles, the less effective on challenging terrain but the more durable overall. One option is to take hiking boots for those situations and approach shoes for the more difficult terrain. This means you'll have to attach your boots to your backpack and handle the extra weight, but it's a small price to pay to have the benefits of both types of footwear.

The decision to use approach shoes regularly is very much a personal one. Some people will fall in love with them (as I did until I rolled my ankle!), while others will have no use for them whatsoever. There are definitely worth a try, however.

HIKING POLES

Hiking poles almost seem mandatory for scramblers these days. Descending steep terrain is often much easier with poles and they also can take pressure off your knees (increasingly important as you age). As well, poles are invaluable for river crossings. The only downside of hiking poles is that they can sometimes get in the way when scrambling up or down rock bands that require the unimpeded use of both hands. In such cases, it is best to put the poles in or on the side of your pack so that both your hands are free. I never leave the parking lot without a set of hiking poles.

CLOTHING

Dressing for success is very important in the mountains and layering is the key. Typically, for the upper body, those layers include a synthetic, wicking base layer, an insulating mid-layer (can be fleece) and a waterproof, breathable shell or jacket.

A lightweight down jacket is also always in my pack, for those chillier summit stays.

Lower-body coverage is a little simpler. Lightweight, breathable synthetic pants are usually the weapon of choice, although I love wearing fleece pants year-round (must be the Englander in me!). Long underwear may be necessary for late season ascents.

Other items that should always be readily available in your backpack are a raincoat, windpants, toque, neck gaiter and gloves. In regards to the weather (which is often very unpredictable), it is far better to be overequipped than underequipped. I'll never forget a July ascent of "Noseeum Peak," where less than a minute after I reached the summit it started to snow! Thankfully all of the above were in my pack, so I was able to sit at the top, in a whiteout, by myself, getting snowed on. It doesn't get any better than that, does it?!

Lastly, and perhaps it goes without saying but should be said anyway: avoid wearing anything made from cotton. Cotton will not keep you warm and in fact can lead to hypothermia if it gets wet and remains on you.

OTHER GEAR

In addition to extra clothing and the items mentioned above, your backpack should also include sunblock, sunglasses with 100 per cent UV protection, a small first aid kit, a headlamp and extra batteries, a lighter or matches in case you need to start a fire, a compass, a map of the area you are scrambling in, toilet paper and a plastic bag to pack it out, and any form of technology you may be using (see the **Technology** section on p17). Of course, it goes without saying that food and water also are going to be coming with you!

MAPS

Although technology is quite convincingly replacing paper maps for navigation, it is still strongly recommended that you carry a topographical map of the area in which you will be scrambling or hiking. I take a map on all trips, regardless of whether I am familiar with the terrain or not. You never know when you might want to take an alternative descent route or change your objective, and sometimes only a map that reveals the exact lay of the land will tell you if your new plan is feasible or not.

At present, there are two brands of maps available that are useful for these scrambles: NTS maps from Natural Resources Canada, which cover all areas of the Canadian Rockies; and Gem Trek maps, which are specific to popular outdoor recreation areas. Both are available at Mountain Equipment Co-op and Maptown in Calgary as well as other outdoor-sports retailers. The following NTS maps are specific to this guidebook and should be in the possession of all who use routes covered in this book:

- 82 H/04 Waterton Lakes
- 82 G/01 Sage Creek
- 82 G/08 Beaver Mines
- 82 G/10 Crowsnest
- 82 G/16 Maycroft
- 82 J/01 Langford
- 82 J/07 Mount Head
- 82 J/10 Mount Rae
- 82 J/11 Kananaskis Lakes
- 82 J/14 Spray Lakes Reservoir
- 82 J/15 Bragg Creek
- 82 O/03 Canmore
- 82 O/04 Banff
- 82 N/01 Mount Goodsir
- 82 N/07 Golden
- 82 N/08 Lake Louise
- 82 N/09 Hector Lake
- 82 N/10 Blaeberry River
- 82 N/15 Mistaya Lake
- 82 N/16 Siffleur River
- 82 C/03 Columbia Icefield

Most NTS maps have contour lines that represent 40 m changes in elevation. Useful as this information is, it is important that you not rely completely on the relative spacing of contour lines to choose a line of ascent or descent. An apparently low-angled route could be interrupted by a 20 m vertical rock band which will not show on the map. Neither are these maps water- or tear-resistant, so it is a good idea to carry them in a plastic bag. The red-lined map reproductions in this volume are taken from NTS maps, so using the actual maps in conjunction with the photos in the book is ideal. Please note, however, that the red-lined topographical maps display the general routes to the summits and should be used in a general context only, not a specific one.

Gem Trek maps provide another option for the majority of trips in this book. Most Gem Trek maps have contour lines that represent 25 m changes in elevation and therefore contain a little more detail than their NTS counterparts. However, once again you should be careful not to rely on contour lines alone to make a judgment about a route. In truth, a map displaying that kind of detail simply doesn't exist at present. After all, a day of scrambling could come to an abrupt end upon reaching a vertical rock band of no more than 2 m if there are no good hand or footholds – and there's no way a 2 m rock band is going to appear on any map! Gem Trek maps are quite detailed and display both maintained and unmaintained trails, official and unofficial peaks, and other points of interest. Though there may be minor differences when compared to their NTS counterparts, Gem Trek maps can also be used in conjunction with the red-lined photos in this book. Many Gem Trek maps are water- and tear-resistant and therefore very durable. The following Gem Treks are very useful for ascents in this book:

- Waterton National Park
- Highwood and Cataract Creek
- Kananaskis Lakes
- Canmore and Kananaskis
- Bragg Creek
- Banff and Mount Assiniboine
- Kootenay National Park
- Lake Louise and Yoho
- Bow Lake and Saskatchewan Crossing
- Columbia Icefield

At the time of printing, there was no Gem Trek map available for the Castle area.

Regardless which brand of map you are using, it will show blue grid lines on the actual map and blue grid reference numbers on the sides of the map – the key to identifying a specific location on the map. On most maps, one square represents 1 square kilometre, though some may be 2 square kilometres. Grid reference (GR) numbers contain six digits. The first two indicate the west/east coordinate (located at the top and bottom of the map), and the third digit is an approximation of the distance east of the first two, with the square being divided into ten equal divisions (100 m each). For example, if the first three digits are 835, find 83 on the top or bottom of the map; the 5 indicates that the point you want is halfway (500 m) between 83 and 84. The fourth, fifth and sixth digits operate in

exactly the same way, but refer to the south/north coordinate on the sides of the map.

As we move to a paperless society, there is now the option to buy CD-ROMS that contain topographical maps along with software that enables you to zoom in on a specific area and print a small map just for that trip. This technology is still relatively new and some of the maps might not contain the detail you would like, but improvements are being made every day and the aforementioned problem should soon be solved.

TECHNOLOGY

The days of navigating mountain terrain with a map and compass – and a healthy dose of fear that you may get lost and never see humanity again – are fading rapidly, if not completely gone. From an idealistic standpoint, everyone would know how to get around using these "old-school" (but also "good-school") methods. But realistically, advances in technology have rendered them, if not obsolete or undesirable, simply impractical. In addition to a map and compass, my backpack or person now routinely carries three additional forms of navigational technologies: a handheld GPS, a SPOT device and my cellphone.

GPS

The Global Positioning System has revolutionized the way we move around this planet. GPS uses satellites orbiting the Earth to triangulate your exact position, down to the nearest metre. It is remarkably accurate and reliable these days. Some form of built-in GPS is now the standard on many cars, cellphones and even cameras.

Most mountain enthusiasts now carry a handheld GPS. While older units were limited to giving location coordinates (GR numbers or latitude–longitude coordinates), with some route-mapping features, the newer models will pretty much do everything except make your breakfast! Most GPS units now show your exact location and elevation on a topographical map, allow you to download routes and waypoints into the unit, and enable you to access geocaching information.

In regards to elevation readings, most current handheld GPS units could be off by as much as 10 m in either direction. At the summit of Lys Ridge, for example, Dave McMurray, Jollin Charest and the author recorded elevations of 2526 m, 2524 m and our respective GPSes. In other words, ... the readings on your unit as gospel – ...n't break out that bottle of champagne you always carry in your backpack – when at the summit of some unknown mountain your GPS reads 3353 m or over (the infamous 11,000-foot mark!).

SPOT

SPOT stands for Satellite PersOnal Tracker and has widely become the weapon of choice for location tracking and for calling for help if necessary. The device uses a GPS signal to communicate with satellites and so cellphone coverage is not required. You can also use SPOT to notify friends and family of your GPS position and status, mark waypoints, or track your progress on Google Maps. The device is extremely light and easy to use and the yearly fee is a very small price to pay for the peace of mind and access to help that SPOT gives you.

Up to late 2016 I had yet to use my SPOT for an emergency, but I will never go into the mountains without it anymore. SPOT can save your life – period!

Cellphones

I obstinately denied myself a cellphone ("mobile phone" for all my dashing relatives in England!) until 2010, but now that I have the little gizmo, it's hard to imagine life without it. I likewise denied myself the use of that phone in the mountains until late 2013, but now that I do use it,…well, you get the picture!

Very simply, the cellphone has singlehandedly replaced maps, a compass and for some even a separate GPS unit. Utilizing satellite signals rather than cellular ones, the *Topo Maps Canada* app on my phone shows a topographical map and pinpoints my exact location on that map, all far out of the range that any cellphone signal can reach. Newer versions of this app include trail and mountain routes and greater map detail.

As well, cellphone signals are now covering areas that were previously "dark." I've been shocked and pleasantly surprised on many occasions to find myself "FaceTiming" my nephews and niece from atop some fairly remote mountains.

The major limitations of cellphones in the mountains, and especially in regards to winter scrambling, is cold weather. The lithium-ion battery that most cellphones use for power drain much faster in cold weather. In fact, even with a full charge your cellphone can lose power within minutes in very cold temperatures – a compelling argument for never relying solely on a phone in the mountains. Carry your phone as close to your body as possible to keep it warm when the temperature drops below zero degrees Celsius.

New technologies, such as dongle devices for smartphones (check out Bad-Elf.com) and additional global satellite navigation systems (e.g., Galileo), are further increasing mobile connectivity to unprecedented levels. The day when the cellphone in your pocket will have the capabilities of all the above devices is close at hand, if not already here.

Apps

In addition to the *Topo Maps Canada* app, here are a few other apps you may find useful (as of mid-2016):

1. *ViewRanger* – similar to *Topo Maps Canada* but also allows you to upload and download routes from and to your phone.
2. *SunCalc* – great app that displays sunrise, sunset and the path of the sun on a topo map, for any day of the year. Very useful in helping to decide what time of day and what time of year to do routes in order to get the best sun.
3. *Accuweather* – weather forecasts for all mountain areas pertinent to this book.
4. *Avalanche Canada* (by Avalanche Canada) – if you are scrambling in the winter, this is an important app to acquire and use.

Conclusion

As wonderful as the technological world can be, overwhelming is also often an appropriate adjective to describe it. Embracing technology is a good thing, but relying on it completely may not be. Self-reliance in the mountains is paramount, and that includes the ability to navigate the terrain without the latest gizmo or app.

Personally, I love all the new technologies, but with all the new tools available to me, a paper map and compass have been, presently are and probably always will be in my backpack on every trip I take into the mountains. As stated, "old-school but good-school"!

MOUNTAIN-BIKE APPROACHES

Like most of the trips in Alan Kane's book, bike approaches are not feasible or permissible for the majority of the trips in this volume. There are notable exceptions, however, and for many of the mountains in south Kananaskis that are on the Continental Divide a bike is almost necessary. Most of these bike approaches are on old logging roads, which vary from smooth and gentle to steep and rocky. Often you may encounter, on the same trail, terrain that is awesome for bikes and terrain that is terrible for bikes. In addition the trails are often interrupted by river and creek crossings. Investing in a pair of hip waders is recommended. You can do the entire approach wearing them, saving time and energy when you arrive at a crossing. The waders can then be left with your bike when that part of the trip is over. A pannier on your bike provides a good place to securely fasten your scrambling boots while you are riding.

Below are trips for which a bike is strongly recommended, as well as trips where one is suggested.

Strongly recommended
- Vimy Peak/Ridge
- Mount Loomis via Loomis Creek Trail
- Mount McPhail
- Mount Muir
- Mount Strachan
- Mount Armstrong
- Threepoint Mountain
- Mount Rose
- Mount Burns
- Mount Fortune
- Mount Turbulent

Suggested
- "Deadman Peak"
- "Racehorse Peak"
- Chinook Peak
- "Mount Racehorse"
- Newman Peak
- Victoria Peak
- Victoria Ridge
- Pincher Ridge – centre and south peaks
- Loaf Mountain – both routes
- Middle Kootenay Pass – all routes
- Andy Good Peak
- Mount Coulthard
- Mount McLaren

- Mount Bishop
- Snow Peak
- "Piggy Plus"
- Wind Mountain
- Ribbon Peak
- Eagle Mountain
- Mount Howard Douglas

WINTER SCRAMBLING

Scrambling during the winter months or in winter conditions can often provide an infinitely more rewarding experience, both visually and aesthetically, than the same trip in summer. Of course, winter trips are also infinitely more dangerous, and the appropriate training and knowledge are absolutely essential should you choose to venture out in winter conditions.

The line between scrambling and mountaineering can be a blurry one. Mountaineering usually implies glacier travel, including roped and often belayed climbing using snow pickets, ice screws and other methods of belaying. These techniques are far beyond the scope of this book. To learn more about mountaineering, pick up the latest edition of *Mountaineering: The Freedom of the Hills* or Craig Connally's *The Mountaineering Handbook* and seek training from a professional.

Winter scrambling – or perhaps more accurately, snow and ice travel that is not mountaineering – usually requires only an ice axe and maybe crampons and of course knowledge of how to use both. Learning how to self-arrest with an ice axe is a skill that no one travelling in the winter should be without. Self-arrest techniques can be learned from books, but they must be practised so that they become intuitive and reflexive. If you have never done a self-arrest, don't expect to be able to successfully execute one when required.

The ability to accurately assess snow conditions and avalanche potential are also skills imperative for safe winter travel. Even with these skills, many an experienced mountaineer or winter traveller has perished in an avalanche – very simply, avalanches are that unpredictable. Taking an avalanche safety course is absolutely essential. Wear an avalanche beacon; take along a shovel and probe and know how to use them. The best way to avoid being caught in an avalanche is to stay away from terrain that has the potential to slide. Again, this knowledge is best gained from taking a course – the

Views such as this one on "Smutwood Peak" are the reward for winter scrambling. The price for that view is having to carry crampons, an ice axe, snowshoes, avalanche gear and possibly climbing equipment – in my opinion a very small price!

modest fee for such training could save your life. It may seem obvious, but travelling alone in suspect areas is downright foolish – who's going to dig you out when you're lying helpless beneath a metre of hard-packed snow? And, as always, let someone know where you are going.

Although officially winter lasts from December 21 and March 20, from a practical standpoint it can extend far beyond those limits. One can encounter winter-like conditions in any month of the year, but November to May is a more reasonable guideline than December to March. Location also plays an important role. As a general rule, farther west means more snow. The Continental Divide holds snow far longer into the season than the Front Ranges do, and if you're

looking for less or no snow, the Eastern Slopes is the place to go.

Mountains of the Front Ranges often make the best choices for winter ascents, primarily because, at any given time of the year, they can be relatively snow-free and have the least avalanche danger. Chinooks can quickly clear snow off these peaks, rendering them far less dangerous than their counterparts farther west.

Front Range mountains are also the best choice when areas farther west are socked in. It is not at all uncommon for heavy clouds to completely dissipate upon reaching the Front Ranges, granting clear skies to those in the area.

Those with cross-country skis or AT skis – multi-purpose skis that can be used as either cross-country (heel free) or downhill (heel locked in) – and a modicum of skiing ability can also complete the approach (or the entire ascent) on skis. Again, ski mountaineering falls outside the scope of this book. Ski mountaineering guru Chic Scott has written several excellent guidebooks on this subject.

Snowshoes are another terrific option for a mode of travel during the snow months. Two new RMB books have just become available for those wanting to get out on snowshoes: *Snowshoeing in the Canadian Rockies* and *A Beginner's Guide to Snowshoeing in the Canadian Rockies*. The former book is well suited to scramblers looking to get out in winter.

SCRAMBLING vs. CLIMBING

The line between scrambling and climbing is even blurrier than the one between scrambling and mountaineering. Some people can scramble up terrain that others will require a rope to ascend. Certainly, a traditional climber who regularly manages 5.10 and above would more than likely be quite comfortable on low class 5 terrain without a rope. Conversely, someone with very little experience could be completely out of their element on class 3 terrain. This is where self-awareness and the ability to objectively assess your own climbing ability are so vitally important. Just because your best friend or some Joe Schmo in front of you scrambled easily up a steep section doesn't mean you should. A scramble for some might be a climb for others and vice versa.

Ego and pride can be your worst enemies in the mountains. Don't do anything that is clearly beyond your level of comfort, even if everyone else has done it. This seems obvious, but it's amazing what people will push themselves to do in order

This short but steep step on Devil's Head puts the ascent right on the border between scrambling and climbing. Getting up it was tricky but not terribly difficult. However, most people would want to rappel down the step, and thus the trip is not included in this guidebook.

not to appear weak, nervous or scared in front of their friends. Better weak than dead!

Downclimbing is one of the true tests of scrambling ability. It is also the most consistent weakness of scramblers in general. A good friend of mine taught me a technique where you ascend a few steps and then downclimb it right away. Then climb higher and downclimb that section also. Repeat this until you get to the top. Yes, it's time-consuming, but it's almost guaranteed you'll have no problem downclimbing the whole section on return, and you'll improve your downclimbing confidence in the process. All the top-notch scramblers I know are also great downclimbers. If possible, find some time to practise this vital skill in a safe environment.

Scrambles in this edition (and also in Alan Kane's book) that receive the qualifier "a climber's scramble" do so for a very good reason. Any minor mistake or slip on one of these routes could very quickly end your life. If you are not comfortable with exposure, very steep terrain, loose rock and difficult and exposed downclimbing, climber's scrambles are best avoided until you gain more experience and comfort with those situations.

Below is a list of the most difficult and dangerous of the scrambles in the book (in alphabetical order). Most of these scrambles involve not only steep and exposed scrambling but also a great deal of route-finding and decision-making. Thus their route descriptions are more general in nature. For example, a detailed description of Mount Dungarvan's south ridge would not only be complicated and difficult to follow, but may also detract from the route-finding experience itself.

Scramblers who tackle the routes below should be confident in their abilities in all aspects of scrambling. For your own safety, it is also recommended that these routes be done in pairs or groups and not as solo trips. Wearing approach shoes (see page 15) for the difficult sections is rarely a bad idea. Also, ropes, harnesses, a small amount of climbing protection and rappel gear would not be out of place in your pack for these trips.

- Mount Baldy – west ridge of west peak
- Mount Coulthard – west ridge
- Mount Dungarvan
- GR628936 of "Lineham Creek Peaks"
- Mount Loomis – southern outlier
- Mount Lougheed traverse
- Pulpit Peak (difficult route)

- Mount Richards (via the north ridge)
- Scarpe Mountain

ROPE

Carrying a rope is another issue that deserves some attention. By its very definition, scrambling (unroped climbing) precludes the use of rope. But this doesn't mean that a short length (10 m or so) of 8 or 9 mm rope is out of place in your backpack. It will probably stay there on every one of your trips, but unforeseen circumstances may change the nature of a trip: drifting off route, forced change of route, changing weather, wet or icy rock, a group member getting stuck on tricky or exposed terrain. These are situations where, as a last resort, it may become necessary to use a rope.

Learning how to use a rope properly (belaying, setting up anchors/protection and rappelling) are all skills that require formal training. Take advantage of the relatively small fees charged for introductory rock-climbing courses and get some professional training. You will likely never use these techniques on any of the scrambles in this book, but it is certainly comforting to possess the skills and know you will be able to use them in unforeseen or emergency situations.

Having said all of the above, one should add that a rope in your pack may lull you into a false sense of security that induces you to ascend terrain that you perhaps shouldn't. I carry a rope less and less these days, simply because experience has taught me when to back down and when the risk is acceptable and/or minimal. There is no substitute for getting old!

UNOFFICIAL, UNNAMED HIGH POINTS AND GRs

You may have noticed there are a few unnamed peaks in this book, especially in the Kananaskis and Castle regions and also along Highway 93 North. "Unnamed" is not synonymous with "not worth ascending." The process and/or criteria for naming mountains can often appear arbitrary and illogical. For example, why are the five most significant high points of the Mount McDougall range all unnamed except for Mount McDougall? McDougall isn't even the highest point of the massif. Having ascended all of them, Mark and I agreed that the most interesting and gratifying was "Kananaskis Peak" at GR345444, not McDougall.

Who wouldn't want to ascend this beauty?! "Jake Smith Peak" (right) is the highest mountain in the area and yet lacks an official name. This colourful view is from the summit of Scarpe Mountain.

Similarly, "Jake Smith Peak," in the Castle, exceeds everything in the area in height and yet has been denied an official name. The highest does not necessarily mean the best, and in the case of "Jake Smith" the scrambling on the actual peak is far from aesthetic. However, the trip as a whole is rich in exquisite scenery and views, rendering it one of my favourites in all of the Rockies.

Interestingly, six of the nine trips identified in the preface as some of my new favourites are unofficial. Don't deny yourself an enjoyable and worthwhile summit just because no one has chosen to give it an official title or it appears to be simply an insignificant high point of a larger mountain. After all, there are plenty of named and official summits out there which really aren't worth a trip up. Also, it often really is about the journey, not the destination.

HAZARDS

If you go into the mountains looking for a hazard-free environment, boy have you come to the wrong place. Rockfall that could level a small city,

weather more hostile than a chicken at a KFC convention, man- (and family-) eating bears, avalanches that can swallow large towns, insects so big they have their own dogs – we've got it ALL in the Canadian Rockies! (Although I'm not sure that a bear encounter in the mountains is any more dangerous than rush hour on Calgary's Deerfoot Trail!) All exaggerations and falsehoods aside, the hazards of scrambling are generally easy to foresee and manage and the tools to help minimize much of the risk are easy to acquire and employ: knowledge, common sense and, eventually, experience.

Rockfall

Loose rock is simply what the Canadian Rockies have been reduced to. If ascending seemingly endless and steep slopes of unstable rubble and scree and then having to dodge falling rocks from above isn't your cup of tea, choose another hobby. Unfortunately the limestone that makes up most of the rock of the Rockies does not react well to the extreme range of temperatures in this part of the world. It fractures and breaks easily, leaving behind massive areas of shattered rock – some of it fairly stable and some very unstable.

Short of wearing a full suit of armour, the most logical form of protection against rockfall is a helmet. Wearing one simply makes sense. Increased use of helmets can be seen in a significant number of sports nowadays, including biking, skiing, snowboarding and rollerblading. There are two extremes: those who never wear a helmet, and me! I've been known to don the headgear even on the simplest and most innocuous hike, and of course anything more involved means I bring a helmet and use it without question or hesitation.

A helmet will protect you if you fall or knock your head while scrambling up or down steep rock. More common, however, is the need for protection from objective hazards. The "rotten" Canadian Rockies come by that name honestly, and rockfall from above is a serious concern. Unfortunately, most of it will come from scramblers above who may accidentally dislodge rocks. This is especially dangerous when ascending gullies that funnel falling rocks and make dodging them or finding a quick escape route difficult. Be aware of this as you ascend a gully and also be super aware that there may be parties coming up behind you. Don't end someone's day (or life!) prematurely by carelessly dislodging rocks. If you are the upper party it is your responsibility to avoid knocking rocks down, not theirs to dodge what you have negligently displaced.

At other times the freeze–thaw action of snow and ice will loosen sections of rock and send them hurtling down the mountain, though this is more of a concern for mountaineering trips in heavy snowfall areas.

Slipping on scree or wet, loose rock, as well as general carelessness due to fatigue or complacency, are also good reasons to wear headgear. Helmets are neither heavy to carry nor uncomfortable to wear. They should be an integral part of your scrambling gear.

Weather

If you think predicting the stock market is tricky, try predicting the weather in the mountains. Everyone who experienced the volatile summer of 2016 will understand exactly what this means. No one has yet to figure out how to definitively forecast the weather in the Canadian Rockies and it is unlikely that such a level of precision will ever

be achieved. The only accurate prediction one can make about the weather is that it is going to be unpredictable! Thunderstorms can materialize without warning, snow can fall during any month of the year, and you may leave your vehicle enjoying balmy +20° weather, only to arrive at the summit several hours later in temperatures below zero and winds that make things feel even colder.

Thus the keen scrambler needs to be prepared for all types of weather – good and bad. This doesn't mean you have to fill your pack with clothing to handle every potential nasty weather event, but it is prudent to have such items in the car, just in case. It is also prudent to do your homework, regardless of the inherent weaknesses of weather forecasting. Several days before – and most importantly the morning of – your trip, check a variety of different forecasts and look at the satellite photos (satellite animations are often very telling).

The good news regarding weather in the Rockies is that periods of very stable and beautiful conditions (high-pressure systems) are fairly common (except in the summer of 2016!) and make for a fantastic scrambling experience. Save up your sick days and keep an eye out for those systems!

River crossings

I bring up this topic only because a number of scrambles in this book require crossing one of two major rivers in Kananaskis Country: the Kananaskis and the Highwood. The fordability of these two streams can vary greatly according to the time of day and time of year and can also depend on the amount of precipitation during the year.

The Kananaskis River can be especially tricky for the simple reason that its volume can vary greatly during the day. Water released from the dam at the Kananaskis Lakes can dramatically raise the river from morning to evening. Even if the level is low in the morning, it may be dangerously high in the evening and may have to be reassessed at that time. If necessary, be prepared to hike out via Stoney Trail and then back along Highway 40 to your vehicle.

Keep in mind that for ascents of Lorette, "Skogan" and "Mary Barclay," the river crossing can be avoided by hiking or biking Stoney Trail and starting from the Stoney day use area, about 1 km along the road to the Nakiska ski hill.

Hip waders are ideal for the above three ascents. For Lorette and "Skogan," the parking area is no more than 50 m from the river and only a few hundred metres for "Mary Barclay." Put the waders on at the car, cross the river and leave them on the other side for the return crossing. The water in these rivers is always painfully cold.

The Highwood River is less problematic than the Kananaskis, but there is no way to avoid crossing it for Odlum, Loomis (via Loomis or Odlum Creek trails), McPhail, Muir, MacLaren, Strachan and Bishop. This river can be quite high in the spring and is best avoided at those times. In addition, many of the approaches mentioned above are best done on bicycle. Trying to get you and your bike across the Highwood safely can be especially dangerous when the water is high. Once again, hip waders are a great idea.

For ascents of Junction Mountain, Pyriform and Shunga-la-she, the Sheep River may also be impassable, especially in the spring. Having a backup plan for all the ascents mentioned above (in case the river is too high) is always a good idea.

Avalanches

If you enjoy the winter and snow as much as I do, then making yourself aware of all the dangers that avalanches pose is absolutely mandatory. The best way to do this is by taking Avalanche Skills Training (AST) 1 and 2 courses. These courses place heavy emphasis on learning how to recognize and then stay out of avalanche terrain. Detailed information about terrain recognition is beyond the scope of this book. If you don't have the training, simply stay off snow slopes and avoid winter scrambling altogether.

There are a few peaks described in this book that offer fantastic glissades if enough snow remains on the slopes ("Chimper Peak" and "Ochre Spring Peak," for example). Note, however, that these mountains are still intended to be ascended in late spring, when snow often remains but is less of an avalanche concern, or in summer, when there is no snow. There are many scrambles in the book that I would tackle in the dead of winter, but I wouldn't go anywhere near Chimper or Ochre during avalanche season (December to April).

(See also **Winter scrambling** on page 19)

Wildlife

The rules regarding wildlife are very simple: stay away from **all** wildlife and make lots of noise so it stays away from you. This is especially true for any animal that has offspring in tow. Moose, elk and bears are of particular concern. If you get between one of these animals and their young, you will be perceived as a threat and they will protect their young, possibly in ways that will be severely detrimental to your immediate health! A mother bear could attack even if you are just in the vicinity of her young. The good news is that this is very unlikely to happen if the wildlife hears you coming well in advance. So make noise!

Carrying bear spray is a great idea. However, unless you are related to Wyatt Earp, Billy the Kid or Quick Draw McGraw (I would pay to see that last one!), getting your bear spray out takes time – time you may not have when you need it. But if you make noise, an encounter is far less likely to even occur. Bear spray is a last resort.

If you do have to draw your spray, it is imperative that you know how to use it correctly. In short, be aware of wind direction, hold the can with both hands, wait until the animal is approximately 10 m away and spray above the bear (to account for gravity doing its thing). The goal is to get the pepper component of the spray into the bear's eyes and nose. When the animal backs away (and pray that it does), leave the area immediately.

Be sure you can tell the difference between a black bear and a grizzly. Grizzlies have a broader, dished face and a shoulder hump. Black bears are smaller, have a forehead "bump" and the shoulder is not humped. The general rules are different for each: fight, throw things, yell and scream if it's a black bear; play dead (and, once again, pray) if it's a grizzly.

Familiarize yourself with the signs that a bear has been or is in the area, such as what bear scat and grizzly diggings look like. If you are camping (at a drive-to campsite or in the backcountry), practise "smart camping" habits. That is, hang all food high in a tree and some distance from your tent and keep your campsite clean. You yourself may not be on the bears' menu for the evening, but even your average *Ursidae* love Cheez Whiz sandwiches.

Here are some personal statistics that may support the practice of making lots of noise in the backcountry. Since 2001 I have ventured out into the mountains approximately 900 times, with approximately 300 of those trips being solo. When I hike alone I make a great deal more noise than

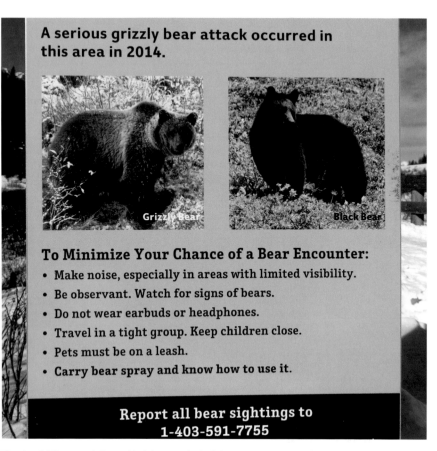

A serious grizzly bear attack occurred in this area in 2014.

Grizzly Bear

Black Bear

To Minimize Your Chance of a Bear Encounter:

- Make noise, especially in areas with limited visibility.
- Be observant. Watch for signs of bears.
- Do not wear earbuds or headphones.
- Travel in a tight group. Keep children close.
- Pets must be on a leash.
- Carry bear spray and know how to use it.

**Report all bear sightings to
1-403-591-7755**

The visual differences between black bears and grizzly bears, as seen on a trailhead sign in Kananaskis.

when I am with others. Of those 900 trips, I have seen and/or encountered a bear on just 12, and not a single one of those sightings or encounters occurred when I was alone – 0 out of 300 – a Vegas bookie would be drooling at those odds!

An excellent source of all relevant information about bears in the Rockies is *Bear Attacks: Their Causes and Avoidance*, by Stephen Herrero.

Insects

Most insects encountered in the Canadian Rockies are simply an annoyance and pose little health threat to humans. In late spring/early summer mosquitos can be ravenous and relentless.

Black flies and horseflies may be issues later in the season.

Ticks, on the other hand, are an insect to be concerned about. Although it has long been advertised that Lyme disease does not exist in Alberta or our neighbour province to the west, that fact is now in question. Multiple cases of Lyme disease have been reported in Alberta and BC. The source of those infections is debatable, but this is one case where safe is better than sorry. Products containing DEET can be applied directly to the skin to ward off ticks as well as mosquitos and other pests. Unfortunately, DEET can ruin clothing. Permethrin-based products actually kill ticks, not just repel them, and can

A typical Rockies wood tick. They are very small and difficult to see on darker clothing.
Photo: Sonny Bou

be used on clothing. Do not, however, apply them to your skin.

Ticks are primarily active from March to July in the Rockies. Wearing light coloured clothes will make it easier to spot them if they get on you. After a trip, always thoroughly check yourself, your clothing and your backpack for ticks. If a tick has attached itself to you, remove it by gently tugging on it with a pair of tweezers. Saving the tick for analysis may be prudent. Look for a rash or ring around the bite and see a doctor if you see that and/or experience headache or flu-like symptoms.

DRINKING-WATER

Be very careful about the Rockies water you choose to drink. There does exist the potential for contracting giardia, commonly known as beaver fever, if you drink from a contaminated source, although cases are rare. Symptoms can take up to 15 days to appear and include persistent diarrhea, cramps, weakness, and loss of appetite. The general rule is that the higher up in the mountain you are, the safer the water is to drink. Getting water from running streams is better than still lakes or tarns.

If you are suspicious about a particular water source, purify it using a commercially purchased filter, boil it for 10 minutes, or treat the water with iodine drops or tablets in order to kill anything that can make you sick.

The parasite can also be present in feces of dogs, beavers and humans as well as other animals. Therefore, proper disposal of human waste is very important. Bury it at least 15 cm deep, well away from trails and at least 60 m away from all water sources. If burying the waste is not an option, use a rock to smear the feces on other rocks. The UV from the sun will then biodegrade the waste naturally. Of course, you'll want to do this well off the usual path that scramblers and hikers might take. Pack out or burn any toilet paper.

ENVIRONMENTAL SENSITIVITY

Admittedly I feel a little hypocritical about addressing this subject, since this guidebook promotes human activity in the mountains. In truth, our best means of exercising "environmental sensitivity" to the mountain environment is for all humans to simply get out of the mountains and stay out – no residents, no tourists, no hikers, no scramblers, no climbers, no skiers. Leave the mountain environment to those it belongs to: animals, plants and nature itself.

However, that is a less than realistic ideal and therefore it is absolutely our obligation, as guests, to treat the mountain environment with the utmost care and respect. Here are a few general guidelines to follow when in the mountains:

- Always use trails (whether animal or human) where they are available and never shortcut over untouched terrain unless it is absolutely necessary.
- Pick up garbage if you see any. Fortunately, garbage is not a serious issue in the Canadian Rockies right now, so let's keep it that way.
- Avoid interacting with any kind of wildlife, not just the obvious species such as bears, moose etc.
- Avoid trampling or damaging nests, dens and other forms of animal dwelling.
- Leave the mountain exactly as you found it. It should be as though you were never there.

On a personal note, one very positive side effect of becoming a regular visitor to the mountains is that I have become far more cognizant of the planet's environmental concerns and therefore a more environmentally conscious person. My consumption of resources has been dramatically reduced. I recycle everything I can and I try to consider the environmental consequences of the activities I'm involved in. Hopefully, if we all do what we can to minimize our own negative impact on the environment, the mountains will continue to be a viable habitat for humans, animals and plants and will provide a clean, spectacular environment to appreciate and enjoy.

WATERTON

Waterton Park is one of my favourite areas of the Canadian Rockies: beautiful mountains, beautiful lakes, beautiful scenery and unbelievable colours. The park also contains two of my favourite scrambles of this book: Mount Dungarvan and Mount Glendowan (Irish names, not Scottish as is sometimes thought). A new route up Anderson Peak, described in this edition, also makes that list.

A well-used and well-maintained system of trails makes access to most of the peaks quite easy and though you will probably run into other people on the trails, it is likely you will have the actual mountain to yourself. Waterton has become increasingly popular with hikers, sightseers and tourists, but it is still relatively quiet when you leave the trails in search of a summit. Poor rock keeps climbers away and the disappearance of any glaciation means the area offers nothing for mountaineers. Never mind – that's all the more room for scramblers!

Between this edition of *More Scrambles* and Alan Kane's *Scrambles*, all official peaks in Waterton National Park (and several unofficial ones) are now described. Although completing the entire list will not likely secure you a spot on the next Canadian Mount Everest ascent team, it may be a small feather in your cap to accomplish the feat.

For those who appreciate the unspoiled beauty of Waterton, remember that the park is but the northern tip of a much larger area, mostly located in Montana – the absolute gem that is Glacier National Park (not the Canadian Glacier National Park in British Columbia). If you enjoy Waterton and the Castle, grab your passport and take a trip down to Glacier – it is magnificent! A copy of Gordon Edwards's *A Climber's Guide to Glacier National Park* is invaluable for scramblers going to this area.

One unpleasant aspect of the Waterton area (and the Castle: see next section) is ticks. Both areas are notorious for high populations of ticks from mid-March to July. There has been much discussion and controversy about ticks' capacity to pass on Lyme disease to their host. Regardless of whether they carry the virus or not, it is better to check yourself thoroughly at the end of each trip and use the correct procedure for removing any unwanted intruders that have attached themselves to you. If a tick has been feeding on you, it may be prudent to keep it for testing after removal.

GEOLOGY

You will probably immediately notice a significant difference in the geology of the Waterton area compared to that of the Rockies farther north. The rock is laid primarily horizontally and the variety of colours of it is astounding. The horizontal bedding is explained by the Lewis Thrust. A few years ago (about 75 million, to be more exact), a huge slab of layered rock was thrust upward and northeastward, over the younger rock. For this reason, the rock in Waterton is some of the oldest in the Rockies. The slab was displaced about 100 km, ending up where Waterton, Glacier National Park and much of their surrounding areas presently sit. This process took a mere 15 million years. Whereas most of the mountains of the Rockies were formed by thrust sheets being piled up against one another, the slab of the Lewis Thrust moved more or less as a single unit, causing the rock to maintain its horizontal orientation.

The horizontal bedding is certainly a benefit for scramblers, who will enjoy sections of terrific hands-on scrambling on a number of ascents (Mount Dungarvan definitely provides the best example). The step-like terrain often enables you to ascend in places that may appear to be too steep. Unfortunately, the quality of the rock is dismal, explaining the lack of rock-climbing routes in the area.

The colour of the rock in Waterton is arguably the area's best feature. Nowhere in the Canadian Rockies will you find such an amazing variety of rock and rock colours. The specific rock that is primarily responsible for this is argillite (the "g" is pronounced as a "j"). The argillite of Waterton comes mostly in two colours, red and green. Often they are seen together and it is not uncommon to see visually striking examples of alternating layers of red and green argillite. The rock is basically hardened mud. A small amount of iron in it is the cause of the unique colours: red if the iron is oxidized, green if not.

In addition to the argillite, various shades of brown, grey and beige limestone and dolomite are also found in the Waterton area. The very distinctive band of black to dark-grey rock – noticeable near and at the summits of Dungarvan, Glendowan and many others – is an igneous rock, resulting from molten magma having been injected between sedimentary layers. Put this variety of colourful rocks side by side and you're guaranteed a visual feast which simply can't be beat.

CLIMATE AND WEATHER

Chicago may be "The Windy City," but Waterton could certainly earn the title "The Windy National Park." The average daily wind speed in Waterton is 32 km/h, and speeds of up to 120 km/h are not uncommon. Gusts have been measured at a violent 150 km/h. You might want to stay well clear of cliff edges when the wind picks up. Before you leave home, check the weather forecasts, which often give high-wind warnings when applicable.

WATERTON				
Lakeview Ridge		1945 m	easy/moderate	p. 31
"Rogan Peak"		2442 m	easy	p. 35
Bellevue Hill		2112 m	easy/moderate	p. 37
Mount Dungarvan		2614 m	difficult	p. 39
"Dundy Peak"		2480 m	moderate/difficult	p. 43
Cloudy Ridge		2607 m	moderate	p. 47
Mount Glendowan		2677 m	moderate	p. 50
Newman Peak		2515 m	moderate	p. 52
	Spionkop Ridge	2576 m	easy/moderate	p. 53
	Avion Ridge	2440 m	easy/moderate	p. 54
Anderson Peak		2698 m	moderate/difficult	p. 55
Lost Mountain		2509 m	easy	p. 58
	Mount Bauerman	2409 m	easy	p. 59
Lone Mountain		2420 m	easy	p. 60
Kishinena Peak		2440 m	moderate	p. 62
Ruby Ridge		2420 m	easy	p. 65
Mount Rowe (via Rowe Lakes)		2469 m	moderate	p. 67
Mount Rowe (southeast route)		2469 m	moderate	p. 69
	Festubert Mountain	2522 m	easy/moderate	p. 70
"Carthew Minor"		2330 m	easy/moderate	p. 72
Mount Richards (north ridge)		2416 m	difficult	p. 77
Mount Richards (north face)		2416 m	moderate	p. 79
Mount Boswell		2439 m	moderate	p. 81
Vimy Peak		2379 m	moderate/difficult	p. 83
	Vimy Ridge	2500 m	easy	p. 85
Sofa Mountain		2515 m	moderate	p. 86

It may surprise you to find out that Waterton receives more precipitation than any other area in Alberta: an annual average of 1072 mm, compared to 930 mm in the Columbia Icefields. April and June are the wettest and cloudiest months of the year. Average snowfall in winter amounts to 575 cm in the townsite.

Mount Cleveland and Upper Waterton Lake provide a perfect background for the final push to the summit of Mount Richards.

ACCESS

From Calgary, drive south on Highway 2, then west on Highway 3 (towards Pincher Creek), then south on Highway 6 to Pincher Creek. From Lethbridge, take Highway 3 west and turn south on Highway 6. Turn left to remain on Highway 6, and continue southward about 50 km. Turn right to enter Waterton Park. A park pass is required, and can be purchased shortly after the turnoff.

ACCOMMODATION

The town of Waterton has several hotels and lodges, including the famous Prince of Wales Hotel. The townsite has one campground and there are a few others in the area. Just before the turnoff to the park you'll find Waterton Springs Campground, and in the park Crandell Campground is ideal for any peaks along the Red Rock Parkway. Check for seasonal closures.

1. LAKEVIEW RIDGE 1945 m

(MAP 1, PAGE 448)
Rating easy; options to do some moderate scrambling
Round-trip time 6–9 hours
Elevation gain ~800 m for the full loop
Maps 82 H/4 Waterton Lakes; Gem Trek Waterton National Park

Lakeview Ridge shares a great deal in common with its northerly neighbour Prairie Bluff: both are on the very edge of the Front Ranges and look fairly boring from afar. However, they are wonderfully scenic trips with some of the best rock vistas you are ever likely to see in the area. The recommended route does not take the more obvious south or west ridge but instead goes to the southeast face, where the impressive rock sits. Early spring or autumn are often the best times to do the trip, and as usual, clear skies are almost a must to get the most out of the scenery. A loop route enables you to take in as much as possible. Try from mid-April on. Snowshoes may be necessary if the ridge is still snow-covered in early spring. The south and west ridge routes are also outlined.

A few kilometres north of Waterton Park on Highway 6, take the turnoff to the bison paddock. Follow the road around, but don't turn left into the actual paddock. Instead, keep going straight along the north border of the paddock and park on the side of the road just before the gate. Do not park right in front of the gate.

The loop route can be done in either direction but counterclockwise is recommended. This means that, hopefully, the sun will be lighting up the spectacular rock of the southeast face.

Go through the gate and hike west, along the north side of a usually dried-up tarn. Turn right at the end. Find the "HORSESHOE BASIN LOOP TRAIL" sign. Take the right fork, heading north. The trail eventually descends to Galwey Creek, where you must cross to the other side and then continue going north.

The variety of routes to Lakeview Ridge. The recommended ascent route is via the steep gully **G**. The scree route **S** is a little easier. For those wanting to explore the colourful rock from below, the alternative route **A** is an option. **ES**: east summit of Lakeview Ridge.

The gully route up and through the fascinating layered rock. We went right up the snow, which in April can be quite hard. An ice axe and crampons were very much welcome here.

About 30–40 minutes from the start, an opening in the trees appears to the left, where you can see the objective. Staying on the trail, go past this opening, through the next set of trees and on to the next opening (GR903482), where there is a clear route to any part of the east side of Lakeview Ridge (see photo on page 31). Choose your route and off you go. There are several steep, but straightforward scree gullies below the summit. Steeper scrambling routes exist to the right (north). Arguably the best part of the trip is right in front of you. Ascend the steep scree to the base of the rock bands and take as long as you need to explore the fascinating layers of exposed rock. When satiated, pick one of the scree slopes/gullies and ascend to the ridge, close to the southeast summit. Backtrack if necessary to the summit. Almost the entire loop route is visible from the high point. The true summit does not look like the highest point and lies about 1.3 km southwest of the higher-looking north summit.

Instead of visiting the southeast summit as outlined above, another equally interesting option is to traverse north, below the rock bands of the southeast face. This allows you to see more of the east face. At the far north end, the rock bands start to diminish and easy routes to the ridge appear. Take one or go around to the north end, where it's a veritable cakewalk to the ridge.

Regardless of whether you visited the southeast summit or not, the route is obvious once you're on the ridge. Follow it north, then west, then slightly southwest, around to the north summit. Stay near the edge of the ridge to best enjoy the variety of colourful rock, especially near the southeast summit.

As the name implies, views from the north summit towards the Waterton Lakes are very respectable, although those who have seen the water from Crandell, Richards, Vimy or Boswell may wonder what the fuss is all about! Nearby Mount Galwey, "Rogan Peak" and Mount Dungarvan will also warrant some attention.

You may be less than thrilled to see that the

continuation of the loop requires a 200 m elevation loss followed by an almost equal amount of gain to the true summit. Descend scree slopes to the intervening col. If you have had enough at this point, it is possible to descend southeastward to Galwey Brook and follow it back out. However, continuing on to the true summit and then down the south ridge is definitely worth the effort, featuring the best scenery and a straightforward descent.

Providing the ridge to the true summit is snow-free (if not, let's hope you brought your snowshoes), the ascent is very easy. The summit view is not terribly different from that of the north summit, although the lakes are noticeably lacking. For the remainder of the loop, continue following the ridge southward, up and down over several bumps. Note that at almost any point it is possible to descend west to the Horseshoe Basin Trail. Better to go all the way to the end of the ridge, however, and then descend scree slopes to your right. The Horseshoe Basin Trail is visible in the valley below and that's what you should aim for. Once on the trail, follow it through more grassy meadows and poplar stands. Watch you don't inadvertently take the southbound turnoff onto Bellevue Prairie Trail, unless you intend to ascend Bellevue Hill also.

South ridge route

The route below (south ridge) is actually the descent route for the route described previously. It follows the Horseshoe Basin Trail into the scenic valley south of the summit and is slightly shorter than the southeast face route and easier in regards to route-finding and terrain.

From the parking area, hop over the gate and hike west alongside a barbed wire fence and on the north side of a small tarn. If the tarn is full you may have to hike around it on the south side or climb over the barbed wire fence to drier ground. At the end of the fence you'll see a "HORSESHOE BASIN LOOP TRAIL" sign to your right. Go to the sign and turn west onto the trail. The trail is generally very easy to follow, through open areas and then through trees. It takes a few turns which seem to be going in the wrong direction, but eventually it resumes heading upward into the Horseshoe Basin valley. The objective and the south end of Lakeview Ridge soon come into view (see photo on page 34).

Once in view, the route up the south ridge is quite obvious. Make your way toward the south face, cross the creek and up you go. Atop the ascent slope, follow the ridge for about 1.8 km to the summit. Either return the way you came or complete the route described previously, but in reverse.

West ridge route

A third option to reach the summit of Lakeview Ridge is to follow the Horseshoe Basin Trail all the way to the Lakeview Ridge/"Rogan Peak" col and then the west ridge to the summit. It's about 10 km to the col, so expect to take at least a couple of hours to get there.

Follow the route above (south ridge), but instead of leaving the trail toward the south face, stay on it as it heads west past the south face. Eventually the trail turns north, paralleling the south ridge of Lakeview. Before this, watch for the sharp switchback shortly after crossing the creek (possibly dried up).

From the east summit the horseshoe route is obvious. The summits of a few Kane and Nugara scrambles are also visible. **GP**: Galwey Peak; **RP**: "Rogan Peak"; **MD**: Mount Dungarvan; **TS**: true summit; **MR**: Mount Roche; **NS**: north summit.

In Horseshoe Basin, with several objectives visible. The south end of Lakeview Ridge lies to the right.
RP: "Rogan Peak"; **MD**: Mount Dungarvan; **LR**: Lakeview Ridge.

Two kilometres of pleasant hiking up the valley precedes the steeper switchbacks up to the col. At the high point, continue going east and up, directly to the summit, less than a kilometre away.

Enjoy the view and then either **return** the same way, use the south ridge descent route or complete the loop route in reverse. The south ridge is highly recommended.

2. "ROGAN PEAK" 2442 m

(MAP 1, PAGE 448)
Rating easy via the north ridge
Round-trip time 6–8 hours
Elevation gain ~1100 m
Maps 82 H/4 Waterton Lakes; Gem Trek Waterton National Park

*Although I originally (and unofficially) gave this peak the name Dunwey Peak (Mount **Dungarvan** and Mount Gal**wey**), the birth of my nephew, Rogan, prompted me to rename it after him, since he is such a cool little man! The peak can be reached as part of an awesome high-level traverse from Galwey to Dungarvan or in much quicker fashion from the east. The route described below is the easiest, if more circuitous, one via the pass due west of the summit of Lakeview Ridge. The Horseshoe Basin Trail allows easy and scenic access to the pass. "Rogan" is a good objective by itself or in conjunction with Lakeview Ridge. Late-season ascents are preferable, in that Galwey Brook will be easier to cross then.*

A few kilometres north of Waterton Park on Highway 6, take the turnoff to the bison paddock. Follow the road around, but don't turn left into the actual paddock. Instead, keep going straight along the north border of the paddock and park on the side of the road just before the gate. Do not park right in front of the gate.

Hop over the gate and hike west alongside a barbed wire fence and on the north side of a small tarn. If the tarn is full you may have to hike around it on the south side or climb over the barbed wire fence to drier ground. At the end of the fence you'll see a "HORSESHOE BASIN LOOP TRAIL" sign to your right. Go to the sign and turn west onto the trail. The trail is generally very easy to follow, through open areas and then through the trees. It takes a few turns which seem to be going in the wrong direction, but eventually it resumes heading upward into the Horseshoe Basin Valley. The objective and the south end of Lakeview Ridge soon come into view (see photo on page 34).

Eventually the trail turns north, paralleling the south ridge of Lakeview. Before this, watch for the sharp switchback shortly after crossing the creek (possibly dried up). The objective is visible

Uncle Andy at the summit, with the long traverse to Mount Dungarvan stretched out behind.

Rogan's dad at the summit, with the challenging route-finding traverse to Mount Galwey at the left.

throughout, as are several other potential routes to the summit. The east face of the peak does give access to the summit. Although 99 per cent of the scrambling on the face is moderate, there is one rock band that may abruptly stop many parties in their tracks. Judicious route-finding may reveal a scramble route through this band. If confident in your abilities on exposed class 4 or lower class 5 terrain, it's definitely worth a look. Be prepared to retreat if necessary.

For those leery about the thought of getting stranded halfway up a nearly vertical rock band, stick to the original route via the north ridge. Continue hiking north, up the valley. The pass is a fair distance away, but the very pleasant surroundings and views make this one of the more enjoyable sections of the trip. Passing the east face of "Rogan," it becomes clear that going all the way to the pass is not necessary. A wide, rounded ridge sweeps down from the northeast side of the peak and offers a shorter route to gain the north ridge. If time is a concern, leave the trail when feasible and

head up this ridge. A good compromise is to use this ridge as a descent route.

To gain the pass, simply stay on the trail as it winds up the hillside over several large switchbacks. The trail then turns northwest, gains a little elevation and then drops down towards Oil Basin. Instead of dropping down, leave the trail and head west to a high point above. Then follow the ridge as it curves around to the southwest and then south to the summit of "Rogan." Travel is easy throughout.

Enjoy the respectable summit view and then **return** either the same way or by the recommended shortcut down the aforementioned ridge. Routefinding your way back to the trail is very easy.

Of course, there is also the option to continue on to either Dungarvan or Galwey. Expect either option to make for a very, very long day, with difficult, exposed scrambling and route-finding challenges. The trip to Dungarvan is a little more straightforward. The only downside to this route is that it means missing out on the outstanding south ridge of Dungarvan – a must-do for all scramblers.

3. BELLEVUE HILL 2112 m

(MAP 1, PAGE 448)
Rating easy/moderate (depending on the route)
Round-trip time 3–5 hours
Elevation gain 750 m
Maps 82 H/4 Waterton Lakes; Gem Trek Waterton National Park

This "Hill" makes a great trip when time and/or energy are lacking or as an additional trip in conjunction with something close by when time and energy are in abundance. The colourful rock of the east face alone makes this a worthwhile trip. Red Rock Parkway is closed from November to mid-May. Try from June on.

Turn onto Red Rock Parkway, drive 3.4 km and park at a small pull-off on the right side of the road. Check out the route (see photo). Hike along the road for an additional 100 m and ascend grassy, open slopes to reach the rock face. Traverse north alongside the face and pick one of two left-rising ramps to gain higher slopes. Ascend one of the ramps and turn right, traversing wide ledges north and up. From here, your goal is to zigzag your way through colourful bands of rock towards the centre that splits the east face. You can gain the ridge

at any point, but the most scenic and interesting route weaves its way almost to the centre gully and then the ridge just before it. Throughout, there are options to do easy, moderate or difficult scrambling (be careful on the loose rock) – whatever your preference.

Once you've gained the ridge, the fun is over. Turn right and try to enjoy the anticlimactic plod to the summit. The first major high point is a cairned false summit. The true summit lies 25 minutes away, to the northwest.

Ascent routes of the colourfully layered east face as seen from Red Rock Parkway. **R:** ridge; **C:** centre gully.

Route to the summit from the false summit. **S**: summit; **ED**: easy descent route; **G**: Mount Galwey.

While the view may not be one of the most riveting you'll see, the pleasant contrast of grassy plains to the east, the Waterton Lakes and craggy peaks south of the border and the familiar forms of Galwey and Blakiston to the west provides a uniqueness all its own.

Either **return** the same way or, for a much faster descent, start south (the way you came), and instead of turning left towards the false summit, keep going south down the ridge. Trend left where it becomes obvious you must do so to maintain the ridge. Follow the ridge all the way down to the road, turn left and hike about 1.5 km back to your vehicle. This descent route can be completed comfortably in about 1.25 hours.

4. MOUNT DUNGARVAN 2614 m

(MAP 1, PAGE 448)
Rating difficult via the south ridge; a climber's scramble
Round-trip time 8–11 hours
Elevation gain 1160 m
Maps 82 H/4 Waterton Lakes; Gem Trek Waterton National Park

Mount Dungarvan could very well be the best scramble in Waterton National Park. The south ridge is a scrambler's dream of steep, hands-on scrambling on step-like terrain. As well, the scenery throughout is fabulous. The summit block has to be snow-free, so don't attempt it too early. Conversely, late season ascents allow you to do the approach along the wonderfully scenic banks of Lost Horse Creek. September and October ascents are therefore highly recommended, as long as snow hasn't blanketed the mountain. If I could only do one trip in Waterton, this would be it! Red Rock Parkway is closed from November to mid-May. Try from July on, but again, September and October are the best months to make an attempt.

Turn onto Red Rock Parkway, and about 11.8 km along, leave your vehicle at the Lost Horse Creek parking lot. Keep your fingers crossed that the creek is low enough to allow an approach via its banks. If it is, you are in for a real treat! The creek and canyon are absolutely beautiful throughout, easily rivalling and perhaps surpassing its westerly and far more popular counterpart, Red Rock Canyon.

What you will see if you can take the canyon approach.

What you will see if you can take the bushwhack approach!

However, the canyon approach is not without its challenges. Be prepared for frequent creek crossings, some scrambling, walking across narrow ledges and route-finding on sections that may seem impassable. If you do encounter problems, try to escape to terrain above, on the west (left) side of the creek. Depending on the difficulties encountered, the first drainage, coming down from the left side, can be reached in about 40 minutes. Pass this one by and continue up Lost Horse Creek for about 10 minutes, where a second drainage empties into the creek (approximately GR826462). This marks the start of Dungarvan's south ridge.

If the creek is high, it is better to sideslope high on the left side of the creek. Again, look for the second drainage and head up the ridge after this drainage. Unfortunately, this option requires some nasty bushwhacking and climbing over endless deadfall. Allow 2 hours for this approach.

Once at the start of the south ridge, follow it up through thinning forest to the treeline. Here, the trip dramatically improves. For the next several hours, enjoy some of the best hands-on scrambling you're likely to find in the area. For the best bang for your buck, stay on the ridge to scramble up rock bands and pinnacles that may appear too steep for simple scrambling but are in fact very enjoyable to ascend. Although the rock is loose (typical of the area), its horizontal bedding inspires confidence, even when the rock quality doesn't. There may be at least one band that is too steep, but it (and all the others for that matter) can be easily circumvented on the left side.

Higher up, you arrive at a limestone rock band that is clearly not scrambling terrain. Again, traverse left along its base and then ascend one of numerous weaknesses. The farther left you go, the easier the ascent. Once above the band, head right and up to gain the ridge again.

Soon the summit block closes in: a band of black, lichen-covered rock atop a band of burgundy argillite (typical of several mountains in

Above: Upper section of the south ridge. **W**: weakness in rock band (approximate); **G**: ascent gully; **S**: summit; **D**: easy descent route.
Below: Summit block. **G**: ascent gully; **A**: alternative ascent route; **S**: summit; **D**: easy descent route.

the area, like Blakiston and Drywood). The argillite band is easily ascended, but the black band can be a serious endeavour. If snow or ice persist on any of the potential ascent routes, this may become mountaineering, where rope skills – belaying, setting up anchors, rappelling – are imperative. If you are without climbing gear, be very cautious about ascending terrain you may not be able to

The easier descent route. **P**: parking lot; **B**: Mount Blakiston.

downclimb – "play it safe and retreat" is always the best policy.

If you're up for the challenge, traverse several metres on mildly exposed ledges around the right side of the summit block to a steep gully that grants access to the summit. If clear of snow and ice, this is your best bet. Scramble up the gully to a collection of chockstones. Good hand and footholds enable you to climb over the chockstones with relative ease. At the top, turn right and scramble up to the summit within minutes.

If the gully is choked with snow and ice you may have to try the following route. Traverse left along the base of the summit block and look for the easiest of several weaknesses. Even the least steep route

(farthest left) requires steep scrambling and an exposed traverse along the final ridge to make it to the summit. Downclimbing any of these routes will require extra care.

Once at the top, enjoy a magnificent summit panorama before cautiously downclimbing (or rappelling) the summit block. When down, a fast and easier descent route can be found by going straight down scree slopes of the south face of the mountain. Head far to the right to circumvent the limestone rock band and then continue down to the creek below. Follow the creek to where it joins up with Lost Horse Creek and then return the way you came.

5. "DUNDY PEAK" 2480 m

(MAP 1, PAGE 448)
Rating mostly moderate with one difficult, exposed rock band
Round-trip time 6–9 hours
Elevation gain 1025 m
Maps 82 H/04 Waterton; Gem Trek Waterton National Park

Dundy Peak sits inconspicuously between Mount Dungarvan and Cloudy Ridge. The summit can be reached from either summit of Dungarvan or Cloudy or from the Lost Horse Creek parking lot via the route described here. The amazing approach, up Lost Horse Creek, is alone worth the trip. As well, the southeast ridge offers good scrambling, interesting route-finding and an excellent summit panorama. Midsummer/early autumn ascents are recommended. Wear running shoes (or approach shoes if you don't mind getting them wet) for the journey up Lost Horse Creek, and be prepared to wade through knee-deep water. The trip is inaccessible from November to mid-May.

Drive 11.8 km on Red Rock Parkway and park at the Lost Horse Creek parking lot. Put on your running or approach shoes and start hiking up the canyon. Judging by the increased number of rocks strategically placed for crossing the creek, this incredibly scenic hike is becoming quite popular. Water levels can vary wildly from year to year and month to month. You may be able to reach the start of the ridge without getting your feet wet or it may be impossible – be prepared for either. Also

Where you leave the creek. **LH**: Lost Horse Creek; **SC**: smaller, unnamed creek; **SE**: southeast ridge.

Top: Typical terrain on the southeast ridge. Lots of potential for fun, hands-on scrambling. **SE**: southeast ridge; **C**: crux rock band; **FS**: false summit.
Bottom: Approaching the true summit and the approximate alternative descent route and traverse to Mount Dungarvan. **CRS**: Cloudy Ridge Senior; **CRJ**: Cloudy Ridge Junior; **S**: summit of Dundy; **MD**: Mount Dungarvan.

be prepared for some of the best rock and water scenery in the park and some fun route-finding challenges.

Hike/scramble along the creek for about 40–60 minutes to where a much smaller creek comes down from the left (GR822460). This is the base of the southeast ridge of Dundy. Gain the ridge and start upward, going northeast and then north, on easy terrain. Animal trails help, but the bushwhacking is never heavy. Stay to the left side of the ridge as it curves north and then northwest, to avoid any bushwhacking.

Above treeline it becomes clear that following the ridge is way beyond scrambling. Once you get to the rock, the best strategy is to circumvent all the steep sections on the left side and then scramble back up to the ridge when feasible. This provides the best route-finding and scrambling experience but is not the only way up. More direct and easier routes are certainly possible.

Whatever route you choose, you will eventually arrive at an impressively steep, light-grey limestone rock band that runs across the width of this peak and many others in the area. This is the crux of the trip. Make your way over to where the southeast ridge meets the rock band (GR817482). Go about 60 m west along the base of the band and look for a weakness. It is recognizable by sharp, thin slab of rock above. Ascend the rock band on small but solid ledges and then move to the right onto much easier terrain. There are only a few difficult moves but downclimbing this section is considerably more challenging and will feel very exposed. Don't

go up if you can't get down. Note the location of the top, for the return trip.

Above the crux it's a short and easy trek to the false summit and then a slightly longer but equally easy hike to the true summit, at GR818488. The summit panorama is impressive in every direction, but the views of Anderson Peak due west and castellated Mount Dungarvan due east really stand out. In case you were wondering, the distant but distinctive peaks to the left of Anderson are the very rarely ascended King Edward Peak (the pointy one) and Starvation Peak.

Note that it is possible to scramble over to Dungarvan and then down via Lost Horse Creek. Following the ridge in the other direction, to Cloudy Ridge, is also a possibility, but that takes you down to Red Rock Canyon.

The fastest descent route is the way you came, provided you can downclimb the crux. If the prospect of that downclimb doesn't exactly make you feel all warm and fuzzy inside, you can avoid it completely by heading a fair distance towards Mount Dungarvan (moderate scrambling and lots of route-finding throughout) and then through a weakness where the limestone band has completely eroded and been filled in with scree (around GR827486). Then descend to the creek and follow it out to Lost Horse Creek. This adds a good hour to the descent time and but it is very scenic. Also, you get close enough to the summit of Dungarvan that you might as well run up it while you are there, if you haven't already done so. See page 39 for a description.

The new route goes right up the centre of Red Rock Canyon, one of the feature attractions of Waterton National Park. The south ridge and summit can be seen in the background.

6. CLOUDY RIDGE 2607 m

(MAP 2, PAGE 449)
Rating moderate via the south ridge; mild exposure
Round-trip time 7–11 hours
Elevation gain 1500 m, due to losses and regains
Maps 82 G/1 Sage Creek; Gem Trek Waterton National Park

Nestled between the two enjoyable south ridges of Dungarvan and Glendowan, Cloudy Ridge unfortunately falls short of its Irish cousins in terms of great hands-on scrambling. The scenery, however, is terrific and the final ridge and push to the summit is enjoyable in its own way. If you can stomach the necessary 200 m elevation loss on ascent (and regain on descent), this is a good day out. Red Rock Parkway is closed from November to mid-May. Try from mid-June on.

Note: There is now an easier and far more scenic approach up Red Rock Canyon. See below.

Drive to the end of Red Rock Parkway, where you get a good look at a large part of the ascent route (see photo opposite). The goal is to gain the ridge due north of the parking lot, descend to a creek below and then ascend the south ridge of Cloudy Ridge.

Hike the Snowshoe Trail for about 5–7 minutes, looking to your right for the first and very obvious clearing in the trees. Open slopes lead easily to the ridge, about 400 vertical metres above. Expect this ascent to drag on for a while, as there are several false ridges!

From the southeast end of the ridge, the south ridge of Cloudy is clearly visible. Unfortunately, a 200 m elevation loss to the creek below is necessary. There are open slopes available for the descent and it's worth searching around a little for them. As you descend, look for a good place to cross the creek and gain the open slopes of the beginning of the south ridge of Cloudy.

Once across the creek, trudge up grassy slopes to gain easy scree slopes. Soon the route becomes visible. Follow the south ridge (along its edge for the best views and scenery) to the first high point. Turn left and traverse the burgundy coloured ridge towards the summit. Pinnacles and rock bands on the ridge can be circumvented on either side or tackled head-on.

Just before the summit, vertical walls rear up to block the way. Downclimb a short step and look for a small col down and a little to the right. Traverse down to that and then around the summit block (easy when dry, but you may feel a touch exposed if the route is snow-covered). Ascend to a plateau that leads to easy terrain around and up to the summit. The farther you traverse around the block, the easier the terrain.

The summit is a flat and grassy plateau that is great for lounging around on and taking in the pleasant view. To the immediate east lies the slightly lower second summit of Cloudy Ridge. Dungarvan dominates to the southeast and Glendowan lies immediately northwest. As well, this is a great place to view many peaks of the Castle, Waterton and Glacier National Park areas. **Return** the same way. Trying to avoid the necessary elevation gain by sidesloping on either side of Red Rock Creek means a good hour of difficult and strenuous bushwhacking – best to just buckle down and ascend to the ridge again.

Red Rock Canyon approach

There was a time when you could only follow the canyon for a short distance before being halted by a massive log jam. But the log jam no longer exists and therefore it is possible to approach the base of Cloudy Ridge from the canyon, thus avoiding the 200 m elevation loss and regain that was necessary for the original route. Note, however, this super-scenic and interesting hike through the canyon will likely require you to wade through a couple of sections of chilly mid-thigh- to waist-deep water, as well as engage in a few creative scrambling moves to avoid even deeper water holes. If you choose to do this approach route, it is recommended that you wear runners and shorts for the canyon and do the trip later in the season.

From the parking lot descend into the canyon and then hike/scramble up it for about an hour, to GR174475. This point is easily recognizable because

Above: The route as seen from the parking lot. **S**: summit.
Below: The south ridge as seen from the top of the ridge. **S**: summit.

the creek forks. The right fork leads in a few minutes to a waterfall. The fork sits at the base of the south ridge of Cloudy Ridge. Hop onto the ridge and up you go. Refer to "Follow the south ridge (along its edge....)" in column 1 of the Cloudy Ridge route description at page 47 for the details of the remainder of the trip.

Above: The route to the summit from the first high point. **S**: summit.
Below: The crux. **C**: small col; **S**: summit.

7. MOUNT GLENDOWAN 2677 m

(MAP 2, PAGE 449)
Rating moderate via the southeast and south ridges
Round-trip time 7–10 hours
Elevation gain 1175 m
Maps 82 G/1 Sage Creek; Gem Trek Waterton National Park

Mount Glendowan is very similar to its easterly neighbour Dungarvan, but shorter and easier. The ascent features lots of hands-on scrambling and a tremendous variety of rock to keep things interesting. Scenery and views are terrific throughout. Except for a minor stint of tedious bushwhacking, this is an excellent day out. Red Rock Parkway is closed from November to mid-May. Try from June on.

Drive to the end of the Red Rock Parkway and hike the Snowshoe Trail for about 2.2 km to the first drainage (about 30–40 minutes at a moderate pace). Cross the creek (if it hasn't dried up) and turn right. Parallel the creek for several hundred metres. Climbing over deadfall may be tedious but it could be way worse – just ask the British Columbians. You should now be at the start of the south ridge, and as long as you are going upward and staying left of the creek, you should have no route-finding problems. The

right side of the ridge offers occasional sections of relief from the bush.

Above the treeline, scree slopes lead easily to the start of the scrambling. The ridge is studded with interesting rock bands and pinnacles. To enjoy a fair dose of moderate to difficult scrambling, tackle them all head-on. Some are quite steep and the rock quality varies from decent to bad, so use good judgment – all can be circumvented on the left side. After some time, you may discover that the route is a little longer than anticipated, and

The south ridge of Mount Glendowan as seen from Anderson Peak.

The upper slopes and summit block.

although staying on the ridge gives the most enjoyable ascent, it is also time-consuming. Move to the left if you feel the need to pick up the pace.

When the light shades of brown shale give way to the lichen-covered black band, look to the left of the ridge for an obvious, boulder-filled gully. Follow the gully up, trending to the left to avoid steeper terrain. The scrambling here should never be more than easy to moderate. At the top of the black band, regain the ridge to enjoy a stunning view of the lighter-coloured summit block. From this angle the block appears intimidating, but a short traverse (left about 50 m) along the base of the block reveals a weakness. Scramble up this weakness and ascend a scree slope to a high point. From there it's a short and pleasant ridgewalk to the summit.

The summit view is first-rate in every direction. Of special interest are the beautiful hues and contours of the Castle Crown peaks to the north, Dungarvan (yet another terrific Waterton scramble) to the east and a possible extension of the trip to the west, towards Newman Peak.

Return the same way. Once below the black band, it is possible to lose elevation quite rapidly down southwest-facing slopes. Although the creek far below looks like it may offer an easy route back to Snowshoe Trail, the bushwhacking is quite bad, and therefore it is recommended that once you have lost enough elevation to circumvent the more serious rock bands of the ascent ridge, you traverse left back to the ridge and follow the ascent route back to the trail.

8. NEWMAN PEAK/AVION RIDGE 2515 m

(MAP 2, PAGE 449)
Rating moderate with a few tougher, exposed steps
Round-trip time 6–12 hours
Elevation gain 1000 m
Maps 82 G/1 Sage Creek; Gem Trek Waterton National Park

Newman Peak can be easily reached via popular hiking trails. A more interesting scramble route leaves the trail and ascends the southwest slopes. Once at the summit, there are plenty of opportunities to continue to other high points. Red Rock Parkway is closed from November to mid-May. Try from June on.

Park at the Red Rock Canyon parking lot and hike or bike 4.6 km along Snowshoe Trail to the Goat Lake sign. Leave your bike here and hike Goat Lake Trail for several kilometres until it opens up to reveal the southwest slopes of the southeast outlier of Newman. The goal is to ascend these slopes to the outlier and then traverse the ridge northwest to Newman. Stay on the trail until it gets closer to the rock bands, and look for a 10 metre scree ramp on the right that leads to an easy rock band. Start the ascent here, hiking up ledges and small rock bands and trending right as you gain elevation. **WARNING:** this route stays above the popular hiking trail for a long time. It is absolutely imperative

The southwest ascent slopes from Goat Lake Trail.

The very interesting southeast ridge. **N**: Newman Peak; **U**: higher, unnamed high point; **C**: Newman/Avion col; **A**: route to Avion Ridge; **D**: easy descent trail.

that you **DO NOT** dislodge rocks onto unsuspecting hikers and backcountry campers below. Use extreme caution.

About two-thirds of the way up, the easy scrambling is interrupted by a smoother band of limestone. Traverse alongside it and ascend one of numerous weaknesses. Gain the upper ridge and go to the southeast outlier for a splendid view of Anderson, Blakiston, Glendowan and the valley below.

The ridgewalk is probably the most interesting part of the ascent. Some sections look daunting, but generally this is an illusion. Stay on the ridge as much as possible. The odd pinnacle can be circumvented on the left. Near the end the terrain becomes much steeper and the ridge narrows (recognizable by trees on the right side). Again, go around to the left and look for a moderate scrambling route to regain the ridge. Back on the ridge you should see a huge, nearly vertical slab on the left side and treed terrain on the right. It is not necessary to descend to the treed terrain. Scramble up the right side of the ridge on exposed ledges to reach easier ground.

At this point a higher and unnamed bump to your right is closer and you should head there for a quick look. Otherwise, sideslope, trending left to the summit of Newman. From the bump, take in the pleasant view and then go west to Newman.

From the summit of Newman there are several options to extend the day, which are listed below. If **returning**, do not use the ascent route – it will be more difficult to avoid knocking off rocks going *down* the southwest slopes. Instead, descend the west ridge of Newman to the col a few minutes away. Here, a well travelled trail heads down into the valley and arrives at Goat Lake. The trail then continues down and soon you'll arrive at the place where you departed from the trail on ascent.

8A. SPIONKOP RIDGE 2576 m

The shortest and most interesting extension goes north to the summit of Spionkop Ridge. No difficulties. Looking down the length of Spionkop Ridge and Loaf Mountain to the north will be a good reward for the extra effort. If you're feeling really energetic, you can continue north to reach the summit of Loaf Mountain quite easily. This, however, leaves you a great distance from your car and is recommended only if you can travel fast and have plenty of daylight left for the long return trip.

Extension to the north from Newman Peak. **S**: Spionkop Ridge; **L**: Loaf Mountain.

8B. AVION RIDGE 2440 m

A second option from Newman goes southwest to the summit of Avion Ridge. Descend southwest to the col, where a trail curves around the west side of the ridge. If time is a concern, follow this trail – it goes all the way to the summit. A more scenic route stays on the ridge and then joins up with the trail as you descend southwest from the ridge and then on to the summit. **Return** the same way.

9. ANDERSON PEAK 2698 m

(MAP 2, PAGE 449)
Rating moderate to difficult scrambling via the south drainage
Round-trip time 7–10 hours
Elevation gain 1200 m
Maps 82 G/1 Sage Creek; Gem Trek Waterton National Park

Anderson Peak (sometimes called Mount Anderson) is the third-highest in Waterton, behind Blakiston and Lineham, and therefore sports a fine summit view. There are many routes to the top of this striking peak, and after completing a bunch of them, I would characterize this route to be the most enjoyable scramble and one of my favourite routes in the park. Tons of hands-on scrambling. Try from July on. Note that this is a different route than the one described in the first edition of this book.

Start at the Red Rock Canyon parking lot and follow the signs to Blakiston Falls. Continue on the trail past the falls to the second major rocky drainage coming down from Anderson Peak on the right (GR142444). This drainage is recognizable by a steep and usually dry waterfall about 100 m up (see photo). It is approximately 45 minutes from the parking lot.

Hike up the drainage to the smooth rock of the waterfall and then swing around to the right side, ascending steep and loose terrain to gain the first tier. The farther right you go, the gentler the grade.

The ascent route as seen from Blakiston Trail.

A scenic diversion on the way to the east summit.

Don't stray too far away from the drainage, as eventually you'll want to be in it. This first section is tedious, but stick with it – the rewards are soon to come.

Ascend scree slopes to right side of the drainage until you reach a wide scree bowl. Here, the drainage to your left takes on a friendlier appearance. Traverse left into it and away you go. For the next several hundred vertical metres enjoy some of the best moderate hands-on scrambling in the area. The rock is solid, step-like and a sheer joy to ascend. Often, steeper sections may appear to be too steep but are easily ascended. Easier terrain always lies to the right of the drainage if desired. To maximize your scrambling experience and minimize your scree experience, hug the left side of the drainage. As well, the variety of rock visible in this drainage is staggering – if I knew a single thing about geology, I'm sure I'd be salivating the entire way up!

Higher up, numerous gullies appear to the left. Resist the temptation to gain the ridge early by ascending one. These gullies are loose and very steep. Stay in the main drainage. Even as the amount of scree starts to increase, good scrambling can again be found on the left side of the drainage. The top of the route features the signature black igneous rock layer atop a layer of beautiful burgundy argillite, common to many peaks in the area. The easiest line here stays in the centre, but there is much exploring to do should you choose to venture left through these bands – moderate to difficult scrambling.

At the top, the true summit of Anderson sits to the left (light-brown scree) and the lower but more interesting east summit lies to the right. A quick traverse over to the east summit is almost mandatory.

After enjoying a wonderful panorama from the east summit, head west to the true summit. Being

Mark makes his way to the true summit of Anderson. Note the impressively steep walls of Anderson's north face.

higher, the view is a little better from the true summit. The glaciated peaks to the south in Glacier National Park (US) are especially impressive.

The southwest traverse to Lost Mountain takes only 30 minutes and involves easy to moderate scrambling, depending on your line of ascent. If an ascent of Lost is not in your plans, either return the same way you came up or descend southwest to the Anderson/Lost col and then head southeast down scree and grassy slopes to Blakiston Creek Trail. At the trail, turn left (east) and hike back to the parking lot.

10. LOST MOUNTAIN 2509 m

(MAP 2, PAGE 449)
Rating easy via south slopes
Round-trip time 5–9 hours
Elevation gain 1000 m
Maps 82 G/1 Sage Creek; Gem Trek Waterton National Park

Though best combined with an ascent of Mount Anderson and/or Mount Bauerman, Lost Mountain offers an easy scramble with interesting scenery along Blakiston Creek and a decent summit view and is therefore worthwhile by itself. Nabbing Anderson adds only an hour to the trip and heading west to Mount Bauerman a couple more, though the trip from Lost to Bauerman is the most interesting and scenic part of the trip. Lost Mountain is a pleasant day with options for one, two or three summits. Mostly steep hiking. Red Rock Parkway is closed from November to mid-May. Try from June on.

Start at the Red Rock Canyon parking lot and follow the signs to Blakiston Falls. Continue on the trail past the falls for approximately 5 km (about 1.25 hours from the parking lot at a moderately fast pace). Keep checking to the right now and then, looking for an obvious grassy slope that leads easily to the summit block of Lost. As soon as you see it, turn right through light bush and gain the open slopes. Be careful not to overshoot this key point, as you may end up in some fairly dense forest when you turn right. The grassy slopes soon give way to annoying treadmill scree,

where you'll probably want a set of hiking poles. As you gain elevation, trend a little to the left. Near the top, the steep and loose summit block can be easily circumvented on the left side. Once on the ridge, turn right and continue up gentle slopes to the summit.

The view is very pleasant even though the taller Mount Anderson blocks some of the panorama – a good excuse for you to run over to that summit (only an hour round trip). Hopefully, the beautiful red argillite slopes of the unnamed peak to the west will catch your attention and motivate you to

Direct route to the summit as seen from Blakiston Trail.

continue on to it and then to Mount Bauerman. If not, **return** the same way.

10A. MOUNT BAUERMAN 2409 m

To get to Mount Bauerman, you must first gain the higher, unnamed peak between Lost and Bauerman (unofficially titled "Kootenai Brown Peak") by dropping down to the col and then reascending the wonderfully scenic rock to the summit – arguably the best part of the entire day. Unless the characteristically fierce Waterton wind is howling from the west, stay near the edge throughout to enjoy vertiginous views down the north side and more fantastic rock.

At the summit, Bauerman comes into view and it may look to be quite far away at this point in the scramble! Thankfully, the terrain is easy and enjoyable to negotiate, and the grade is so mellow you'll hardly even know you're going up. As well, the scenery changes nicely as you reach the low point and make your way through trees lining the col. Again, the vertical north face of Bauerman provides an impressive diversion as you decide whether your legs are going to get you back to the car after all this.

Right: From near the summit of Lost, "Kootenai Brown Peak" and the route to it are quite obvious.
Below: Jodi starts down towards the col between "Kootenai" and Bauerman. Bauerman rises up to the right.

A well-worn trail takes you all the way to the summit, where a puny cairn and respectable summit view await. Although you can **return** the same way, a far easier and less strenuous option is to descend scree slopes heading directly from the summit. Trend a little left as you rapidly lose elevation on very surfable scree. The scree eventually gives way to grassy and treed slopes. Keep heading down, picking the easiest line with the least amount of trees. Eventually you'll run into Blakiston Creek Trail. Turn left onto the trail and enjoy the 9 km back to your car. Make sure you don't walk right by some of the terrific scenery of Blakiston Creek, including stunning red and green argillite rock.

11. LONE MOUNTAIN 2420 m

(MAP 2, PAGE 449)
Rating easy via the south ridge
Round-trip time 8–11 hours
Elevation gain 1000 m
Maps 82 G/1 Sage Creek; Gem Trek Waterton National Park

Lone Mountain is not going to go down in history as Waterton's best scramble. Reaching a height of only 2420 m, the peak sits below pretty much everything around it. The 32 km round-trip distance may also be a deterrent for some. However, an excellent trail system covers 28 of those kilometres and the summit view is quite unique – well worth the effort of getting there. For peak-baggers, tagging Kishinena Peak on the same trip may also be motivation to run up this isolated little peak. Try from July on.

Park at the Red Rock Canyon parking lot. Hike the full length of Blakiston Creek Trail – 10.1 km. You will pass by the entire north side of Lone Mountain (to your left), starting around the 7.5 km mark. Although several direct routes to the summit appear feasible from the north side, they are not. The vegetation on this side of the mountain is deceivingly thick and high. Resist the temptation to try, no matter how easy it looks. From experience I can tell you this side of the peak is a nightmare!

Upon reaching the signed intersection at the end of Blakiston Creek Trail, turn left towards Lone

The summit cairn and view to the southwest. **KP**: Kinnerly Peak; **FM**: Festubert Mountain; **LKP**: Long Knife Peak; **KEP**: King Edward Peak; **SP**: Starvation Peak.

Lake. Hike another 4.2 km to the shores of Lone Lake, taking a left when you reach the cabin. Fast hikers can make it from the parking lot to Lone Lake in 3.5 hours, though a more leisurely pace is recommended.

The best place to start up the south ridge is right by the posts for hanging food, a few metres back up the trail from the lake. The bush may look thick here but it is surprisingly easy to negotiate. Faint animal trails help. Trend slightly left as you ascend, to avoid ending up too far east of the ridge. The steepest terrain occurs near the bottom. Very soon the grade starts to ease and the trees start to thin. When they do, trend a little to the right to gain the actual ridge, where the ascent is easier and more scenic. Once you are on the ridge, route-finding is not an issue. Simply hike north up the ridge, enjoying the pleasant terrain and the improving views. Expect to take 45 minutes to an hour to reach the summit from Lone Lake.

The most interesting views from the summit belong to the very striking forms of rarely ascended King Edward Peak, Starvation Peak, Miskwasini Peak and Kenow Mountain. Those familiar with the remarkable mountains of Glacier National Park in Montana will recognize Chapman Peak, Mount Kinnerly and Long Knife Peak as well as other distinctive mountains.

Return the same way. Once again, it will look very tempting to descend the north side of the mountain. The upper slopes are in fact quite easy, but the middle and lower slopes are treacherous, involving intense bushwhacking and unseen cliff bands.

This trip can be combined with an ascent of Kishinena Peak for a very long and strenuous but rewarding day. A signed trail to South Kootenay Pass lies about 100 m south of the end of Blakiston Creek Trail. From Lone Lake return to that point (4.1 km) and turn left onto the trail. Hike 1.7 km to South Kootenay Pass and then turn north and hike/scramble up to the summit of Kishinena Peak. The summit is the highest point, not the one identified on some topo maps. For descent, either refer to the Sage Pass descent described in the Kishinena Peak trip (highly recommended) or return the way you came. If you choose Sage Pass, it may be easier to return to Red Rock Canyon parking lot via Twin Lakes Trail and Snowshoe Trail. Regardless of which trail systems you take, it's a very long, feet-numbing hike back to your vehicle!

12. KISHINENA PEAK 2440 m

(MAP 2, PAGE 449)
Rating moderate via the east face
Round-trip time 6–10 hours
Elevation gain 1000 m
Maps 82 G/1 Sage Creek; Gem Trek Waterton National Park

Kishinena Peak may not look like much on a topo map, but its strategic location on the Continental Divide guarantees a wonderful summit view. The round-trip distance is approximately 26 km, but with a bike approach, fast parties can complete the trip in 6 hours. Recommended is a more leisurely pace to enjoy some wonderful scenery. Pick a clear, calm day, take a big lunch and hang out at the summit as the sun highlights many of the awesome colours to the east as it moves to the west. This little peak holds snow far longer into the season than its more statuesque counterparts to the east. Early-season ascents can be thwarted by deep snow. Try from mid-July on. Take an ice axe and crampons if you go early in the season and wish to ascend steep snow slopes to the summit. Note that there is some controversy regarding the location of the official summit of Kishinena Peak. This trip goes to the highest point of the ridge (for the best view, of course!), due west of Mount Bauerman.

Park at the Red Rock Canyon parking lot and bike (strongly recommended) or hike 8 km along Snowshoe Trail to Snowshoe Campground. Leave your bike at the campground, cross the nearby creek on a wooden bridge and hike 3.3 km to Twin Lakes Campground. About 20 minutes into the

A first glimpse of the Kishinena objective. The ascent route goes right up the middle of the face.

hike the scenery opens up and Kishinena appears in front of you (see photo opposite).

Take a few minutes to assess whether snow might be a factor. If the east face is plastered, doing the ascent via Sage Pass (the alternative descent route) is preferable.

Hike past Twin Lakes Campground, following signs and the trail towards South Kootenay Pass. Quickly the other lake becomes visible below you. It is the more colourful of the two. The trail leads to a cairn at the col between Mount Bauerman and Kishinena Peak. At this point, leave the trail and hike west towards the east face of Kishinena. The lightly treed terrain leads quickly to more open slopes. Stay over to the left initially to avoid a rock band.

Past the first rock band, continue up the face, trending right for easier terrain. Although you may have to use your hands occasionally, this is mostly steep off-trail hiking if the easiest route is taken. Choose whatever route serves your purpose to reach the summit. Probably the easiest route stays to the right (north) side of the face.

Two summits only a few metres apart are both worth a visit. From the more southerly one, enjoy terrific views into Montana's Glacier National Park. The rounded form of Chapman Peak and the more striking profiles of Kintla, Kinnerly and Long Knife Peak will probably catch your eye. Just north of the border, King Edward Peak and Starvation Peak are very prominent. The north summit boasts unique views of summits of the Castle area.

Both summits grant a terrific view of three of Waterton's most spectacular and colourful massifs. Due east lies the trio of Anderson, Lost and Bauerman, while to the southeast sits the famous Blakiston horseshoe (a more than worthwhile scramble taking in Blakiston, Hawkins

and Lineham). To the northeast lies the Mount Glendowan massif. This amazing group of mountains starts in the east with Bellevue Hill, travels west and then turns north, extending far into the Castle. There are no less than 10 official summits and numerous unofficial high points worthy of a visit. All are connected with high-level connecting ridges and thus there is no need to descend into a valley to get from one summit to the next – remarkable!

For those concerned about standing atop official summits, you may want to hedge your bets and head southeast for about 1 km to a much lower summit, identified on some maps as the true summit. The view is correspondingly inferior and this side trip is hardly worth the effort, except for the impressive view of Kishinena's steep east side. If this is your route of choice, then it is possible to continue south for a few hundred metres towards South Kootenay Pass, looking for a trail that descends east. Follow this switchbacking track to Lone Lake Trail and turn north. In short order it joins with Blakiston Trail, which then leads easily back to the Kishinena/Bauerman col and Twin Lakes Trail. Note that this alternative descent route will require an additional 150 m of elevation gain.

The recommended alternative descent is super easy and super scenic – who could ask for anything more! The goal is to descend north to Sage Pass, where a good trail takes you back to Twin Lakes Trail. In fact there is a good trail all the way to Sage Pass from the summit of Kishinena. However, for those wanting to get the most out of the day, travelling right on the ridge grants much better views (as well as a much longer death fall, should you misstep while gawking at the views!). Lower down, the well-worn trail will suffice and makes life easier.

A partial summit panorama: Mount Blakiston and the Hawkins Horseshoe are at the left, while peaks of Glacier National Park dominate the right side.

Looking back to the summit, along the Sage Pass descent route. Snow can persist well into July on the mountain, due to its westerly location.

Sage Pass is signed, and from there a good trail, heading southeast, switchbacks down to Twin Lakes Trail. At this intersection, turn left (east), hike easily back to your bike and then prepare for an exhilarating 45-minute ride back to Red Rock. Bear activity is very common in this area. Remember to yell and scream your head off as you zip down the trail at Mach 2!

13. RUBY RIDGE 2420 m

(MAP 3, PAGE 450)
Rating easy via south slopes
Round-trip time 4–6 hours
Elevation gain 870 m to summit; 1020 m for the traverse
Maps 82 G/1 Sage Creek, 82 H/4 Waterton Lakes; Gem Trek Waterton National Park

The two summits of Ruby Ridge sport excellent views of some of the more statuesque peaks in Waterton Park. Although the ascent to the west summit is quite scenic, the highlight of the trip is the colourful traverse to the east peak. An alternative descent route then allows for a very pleasant loop route. Try from June on.

Drive about 9 km on the Akamina Parkway (Cameron Lake Road) and park at the Lineham Creek trailhead, on the right (north) side of the road. Follow the excellent trail as it parallels Lineham Creek, then takes a few switchbacks to higher terrain and eventually breaks out into the open. Once the terrain opens up, you can pick pretty much anywhere to leave the trail and go north, upslope towards the summit. In general, the earlier you leave the trail the steeper the terrain will be, but there is never anything too alarmingly steep on this side of the mountain.

Pick a line of your choosing, avoiding rock bands if they appear and taking time to enjoy the variety of rock types encountered on the ascent. Higher up, depending on your route, you may have to trend either left or right to reach the summit. Route-finding is an easy affair on this peak.

At the summit, if the view of Waterton's highest peak, Mount Blakiston, with Ruby Lake nestled under its steep east face, does not satiate, I'm sure the vistas including Cameron Lake and the peaks to the south, in Glacier National Park, will.

Except for circumventing a few rock bands on the way down to the col, the traverse to the east summit is an easy and very satisfying affair. The colourful red argillite rock bands are encountered right away. Some are easily downclimbed, while routes around others can usually be found on either side, though some searching may be necessary. Don't forget to look back at what you've gone down or around. Below the bands, it is an easy walk down to the col and up to the summit. Expect to take about an hour to complete the traverse.

Return the way you came or complete the very scenic and therefore recommended loop route. For the loop route, simply descend easy slopes, directly from the summit, heading southwest. The goal is

The easy ascent slopes of Ruby Ridge. The rock bands above are avoidable but worth checking out.

to go more or less directly back to the trailhead. You will therefore be traversing slopes (southwest) as you descend. The red argillite scenery is, once again, delightful! You will likely encounter a stint of fairly heavy bushwhacking lower down, but it is short lived. Using GPS or other technology may be of great assistance in getting you through the bush and back to the trail.

Mount Rowe

Like Kishinena Peak, Mount Rowe's strategic location amid grander peaks and lakes makes it a fine objective for the view alone. The easiest route to the summit takes you first to the three Rowe Lakes. An excellent trail leads all the way to these idyllic lakes. From there it's a scree slog up the northeast slopes and then an exciting ridge ascent to the summit.

A more direct route tackles the summit from the southeast side. This way lacks the three lakeshore visits of the previous route, but it does ascend an interesting drainage that has a charm of its own.

From the summit of Mount Rowe there are options to continue to two other high points to the northwest. They are both worthwhile diversions and one is actually higher than Rowe. The ultimate extension is to continue on that northwest ridge all the way to the summit of Festubert Mountain. This makes for a very long but rewarding day. If you intend to go to Festubert, the southeast route up Mount Rowe will shave off several kilometres of road walking on return.

Right: Some of the scenic terrain on the way down to the col.
Below: An excellent summit view of Mount Blakiston and Ruby Lake.

14. MOUNT ROWE (VIA ROWE LAKES) 2469 m

(MAP 3, PAGE 450)

Rating moderate via northeast slopes and the northeast ridge; some exposure
Round-trip time 5–7 hours; add 2–8 hours if extensions are taken
Elevation gain 800 m (Rowe only)
Maps 82 G/1 Sage Creek; Gem Trek Waterton National Park

The easier route that visits the very beautiful Rowe Lakes. Try from July on.

Drive about 10 km on the Akamina Parkway (Cameron Lake Road) and park at the Rowe Lakes trailhead, on the right (north) side of the road. Hike 3.9 km along Rowe Lakes Trail to a junction. Although unnecessary, a quick visit to Lower Rowe Lake from here is almost mandatory. The tranquil lake is only a few hundred metres to the south. Return to the junction and hike another 2.5 km to the even more scenic Upper Lakes. A big chunk of elevation is gained as the trail winds up the headwall.

There are two Upper Lakes. A good strategy here is to visit the slightly higher one, descend to the lower one via a scenic stream on the east side of the lake, and then tackle the ascent of Mount Rowe from the lower lake's south shore. You can then revisit and explore the upper lake using the alternative descent route on return.

The red argillite shores of the lower lake are a treat in themselves. Follow the shore around to the south side of the lake and then ascend relentlessly steep slopes to the gain the northeast ridge. Follow the interesting ridge to the summit. There are a couple of exposed scrambling moves, but none are difficult. Take in a wonderful summit view before deciding where to go next. See the southeast route

The ascent slopes of Mount Rowe as seen from near the south end of the slightly lower Upper Lake.

Looking down on the Upper Rowe Lakes from the alternative descent route.

on page 69 for options to the northwest and Festubert Mountain.

Of course there is the option to return the same way you came, but an excellent loop route exists and is highly recommended. Continue along the summit ridge, heading northwest. When you are due west of the upper lake, follow the wide and easy ridge in a northeast direction, down to the west side of the lake. Early-season ascents may be thwarted by lingering snow patches if there is no easy route around them. Views throughout are splendid. After exploring the largest of the three Rowe Lakes, make your way back to the trail on the north end of the lake and then follow the trail back to your vehicle.

15. MOUNT ROWE (SOUTHEAST ROUTE) 2469 m

(MAP 3, PAGE 450)

Rating moderate via southeast slopes; some exposure if the northeast ridge is followed
Round-trip time 4.5–6 hours; add 2–8 hours if extensions are taken
Elevation gain 800 m (Rowe only)
Maps 82 G/1 Sage Creek; Gem Trek Waterton National Park

The slightly shorter route. A better option if you intend to ascend Festubert Mountain as well. Try from July on.

Park at a pull-off on the right side of the road about 12.8 km along the Akamina Parkway (Cameron Lake Road), right by the winter gates. Walk about 150 m farther down the road, looking for a small, dried-up drainage on the right. This drainage is the key to the ascent and leads almost all the way to the summit. Hike up the drainage, moving to the left or right side whenever vegetation takes over the path. Whenever possible, stay in the drainage to enjoy some easy but enjoyable hands-on scrambling.

Vegetation takes over again, and as you gain elevation the upper slopes and summit of Rowe appear to the left. Move back into the drainage and stay there, making your way easily up the southeast slopes. As you approach the middle of the southeast face, there are two ascent options:

1. Moderate scrambling up the centre of the face: continue up the drainage until another drainage comes in from the left and runs right up the middle of the face. This drainage goes right in between two prominent uplifts of rock to the summit.

2. A scree slog followed by an exciting ridge

The ascent route from the road. **CD**: centre drainage; **NR**: northeast ridge.

Upper ascent routes. **CD**: centre drainage; **NR**: northeast ridge.

scramble to the summit: continue up the drainage as it swings to the right and then becomes a scree slope leading to the ridge and skyline to the right of the summit. Once on the ridge, follow the crest up increasingly narrow and exposed terrain to the top. The scrambling here is never difficult, but do remind yourself of the quality (or lack of it) of the rock you are ascending. All too soon the scrambling ends as you arrive at a cairned false summit. A short hike leads to the true one.

The summit view is quite impressive, though needless to say most of the surrounding mountains are taller than the one you're on. The Upper Rowe Lakes look particularly inviting from this summit – as do the taller peaks south of the border – and impressive colour contrasts of light-brown Lineham, red Hawkins and the greenish outlier to the left of Hawkins make this view notable. Mount Festubert lies farther northwest.

Numerous options and extensions are available when you are ready to continue.

1. **Return** the same way.

2. **Return** via the Rowe Lakes Trail. Descend the northeast ridge until it becomes possible to drop down to easy slopes on your left. Traverse down and northeast, arriving quickly at the Upper Rowe Lakes. Find the trail at the north end of the second

lake and follow it for 6.4 km to the trailhead. Turn right and hike 2.6 km back to your car.

3. Continue west and then north along the Rowe ridge to an unnamed high point at GR136374. The view of the lakes continues to improve the farther along the ridge you travel, and eventually the distinctive Festubert Mountain comes into view to the northwest. Also note the grassy bump that allows you to escape to the Upper Rowe Lakes without having to return to Mount Rowe. At the summit at GR136374, other options are to continue northwest to Festubert or to the high point at GR133382 and then east to Lineham Ridge Trail and out via the Rowe Lakes. Otherwise, **return** the way you came.

15A. FESTUBERT MOUNTAIN
2522 m
Add 400 m of elevation gain. 8.5–11 hours for both peaks.

If you plan to do Festubert at any point, this is the time, given that the best route to the summit traverses the entire ridge from Mount Rowe. The route barely needs a description – from Mount Rowe, follow the ridge northwest until you get there! There are two major high points along the way, both of which surpass Mount Rowe in height. It is worth visiting both, but if you wish to avoid

Mount Festubert from the first high point. It's still a long way from here! **F**: Festubert; **HP**: second high point

the extra elevation gain, sidesloping the second high point is possible. The remainder of the ridge is sparsely treed and the most enjoyable route follows faint trails alongside the edge. The final push to the summit can be tackled along the ridge edge (a couple of sections of moderate to difficult scrambling), or via easy scree by traversing left around the rock bands. The summit view probably won't take you by storm, as it's basically what you've been looking at for the past three hours.

Either **return** the same way (taking into account that this return will add another 350 m of elevation gain to your day) or use the south slopes as follows: descend the way you came for a few hundred metres, looking for the obvious scree slope on your right that goes most of the way to the valley bottom. Head down those slopes, enjoying several hundred vertical metres of excellent scree-surfing. Trend left a little as you descend. Soon the slope narrows into a drainage that can be followed all the way down to Westside Road (trail). Expect a short but nasty stint of bushwhacking alongside a creek. Once you arrive at the trail, turn left and enjoy a mind-numbing 11 km hike to the Akamina Pass trailhead. Another 1.5 km hike north along Akamina Parkway completes a long day.

16. "CARTHEW MINOR" 2330 m

(MAP 3, PAGE 450)

Rating easy via the south face; moderate to Mount Carthew with one exposed downclimb
Round-trip time 3–5 hours; add 2–3 hours for Mount Carthew
Elevation gain 700 m; add 350 m for Mount Carthew
Maps 82 G/01 Sage Creek; Gem Trek Waterton National Park

If, like me, you are a sucker for red argillite and the magnificent scenery it creates, this inno-cent-looking little bump on the southwest end of Mount Carthew is figuratively painted with this beautifully coloured rock.

Alan Kane briefly mentions this route in Scrambles *and a more detailed description is included here. From the summit of "Minor," a traverse to the true summit of Mount Carthew is a scenic and very rewarding extension of the day. Consider a late-September ascent, when the larches on the con-necting ridge will be changing colour.*

A long and strenuous but intensely scenic loop route can be approached by taking the shuttle (departing 8:30 a.m. from Tamarack Outdoor Outfitters, $13.50 as of 2015) from the townsite to Cameron Lake and then following the Carthew/Alderson trail all the way back to the townsite – highly recommended! Try from July on.

Turn onto the Cameron Lake road and drive to the end of it, at the lakeshore. From the head of Cameron Lake, take the Carthew Lakes trail along the left side of the lake. The trail follows the lake-shore for a short distance and then takes a series of very long switchbacks up steep, forested slopes to a plateau before descending to Summit Lake.

From the plateau there are two routes to the south face, both involving a little bushwhacking. The Summit Lake route adds about 30 minutes of extra time, a few more metres of elevation gain and of course extra distance. However, if you have never seen the lake, this is a worthwhile diversion. For both routes, be sure to check out the objective through the trees and note the prominent pinnacle of rock about halfway up the south ridge. The pin-nacle acts as a good route guide. The red argillite boulder field at the bottom of the slope serves the same purpose.

Direct route

Arriving at the upper plateau, where the trail lev-els off, hike for another 5 minutes or so, turning around occasionally to check out the objective, to the northeast. A moderately fast pace gets you there in about 50 minutes from the trailhead. If you reach a large, distinctive rock formation just off the right side of the trail, you have gone a little too far.

At approximately GR173329 it is time to turn to the northeast, leaving the trail to head into the light bush, making your way towards the peak (see photo opposite). Aim for the boulder field at the bottom of the peak as it becomes visible through the trees.

Summit Lake route

Complete the 4 km trail to the serene shores of Summit Lake. On a calm day Mount Chapman and Mount Custer will be reflected wonderfully in the lake. Leave the lake and continue on the signed trail towards Carthew Summit, looking up occa-sionally to note the direction of the objective. In about 10 minutes the trail swings around to the southeast side of Carthew Minor and the scenery opens up to the right. The false summit of Mount Carthew also becomes visible ahead and slightly to the right.

Continue along the trail for a short distance until rock bands appear on the left side (GR178330). This is as good a place as any to leave the trail, hike up the embankment to the left and then go north towards the south face/ridge. Trend slightly left as you approach the face, again taking note of the pinnacle high above and the boulder field at the bottom.

For both routes

Once at the base of the peak, work your way care-fully up and through an interesting, steep field of lichen-covered red argillite boulders. Above the

The direct route. Nicole Lisafeld and Carthew Minor, from the point where you leave the trail.

Above: The Summit Lake route. Once you leave the trail, the objective comes into view.
Left: Nicole enjoying one of many scenic diversions in "The Garden of Red Argillite."

field continue upward, looking for the aforementioned pinnacle. The pinnacle and the terrain to the west of it represent the most interesting scenery of the ascent slope and may be the highlight of the day (I call this place "The Garden of Red Argillite"). Be sure to take some time to explore this fascinating area. Continue up the face and reach the summit in short order. Along the way, more cool scenery can be found by traversing right, onto the ridge.

For the effort expended, the summit view is magnificent. In some ways it is actually superior to the view from Mount Carthew in that a host of beautiful lakes are visible, including Cameron, Summit and Wurdeman (the stunning turquoise lake nestled under the rounded form of Chapman Peak). Other highlights of the summit view include Mount Custer circling

Nicole hikes the wonderfully scenic ridge between Carthew Minor and the false summit of Mount Carthew.

Cameron Lake, statuesque Kintla and Kinnerly to the right of Custer, the red form of Akamina Ridge and the three summits of Long Knife Peak behind Akamina. Return the same way if Mount Carthew is not in your plans.

MOUNT CARTHEW

The traverse from Carthew Minor to the true summit is very scenic and takes a little over an hour. You can then use Kane's route for the descent, eliminating the need for additional elevation gains. At an elevation 300 m superior to that of Minor, the summit view from Carthew is, needless to say, excellent.

One of the highlights of the traverse is getting down to the col. Walk to the edge and look down. The drop initially looks quite daunting, but due to the rock's horizontal bedding, downclimbing it is far easier than it appears. It amounts to moderate scrambling, although the exposure will make it feel difficult. Note that snowy conditions on this downclimb will probably render the terrain too dangerous. If that is the case, play it safe and return the way you came.

Go straight down the centre. At an intermediate col, skirt to the left around a boulder and then back up to the right to finish the downclimb on the right side of the ridge. The rock here is stunningly beautiful, equalling and perhaps surpassing what is seen near the pinnacle on the south ridge of Carthew Minor.

An easy and potentially super-scenic traverse (if the larches are changing colour) to the false summit follows. As you gain elevation on the connecting ridge, stay over to the left for great views of Carthew's brutally steep northwest face. A rock band soon interrupts the ridge but is easily ascended with one or two scrambling moves. The false summit is a great place to catch your breath and soak in the exponentially improving view. Hike easily to the true summit to the northeast, staying on the ridge throughout. Savour another magnificent panorama!

Options for return are numerous:

1. The same way you came.
2. Follow the Kane route in reverse (recommended). Return to the false summit and then drop down in a southeast direction to the col between the false summit and Carthew Summit (the obvious high point farther south along the long ridge). Carthew Summit Trail drops down to the west side of the ridge and leads effortlessly back to Summit Lake.
3. If you wisely took the shuttle from the townsite to Cameron Lake, you can complete a marvellous loop route via the Carthew Lakes and the Alderson Lake trail. Return to the false summit and then drop down in a southeast direction to the col between the false summit and Carthew Summit (the obvious high point farther south along the ridge). Instead of dropping down to the right (west), go left (east) and follow the pronounced trail down to the first of the Carthew Lakes. The first few kilometres of this trail, past the three Carthew Lakes and Alderson Lake, are incredibly scenic, but after that it's a long plod with limited views back to the townsite (still, highly recommended!).
4. Via Buchanan Ridge down to Buchanan Peak, then down to Alderson Lake and out via Carthew/Alderson Trail to the townsite. See Kane's description in *Scrambles* for this route.

17. MOUNT RICHARDS (NORTH RIDGE) 2416 m

(MAP 4, PAGE 450)
Rating difficult, steep, exposed scrambling via the north ridge and southeast ridge; a climber's scramble
Round-trip time 11–14 hours
Elevation gain 1500 m (includes necessary losses)
Maps 82 H/4 Waterton Lakes; Gem Trek Waterton National Park

For a diminutive mountain, Richards packs a real punch. Although there are easier and faster routes to the summit, the one described here is long and physically demanding and requires much route-finding and exposed scrambling. The scenic rewards of the route are tremendous throughout, with awe-inspiring views of the Waterton Lakes, Mount Cleveland and Mount Alderson. Try from July on.

Drive into Waterton and follow Evergreen Avenue to a gravel parking lot on the right, the Bertha Lake trailhead. Hike 5.2 km to Bertha Lake. Continue around the east side of the lake on the shore trail for about 5 minutes. When it becomes obvious, take a sharp left and head up the ramp alongside the treeline, aiming for the point on the north ridge where the treeline ends.

For the next several hours, enjoy the challenge of scrambling the north ridge. At times, it is necessary to lose elevation and circumvent steep rock bands on the right side, but always try to return to the ridge for the best scrambling and fantastic views of Upper Waterton Lake, backdropped beautifully by Mount Cleveland. Route-finding can be a challenge and often you will be required to scramble up steep, exposed terrain. On the way, there are several high points where you can rest and enjoy the scenery. Expect your horizontal progress towards the summit to be very slow.

Eventually you'll arrive at a high point before a low col, followed by a striking ridge of red argillite. Quite obviously, continuing along the north ridge at this point would require technical climbing. Drop down to the col and follow a good trail on the east side. The argillite rock bands along the way

The exciting north ridge as seen from Bertha Peak. **C**: Mount Cleveland; **F**: false summit.

The approximate start of the shortcut route. **U**: short upclimb to the higher ledge.

are stunning. Reascend to a col on the other side (the east ridge), and then turn right and ascend easy slopes to a false summit with a huge cairn. Personally, I call this summit "Little Richards." The view is already outstanding and will get even better once you reach the summit of Mount Richards. From the top of Little Richards descend towards the col between Little Richards and the formidable northeast ridge of Mount Richards. Some scrambling on the right side of the ridge is required and then a scramble back up to the ridge. Once you are there look for a not so obvious slightly descending ledge (see photo above). This is the key to the shortcut route. Descend the ledge and then scramble up to a higher ledge. Follow this slightly exposed ledge around to easier terrain. It's slightly downhill from here, all the way to the southeast ridge.

Upon reaching the southeast ridge, traverse left (west) a fair distance into an easier gully that takes you up past all the difficulties of the ridge. Ascend the gully and then route-find your way back to

the ridge and the summit. There are several rock bands to overcome. You could choose to veer way over to the left to get around the biggest one. The summit view is incredible: Bertha Lake and Mount Alderson on one side, Upper Waterton Lake and an array of spectacular peaks south of the border on the other.

Although the easiest descent is southward, into Glacier National Park in Montana and then back via Upper Waterton Lake, this is a very long trek and requires you to have your passport handy. Therefore this route is no longer recommended. The fastest and still quite easy way is to do the north face route (next trip) in reverse.

Return to the col south of Little Richards and then descend the obvious rubble and scree slopes to the west. Work your way down to Bertha Lake's southwest shore and follow the trail on either side of the lake back to the north end of the lake and down. The east side of the lake is definitely the shortest route.

18. MOUNT RICHARDS (NORTH FACE) 2416 m

(MAP 4, PAGE 450)
Rating moderate via the north face and southeast ridge
Round-trip time 9–11 hours
Elevation gain 1400 m
Maps 82 H/04 Waterton Lakes; Gem Trek Waterton National Park

If the difficult scrambling of Richards's north ridge does not sound appealing, then give the north face a go. This route takes less time but is still extremely scenic and gives you the chance to go around half of beautiful Bertha Lake. It is likely this route will eventually become the approach of choice for Mount Richards. Note that this is not the same way as for "Little Richards" as described in Snowshoeing in The Canadian Rockies, 2nd Edition. *Try from July on.*

Drive into Waterton and follow Evergreen Avenue to a gravel parking lot that is the Bertha Lake trailhead. Hike 5.2 km to Bertha Lake. From Bertha Lake follow the trail around the left (east) side of the lake. Unfortunately the trail is mostly a short distance away from the lake, but there are a couple of places where it descends to the shore and you can take in the colourful scenery.

At the south end of the lake, look for a minor trail heading off to the left (GR843337). Follow this for a short distance. You must now get up to the open terrain and shelf above (see photo next page). This requires a more circuitous track around the trees and foliage to the left or a more direct route through the greenery. Though very difficult to see from below, there is also a trail through the bush above you.

For either route, once you are above the lower

The Alstons (Karen, Jill and Ryan) and Reggie Williams arrive at Bertha Lake's red argillite beach. Mount Alderson is to the left, with part of Bertha Peak to the right.

difficulties, turn left and follow the obvious line of rubble and trees up to the false summit of Mount Richards, sometimes called "Little Richards." This part of the trip is foreshortened and can be tedious. Perhaps the least tedious line is to follow the edge of the treeline.

It is not necessary to go all the way to the huge cairn that marks the summit of Little Richards, but the view from there is extremely gratifying. It will get much better once you reach the summit of Mount Richards.

From the top of Little Richards descend towards the col between Little Richards and the formidable northeast ridge of Mount Richards. Some scrambling on the right side of the ridge is required and then a scramble back up to the ridge. Once you are there, look for a not so obvious, slightly descending ledge (see photo on page 78). This is the key to the shortcut route. Descend the ledge and then scramble up to a higher ledge. Follow this somewhat exposed ledge around to easier terrain. It's slightly downhill from here, all the way to the southeast ridge.

Upon reaching the southeast ridge, traverse left a fair distance into an easier gully that takes you past all the difficulties of the ridge. Ascend the gully and then route-find your way back to the ridge and the summit. There are several rock bands to be overcome. You could choose to veer way over to the left to get around the biggest one.

The summit view is incredible: Bertha Lake and Mount Alderson on one side, Upper Waterton Lake and an array of spectacular peaks south of the border on the other. Return the same way.

The routes to the shelf.

19. MOUNT BOSWELL 2439 m

(MAP 5, PAGE 451)
Rating moderate via the east face
Round-trip time 7–8 hours (doesn't include boat trip of 15 minutes each way)
Elevation gain 1200 m
Maps 82 H/4 Waterton Lakes; Gem Trek Waterton National Park

An ascent of Mount Boswell is an exercise in planning and logistics. The easiest route involves a pleasant boat ride across Upper Waterton Lake, follows a good section of Crypt Lake Trail and then ascends the east face of the mountain. To complete the trip in a day, you must take the 9 a.m. boat and be back at Crypt Landing by 5:30 p.m. for the return sailing. The consequences of missing the boat are: 1. A 40 km hike back to your car; 2. Spending the night at Crypt Landing and taking the boat back in the morning (highly inadvisable and frowned upon by the park). Although sprinting up the mountain is not necessary, a moderately fast hiking and scrambling pace are. Try from mid-July on.

Drive into Waterton and take a left at the three-way stop sign. Drive a few hundred metres to where the road forks and take another left into the marina parking lot. Tickets for the boat can be purchased at the end of the dock. Arrive well before 9:00 to be guaranteed a spot, having checked departure times beforehand in case they have changed.

Once the boat has brought you to Crypt Landing, hike the Crypt Lake Trail to the Burnt Rock Falls viewpoint (about 1.25 hours). Continue along the trail for about one kilometre and then look for a faint trail that heads west at GR918328 – 1740 m. From the lakeshore to this point should take no more than 1.5 hours. If it has taken you longer, it's

The approximate ascent route as seen from near where you leave the trail.

time to pick up the pace or downgrade the trip to a very pleasant and worthwhile visit to Crypt Lake. Head west down the faint trail through light bush. The trail quickly disappears. Keep going west and slightly down towards the stream that splits the valley. Don't veer too far left. The goal is to cross the stream just before the trail starts descending. If you run into a mess of alder bushes, circumvent them around the right side. If you are lucky you will find a couple of trees that have fallen across the stream, making easy work of the crossing. If not, simply ford. Once on the other side, continue heading west and also trend south as the heavily vegetated terrain dictates. Again, avoid the alders.

Start gaining elevation heading southwest towards the obvious gully that goes up the east face from left to right. Once in the gully, follow it up towards the summit ridge. It is also possible to ascend on either side of the gully. Be careful not to dislodge rocks onto your scrambling partners below in this narrow gully. When trees start to appear above you (or to your right, depending on the ascent route you took), start angling to the left towards the summit ridge. Gain the ridge and follow it southwest to a high point and then due west to the true summit. Hopefully you will reach the summit around 1:30 p.m. or earlier.

Needless to say, the strategic location of this peak renders the summit panorama a fine one. Mount Cleveland dominates the view to the south, although Goat Haunt Mountain, Miche Wabun Peak and other striking, unnamed summits in the vicinity also compete for attention. If you descend a short distance southwest, Upper Waterton Lake can be viewed in its entirety. To the east sit Vimy Peak and its long ridge south (Vimy Ridge), with Sofa Mountain behind. The red-argillite-topped mountain above Crypt Lake is unofficially titled "Crypt Peak."

Return the same way, leaving the summit no later than 2 p.m. This will allow you an unhurried descent. If you make it back to Crypt Lake Trail by 3:30, enjoy a pleasant stroll back to Crypt Landing. If it is any later, enjoy a frantic sprint!

Mark ascends typical terrain near the ridge. Crypt Lake is just visible at the left. The summit of the red peak above the lake lies just over the US border.

20. VIMY PEAK/RIDGE 2379 m

(MAP 5, PAGE 451)
Rating moderate with one difficult but avoidable rock band
Round-trip time 7–9 hours for the peak; add 5–7 hours for the ridge
Elevation gain 1100 m for the peak; add 500 m for the ridge
Maps 82 H/4 Waterton Lakes; Gem Trek Waterton National Park

Though the summit of Vimy Peak can be reached by a long but straightforward hiking trail, a more interesting route tackles the scenic north side more directly and is the one described here. The hiking trail then makes for an easy descent. Continuing on to the high point of Vimy Ridge will truly put your stamina to the test. Take a headlamp and twice as much water as you think you'll need. Try from mid-June on.

Drive to Pincher Creek and keep heading south on Highway 6. Still on Highway 6, about 900 m after passing the turnoff to Waterton Park, turn right. Drive 500 m and park at a pull-off on the left side of the road (there is a Wishbone trailhead sign on other side of the road). Hike – or better yet, bike – Wishbone Trail for 7 km (5.5 km to the Sofa Creek crossing and then 1.5 km to a junction). This trail is very narrow. Make lots of noise, not only to warn wildlife but also to alert other people on the trail.

Leave your bike at the signed junction, even though bikes are permitted on Wishbone Trail – you'll be using the easy descent route and the junction is where you'll end up. Take the right fork (Wishbone Trail) at the junction and continue on foot until you reach an unusual clearing strewn with dead trees. Turn left up this clearing, aiming for a rocky drainage at the back right side. Ascend the middle of the drainage. It is possible to continue up the entire drainage, but a more interesting

Ascent route from the clearing. **D**: difficult route to ridge; **E**: easy route.

Above: Preparing to ascend the difficult route to the ridge.
Left: One advantage of taking the difficult route is this scenic diversion, with a great view of the Waterton Lakes and Mount Crandell.

route gains the ridge to the right when a prominent band of alternating layers of light brown and greenish rock appears on the right side. Scramble up this band to reach the ridge, where a good view of the Waterton Lakes awaits. Moderate scrambling up this ridge leads to a rubble slope below Vimy's impressive, vertical north face. Aim for a prominent notch at the left side of the face. This area provides a weakness through the rock band and access to the summit ridge.

At the base of the weakness, assess the terrain. It is steep and involves difficult and exposed scrambling for the first several metres. If not to your liking, continue east to circumvent the band entirely. The best route up the band is right up the middle on small ledges. The rock is generally solid and a few good handholds make life easier. Trend right to easier terrain and then continue up. The towering pinnacles of rock are well worth a visit. Gain the ridge and continue to the summit.

As expected, the view of the Lower and Middle Waterton Lakes and the surrounding peaks is great, but most of the Upper Lake is out of view. Continuing west to a lower summit on the ridge remedies this a little, but it is still a worthwhile and scenic diversion. If satiated, either **return** the same way or take a slightly longer but easier route via Vimy Peak Trail. The trail heads southeast down the peak and then into the treed valley between two ridges. The distance for this return is 5.8 km from the summit to Wishbone/Vimy junction.

20A. VIMY RIDGE 2500 m

The long ridgewalk to the highest summit of Vimy Ridge, at GR939323, is easy but it leaves you a great distance from your car (a solid 18 km if you go to the highest point). Ensure you have plenty of water, and start down the ridge in a southeast direction. Stay on the crest of the ridge throughout. At the first high point, it is easy to bail out and go north down to Vimy Basin and the trail – a popular option for many hikers. Otherwise, keep going and going. The lakes quickly disappear behind other peaks, but the view towards Crypt Lake and Mount Cleveland to the south improves with each several hundred steps!

Technically, the summit of the ridge lies at GR929331, with an elevation of 2416 m. The highest and most scenic summit, however, is the next point to the southeast. If you've made it to the first summit, you might as well finish the job. At GR939323, pat yourself on the back, enjoy the view and then **return** the same way, using the alternative descent down the Vimy Peak trail (see above). It is possible to avoid too much elevation regain by sidesloping the east side of the mountain, but the travel may be slower and self-defeating. **Do not** try to shortcut by descending into the valley north of GR939323 and then directly to the southeast leg of Sofa Creek (unless you're carrying a 300 m rappel rope!).

The long route to Vimy Ridge and beyond. Check your water supply before embarking on this rewarding traverse. **B**: bailout route; **VR**: summit of Vimy Ridge; **HP**: high point of traverse; **C**: Mount Cleveland.

21. SOFA MOUNTAIN 2515 m

(MAP 5, PAGE 451)
Rating moderate via the northeast ridge or east of the northeast ridge
Round-trip time 6–8 hours
Elevation gain 900 m
Maps 82 H/4 Waterton Lakes; Gem Trek Waterton National Park

The northeast ridge of Sofa Mountain offers about 20 minutes of excellent scrambling on solid rock. A good trail takes you quickly and easily to the mountain, and on a clear day the views to the west and southwest are terrific. A slightly shorter route goes up the ridge east of the northeast ridge and has some interesting rock scenery en route. Try from June on.

Drive towards Waterton but do not take the right turn into the park. Instead, continue on Highway 6 for about 1 km and turn right onto Highway 6 South (Chief Mountain Parkway). Drive about 7.2 km and park at a gravel pull-off on the right side of the road. The trail starts here. Hike the trail as it wanders southward up and over hills and through lightly forested terrain and grassy meadows. In about 45 minutes you'll arrive in open terrain, with both routes visible. The trail continues west, heading towards the valley between the northeast ridge and the north ridge.

NORTHEAST RIDGE

Instead of following the trail into the valley, head directly up the steeper, grassy slopes of the northeast ridge. At the top, the rest of the ridge and the route up it become clear. Hike up scree slopes to

The ascent route as seen from a few hundred metres east of the start of the trail. **NE**: northeast ridge route; **EN**: ridge east of the northeast ridge.

Above: In the open. **NE**: northeast ridge route; **EN**: ridge east of the northeast ridge.
Below: Looking up the ridge east of the northeast ridge.

the start of the scrambling. Scramble straight up the first rock band. If it is too steep, traverse left for a short distance and ascend an obvious gully. The rock is solid, with good hand- and footholds. Continue up the ridge by tackling all rock bands head-on or slightly to the left, depending on your preference. At the top of the northeast ridge, turn left and hike easily for 2 km to the summit.

EAST OF THE NORTHEAST RIDGE

Follow the trail to a point above the waterfall that lies to the left. Find a place to cross the creek and then turn south, up the wide north ridge. The route is fairly straightforward, although you may want to be careful about getting onto terrain that is too steep. Also, note the route you are taking up, as it looks very different on descent. At the top, an easy 1 km hike leads to the summit. The summit panorama includes Chief Mountain and Mount Cleveland, two of Glacier National Park's more distinctive peaks, as well as a comprehensive view of most of Waterton Park.

For the **return** trip, it is probably best to retrace the route you took on ascent. For those who took the northeast ridge up, taking the north ridge down is not terribly difficult but may require some careful route-finding. For that route, instead of following the ridge in a northwest direction to the top of the northeast ridge, go north to the end of the north ridge. Route-find your way down the ridge (may be tricky at the top, but it gets increasingly easier lower down) to the valley below.

THE CASTLE

This stretch of land north of Waterton National Park is one of the best-kept secrets in the Canadian Rockies (until now, I suppose!). I would not have known about it if not for the insight and adventurous nature of Linda Breton, who introduced me to the area and a number of ascents within its borders. Host to many interesting scrambles, the area sees little traffic and more than likely you will have the mountain all to yourself. Like Waterton, its neighbour to the south, the variety of rock and rock colours are the highlights of the Castle area. Eye-catching bands of red and green argillite are features of most peaks. As well, there are numerous trail systems that make access and approaches considerably easier. Some of these trails are well suited for mountain bikes.

The area – also called the Castle Crown or Castle Wilderness – encompasses approximately 1000 square kilometres and is about twice as big as Waterton. The diverse ecology of the Castle is remarkable: aspen parklands, fescue grasslands, montane and subalpine forests, alpine meadows, hanging valleys and high-elevation lakes make up the area. The Castle is also home to an incredible variety of plant life, including approximately 120 rare species (about three times as many as are found in Banff National Park). Animal life is equally diverse. Bears, ungulates, wolverines, cougars and wolves, to name a few, are common to the area and use it as a corridor to additional habitat to the south and west.

Unfortunately, the land does not lie within a national or provincial park and therefore does not enjoy the environmental protection that parks afford. Perhaps more than any other area mentioned in this book, preservation of this pristine environment requires special attention from each of us. Environmental groups are presently working to ensure that logging, clear-cutting, mining and oil and gas extraction do not irreparably damage this delicate and precious environment.

Autumn is often the best time of the year for ascents in the Castle. The stunning array of rock colours are still visible, the larches are changing colour, early snowfall can enhance the beautiful scenery even more, creek crossings are easier and ticks are not an issue. Of course, unless you are lucky enough to live in the area, you might be making breakfast at 4 a.m. and leaving the city at 5 in order to get to the trailhead early enough.

The Castle is also home to a handful of amazing **high-level ridgewalks**. See page 127 for details.

GEOLOGY

The geology of the Castle is much the same as that of Waterton. See page 28 for details.

CLIMATE AND WEATHER

Like Waterton, the Castle is subject to very high winds. This can be a double-edged sword. Those high winds can clear west-facing slopes of snow early in the year, making this a good area for early-season trips. Of course, being on a peak during high winds can be dangerous. Gusts of up to

The wild colours, shapes and lines of The Castle area as seen from the summit of Mount Roche. Photo: Vern Dewit

100 km/h are not uncommon in this area and can easily knock you off your feet. Avoiding exposed scrambling situations is strongly recommended when the wind picks up. Before you leave home, check the weather forecasts, which give high-wind warnings when applicable.

ACCESS

From Calgary, go south on Highway 2, west on Highway 3 (towards Pincher Creek), then south on Highway 6 to Pincher Creek. For peaks in the West Castle area, turn right onto Highway 507. For the East Castle, continue south (turning left to remain on Highway 6), through Pincher Creek and towards Waterton.

ACCOMMODATION

The town of Pincher Creek has a number of motels and hotels. For less luxurious accommodations, there are quite a few campgrounds close to the town. If you want to get a little closer to the mountains, there are campgrounds at Beauvais Lake (off Highway 507) and Beaver Mines Lake (Highway 774) as well as several others in the area. Check for seasonal closures.

EAST CASTLE			
Prairie Bluff (south face)	2258 m	moderate	p. 92
Prairie Bluff (south ridge)	2258 m	easy	p. 94
Victoria Peak	2587 m	moderate	p. 96
Victoria Ridge	2530 m	easy	p. 98
Pincher Ridge	2423 m	difficult	p. 101
Pincher Ridge (centre and south)	2430, 2570 m	easy/moderate	p. 103
Drywood Mountain (south side)	2514 m	moderate	p. 106
Drywood Mountain (north side)	2478 m	moderate	p. 108
Loaf Mountain (south side)	2640 m	easy	p. 111
Loaf Mountain (north side)	2640 m	easy	p. 114
Mount Roche	2492 m	moderate/difficult	p. 116
Spionkop Ridge Traverse	2576 m	moderate	p. 120
"Cloudy Ridge Junior"	2585 m	moderate/difficult	p. 123

The peaks in this section all lie in the Front Ranges and are readily viewed when driving south on Highway 6 between Pincher Creek and Waterton. Though not particularly striking from a distance, these mountains are absolutely beautiful up close. Pincher Ridge has a rock band that displays one of the most impressive examples of multicoloured rock layering I've ever seen (see

Part of the spectacular traverse from Victoria Peak to Victoria Ridge.

page 102). A little farther to the northwest sits Victoria Peak/Victoria Ridge, arguably one of the best ridgewalks in the Canadian Rockies. You are unlikely to find another ridge whose views boast such an amazing variety of colours. Every peak in this section offers not only visual spectacles that are guaranteed to impress and delight, but a fair amount of decent hands-on scrambling as well. The rock quality is a little suspect, as expected, but as a good friend of mine always says, "You can't have everything can you? Where would you put it?!"

PRAIRIE BLUFF

From a distance Prairie Bluff, also known as Corner Mountain, doesn't appear to offer much in terms of interest. But over the years, I have found the peak to be as fascinating as any in the area, with numerous ascent routes and a wide variety of terrain to explore. Two routes are described here: the south face and the south ridge.

The outlier of the south face is a geologist's dream of interesting and colourful exposed rock layers. It can be a demanding ascent, with route-finding challenges and steep terrain. Atop the outlier, the remainder of the trip is a hike. A wide gas plant access road makes easy work of the descent. This road is also a good option for a bike ascent if that's your thing.

The south ridge is more direct. This is an enjoyable and stress-free route, with pleasant scenery from bottom to top. As long as the ascent slopes are not plastered with snow, it is a good candidate for winter ascents. Chinook winds can melt much and sometimes all of the snow at any given time. Snowshoes may be helpful for the approach, as that terrain can hold the snow longer.

A panorama of the Front Range peaks of East Castle. **C**: Mount Cleveland; **D**: Mount Dungarvan; **CR**: Cloudy Ridge; **R**: Mount Roche; **L**: Loaf Mountain; **DR**: Drywood Mountain; **P**: Pincher Ridge; **V**: Victoria Peak.

22. PRAIRIE BLUFF (SOUTH FACE) 2258 m

(MAP 6, PAGE 452)
Rating moderate, with a few short tougher steps, via the south face
Round-trip time 6–8 hours
Elevation gain 700 m
Maps 82 G/8 Beaver Mines

Not for those who want a trail all the way up. A steep and loose ascent up the outlier, followed by an easy walk on a wide road to the summit. Try from May on.

From Pincher Creek, head south towards Waterton. About 20 km south of the south end of Pincher Creek, turn right (west) onto the Shell Waterton Complex road (Twp. Rd. 4-3A; the sign is on the east side of the road). Follow the road for about 9 km, past the complex, and turn left at the Forest Reserve sign onto Twp. Rd. 4-3. Drive 5.4 km to the Victoria Ridge trailhead (just beyond the gas plant). You may have to park outside the gates, about 50 m before the locked gate.

Hike the gas road for about 1.5 km, looking to your right for a clearing in the trees that leads towards the southern outlier of the main peak (see top photo opposite). Hike easily to the base, aiming for the left side of the face. This is not the most direct route, but it offers the opportunity to explore some of the most interesting layered rock you are ever likely to encounter. There are numerous gullies that can be taken to reach the gentler upper reaches of the southwest slopes of the outlier. The trick is to find one you can safely upclimb. Although the rock is stunning to look at, it is also stunningly loose! As well, many of the gullies are steeper than they appear from below and have even steeper sections at the top – be very confident if you choose to take a different route from the one described below.

Traverse along the base or explore a little higher up on the face, trending in a northeast direction. Attempting to describe the exact route here is self-defeating due to the complexity of the gully systems. Suffice it to say there is a pleasant scramble route that goes back up to the northwest. A few steps of difficult scrambling are very short but a tad exposed. Again, easier terrain exists to the northwest if you wish, though getting there may require some elevation losses.

Once you are above the colourful rock bands, the terrain levels off a little, though it does get steeper again towards the top. Choose one of many routes to the west ridge. The large summit block is comprised of grey igneous rock. Once you reach that, scramble straight up the ridge or duck around the southwest end (to the left) on easier terrain. Continue without difficulty on pleasant rock to the summit of the outlier.

By this point the scrambling is all done. The true summit lies to the north and, at a good pace, is just over an hour away. Depending on your perspective, you may find that hour to be a pleasant, scenic and stress-free jaunt to the top or tedious hiking along a boring gas plant road – I certainly found the former to be true and strongly recommend completing the ascent. The gas road is clearly visible from the summit of the outlier. Hike over to it and then simply follow it almost all the way to the true summit (take a left turn when the road comes to a T-intersection). The fenced gas plant can be circumvented on either side. If you are a fan of red argillite, this traverse to the summit will not disappoint.

The shapely northeastern profile of Victoria Peak provides the highlight of the summit view, with distinctive Windsor Mountain and Castle Peak to the right of Victoria. To the distant northwest lie peaks of the Crowsnest area and farther north, Tornado Mountain, the highest of the High Rock Range, can be seen.

Multiple descent routes exist. The most direct route is to follow the south ridge down to the approach road and back to your vehicle. Another option is to follow the gas road all the way back to the approach trail. This option is as easy a descent as you can get, though it is longer than the south ridge. The third option is to return the way you came.

Opposite above: The exciting and colourful south face of the objective's southern outlier. **SR**: scenic route; **DR**: direct route; **S**: summit of the outlier.
Opposite below: Mark completes the ascent in very easy fashion. Victoria Peak dominates the background.

23. PRAIRIE BLUFF (SOUTH RIDGE) 2258 m

(MAP 6, PAGE 452)
Rating easy via the south ridge
Round-trip time 4–6 hours
Elevation gain 700 m
Maps 82 G/8 Beaver Mines

A fast, easy and scenic ascent route that can sometimes be completed in any month of the year, though snowshoes may be needed. In terms of rock scenery, perhaps not as interesting as the south face route, but several striking examples are available to see. For later-season ascents, try from May on.

From Pincher Creek head south towards Waterton. About 20 km south of the south end of town, turn right (west) onto the Shell Waterton Complex road (Twp. Rd. 4-3A; the sign is on the east side of the road). Follow the road for about 9 km, past the complex, and turn left at the Forest Reserve sign onto Twp. Rd. 4-3. Drive 5.3 km to the gas plant, turning right just before it. Drive that road for 400 m and park at a clearing on the other side of the road, where a double track leads north towards the objective.

Follow the double track for a 100 or so metres and veer off left onto a narrow but obvious single-track trail. Follow this through light forest and up a hill. Hop over a barbed wire fence and continue going northwest towards the base of the south ridge. Dense forest appears to block the route, but there are places where the trees are very sparse and easy to get through. Make sure you find one.

Another fence must be hopped and then it is fairly obvious route-finding to the base of the mountain. At the base, route-finding is again straightforward. Go right up the middle of the broad ridge/face. A fascinating rock band of exposed, clearly defined, layered rock is well worth a quick diversion to the left on the way up. It may not look like much at a distance but it is fairly impressive close up. After visiting the rock band, continue going up, red argillite now underfoot.

More interesting rock can be found as you near the upper ridge. Lichen-covered, black igneous rock lies to the right and also warrants a visit. After

The south ridge route as seen from the parking area. Not much snow for late December. **S**: summit; **1**: first rock band; **2**: second rock band.

that, plod your way north to the summit. Staying near the ridge grants good views of the mountain's impressive east face.

The view is unlikely to knock you off your feet (leave that to the wind!), but it is very pleasant – a mix of prairies to the east and shapely mountains in the other directions. Victoria Peak is close by and will definitely catch your attention.

To **return**, either go back the way you came or, for a little variety, descend the obvious drainage immediately west of the summit. When you get near the base of the mountain, trend to the left (east) to rejoin your ascent route.

Above: The first diversion of interesting rock.
Below: The alternative descent route, right down the centre. Recommended for ease and variety.

24. VICTORIA PEAK 2587 m

(MAP 6, PAGE 452)
Rating moderate via southeast slopes
Round-trip time 4–7 hours
Elevation gain 1100 m
Maps 82 G/8 Beaver Mines

Victoria Peak is a thoroughly enjoyable scramble, best done in fall when the larches are changing colour. On a clear day the variety of colours you'll see is fantastic. There is also the option to extend the trip to Victoria Ridge for a full day of such colour. That trip is possibly my favourite ridgewalk/ scramble in the Rockies. Try from mid-June on.

From Pincher Creek, head south towards Waterton. About 20 km south of the south end of Pincher Creek, turn right (west) onto the Shell Waterton Complex road. Follow the road for about 9 km, past the complex, and turn left at the Forest Reserve sign, onto Twp. Rd. 4-3. Drive 5.4 km to the Victoria Ridge trailhead (just beyond the gas plant). You may have to park outside the gates, about 50 m before the locked gate.

Hike or bike the road for approximately 3.5 km. Victoria Peak is the tallest and most shapely peak in the area and lies on the north side of the trail. Several ascent routes are possible, but the best one stays on the ridge immediately to the left of the major drainage that divides the mountain. Scramble easy slopes, picking up the odd trail here and there. Higher up you come across several bands of rock which can be tackled head-on or circumvented on the right. A line of trees to the right marks the route.

Once above treeline, enjoy the wonderful variety of colourful rock as the terrain becomes steeper. Again, small rock bands can be ascended via weaknesses or you can keep to the left to avoid them. A short section of moderate scrambling will lead you to the ridge only minutes away from the summit. Turn right and you're practically there.

The colourful summit panorama is quite impressive and includes Pincher Ridge to the southeast, Mount Gladstone to the northwest and Prairie Bluff to the northeast. Most notable, however, is the striking form of Castle Peak connected to Windsor Mountain to the west.

Return the same way or, for an easier descent, trend left once below the rock band at the top. Find scree slopes that lead all the way down to the major drainage. Near the bottom you may want to traverse to the right through the trees and back to the original ascent route. This helps avoid some potentially annoying bushwhacking farther down.

For a scenic and more than worthwhile extension of the trip, head southwest from the summit and follow the long ridge – appropriately called Victoria Ridge. Initially the ridge is undulating and jagged, with a precipitous drop on the east side, but it soon flattens out. Throughout, the extension is mostly hiking, with some easy scrambling and no exposure. See the Victoria Ridge description, next, for the remainder of the details.

Opposite above: The ascent and descent routes from the approach trail.
Opposite below: Part of the amazing high-level traverse from Victoria Peak to Victoria Ridge.

25. VICTORIA RIDGE 2530 m

(MAP 6, PAGE 452)
Rating easy; mostly hiking
Round-trip time 5–10 hours
Elevation gain 1050 m
Maps 82 G/8 Beaver Mines, 82 G/1 Sage Creek

Victoria Ridge extends south from Victoria Peak, eventually forming a horseshoe with Pincher Ridge. The trip can be done in conjunction with an ascent of Victoria Peak or by itself. Either way, the spectacular scenery and colours put it in the "must do" category, even though the ascent would more accurately be described as a hike, not a scramble. Wait for a blue sky day. Try from June on.

Park as for Victoria Peak at the Victoria Ridge trailhead. Hike or bike the gravel road for 4 km until it ends and becomes a trail. Leave your bike here and hike the pleasant trail through the valley. Eventually it curves right, heading uphill through the trees. Higher up, the trail goes left under the impressive walls of one of the many high points along the ridge and then goes south, paralleling the ridge.

At this point it is best to turn right and ascend easy slopes to the ridge. This route is more scenic than remaining on the trail below the ridge, but it will require additional elevation losses and gains. Once on the ridge, turn left and head south towards the high point of the ridge some distance away. You will have to drop to a low col before making the final push to the summit of Victoria Ridge. Be sure to stop occasionally and enjoy the colourful views of Pincher Ridge. **Return** the same way, but follow the directions below to get the most out of the trip by traversing a portion of the ridge towards Victoria Peak.

If you don't feel like completing the long ridgewalk all the way to the high point, gain the ridge and turn north instead of south. The first cairned high point is easily gained. Continue north along the jagged ridge, which now has a precipitous drop on the right. A few small drop-offs can easily be circumvented by dropping down a short distance to the left. Upon reaching the next and most prominent high point, the ridge descends to a low col that separates Victoria Ridge from Victoria Peak. If you have the energy, it's a straightforward scree ascent to the summit of Victoria Peak from here. If not, pick one of several descent routes back to the trail (see photo). If snow persists in the valley

The first major high-point along the ridge. The trail traverses the lower slopes. Route line is approximate. Photo: Dinah Kruze

Above: Linda Breton on the ridge connecting Victoria Peak to the summit of Victoria Ridge. **VR**: summit of Victoria Ridge.
Below: Many choices for descent. **C**: low col; **VP**: Victoria Peak; **V**: valley; **H**: high descent route. Photo: Bob Spirko

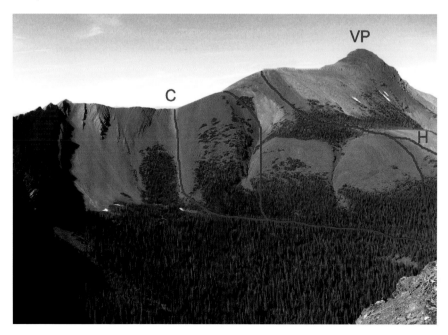

The breathtaking colours and shapes of a late September ascent. Photo: Vern Dewit

below you, one of the routes that stays high and avoids travel through the trees is recommended. The high road will also maximize your exposure to the terrific scenery.

26. PINCHER RIDGE 2423 m

(MAP 6, PAGE 452)
Rating difficult; sections of steep, exposed scrambling; route-finding challenges
Round-trip time 6.5–8 hours
Elevation gain 900 m
Maps 82 G/8 Beaver Mines

When seen from Drywood Mountain, Pincher Ridge presents the beautifully rounded contour and spectacular colours of its south side. And like Drywood, there is also a more challenging ascent route, followed by a much easier descent route. The rock is loose, but the interesting scenery and amazing colours should be more than enough motivation to try this peak. Try from June on.

From Pincher Creek, head south towards Waterton. About 20 km south of the south end of town, turn right (west) onto the Shell Waterton Complex road (Twp. Rd. 4-3A; the sign is on the east side of the road). Follow the road for about 9 km, past the complex, and turn left at the Forest Reserve sign onto Twp. Rd. 4-3. Drive 3.8 km and turn left onto Rge. Rd. 1-2A. Follow this for 2.1 km and park to the right of a locked gate.

From the parking area, head northwest to gain the east ridge. There are many possible routes to the ridge, but the most visually rewarding one intersects the prominent rock outcrop lining the upper section of the ridge (see photo).

Once at the rock, be sure to explore the terrain a little before cutting through the rock bands to gain the ridge. Either continue up to the most easterly high point of the ridge or trend left, sidesloping towards a point on the ridge farther west. On the ridge, head west towards a series of bands of rock that line the striking east ridge.

Eventually you'll arrive at a vertical rock band that bars the way. Traverse along and down it on the left side. Once around, start sidesloping the scree (heading southwest), passing by one rib. It is possible to continue sidesloping and then gain the ridge closer to the summit; however, the most interesting route gains the ridge quickly. Look for a water-worn, grey rock gully and ascend its step-like terrain to an obvious weakness (break) in the

Three routes to the ridge. The middle one is the most scenic. **R**: colourful rock bands; **HP**: easterly high point of east ridge; **ER**: east ridge.

Above: One of the most beautiful rock bands I've ever encountered. Well worth the small diversion.
Below: The approximate route up the east ridge. **G**: gully; **S**: summit.

rock band to the left. Go up this rock band. It is steeper than it looks and involves a few difficult moves, but the rock is solid.

Gain the east ridge again and continue up until the next band rears up. A detailed description from here is unnecessary. Ascend the ridge by circumventing steeper sections on either side (which side is usually obvious). Higher up, the right side is best.

About 40 vertical metres from the summit, detour onto the north side of the mountain and route-find your way up steep, grassy slopes towards the ridge. This may require a couple of short but necessary elevation losses as well as a few exposed moves up very steep terrain right before the ridge. Upon gaining the ridge, the summit is only a short distance away to the east.

The west ridge and southwest slopes offer an easy and stress-free **return**. Follow the ridge west until you can trend left onto the light-brown slopes of shale. Descend these gentle grades more or less directly to the gravel road far below. Expect a short stint of bush-bashing just before the road. It's 4 km back to your vehicle once you reach the valley bottom.

27. PINCHER RIDGE CENTRE PEAK 2430 m and SOUTH PEAK 2570 m

(MAP 6, PAGE 452)

Rating mostly hiking, with a few scrambling moves (moderate, but a little exposed)
Round-trip time 5.5–7 hours for the centre; add 2–3 hours for the south
Elevation gain 870 m for the centre; add approximately 350 m for the south
Maps 82 G/8 Beaver Mines, G/1 Sage Creek

When the larches are turning in late September/early October, this can be one of the most scenic trips in the Castle. The easy extension to the south peak is well worth the extra time, and for those with endless energy and knee cartilage, continuing all the way to Victoria Ridge is a possibility. Save the trip for a clear day and take a bike for the 3.7 km approach. The description that follows is the descent route for Pincher Ridge. It does not go to the true summit of Pincher Ridge, though the option to do that does exist. Try from June on.

Centre peak

Park as for Pincher Ridge. From the trailhead, hike or bike (preferred) the road for about 3.7 km to a point where it starts to drop down to a large clearing (former gas well site). Before losing elevation, look to the right (northwest) for flagging and a faint trail through the trees. It is not absolutely necessary to find this trail, but it does make the initial bushwhack a little more tolerable. Head into the trees and bushwhack up to more-open terrain on the south slopes of Pincher Ridge. Once out of the trees, keep going up but also start to trend to the left. That is, unless you also want to tag the true summit of Pincher Ridge. If that is the case, slog your way up vegetated terrain and onto an endless

The centre peak as seen from approximately the point where you leave the road. The dismal weather would soon reveal some pretty cool scenery on this day.

Above: Low-lying clouds crawl over the col between the true summit and the centre peak.
Below: The visually rewarding view back to the centre peak (right), from the traverse to south peak.

scree slope that eventually leads to the summit ridge and then the summit.

If your plans are to go straight to Pincher Ridge centre peak, the goal is to sideslope to the low col between the true summit and the centre peak. After gaining some elevation and traversing left for a distance, the route will become obvious. Find and follow one of several animal trails going exactly in the direction you want to go, to ease the ankle-jarring traverse.

At the col, route-finding becomes a no-brainer: simply follow the ridge southwest up to the centre peak. A rock band interrupts progress just before the top. Start on the right side of the band; then work your way back onto the ridge and make a few steep scrambling moves to get up to easier terrain. The summit is only a short hike from there. Be sure to look back at the wonderfully colourful slopes behind you. After taking in the fine view, return the same way if you have had enough. On return, once below the rock band it is possible to take a more direct route down the valley by following the obvious descending scree ridge. Lower down, some judicious route-finding is required to avoid heavy bush. There is a trail that is visible from high above to aim for. This track takes you easily back to a large clearing (former gas well site) and the approach road.

South peak

The traverse to the south peak is easy, scenic and very straightforward. Simply follow the wide ridge in a southwest direction, up and over a high point and then onto the summit at approximately GR082590, 2670 m. Again, the colourful surrounding scenery is remarkable and will probably be the highlight of the traverse. The summit, however, is somewhat unremarkable, lacking in a single high point from which to enjoy the panorama. A little wandering around resolves that issue. Return the same way unless you are bound for Victoria Ridge.

Victoria Ridge

Given its close proximity, those who haven't visited the summit of Victoria Ridge may want to make the effort from the south peak of Pincher Ridge. The hike over there takes about 60–90 minutes and requires an additional 200 or so metres of elevation

gain. Yet again the route is very obvious, as there really is only one way to go: southwest and then south. Note, however, that the most scenic route to reach the summit of Victoria Ridge is via Victoria Peak and Ridge. That trip remains the premier ridgewalk in this part of the Rockies.

If you do reach the impressive vantage point at the apex of Victoria Ridge, there are several return options, all very long and demanding.

- The easiest way back is to return the way you came.
- Via Victoria Ridge (see the Victoria Peak and Victoria Ridge trips on pages 96 and 98). This makes for a most impressive and intensely scenic day that **will** leave you "dead on your feet"! The crux of this route is the very long walk back to your vehicle, having already completed a very, very, **very** long hike. If your intent is to nab both the centre and south peaks of Pincher, Victoria Ridge (and possibly Victoria Peak), it makes far more sense to start the trip from the Victoria Peak trailhead (see **Ultimate High-Level Ridgewalks**, at page 127).
- Via Drywood Mountain. This route makes the most sense, since you end up on the same approach road as you started from, but it still makes for a very long day. As well as the approximately 27 km of horizontal distance, the total elevation gain for the day will be well over 2000 m. See Drywood Mountain (North Side) on page 108 for details.

Drywood Mountain

Drywood Mountain is another of my favourites in the Castle, and like Loaf Mountain it can be ascended from numerous sides and several valleys. The mountain has an east and west summit, of very similar heights. Between those summits is a highly enjoyable and easy hike. It involves an additional 500 m of elevation, but the scenery is excellent.

The south side of the peak is the preferred route for interesting scrambling and beautifully coloured rock. The north side has an advantage in that it can be accessed year round. The route is a sentimental favourite of mine. A November ascent in 2011 was characterized by amazing cornice and snow scenery as the wind wreaked havoc on the mountain (and on me!).

28. DRYWOOD MOUNTAIN (SOUTH SIDE) 2514 m

(MAP 6, PAGE 452)
Rating moderate via south slopes
Round-trip time 7–10 hours for the loop
Elevation gain 840 m; 500 m loss and gain to west summit
Maps 82 G/8 Beaver Mines, 82 G/1 Sage Creek

This route offers the typical fare of amazing colours and interesting scenery that is common to peaks in the area. The loop route features a more challenging ascent with an easy and scenic descent and is the recommended route. Fit parties can continue on to the summit of Loaf Mountain to the south. Try from June 15 on. The road is closed until then. Earlier or later season ascents can be made from the north side, described on page 108.

From Pincher Creek, head south towards Waterton. About 20 km south of the south end of town, turn right (west) onto the Shell Waterton Complex road (Twp. Rd. 4-3A; the sign is on the east side of the road). Follow the road for about 9 km, past the complex, and turn left at the Forest Reserve sign, onto Twp. Rd. 4-3. Drive 3.8 km and turn left onto Rge. Rd. 1-2A. Drive 1.4 km and turn left onto Twp. Rd. 4-2. Follow this road for 5 km and turn right. You'll find the Bovin Lake trailhead sign about 200 m along. If the gate is open (June 15 to September 1), drive 4 km to the final gas well and park near the road (trail) that veers off to the right.

Hike for several minutes along Bovin Lake Trail, looking to your right for an obvious ascent line that has been cut through the mountain by water (see photo). Turn right and make your way through light bush to the start of the drainage. Enjoy easy to moderate scrambling as you ascend the water-worn rock of the gully. The only major obstacle is a steep band of rock that lines the south face, going up to the right. Water may be pouring down this step when you reach it. If not, scrambling straight up the steep terrain is the easiest way to go. If water stops you, there are two ways to get above the band. Either back down a little and look for a weakness on the left side of the watercourse or traverse up and along the base of the band until you arrive at another weakness. Ascending this step involves several exposed moves on steep rock. If that's not to your liking, return to the watercourse and go up the left side.

Above the band, continue following the watercourse up more steppy terrain until you reach a band of burgundy argillite. Start trending left towards easier terrain marked by a black band. Ascend this band to the ridge and turn right. Follow the ridge easily to the summit.

Either **return** the same way or extend your day by choosing the longer but easier descent route along the west ridge. Start by heading back the way you came, but instead of cutting left onto the south-facing descent slopes, keep going straight in a westerly direction towards the slightly higher west summit. This traverse is long and involves approximately 500 m of elevation loss, which all must then be regained. Fortunately the terrain is easy and very scenic, with no route-finding. Expect to take 2–3 hours from the east summit to the west one. At the west summit, continue heading west along the ridge towards Bovin Lake. When the lake becomes visible, turn left and head down easy slopes to hook up with Bovin Lake Trail. Turn left onto the trail and hike the easy route back to your vehicle.

Opposite above: Drywood Mountain as seen from the east end of Loaf Mountain. **CR**: crux rock band; **S**: summit; **LR**: loop route; **FS**: false summit of west end.
Opposite below: Left in the dust. The author (little orange helmet) lags behind speedy Scott, Amber and Janine heading to the west summit. Photo: Amber Kunimoto

29. DRYWOOD MOUNTAIN (NORTH SIDE) 2478 m

(MAP 6, PAGE 452)
Rating steep hiking with a few moderate scrambling sections
Round-trip time 6–8 hours; add 2–4 hours for the west summit
Elevation gain 940 m; add 500–1000 m for the west summit
Maps 82 G/8 Beaver Mines, G/1 Sage Creek

While not as colourful and challenging as an ascent of the southeast face, the north side gives relatively easy access to the summit and can be done year round. If you do choose to go during the snow season, be aware the ascent slopes could be very avalanche-prone. Take the necessary precautions and stay away if the avalanche hazard is "considerable" or higher.

From Pincher Creek, head south towards Waterton. About 20 km south of the south end of town, turn right (west) onto the Shell Waterton Complex road (Twp. Rd. 4-3A; the sign is on the east side of the road). Follow the road for about 9 km, past the complex, and turn left at the Forest Reserve sign onto Twp. Rd. 4-3. Drive 3.8 km and turn left onto Rge. Rd. 1-2A. Follow this road for 2.1 km and park to the right of the locked gate.

Hike or bike the gravel road for about 1.8 km to a rocky drainage coming down from the north side of the mountain around GR127621 (see photo). Follow the drainage southeast, going right up the centre or on either side, wherever the water level dictates. The drainage soon becomes more canyon-like, as walls of colourful argillite line the sides.

Continue up the canyon until the red cliff bands

The rocky drainage and approximate ascent route. Many variations are possible.

Top: Snow and wind combine to create magical scenery on the north ridge.
Bottom: View to the southwest summit of Drywood Mountain (left). With this much snow, a traverse to that summit would be extremely strenuous if not impossible.

are replaced with more-open slopes to your right. These are the slopes that lead to the north ridge. Do NOT leave the canyon too early, as rock bands above the open slopes are far steeper than they appear. Instead, be patient and choose a line where you can see most of the ascent before you start. Always pick the easiest-looking line – though it may turn out to be "not so easy"!

Work your way up these steep slopes to the northwest ridge. Turn left and embark on another slog up the northwest ridge to the north end of the mountain. Views to the north and northwest will really start to improve here. You can go straight up the northwest ridge (recommended) or angle slightly to the right as you ascend if you want to go more directly to the summit. The former route may take a few minutes longer but it can pay dividends in fantastic scenery if the north ridge traverse to the summit is snowy. For this route, follow the northwest ridge up to the north ridge and then turn right and travel south for about 600 m to the summit. A couple of moves of moderate scrambling are required to surmount the summit block. Return the same way or continue the trip to the west summit.

The traverse to the slightly higher west summit is very straightforward, as described on page 106. If the route is snow-free, it makes for a long and wonderful trek. Since the return trip involves retracing your steps, the price of the west summit is an additional 1000 m of elevation gain.

For the ultimate extension of this trip see **Ultimate High-Level Ridgewalks**, at page 127.

Loaf Mountain

Loaf Mountain is the highest peak in the Castle and, needless to say, boasts a magnificent summit view. There are a number of routes to the summit, including traverses from either Drywood Mountain or Spionkop Ridge. The two ascent routes described here approach the summit from different valleys. The new route up the south side is a wonderfully scenic trip and highly recommended over the more mundane north side. Biking the approach is also strongly recommended for both trips. Regardless of the route you use to reach the summit, once there, looking east along the huge, red, winding ridge is a rare treat.

30. LOAF MOUNTAIN (SOUTH SIDE) 2640 m

(MAP 6, PAGE 452)
Rating easy via the southeast face and the east ridge
Round-trip time 8–10 hours
Elevation gain approximately 1000 m
Maps 82 G/8 Beaver Mines, 82 G/1 Sage Creek

Of the two routes up statuesque Loaf Mountain this is the recommended one. It is considerably more interesting and scenic than the slog up slopes on the north side of the peak. If you like terrific rock scenery, this is an excellent trip. Try from June on.

From Pincher Creek drive approximately 30 km south on Highway 6 and turn right onto Twp. Rd. 3-4 (4.3 km south of the general store in Twin Butte). Drive 7.8 km to the end of the road. Turn right onto Yarrow Road and go 4 km to the bridge that crosses Spionkop Creek. Continue around a hairpin turn, take the first left and park off the road at the locked gate of the Spionkop Creek trailhead.

From the gate, hike or bike (preferred) the gas road west to the last gas plant (approximately 4 km). Ignore all sideroads. The road turns into a trail at the west end of the plant. Hike the trail

for about 15–20 minutes to the base of the second major drainage coming down from the south face of Loaf Mountain (approximately GR144563 – see photo). Hike up the slope on the left (west) side of the drainage, towards a very distinctive, dark, lichen-covered rock band above.

The right side of the rock band is the key to the ascent. Between the main section and a smaller but very striking pinnacle of rock lies a passage through both. This weakness is quite obvious – no scrambling required; just steep hiking (see photo next page). Stay to the right side of the passage for

The ascent route as seen from the trail.

Above: The passage.
Below: The incomparable summit view from the summit of Loaf. **RD**: route down; **VP**: Victoria Peak; **PR**: Pincher Ridge; **DM**: Drywood Mountain; **MR**: Mount Roche. Photo: Matthew Clay

the least steep terrain. Follow it to the ridge, heading north. The true summit of Loaf soon makes an appearance to the west.

Eventually it becomes clear that it is not necessary to go all the way to the middle summit of Loaf, to the north. Instead, when it is obvious, start sidesloping to the left to gain the main east/west-trending ridge of the mountain. Although travel is easy and route-finding obvious, the summit is farther than you may think. The increasingly impressive view in all directions should alleviate some of the tedium along the way.

As the highest mountain in the area, Loaf sports a magnificent summit panorama. The colourful forms of Drywood Mountain, Pincher Ridge and Spionkop Ridge are especially striking. The red, snaking ridge of Loaf itself is likewise a treat to see from this vantage point.

Options for return are numerous:

- The way you came up. Besides the unwelcome but necessary elevation gains, this route has the advantage of keeping you at a relatively high elevation, to again take in the wonderful views.
- Via the Loaf/Spionkop col. This route adds a little horizontal distance to your return, but it eliminates the elevation gain and is very scenic. From the summit, travel southwest and then south to the Loaf/Spionkop col. Turn east and drop down into the Spionkop Creek Valley. Stay on the left (north) side of the valley and look for the trail that leads back to the gas plant.
- Via the bowl to the east of the summit (recommended). No extra elevation gain, minimal additional horizontal distance and more terrific scenery are enough to make this the preferred descent route. Start by returning the way you came. Once you are almost to the col between the summit of Loaf and the next high point to the east, turn south and descend the red argillite slopes into the bowl below. Follow the valley as it trends to the southeast. A pretty significant and vertical rock band lies ahead, but more gentle slopes on both sides of the band offer an easy path past it. I would recommend staying to the right (west) side of the valley to find the route. Once past the rock band, veer to the left and down the valley, looking for the trail that leads back to the gas plant. The rock scenery on both sides of the valley is terrific.

For all return routes, once back to the gas plant, enjoy a coasting, 10-minute cruise back to the gate if you biked. If you hiked, enjoy 45 minutes of cursing and swearing the fact that you didn't bring a bike – that's exactly what I did all three times I hiked this valley!

31. LOAF MOUNTAIN (NORTH SIDE) 2640 m

(MAP 6, PAGE 452)
Rating easy via northwest slopes
Round-trip time 6–8 hours
Elevation gain 1000 m
Maps 82 G/8 Beaver Mines, 82 G/1 Sage Creek

From a scenery point of view this route pales in comparison to the previously described route on the south side of the mountain. However, it is a slightly faster way to get to the summit, and the route-finding is easy. The advantage here is that upon completing the ascent, you have the option to tag Drywood Mountain also. Having said that, a far superior option (for very fit parties) is to ascend Drywood, traverse over to Loaf and then use this route for descent. Save it for a clear day. Try from June 15 on. The road is closed until then.

Follow the driving directions for Drywood Mountain (south side). From the gate, go 4 km to the final gas well. The road/trail that veers off to the right just before the gas well is the trail you'll be on. Unless your vehicle has monster-truck tires and 4 feet of ground clearance, don't even think about trying to drive it.

Hike or bike the trail for several kilometres, keeping your eye on the "loaf" shaped mass on the left (see photo below). Coincidentally, this is a false summit, which, like the true summit, resembles a rising loaf of bread. You'll be ascending easy slopes to the east of this mass. Look for a good place to cross the creek and gain these slopes without too much bushwhacking (see photo next page). There is a good drainage you'll want to aim for.

The slopes are tedious, but at least the drainage offers a little visual interest and the feeling that

The false summit from the approach trail and approximate ascent route. **FS**: false summit. Photo: Matthew Clay

The ascent drainage and approximate route to the ridge. Photo: Matthew Clay

you are actually scrambling, if only in a minor way. Once you gain the ridge, if you have time, turn left and follow the beautiful and very wide red argillite ridge to a high point that overlooks the east end of the mountain. This diversion is simply for the view. If that doesn't interest you, turn right upon gaining the ridge and follow it up and over the false summit and then easily onto the true summit.

Second in elevation only to Mount Glendowan in the general area, Loaf is a splendid viewpoint. To the south lies lengthy Spionkop Ridge, with the equally interesting Drywood Mountain immediately to the north. Most eye-catching, however, is the snake-like contour of Loaf to the east.

Returning the same way is fast and easy. A more interesting and longer but still very easy descent is to continue down the gentle southwest slopes. At the bottom, curve around to the northwest and either find the trail (easily visible from above) that joins up with the Bovin Lake Trail via forested terrain, or continue northwest up to the next high point for a good aerial view of Bovin Lake. Traverse the ridge and then drop down to the lake through light forest. At the lake, walk around to the northeast side, where you'll find Bovin Lake Trail. It's 6.4 km back to your car from there.

It is also possible to stay on the ridge, circle Bovin Lake from above and head northeast to the two summits of Drywood Mountain. This option, however, is far more enjoyable when done in reverse.

Another extension for the day is to descend the southwest slopes and then continue south to the summit of Spionkop Ridge (2576 m). You can then avoid too much unnecessary elevation gain on return by using the alternative descent route described above.

32. MOUNT ROCHE (SPREAD EAGLE MOUNTAIN) 2492 m

(MAP 6, PAGE 452)
Rating moderate, with one difficult step, via the northeast ridge
Round-trip time 7–10 hours
Elevation gain 1000 m
Maps 82 G/1 Sage Creek

Mount Roche (locally named Spread Eagle Mountain) is a prominent high point at the east end of 7 km long Spionkop Ridge. The scrambling is generally excellent and interesting throughout, though much of the rock is covered in lichen and is very slippery when wet. Wait for a dry day to best enjoy the scrambling and a clear day to best enjoy the colourful scenery and views. Try from July on.

From the south end of Pincher Creek, drive 30.6 km south on Highway 6 and turn right onto Spread Eagle Road (Twp. Rd. 3-4, 4.2 km south of the general store in Twin Butte). Drive about 8 km to the end of the road. Turn right onto Yarrow Road and go 4 km to a bridge over Spionkop Creek. Park at the hairpin turn immediately after the bridge. The trail starts here and heads west between Loaf Mountain to the north and Mount Roche to the south. Hike the trail, eventually crossing to the south side of the creek. Continue west for a while, ignoring the multitude of animal trails heading south. Soon the trail does turn south and

up. Follow it through light forest until the terrain opens up with a rocky hill to your right. Either go up the hill right away or traverse the east side of it for a few hundred metres and then pick a line of ascent. This will put you at the far east end of Spionkop Ridge (Mount Roche).

Follow the ridge west, up and over a couple of bumps to the start of the scrambling. When it does start, the best (and steepest) scrambling is found on the edge of the ridge. Go to the right for easier terrain. A steeper rock band soon comes up and can be ascended via one of several weaknesses. Traverse alongside the band to find one to your

Both ascent and descent routes from the gas road. **S**: summit; **D**: descent route.

The summit block of Mount Roche.

liking. Your best bet may be the second gully from the south end. If this band gives you problems, you may want to consider an alternative objective, as the crux will prove to be more difficult and exposed.

Continue up the ridge to arrive at the crux – a high, vertical band of rock that is a staple of many of the surroundings mountains (Loaf, Drywood, Dungarvan, Glendowan etc.). Head north (losing elevation) alongside the band for several hundred metres to find the weakness. It is characterized by a small but noticeable example of rock folding, seen when you scramble up to the base. This crux step only involves a couple of tricky moves, but it is steep and exposed. Descending this step would likely require a rope. Fortunately, an alternative descent route eliminates that need – provided you make it to the top!

Regain the ridge and continue on to the summit. Choose your own line from here. The fastest but least interesting ascent takes a line that sideslopes

and stays well right of the ridge on easier terrain. Stay on the ridge as much as possible to maximize your scrambling experience. The summit view features mountains of Waterton to the south and southwest and other familiar peaks of the Castle to the north and northwest. This is a good vantage point to see the entire length of Loaf Mountain and scope out potential routes from the south side (the ascent route described in this book goes up the north side). The lower connecting peak a few hundred metres to the southeast is another unofficial summit, called "Mount Yarrow," and can be reached easily from the top of Roche.

Either **return** the same way – provided you can downclimb or rappel the crux – or for a much easier escape off the mountain, start heading west. Drop down to a col and then up to the next minor high point, where the descent route is visible to the northwest: a hanging valley with a drainage in the middle. Descend easy slopes in a northwest direction alongside a small forest of larches on the way

Above: The alternative descent route and start of the Spionkop Ridge Traverse. A wonderful photo by Vern Dewit, who knows how magical autumn can be in the Rockies. **WS**: west summit of Spionkop Ridge. **L**: summit of Loaf Mountain.

Below: The view back to Mount Roche from near the summit of Yarrow, with much of the incredibly scenic Spionkop Ridge Traverse in full view at left. **R**: Mount Roche; **L**: Loaf Mountain; **S**: summit of Spionkop Ridge. Photo: Vern Dewit

to the drainage. There is an animal trail on the other side of the drainage, but eventually you'll want to be on the side you're already on (the right-hand side). Follow the drainage out (now heading northeast), staying above the trees and vegetation. The drainage soon drops off, but you can traverse under the growing rock bands on the right to scree slopes that go all the way down to another drainage. Follow that drainage out to the trail or the easier gas well road. A 4 km walk takes you back to your vehicle.

"MOUNT YARROW" 2380 m

If you are looking to increase your count of ascents of official mountains, you need not extend the Roche trip by nabbing Mount Yarrow. Yarrow is merely the southeast tip of another unofficial mountain – the one you are standing atop! However, for those looking to get some extra exercise while enjoying the strikingly colourful views of the surrounding mountains, Yarrow is a terrific extension.

The extension is about 1.4 km in length and will take about an hour round trip. Simply follow the ridge southward, then southeastward. It's a little more involved than appearances disclose and will require some route-finding and moderate to difficult scrambling. Return the same way. If you want to avoid extra elevation gain, it is possible to side-slope directly to the col southwest of Roche and then complete the alternative descent route.

33. SPIONKOP RIDGE TRAVERSE 2576 m

(MAP 6, PAGE 452)

Rating mostly steep hiking, with a few moves of moderate scrambling via the long northeast ridge; moderate for the alternative descent via Spionkop/Loaf col
Round-trip time 8–11 hours
Elevation gain Approximately 1300 m; 1700 m if continuing to Loaf Mountain
Maps 82 G/1 Sage Creek, G/8 Beaver Mines for Loaf Mountain

The lengthy east to west, high-level traverse of Spionkop Ridge makes for a wonderfully scenic and colourful trip. Except for the few moves of moderate scrambling, with mild exposure, the trip is all hiking, though much of it is very steep hiking. Clear skies are mandatory. The ascent route described here is the alternative descent route for Mount Roche. You can use the Mount Roche description if you also want to tag that summit. However, be prepared for a very long day. Of course, it is also possible to use the descent route for Roche and then backtrack to the summit. Even with the backtracking, this will probably be faster than ascending Roche via the normal route.

From the south end of Pincher Creek, drive 30.6 km south on Highway 6 and turn right onto Spread Eagle Road (Twp. Rd. 3-4, 4.2 km south of the general store in Twin Butte). Drive about 8 km to the end of the road. Turn right onto Yarrow Road and go 4 km to a bridge across Spionkop Creek. Continue around a hairpin turn, take the first left and park off the road at the locked gate of the Spionkop Creek trailhead.

Hike or preferably bike the gas road for about 3.75 km. The road forks, with the left fork heading downhill to Spionkop Creek. If biking, leave your bike at the top of the hill, as most parties will want to return via Spionkop Creek, not the way they came. Hike down the gas road and cross Spionkop Creek. On the way there, look for the obvious wide, rocky drainage that is the key to the ascent. A smaller rocky drainage goes generally in the same direction but leads to steep bushwhacking – avoid that one.

Boulder-hop up the drainage into the bowl beneath the summit of Mount Roche. Look for an obvious scree slope to your right. This slope goes up to the hanging valley to the west of the bowl you are presently in. Turn right and ascend the scree slope, passing under a significant rock face. Animal trails make the work a little easier. Soon another drainage becomes visible to your right. Stay high on the slope, above the drainage. Sideslope to avoid minor bushwhacking. When feasible descend into the drainage and follow alongside it into the upper valley.

The high point west of Roche soon becomes visible. If you want to tag Roche, trend left up to the ridge and then follow it east to the summit. If not, go straight up to the ridge and follow it west to the stunning red argillite rock band that guards the summit ridge. Pass two unusual pinnacles and then scramble up to the summit ridge with a couple of moves of moderate scrambling. The exposure down the north (right) side here is thrilling. The summit of the west peak is only a few metres away.

Most of the remainder of the route is visible from the west summit. There's really only one way to go: southwest, along the ridge. The ridge is wide and the flattened scree is easy to travel on. You'll want to make good time as you lose elevation. Note the interesting changes in colour of the rock underfoot.

The ridge eventually starts to narrow near the low point but is not at all exposed. A couple of small notches are also encountered. Again, they are inconsequential and easily worked through on the left side. The red argillite rock band up ahead is a formidable obstacle and must be circumvented on the left side. Stay close to the base of this impressive band. Several gullies to the right appear to offer routes back up to the ridge. Many of these gullies get quite steep at the top and are not recommended. Instead, wait for a gully that looks easy and then regain the ridge.

Back on the ridge, you'll see the highest point of Spionkop is now only a steep hike away – albeit a fairly long one. The summit view is terrific, especially looking northeast at the long, red fingers of Spionkop and Loaf stretched out in front of you.

Returning the same way is certainly possible, but not very logical. There exists an easier descent

Above: The ascent route to the west summit (alternative descent route for Mount Roche). **MR**: Mount Roche; **WS**: west summit.

Below: A good portion of the interesting northwest ridge. Contrary to its appearance, the route is not exposed. **S**: summit.

One of the best summit views in the area. If it seems like your vehicle is a long distance away, that's because it is! The valley below provides an easy descent route.

route and also the option to make a loop route by ascending nearby Loaf Mountain. If the weather and your energy are cooperating, the loop route is highly recommended.

Via the Spionkop/Loaf col. This is the easiest descent route. Follow the ridge north, descending to a col. This descent can be a little tricky. Stay near the ridge, circumventing steeper sections mostly on the left side. Try to avoid going too far out onto the west slope. Always return to the ridge. There is only one steep section and then the grade eases up. From the low point, ascend easily to the bump to the north. This gives you a good look at the remainder of the route, which basically goes straight down the valley.

Don't go straight down from the bump. Instead, follow the ridge northwestward for a short distance until an easy route becomes obvious down the argillite slopes. Turn right (east) and hike down into the valley. Game trails can be followed. Stay to the left (north) side of the small drainage that bisects the

upper slopes. As you lose elevation look for the trail that leads all the way back to the start of the trip. The trail is on the left side of the creek and stays relatively high on the south slopes of Loaf Mountain. Find the trail and follow it back to your bike and/or vehicle. Due to the significant distance you have already travelled, the hike down the valley will probably be taxing.

Loaf Mountain. Tagging Loaf adds an additional 350 vertical metres to the trip and is well worth the extra effort. Descend Spionkop as described above. Ascend north to the bump or sideslope to the low col to the northwest. Follow the wide ridge up as it arcs around from northwest to north to northeast and on to the summit. Take in another magnificent summit panorama before continuing the loop route. The best way back to your vehicle from the summit is to follow the alternative descent route for Loaf Mountain South described on page 113.

34. "CLOUDY RIDGE JUNIOR" 2585 m

(MAP 1, PAGE 448)
Rating mostly moderate with a few difficult moves
Round-trip time 8–10 hours
Elevation gain 1100 m
Maps 82 H/04 Waterton; Gem Trek Waterton National Park

The two summits of Cloudy Ridge are clearly visible north of Mount Dungarvan when driving to Waterton from the north. The higher summit ("Senior" if you wish) is approached from Red Rock Canyon. The lower (Junior) is best approached from Highway 6. Even if you have completed an ascent of Senior, Junior is well worth the effort, as the trips are totally different from one another. The start is the same as that described by Mike Potter in Ridgewalks in the Canadian Rockies, *2nd Edition, but the end is different, as it continues on to the highest point of the ridge. Parts of the approach trail are severely overgrown, with chest-high foliage. If it has rained the previous night, nothing short of a full drysuit (wetsuits keep you wet!) will keep you dry – pick your ascent day carefully! Try from July on.*

From the south end of Pincher Creek, drive 30.6 km south on Highway 6 and turn right onto Spread Eagle Road (Twp. Rd. 3–4, 4.2 km south of the general store in Twin Butte). Drive about 8 km

A good look at the objective from the gate. Note that the route through the trees goes east before turning back southwest. **G**: gate; **S**: summit.

From just below the ridge the approximate route loses elevation and then ascends to the ridge above. **GR1**: GR845529; **GR2**: GR842527.

to the end of the road. Turn left onto Yarrow Creek Road (Rge. Rd. 30-3) and go 1.2 km to the end of it. Park here and start hiking south on the obvious trail, often heavily indented by cattle hooves! Go through a barbed wire gate (close it behind you, please) and continue on the trail.

Eventually the trail starts to descend towards Yarrow Creek. When possible it is a good idea to check out the gas well access road that parallels Yarrow Creek. You will be aiming for the point where the road bends to the west. As the trail nears Yarrow Creek, cut to the left, cross the creek (often dry by midsummer), and make your way to the gas road. Hike down the road to where it bends west (GR832538) and find an unmarked gate in the barbed wire fence (see photo).

You have now arrived at the crux of the trip: finding and following the unmaintained and infrequently used trail up and over the east end of Cloudy Ridge. This trail is the only way to get to the

summit. Bushwhacking more directly to the ridge is a nightmare I wouldn't wish on anyone!

On the other side of the gate, the trail goes to the right and into the forest. Within 5 minutes you will arrive at an open area, with a picnic bench (as of summer 2016). The trail disappears momentarily, then continues on the other side of the clearing, a little to the left, where a "MONITORING OUR TRAILS" sign is attached to a tree (GR831536).

The trail is actually easy to follow from here, as it goes up and into the forest. It heads east (seemingly the wrong direction), slowly gaining elevation. There are several sections where foliage has overgrown the trail, but navigation is still easy if you keep your eyes down, looking at the trail.

Eventually you will come out into the open and find yourself at a high point at the far northeast end of Cloudy Ridge (GR844535). As tempting as it is to turn southwest and start following the ridge, this leads to intense bushwhacking or dreadful

The grassy and relentlessly steep slopes to the ridge.

sidehilling. Instead, stay on the main trail, losing some elevation on the other side of the ridge. The trail heads south, more or less following the contour of the ridge above (see photo opposite).

About 800 m along, after another stint of wading through foliage, you will come out into the open (GR845529). Time to finally leave the trail. Look to the right and ascend relentlessly steep, grassy slopes to the ridge above (see photo this page). Aim for GR842527. When you get there, breathe a sigh of relief, as the most challenging route-finding part of the day is done.

Follow the easy and pleasantly scenic ridge southwest. Unfortunately, trees are going to interrupt progress one more time. Here, it is best to lose elevation on the left side of the ridge to get around them. Return to the ridge and continue upward.

Above treeline it is best to stay close to the edge of the ridge. This allows you to take advantage of the step-like terrain and also to see the impressive and precipitous cliffs on the left side. All rock bands can be ascended directly or to the right for easier terrain.

Up high, a beautiful band of red argillite leads to a large cairn at GR818511. The terrain from this cairn to the true summit is convoluted and complex. A specific route description would be confusing. Instead the following general description is offered. After you've descended into a red argillite notch, the first minor and first major obstacles can be circumvented on the left side, all others on the right side of the ridge. Always pick the easiest line back to the ridge and make sure you can downclimb what you choose to upclimb. The scrambling should be moderate throughout, with perhaps one or two difficult moves. The true summit lies at GR815508.

After enjoying the terrific summit view from the high point, continue heading southwest for a few hundred metres to check out the continuation of the ridge to Cloudy Ridge (Senior). This is actually where the best views are and a great place to

From near the large cairn, the first part of the summit ridge looks quite daunting. Circumvent the first two obstacles on the left side.

relax, have lunch and enjoy the vistas. Although it appears there may be a possible scramble route to the summit of Senior, the trip would involve big elevation losses, traversing annoying scree and doing a lot of route-finding, not to mention the ridiculously long return trip. Not recommended!

Return the same way. Don't attempt any bush-whacking or creek-following shortcuts – Mr. Potter and I both learned the hard way on this! Also note that once you are back to the base of Cloudy Ridge at GR844535 and starting down the other side, the trail forks about 65 m along. Take the left fork (the trail you came up on) – it's an easy one to miss.

ULTIMATE HIGH-LEVEL RIDGEWALKS

The Castle and Waterton areas feature many of the best high-level ridgewalks the Canadian Rockies have to offer. The following recommendations describe terrific loop routes of unparalleled scenic beauty. They are all extremely long, involve tremendous amounts of elevation gain and will challenge the fittest of the fit. Specific routes descriptions are not given. You can simply piece together parts of other descriptions in this section of the book to get an idea of the route. There are numerous permutations and variations of routes and attained peaks, often ending in different valleys and requiring very long road hikes to get back to your vehicle. However, the routes described below start and end in the same valley, thus eliminating the dreaded 10–20 km road hike at the end of your day!

In general, route-finding is straightforward throughout and the scrambling rarely goes above "moderate." Expect 90 per cent hiking and 10 per cent scrambling, though there are exceptions where there is more scrambling.

Mount Roche to Spionkop Ridge to Loaf Mountain. Park as for Mount Roche, page 116, and ascend Roche via the normal route or the descent route in reverse. Complete the ridgewalk to the summit of Spionkop Ridge, page 120, and then swing around to the north to reach the summit of Loaf Mountain. There are two routes back to the starting point. Longest but easiest is to return to the low point between Loaf and Spionkop and then descend eastward into the valley, eventually finding Spionkop Creek Trail. A more adventurous and exciting route is to follow the alternative descent route for Loaf Mountain South described on page 113.

Drywood Mountain to Loaf Mountain. Park as for Drywood Mountain (south side). Ascend Drywood and traverse over to the west summit. Stay on the ridge and circle around Bovin Lake, high above it, to Loaf Mountain. Descend the ascent route for Loaf (north side) and return to your vehicle.

Drywood Mountain to Victoria Ridge to Pincher Ridge. Park as for Pincher Ridge. Follow the north route to the east summit of Drywood and then traverse the long distance to the west summit. Stay on the ridge, high above Bovin Lake, and continue on to the summit of Victoria Ridge. From Victoria, hike north to the next high point, then turn east and go to the south peak of Pincher Ridge. Continue over to the lower centre peak and keep going east. Those with unbelievable stamina will make it all the way to the true summit of Pincher Ridge and then return to the centre/true summit col

The gorgeous view from near the summit of Loaf Mountain. Mount Roche and a big section of the Spionkop Traverse are visible.

before making their way southeastward back to the approach road. A 4 km hike ends the day. A more modest, but still incredibly long, variation is to leave the true summit of Pincher out and simply head down to the trail from the centre/true summit col.

Victoria Peak to Victoria Ridge to Pincher Ridge. Park as for Victoria Peak. Complete the Victoria Peak to Victoria Ridge trip as described beginning on page 96. From the summit of Victoria Ridge return to the next high point to the north and then turn east towards the south peak of Pincher Ridge. Follow Pincher Ridge over the south peak, the centre peak and onto the true summit at the far east end of the ridge. To descend, backtrack to the low point between the true summit and the centre peak. Hike north to another high point and then follow the ridge northeastward. When feasible, leave the ridge and descend north to Pincher Creek. Ford the creek and make your way back to the approach trail.

WEST CASTLE				
Mount Gladstone		2458 m	moderate	p. 130
Table Mountain		2225 m	easy	p. 133
Whistler Mountain		2214 m	easy	p. 135
	GR978676	2284 m	easy	p. 135
	"Frankie Peak"	2375 m	easy/moderate	p. 136
	"Larry Mountain"	2375 m	moderate/difficult	p. 137
	North Castle	2327 m	moderate	p. 138
Lys Ridge (north ridge route)		2520 m	moderate	p. 140
Lys Ridge (Ruby Lake route)		2520 m	moderate	p. 142
Syncline Mountain		2500 m	easy/moderate/difficult	p. 145
St. Eloi Mountain		2500 m	easy	p. 148
Mount Haig		2618 m	moderate	p. 150
	Gravenstafel Ridge	2394 m	easy	p. 152
"Boot Hill"		2498 m	easy	p. 153
Tombstone Mountain		2515 m	moderate	p. 154
Barnaby Ridge		2471 m	moderate	p. 156
	Southfork Mountain	2350 m	easy	p. 157
Rainy Ridge		2469 m	moderate	p. 159
Three Lakes Ridge		2492 m	moderate/difficult	p. 163
"Jake Smith Peak"		2630 m	easy/moderate	p. 166
Scarpe Mountain		2617 m	difficult	p. 168
"Middle Kootenay Mountain"		2512 m	easy/moderate	p. 170
"Mount Miles"		2470 m	moderate	p. 172
	"Krowicki Peak"	2440 m	moderate/difficult	p. 174

Over the past eight years, the West Castle has asserted itself as one of my favourite areas in the Rockies. The landscape is rugged and untouched; the mountains are beautiful, their colours exquisite and vibrant; and solitude is almost a foregone conclusion. There are several significant trail systems and one major commercial development (Castle

Above: Hours and hours of this type of scenery can be the reward for completing a high-level ridgewalk. Mark enjoys the red argillite slopes between Victoria Peak and Victoria Ridge.
Below: The exquisitely beautiful west ridge of Rainy Ridge as seen when returning from an ascent of "Mount Miles."

Mountain Ski Resort) here, yet the area maintains a remote feel that is very compelling.

This edition includes a handful of peaks around Middle Kootenay Pass, including the unofficial "Jake Smith Peak," the highest summit in the area and yet another of my favourite mountain trips. Also strongly recommended is an autumn visit to Middlepass Lakes when the larches are turning yellow. Whether you complete an ascent of Rainy Ridge or Three Lakes Ridge, or both or neither, the three small lakes are worthwhile destinations in themselves.

These peaks are accessed from Highways 507 and 774, west of Pincher Creek.

35. MOUNT GLADSTONE 2458 m

(MAP 7, PAGE 453)
Rating moderate via southeast slopes
Round-trip time 5–8 hours
Elevation gain 1000 m
Maps 82 G/8 Beaver Mines

The scrambling on Mount Gladstone is minimal, but the mountain does offer interesting scenery, varied terrain, a fine summit panorama and a terrific alternative descent route. A clear autumn day, when the creek is low and the colours are changing, may be the best time of the year for this trip. Try from June on.

Drive to Pincher Creek and turn right onto Highway 507 west. Drive 15.2 km and turn left onto Gladstone Valley Road. Follow this gravel road for 13.6 km and turn right at an unmarked intersection 600 m after the second bridge. Drive another 3.2 km along this road, staying right when it forks to a gas well site, and arrive at a small grassy parking area by the ATV trail signs.

Hike 100 m alongside a barbed wire fence

to a small grassy clearing. Find a wide trail that curves left, continues for 50 m and then becomes a horse trail as it turns right and heads into the forest. This track is a little more circuitous than the ATV trail, but it is easy and straightforward and means you'll only have to cross Mill Creek once. Hike this trail for about 35 minutes (it eventually merges with the ATV trail) until you arrive at Mill Creek (GR038676). Across the creek, a distinctive,

The ascent route from the trail. **S**: summit.

Above: Starting down the alternative descent route. **WM**: Windsor Mountain; **CP**: Castle Peak.
Below: Mark bombs down the alternative descent route, one of the best scree runs in the Rockies.

unnamed outlier will be to your left, the east slopes of Gladstone to your right. You will be heading directly between these.

Cross Mill Creek – it may be flowing, it may be dry, it may be low, it may be high (watch out, Shakespeare!). Find the trail on the other side. Cross another dried-up creekbed and follow the trail back into the trees as it starts to head up and alongside the slopes of Gladstone. Soon the trail takes a sharp right and starts to traverse Gladstone's east slopes. From the crossing of Mill Creek, hike the trail for about 50 minutes to one of several rocky drainages (see photo opposite). The entire ascent route is visible from here.

Ascend the drainage, either straight up the middle or on the right side. The ascent is mostly steep hiking but the interesting rock is enough to entertain. Higher up, two significant bands of black rock are visible to the left. The top of the first is easily gained by traversing left before it starts to become significant. Continue up alongside the second black band (and last obstacle before the summit) until you reach the ridge. Then back down a few metres to find an obvious weakness in the band. The last few metres takes you up a groove of smoother rock that is steeper but has good holds. Once at the top of this, the summit is only a few metres away.

Undoubtedly, the splendid view of the striking Castle Peak and its partner Windsor Mountain to the left will garner most of your attention. Table and Whistler mountains are immediately north, with the familiar peaks of the Crowsnest beyond. The tall summit to the southeast is Victoria Peak, with Victoria Ridge heading west from it – two outstanding trips in themselves.

The alternative **return** route is a must-do. Continue southwest along the ridge and then down rubble, grass and scree slopes to a low col characterized by red argillite scree. Turn southeast down the argillite slopes. Scree surfing this slope is not only super fast and fun but a colourful visual reward as well. When the red argillite runs out, traverse left onto light-brown scree and continue down, paralleling the drainage. Near the bottom, cross to the right side of the drainage and continue down along the left side of thick foliage. Arrive shortly at the trail, turn left and it's an easy hike back to the parking area.

36. TABLE MOUNTAIN 2225 m

(MAP 7, PAGE 453)
Rating easy via southwest slopes
Round-trip time 3.5–5 hours
Elevation gain 740 m
Maps 82 G/8 Beaver Mines

A great choice if time and/or energy are limited. Table Mountain has a very short approach, interesting scenery and varied terrain and it won't leave you searching on eBay afterwards for a new set of lungs. Yet again, doing the ascent in autumn rewards you with the beautiful yellows of changing larches. Try from June on.

Drive to Pincher Creek, turn right onto Highway 507 and follow signs for Castle Mountain Ski Resort. At a T-intersection, turn left to head southwest on Highway 774 and drive 14.8 km to the Beaver Mines Lake turnoff. Turn left and go 5.4 km, arriving at a pull-off on the right side with a Table Mountain trailhead sign.

Hike Table Mountain Trail for about 20 minutes. At the second big clearing, leave the trail and head up slopes on your left (see photo next page). The ascent route goes up between the two outliers visible ahead. Either go straight up towards the western outlier (left) or traverse right to find a trail that makes life a little easier. Either way, you will eventually have to work your way to the right in order to find a weakness on the left side of the gully which grants easy access to the upper slopes.

Ascend this weakness. Once above the weakness, either continue straight up the middle of the upper slopes or trend left to gain the west ridge. Both routes join up later as you head to the left side of the interesting summit block of the western plateau (not the true summit).

Though this block may appear intimidating from afar, there is a weakness at the far left. It is possible to bypass the block altogether by heading to its right side, but the layers of beautifully coloured rock are definitely worth a look close up. At the top of the western plateau, the rest of the route is obvious, easy and not as far as it looks. On the way, you pass through a small larch forest (very pleasant in late September, when the trees are changing colour). The summit view is decent, though perhaps a little anticlimactic after the interesting ascent.

Table Mountain as seen from Highway 774. **S**: summit; **WP**: western plateau.

Above: Looking up the ascent gully. Photo: Vern Dewit
Below: The upper slopes. **G**: gully; **WP**: western plateau.

Return the same way. It is not necessary to go all the way back to the western plateau. Once back at the col, simply sideslope scree on the left side of the plateau back to the ascent slopes. Everything is the same after that.

37. WHISTLER MOUNTAIN 2214 m and beyond

(MAP 7, PAGE 453)

Rating easy to Whistler; moderate to "Frankie"; difficult to "Larry"; moderate to North Castle
Round-trip time 3–5 hours for Whistler; 9–12 hours for the full loop
Elevation gain 700 m to Whistler Mountain; approximately 1350 m for the full loop
Maps 82 G/8 Beaver Mines

The crux of Whistler Mountain is getting to the trailhead. The rest is just a steep hike. Lack of scrambling means you'll want decent weather to enjoy the views and extraordinary colours that are characteristic of the area. Extending the trip to the higher summit of "Frankie Peak" (named after my mum) and beyond – "Larry Mountain" (named after my stepdad) – is definitely recommended, the effort being rewarded with even better views of this beautiful area. In dry years the approach may be driveable by mid-April. A bike provides an alternative means of transportation to the trailhead.

From Pincher Creek, turn onto Highway 507 heading west. At a T-intersection, turn left onto Highway 774 and drive about 14.8 km to the Beaver Mines Lake turnoff. Turn left onto Beaver Mines Lake Road, drive for about 3.7 km and turn right onto an unsigned road. Follow the road for 600 m to arrive at a stream crossing. At most times of the year, the stream is low enough to drive through, even for low-clearance vehicles. Get out and check before crossing, though, just in case. If driving through the stream and then along an additional 5.4 km of rough road doesn't appeal to you, park in the clearing on the right side just before the stream and continue on foot or bike (preferable).

Once across the stream, follow the road for about 5.4 km to the unsigned Whistler Mountain trailhead at GR947666. This not so easy to find trailhead lies on the east (left) side of the road just before a more serious creek crossing where a high-clearance vehicle is mandatory. If you are driving the 5.4 km, go very slowly, as the road is rough and severely potholed in places. Deep, muddy puddles may halt your progress, in which case you will have to walk the rest of the way.

As mentioned, the trailhead is not obvious. From the road, simply head into the bush, going up and slightly left. This section is short and quickly leads to open terrain. Head upslope and then trend left through another patch of trees. More open slopes follow, at which point the trail should become obvious over to the left. Once you find it, the remainder of the ascent to Whistler Mountain is as easy as it gets. As the trail winds up the mountain, views start to open up to the west. The track eventually turns into beautiful red argillite and

then swings around to the east (right) towards the ridge.

Once on the ridge, if you want to visit the former site of the Whistler Mountain Lookout, turn in almost the opposite direction and walk easily to the summit in a northwest direction. The view from the lookout is very nice, and if you only plan on visiting the summit of Whistler, the diversion to the lookout is definitely recommended. Those planning on going farther than Whistler may want to save their energy and bypass the lookout. Regardless, the false summit of Whistler (GR965681) is clearly visible from the ridge and offers no resistance.

Take in the decent views for a minute and then follow the ridge southeastward to the true summit (GR967677, 2206 m), about 500 m away. The summit view is respectable, but still lies below treeline and is therefore slightly obstructed by forest. This problem is easily solved by continuing the trip to the higher peak to the east at GR978676. If the summit of Whistler was enough, **return** the same way.

37A. GR978676 2284 m
(steep hiking)

The traverse to the next high point east of Whistler offers a much improved view and is well worth the minimum effort required to get there. Simply follow the ridge, losing elevation to a col and then regaining it and more to the summit at GR978676, 2284 m.

With some planning it is possible to head north from here, to the summit of Table Mountain. This will require another vehicle or a bike to be left at the Table Mountain trailhead. Most parties will probably choose to either go south to the next and highest

From near the summit of Whistler Mountain, the remainder of the route unfolds. **LM:** "Larry Mountain"; **FP:** "Frankie Peak"; **CP:** Castle Peak. Photo: Matthew Clay

summit of the day ("Frankie Peak") or call it quits. **Return** the same way if you're done.

37B. "FRANKIE PEAK" 2375 m
(easy/moderate scrambling)

"Frankie Peak," named after my wonderful mum, offers an even finer viewpoint than the previous GR and is easily reached in under an hour. Simply hike south, losing elevation on the wide ridge. The ridge narrows as it starts to go up and there is even some very mild exposure. However, the scrambling is very easy. A more serious rock band soon rears up. It is easily avoided by going around the left side and then immediately back up to the ridge. Keep following the ridge as it curves around to the east and then to the summit at GR987665, 2375 m. For the final section, again try to stay on the ridge for some fun scrambling. A faint trail on the right side of the ridge offers easier but less enjoyable access to the summit. Reaching the summit, the unique form of Castle Peak will likely be the subject of most of the picture-taking. Mount Gladstone and Victoria Peak lie to the east. Pyramidal Mount Haig and the

vertical north face of Tombstone Mountain are just visible beyond Barnaby Ridge.

Yet again, you are now faced with the decision of whether to continue along the loop route or turn around. Be sure that time, energy and the weather are on your side if continuing. If you are done for the day, retracing your route back to the trailhead is straightforward and has the added benefit of keeping you above treeline for an additional hour or so. With good weather this is probably the best idea. However, for those who wish to avoid regaining elevation to the summits of GR978676 and Whistler there is an optional descent route. Tedious rubble at the top and a good dose of sidesloping make this a less than aesthetic route, but it is faster than following the ridge back.

For the alternative route, descend rubble heading southwest, aiming for the drainage far below (at about GR985656). It is probably best not to descend all the way to the drainage, as the bush and deadfall down there can be tedious. Instead, stay about 100 m above the drainage and sideslope, following the direction of the drainage westward. There may

On my first ascent of "Frankie Peak," I was treated to this rare and sublime view of the area. "Frankie" and "Larry" are to the left, with the super-distinctive form of Castle Peak to the right.

be easier options by turning west even earlier if you feel lucky. All routes will eventually dump you out onto the road near or at GR970649. A 3 km walk along the road leads back to the trailhead.

37C. "LARRY MOUNTAIN" 2375 m
(moderate/difficult but exposed scrambling down to col)

The traverse to "Larry Mountain" is short and very scenic – well worth the 30 minutes required to do the job. Continue east along the ridge of "Frankie Peak" for a short distance until the mountain suddenly drops off. Although these cliff bands may seem impossible to downclimb, there is a weakness close by. Descend to the right, staying close to the edge. About 50 m down, a left-trending ramp offers access to the slopes and col below. Carefully downclimb this ramp. There are no really difficult moves, but the exposure is significant. The last few moves down to the slope are a little more difficult. If descending this ramp does not appeal to you, the

cliff band can be circumvented by continuing to lose elevation along the edge of the cliff band and then around where it peters out.

Return to the ridge and continue east towards the summit of "Larry Mountain." Be sure to check out the vertigo-inducing drop down the north side of the mountain, and also the beautiful strata of "Frankie Peak's" north face.

The view from "Larry Mountain" is not significantly different from that of "Frankie Peak"; however, the ridge that continues in a southeast direction will certainly be of interest to you. If you have come this far, the loop route via North Castle is the logical way to complete the trip. There is the option to descend south into the valley and then follow the drainage, mentioned above, out to the trail. However, this is a tedious trek with route-finding, ups and downs and bushwhacking and is therefore not recommended. If you do not want to reascend "Frankie Peak" and Whistler Mountain, follow the directions below.

The first section of the alternative descent route. **R**: rock band that can be circumvented on left side; **VP**: Victoria Peak, one of the best scrambles in the Castle.

Alternative descent via North Castle 2327 m
(moderate with route-finding)

Continuing around the horseshoe-shaped ridge is as straightforward as it looks. From afar, a light-coloured rock band at the low point appears daunting but is easily circumvented around the left side. Follow the colourful ridge to a high point between Mount Gladstone and North Castle. For those with boundless energy (or another vehicle stashed at the Mill Creek parking lot – see Mount Gladstone, page 130), there is the option to run up to the summit of Gladstone. If you are returning to your vehicle in West Castle, this extension will make for a very long and physically strenuous day.

From the high point between Gladstone and North Castle, turn southwest and follow the ridge to the treed summit of North Castle. One obvious rock band must be tackled by going to the right for a short distance and then scrambling up loose scree gullies back to the ridge. Take all your photos before reaching the treed section of the ridge and summit.

For descent, follow the ridge southwestward to more open slopes until it starts to curve to the south towards Castle Peak. From here, start trending more to the west, going back into the trees and then out onto more grassy, open slopes. It is important to find these slopes. If you go too far south, you'll end up in the trees and have to sideslope numerous drainages to get over to easier terrain. Avoid dropping into any drainages. Continue going west, back into the trees, joining up with the road in several kilometres. Hike northwest along the road for about 4 km back to your vehicle.

LYS RIDGE

Lys Ridge is one of the many hidden gems of the Castle. More or less sandwiched between Barnaby

Typical colourful scenery along Lys Ridge, looking north from the summit of West Castle.

Ridge to the northwest and Windsor Ridge to the east, this almost 9 km long spine offers some of the most delightful ridgewalking/scrambling in the Canadian Rockies, right on par with my other favourite ridgewalk/scramble, Victoria Peak to Victoria Ridge. Since official West Castle sits in the middle of Lys, this is technically a two-peak day (and believe me, it feels more like ten!).

Two routes are described here and neither is for the scrambler looking for a short, easy day with a mid-afternoon start. Although the actual scrambling never goes above the moderate level, the sheer length of these routes requires that anyone attempting them get an early start and have a fairly high level of physical fitness (but then, don't all scramblers?!).

Larches are rivetingly abundant throughout and therefore late September/early October ascents will increase the scenic rewards exponentially, as will waiting for a bluebird weather day. Also, the Castle River is more easily forded late in the season.

As for which route to use, it's a toss-up. Both have fun and interesting ascent lines and both can be made into loops. The north ridge way gets you up high quickly, where you can then enjoy several hours of mainly uphill travel to the summit of Lys Ridge, with terrific views throughout. The Ruby Lake option takes you more directly to the summit, where you then enjoy mainly downhill travel to the north end of the ridge, again with awesome scenery, but later in the day. If a traverse of the entire ridge is not on the agenda and your goal is only one of Lys Ridge or West Castle, then use the Ruby Lake route for the summit of Lys Ridge, and the North ridge route for West Castle.

In addition, although a low-clearance vehicle can get you to the Ruby Lake trailhead, a higher-clearance one is recommended for the North ridge trailhead.

Lastly, a big thank you to Dave McMurray for pioneering the north ridge route and Jollin Charest for accompanying us on that trip.

38. LYS RIDGE (NORTH RIDGE) 2520 m

(MAP 8, PAGE 454)
Rating moderate
Round-trip time 11–16 hours
Elevation gain 1765 m
Maps 82 G/08 Beaver Mines, G/01 Sage Creek

This fantastic route, pioneered by Dave McMurray, has the advantage of gaining most of the day's elevation right away. Thus, within a couple of hours you are atop a beautiful ridge, with awesome views in every direction. Expect an ascent time of 6–8 hours. Bring a change of pants and socks, as you will have to ford the river without hip waders at the end of the day if you choose the Ruby Lake descent option.

After turning south onto Highway 774, drive 14.9 km and turn left onto the Beaver Mines Lake gravel road. Drive 3.7 km and turn right onto an unsigned road and continue for about 7.5 km to an obvious clearing on the west side of the gravel road. About 600 m along you will have to drive across a creek. It may be flowing or completely dry. If the water is too high (early season), you may have to ford the creek and hike or bike the additional 6.9 km. If that is the case, change your plans and do Whistler Mountain or another nearby objective instead.

The drive to the trailhead is slow due to an abundance of huge puddles to drive through. Note the cattle grating you will pass by. The trailhead is on the right (west) side of the road, about 3.3 km after you pass the grating. Shortly before reaching the parking area, you'll come to a washout where you have to stay to the right and drive down into a drainage and back up the other side. It's short, but higher clearance on your vehicle is preferred.

The ascent route is clearly visible from the parking area (see photo opposite). Before leaving your vehicle, put on whatever you'll be using to ford the river (hip waders, runners etc.). Hike down to the river and ford it (the first of four potential crossings), leaving your waders on the other side. Follow the river upstream for several hundred metres. Turn right (southwest) and bushwhack uphill to the open boulder slope as seen in the photo. The best way to ascend from here is right up the boulders. Most of them are very stable and provide a stair-like and fun ascent. The lichen-covered rock wall to your left and larches to your right further enhance the scenery. It's about 600 vertical metres to the ridge, so expect to take more than an hour to get there.

Atop the ridge, turn south. The dark rock band in front is easily surmounted via a weakness on the

right (west) side. It is now just a matter of following the ridge south until you reach the summit of West Castle at GR957622. The scrambling throughout should only be moderate and route-finding challenges are few.

West Castle may be considered a double summit, a yellow one and red one (GR957622), separated by about 450 m. The red is marginally higher. If this is enough for the day, then return the same way.

To complete the full traverse, continue following the ridge. Although some sections ahead may appear to be difficult, they are not and easy routes exist throughout. If you stay on the ridge, you will eventually arrive at a dead end, where the mountain suddenly drops away. Lose elevation to the left (east) until an easy to moderate route to circumvent the wall below you presents itself. The lower you go, the easier the terrain. Then sideslope back to the ridge. Once again, the lichen covered rock is incredible to look at.

Back on the ridge, gain the next high point to a wide plateau and then hike about 2 km to the true summit of Lys Ridge, at GR959577 (easy to recognize because there is a repeater station there). Before you get there, go to the left (east) side of the ridge, where you will get a good look at beautiful Lys Lake to the east.

The summit view is remarkable, especially if you are familiar with other scrambles in the immediate area, such as Mount Haig, "Jake Smith Peak," Rainy Ridge and Three Lakes Ridge. Note the huge chunk of rock missing from the side of Jake Smith, the area's highest mountain. Other notable summits in the vista include Castle Peak and Windsor Mountain, Loaf Mountain and a bunch of huge peaks down in Glacier National Park, Montana. It's

The ascent route as seen from the parking area. **CR**: Castle River; **R**: ridge.

also nice to get a look at some of the lesser-known mountains: La Coulotte, Jutland, Matkin, Font and Sage.

There are two viable return routes. Even with the extra elevation gains, perhaps the fastest way back is to retrace the route. This may also be a good idea if weather conditions have improved or are improving.

To fully experience this area, the recommended descent route is via Ruby Lake. This does require extra hiking distance and you will have to ford the Castle two or three times without your hip waders. However, the trail from Ruby Lake back to the road is excellent and therefore travel is quite fast.

From the summit of Lys, descend scree slope to the west. Ruby Lake will soon be visible. As a general guide, aim for the eastern shoreline. There are several rocky gullies that offer easy ways down the mountain and your goal is to find one. The scrambling should never be more than moderate and not exposed.

You will pass through a band of diorite (a very hard, greenish-grey igneous rock) and then hopefully the RASC below that. "RASC" stands for "red argillite staircase" and this one is a beaut! It is actually easier to use scree slopes on either side of the RASC to descend, but it is also easy to see why this gully makes an awesome ascent route. It literally is a staircase of red argillite.

Lower down, trend a little more to the left, again aiming for the shoreline of Ruby Lake. Upon reaching Ruby Lake, follow the shoreline or a trail near the shore around the north side of the lake, over the lake outlet and to a backcountry campsite (at this point in the day, you may be wishing you had brought a tent!). The lake itself is fantastic, backdropped by steep, colourful walls of nearly vertical rock. If time permits, it is definitely worth checking out the views from various points around the lake.

The return trail leaves from the campsite and is very easy to follow. When you arrive at an intersection with an orange hiking sign on the left fork (which leads to Grizzly Lake), take the right fork. The trail now drops down to Grizzly Creek, crosses it and then gains elevation, seemingly going in the wrong direction. This is not the case, however, and you reach another intersection, where you turn left, now going north and traversing the side of Lys.

The remainder of the trek is long but easy. A few hours later the trail will empty you out back at the Castle River, about 2 km north of where you crossed the river in the morning. Ford the river again (sans hip waders!) and find the trail on the other side (more to the left) that leads within minutes back to the gravel road. Hike about 2 km southeast on the road, back to your vehicle. Don't forget to retrieve your hip waders if you used them.

39. LYS RIDGE (RUBY LAKE) 2520 m

(MAP 8, PAGE 454)
Rating moderate
Round-trip time 11–16 hours
Elevation gain 1765 m
Maps 82 G/08 Beaver Mines, G/01 Sage Creek

The advantages of this route are that you get to ascend the RASC (preferable to descending it), experience the awesome summit view a little earlier in the trip and then spend the remainder of the day going downhill, more or less, along the stunning north ridge. It also means the sun will primarily be at your back as you descend the ridge.

After turning south onto Highway 774, drive 14.9 km and turn left onto the Beaver Mines Lake gravel road. Drive 3.7 km, turn right onto an unsigned road and continue for 5.8 km to the parking area. About 600 m along you will have to drive across a creek. It may be flowing or completely dry. If the creek is too high (early season), you may have to ford it and hike or bike the additional 4.8 km. If

that is the case, change your plans and do Whistler Mountain or another nearby objective instead. The trailhead is on the right (west) side of the road, 1.2 km after passing a cattle grating.

While still at your vehicle, put on whatever you will be using to ford the river (hip waders, runners etc.). Then hike down the trail, take a left when you arrive at an ATV trail, and make your way to the

The ascent line up the RASC as seen from the shore of serene Ruby Lake. Jollin Charest and Dave McMurray model perfect scrambling attire by the lake!

Castle River within minutes. Ford the river and find the trail (a little to the right) on the other side. It's marked with an orange hiking sign. The trail parallels Grizzly Creek, crosses it and continues on the other side.

Follow this excellent trail for the next 11 or so kilometres. It wanders a little but eventually goes due south, paralleling Grizzly Creek at various distances from it. Hiking trail signs and bridges make the trip that much easier. The occasional open sections reveal great views of the southeast side of Barnaby Ridge to the right and Lys Ridge to the left.

Around GR950587 (the 11 km mark), the trail forks. Straight leads to the dead end; right and down leads to Grizzly and Ruby lakes. Rocks have been piled across the trail to prevent hikers from going straight. There is also flagging in the trees and another hiking trail sign. Descend to and cross Grizzly Creek. Another fork is quickly reached. Turn left and follow this trail to a campsite by Ruby Lake.

If you have the time, Ruby Lake is definitely worth exploring. You can go completely around it in a counterclockwise direction if desired. The views of the lake, surrounded by forest and the steep walls of Lys Ridge are excellent. If you do go around the west side, be sure to check out the location of the RASC (see below) for your ascent line.

From the campsite, head east and cross the lake outlet on fallen trees. Go immediately to the lakeshore so you can identify the location of the red argillite staircase (at last, the acronym is decoded!). There are actually a couple of RASCs, but the northern one is what you will be aiming for (see photo). Follow a faint trail around to the northeast side of the lake, looking left for a good view of the RASC, around GR951574. Bushwhack to the staircase and start up it. Initially the terrain is tedious, but as soon as the scree gives way to more solid rock you are in for a real treat.

The ascent line really is a staircase of red argillite. Water has simply eroded and cleared all the

The "minor hiccup.

debris way. The ascent is fun and easy from here. A steep rock band is quickly encountered and can be ascended head-on or circumvented in the trees on either side. More red argillite steps follow.

Eventually a solid band of diorite is reached (a very hard, greenish-grey igneous rock). Scramble up the rock band and finish the ascent on steep scree and rubble that is less fun. Grovel your way up to the high point, complete with its own repeater station, at GR959577. Besides the unsightly but necessary structure, the view is outstanding, especially if you are familiar with other scrambles in the immediate area, such as Mount Haig, "Jake Smith Peak," Rainy Ridge and Three Lakes Ridge. Note the huge chunk of rock missing from the side of Jake Smith, the area's highest mountain. Other notable summits in the vista include Castle Peak and Windsor Mountain, Loaf Mountain and a bunch of huge peaks down in Glacier National Park, Montana. It's also nice to get a look at some of the lesser-known mountains: La Coulotte, Jutland, Matkin, Font and Sage.

After checking out North Scarpe Lake to the southeast, you have to traverse over to the lower summit to the north. Here you get an amazing view of larch-surrounded Lys Lake, below the ridge to the east.

If satiated, return the same way. However, the full traverse of the ridge is an incredible experience you won't soon forget. A detailed description is hardly required, as there is only one way to go – north. There is one minor hiccup, about 3 km along, where a nearly vertical and extremely colourful rock band halts progress (see photo on page 143). Here you will have to either leave the ridge and sideslope over to a weakness in the rock band or follow the ridge and then lose elevation alongside the rock band until a feasible route appears to get around it. Return to the ridge and continue along it, enjoying more great views and ridgewalking. The scrambling is generally easier than it looks and should never be exposed or difficult.

The red and yellow double summit of West Castle is eventually reached, at GR957622 (the red one). Continue following the ridge as it turns northwest. At the far northwest end, open slopes give way to forested ones. Try to spot the Grizzly Lake trail far below, on the west side of the ridge. Pick the least steep line, down through the trees, trending slightly left as you go. Eventually you will intercept the Grizzly Lake trail. Follow it back to the Castle River and then to your vehicle.

40. SYNCLINE MOUNTAIN 2500 m

(MAP 9, PAGE 454)
Rating easy to 1st summit; moderate to 2nd; difficult (but avoidable) scrambling to 3rd
Round-trip time 3.5–5 hours to 1st summit; 9–12 hours for all three
Elevation gain 1020 m to 1st summit; add ~400 m for 2nd and 3rd
Maps 82 G/8 Beaver Mines

Syncline Mountain sports three separate summits. Inexplicably, the lowest of the three is actually the true summit. This one can be easily reached from the road in short order. The best part of the trip, however, belongs to ascents of the second peak and the third, which is the highest. The rock scenery along the way is absolutely wonderful. Try from July on.

Drive to Pincher Creek and turn right onto Highway 507, following the signs for Castle Mountain Ski Resort. At a T-intersection, turn left and head southwest on Highway 774. Drive southward for about 23 km and park on the side of the road at GR881700. As you approach the parking area, the entire route to the first summit is visible from the road.

Head west through light forest, aiming for the northeast ridge. Once on more open slopes, trend a little left and ascend the left side of the slopes all the way to the summit ridge – this will at least give you some decent views along the way. Gain the summit ridge through an obvious weakness between two outcrops of rock; then turn left and walk to the summit cairn a couple of minutes away. Technically, you have now reached the true summit

of the mountain. It is, however, not the highest one and certainly not the most interesting of the three. If content, **return** the same way.

The two higher summits of Syncline can be seen to the SW and NW of the first summit. The most interesting route follows the ridge for some sections and traverses below it for others. Continue south along the ridge (don't be tempted to take a more direct route down to the valley to the west) and drop down to a col. Gaining the high point in front of you is a worthwhile diversion, requiring minimal effort, but you will have to return to the col. Once back at the col, descend slopes to the right and traverse along the base of the huge rock outcrop. This takes you to another col and another rock outcrop.

From here it is possible to pick your way down

The three summits of Syncline from Highway 774. **AD**: alternative descent route.

Above: The route to the second summit from the first. **HP**: worthwhile high point; **T**: traverse around high point.

Below: The view from the second summit towards the highest summit. **S3**: third summit; **AD**: alternative descent route; **WW**: wrong way – mountain drops off.

the right side of the mountain to the low col that separates the two summits. A more scenic (but longer) option goes around the other side and is described here. Both options require a significant elevation loss. Go around to the left (south) side of the ridge and traverse below it until you arrive at a severe drop-off. You now have to head down scree slopes to your left until a feasible route around the cliffs presents itself. Once low enough, traverse along the base of the impressive and colourful cliffs back to the ridge, staying high on the slopes. A scree slog then leads easily to the second summit.

The view from the second summit is splendid, especially south towards Eloi, Gravenstafel and Haig. Farther southwest, Tombstone Mountain is easily recognizable because of its suggestive shape. The best view is looking back to the first summit and the scenic ridge you've negotiated to get to the second.

Yet again you now have the option to call it a day or continue on to the third and highest summit. To **return**, go back down to the low col and then southward down scree slopes into the drainage that eventually leads to Syncline Brook Trail. Turn left onto the trail and follow it back to the road. Your vehicle will be about 1 km north.

The trickiest part of the traverse to the third summit comes right at the beginning. Don't head north along the ridge – you'll get cliffed out within minutes. Instead, scramble down to the southwest, looking for a steepish scree gully which gets you below the steep layers of rock that surround you. Once on easier terrain, turn north and traverse

scree slopes to the connecting ridge. Follow the ridge to the summit. Two rock bands rear up just before the top. Both are easily circumvented by going onto scree slopes to the right. It's far more enjoyable, however, to tackle them head-on. Both involve steep, exposed scrambling, so you'll want the rock to be dry.

The first rock band is initially overhanging. Traverse to the right a few metres and a steep crack becomes visible. Ascend the crack, making one or two awkward moves over a chockstone, and then continue up another steep band of brown rock. The second, a lichen-covered black rock band, is a little more serious. Once you start up, you won't want to back down, so be sure of your route. At the top, the summit is only minutes away.

Getting back to your vehicle from the third summit may be the crux of your day. There are several options:

1. **Return** the same way (recommended only for those with Herculean endurance!).

2. **Return** to the second summit and use the descent route described above.

3. From the summit, descend southeast-facing slopes into the valley below. Follow the creek out (Suicide Creek). Be prepared for sections of downright nasty bushwhacking. Much lower down, ATV trails appear on the left side of the creek. If you're lucky, you'll find one right away. If not, stay near the creek as much as possible and eventually you will run into a trail. Turn right and follow ATV and hiking trails back to the road, coming out of the forest about 1.3 km north of your vehicle.

41. ST. ELOI MOUNTAIN 2500 m

(MAP 9, PAGE 454)
Rating easy via the northeast ridge
Round-trip time 5.5–7 hours
Elevation gain 1100 m
Maps 82 G/8 Beaver Mines

In between the more challenging scrambles of Syncline and Haig sits St. Eloi Mountain. It is long enough and scenic enough to be listed as a separate trip. Only very fast and very fit parties will want to consider continuing north to Syncline or south to Haig. Try from June on.

Drive to Pincher Creek and make a right onto Highway 507, following signs for Castle Mountain Ski Resort. At a T-intersection, turn left, heading southwest on Highway 774 for approximately 24 km. Park on the side of the road at the unsigned Syncline Brook trailhead (simply a clearing on the west side of the road).

Hike the trail for about 1.5 km (20–30 minutes), arriving at a large, rocky drainage with flagging on either side. Turn right and hike up the drainage a fair distance, looking for open slopes on the left that lead to the ridge that connects Eloi (left) to Syncline (right). Ascend the foreshortened slopes to the ridge and turn left towards St. Eloi. Follow the ridge to the summit. Though an intervening high point can be sidesloped on the left side, gaining the high point requires minimal effort and is worth a quick visit.

Shapely Mount Haig dominates to the south, with the appropriately named Tombstone Mountain farther west. To the north, the three summits of Syncline are particularly pleasing to the eye. **Return** the same way.

Opposite above: Route from the ridge. **HP:** subsidiary high point; **S:** summit of St. Eloi.
Opposite below: The ascent drainage. **D:** drainage; **R:** ridge; **SS:** Syncline's second summit.

42. MOUNT HAIG 2618 m

(MAP 10, PAGE 455)
Rating moderate via the northeast and east ridges
Round-trip time 6–8 hours; add 1–2 hours for Gravenstafel Ridge
Elevation gain 1400 m; add 300 m for Gravenstafel Ridge
Maps 82 G/8 Beaver Mines

Mount Haig is the second-highest mountain in the area ("Jake Smith Peak" is the highest) and a very worthwhile scramble. The summit view is excellent and once there you have options to continue peak-bagging by going north to Gravenstafel Ridge (highly recommended) or southwest to "Boot Hill" and Tombstone Mountain (also highly recommended, but it's a long trip!). Try from July on.

Drive to Pincher Creek and turn right onto Highway 507, following signs for Castle Mountain Ski Resort. At a т-intersection, turn left, heading southwest on Highway 774 to the Castle Mountain Ski Resort parking lot. At the southwest end of the parking lot a road continues south. Follow this for about 100 m, taking the first right and then a left to arrive at a bridge over Gravenstafel Brook. Park here.

While it is possible to bike some of the approach, this would preclude the option to do the loop route via Gravenstafel Brook or Gravenstafel Ridge (either one is highly recommended). The gravel approach road is the access to the chairlift and basically parallels the lift in long switchbacks. Make your way to the top of the lift and leave your bike here if you rode.

Mount Haig as seen from the Castle Mountain parking lot. The red line up the northeast ridge to the terminus of the ski lift is approximate. **T**: ski lift terminus; **S**: summit of northeast ridge; **TS**: true summit.

Route down to the tarn and up to the east ridge, as seen from the northeast ridge.

The ascent continues behind the lift. Note that further development of the ski hill may alter this terrain in the future. The road here is rocky and steep but easy to follow. It goes most of the way up the northeast ridge. When it ends, continue going up and to the right to the highest point of the ridge. Even at this point, you are privy to a great view of Haig's awesome northeast face, the east ridge route (which you'll shortly be on), the alternative loop descent route and the extension to Gravenstafel Ridge.

Now comes the unpleasant part: a necessary elevation loss down to the tarn in between the northeast and east ridges. Descend to the col and then down easy slopes to your left to the beautiful turquoise waters. You may want to take a break here to contemplate the remaining 800 metres of elevation still to gain!

From the tarn, gain the east ridge and follow it to the summit. There are a few opportunities to enjoy some hands-on scrambling up minor rock bands, so take advantage of them. For easier terrain, traverse left alongside the bands until you find a weakness to your liking. Most notably, the summit view includes mountains in Waterton (SE), Castle (E) and Crowsnest (N and NW). St. Eloi and Syncline, two other worthwhile scrambles, sit immediately to the north.

Either **return** the same way (remember that you will have to regain about 300 metres of elevation for this option), or do the loop route, which is easier, interesting and therefore recommended. Continue down the north ridge, keeping the col between Haig and Gravenstafel Ridge in mind – that's where you're heading. As you approach the first low point on the ridge, look to the right for an obvious trail that starts heading down to the col. The following section is the only one of consequence, as the terrain gets steeper and there is even a touch of exposure! The route down is well marked by the trail and shouldn't pose any problems.

The alternative descent route(s) as seen from the summit of Haig. **C**: Haig/Gravenstafel col; **L**: route to lake; **G**: summit of Gravenstafel Ridge; **S**: Syncline; **E**: St. Eloi.

42A. GRAVENSTAFEL RIDGE 2394 m

If you've had enough, make your way down to the small lake nestled under the northeast face of Haig, find the trail at the lake's east side and follow it back to the parking area. If you're up for an easy additional 300 metres of elevation gain and another summit under your belt, continue north up the south ridge of Gravenstafel. Stay on the ridge and tackle all bands head-on. One rock band about halfway up is a little more challenging, but there are weaknesses and easier routes on both sides. A few false summits later and you're up (40–50 minutes from the col).

Getting down is easy. Continue north along the ridge for a few minutes until a maze of ski runs and maintenance roads become visible. Choose whatever line you like to the bottom. The maintenance roads are less steep, though circuitous, but going straight down is never difficult either.

43. "BOOT HILL" 2498 m

(MAP 10, PAGE 455)
Rating easy from Mount Haig (which is moderate)
Round-trip time 9–11 hours
Elevation gain add 700 m from Mount Haig; approximately 2100 m in total
Maps 82 G/8 Beaver Mines

This is the unofficial peak that sits between Mount Haig and Tombstone Mountain. The comical and very fitting name can be attributed to the amazing Rick Collier, possibly the most prolific mountaineer in Canadian Rockies history. Mr. Collier sadly passed away in 2012. If you are at the summit of Haig, the traverse over to "Boot" is an excellent extension and also the best way to get to Tombstone. A route to the summit via the Haig/Middle Kootenay col has far less elevation gain but is a bushwhacking, route-finding nightmare – not recommended!

See route description #42, for Mount Haig. From the summit of Haig, descend the wide south ridge and then ascend a very short distance to the first insignificant high point, around GR854616. At the high point turn west and scramble easily down to the col between the high point and "Boot Hill." Continue going west up the east ridge of "Boot Hill." Choose whatever line you see fit. Traversing more onto the southeast face means more scree and

less hands-on scrambling, though the scrambling is minimal.

Slog your way up to the false summit and then continue going west to the true summit at GR841612. The view of Tombstone Mountain is fantastic and worth every minute of the trudge. Return the same way or consider continuing on to the summit of Tombstone (see next description).

The straightforward route to "Boot Hill" as seen from Mount Haig. **MK**: "Middle Kootenay Mountain"; **TM**: Tombstone Mountain; **BH**: "Boot Hill."

44. TOMBSTONE MOUNTAIN 2515 m

(MAP 10, PAGE 455)
Rating moderate from "Boot Hill"
Round-trip time 12–15 hours
Elevation gain add 550 m from "Boot Hill"; approximately 2650 m in total
Maps 82 G/8 Beaver Mines

From "Boot Hill" the ascent of Tombstone Mountain is fairly straightforward but makes for an extremely long and physically demanding day, with almost 3000 metres of elevation gain. Only the fittest and/or most persevering of people need apply for this one! Nevertheless, in dry conditions it's mostly a steep hike with a few moves of moderate scrambling. In snowy conditions, the traverse along the east face will be pretty sketchy and is not recommended. The summit view is actually slightly inferior to that of "Boot Hill," but the ascent of this striking and remote peak is still more than worthwhile if you are in the area. Water sources are scarce. On a hot summer day I would recommend carrying at least 4 litres to complete the Haig–"Boot Hill"–Tombstone trip. A much shorter route up Tombstone is possible from logging roads on the west side. Consult other sources for that information.

Tombstone Mountain from near the col. The point where you start the traverse left may change according to conditions.

Exquisite colours of the Castle mountains. The length of Barnaby Ridge, with its summit near the right, dominates the scene. The peak at the distant far right is Mount Gladstone.

See the route descriptions for Mount Haig and "Boot Hill," at pages 150 and 153 respectively. Leave the summit of "Boot Hill," heading down the southwest ridge. The Tombstone/"Boot Hill" col, 300 vertical metres below, is easily reached in short order. Ascend towards the impressive face of Tombstone until a sidesloping route to the left becomes visible. Traverse the east face on this down-sloping terrain to get to the southeast corner of the mountain. Again, a reminder that snowcover may render this traverse a very dangerous one. In that case, either retreat or descend southeast into the valley, cross it and look for a safe route to gain the southeast corner. The third option is to get out your crampons and ice axe and traverse high on the slope, but this will still be a risky and perhaps unnerving affair.

From the southeast corner continue traversing around the peak to the south face. Look to the right for a feasible route up. There is a band of black rock that provides the only real scrambling challenge. Ascend it and then continue up on easier terrain.

Although not apparent from the lower slopes, the summit lies to the left (west) side of the mountain – trend in that direction as you go up. The summit view is similar to that of "Boot Hill."

After taking a break to contemplate the monumental task of now getting back to your vehicle, **return** the same way you came. Keep in mind that the return trip will require another 900 metres (approximately) of elevation gain. You can avoid some of that by traversing around the south and east side of "Boot Hill" and then regaining the "Boot"/high point col, instead of reascending "Boot Hill." A good trail makes easy work of this, as long as you can find one. The trail is above the prominent cliff bands and about halfway up the peak from the valley floor. There are other routes back to your car that minimize elevation gain. However, the bushwhacking and route-finding challenges ("horrors" would be more fitting, actually) of these routes nullify any advantage over the recommended way.

45. BARNABY RIDGE 2471 m
and SOUTHFORK MOUNTAIN 2350 m

(MAP 10, PAGE 455)
Rating moderate via west slopes and the north ridge
Round-trip time 6–11 hours
Elevation gain 1100–1300 m, depending on route
Maps 82 G/8 Beaver Mines

From the road, this long ridge appears to provide a plethora of dull and tedious ascent routes. Such is not the case, and as long as you go looking for it, interesting scenery is abundant. The loop route (with the short descent) is not terribly strenuous, nabs you two peaks (Barnaby and Southfork) and avoids a ford of the West Castle River. It is therefore the recommended route. Try from June on.

Drive to Castle Mountain Ski Resort. Instead of turning right to enter the resort, stay left on the gravel road. In several hundred metres this road trends left and then crosses a bridge. Drive 1.1 km past the bridge to open meadows on the left, below the west face of Barnaby Ridge (GR887649). The road is decent, even for low-clearance vehicles, but

may have large, deep puddles. If such is the case, you may want to back up, park at the bridge and walk the paltry 1.1 km.

The ascent route follows the open drainage immediately northwest of the summit and is visible from the road. Before embarking, be sure to look for the distinctive triangular rock face, high

Much of the ascent route is visible from the parking area. **TR**: triangular rock face; **SR**: scenic route (recommended); **DR**: direct route; **S**: summit.

on the mountain, to the left of the ascent gully (see photo opposite). This rock face provides a very scenic diversion and maybe the highlight of the trip, if you wish to visit it.

Hike east over the meadows and into the trees. The bush is light and very soon you reach a trail (clear-cut) heading north/south alongside Barnaby Ridge. Turn right (south) onto the trail and follow it directly into the ascent drainage. Ascend the drainage until it becomes too difficult. Move into the brush on the left side of the drainage and continue upward. Animal trails are evident all the way up and will make travel a little easier.

As you gain elevation and pass treeline, look to your left for the aforementioned rock face – it's fairly prominent and pretty hard to miss. Keep paralleling the main ascent drainage until you come across a much smaller drainage coming down from the left. This one leads right to the interesting rock. Go straight up the middle on step-like terrain. Note that if you have no interest in the rock face, continue upward, paralleling the main ascent drainage. Circumvent the odd rock step if necessary and eventually gain the ridge, just north of the Barnaby's summit.

Back to the rock face: once there, you may want to take a few (or many!) minutes to check out the lichen-covered rock. When satiated, you'll find the easiest route is the scree gully to the right (south) side of the rock band. The most interesting route (having the best sections of lichen-covered rock) is the obvious weakness near the right side. The gully has some moderate scrambling and is mildly exposed but quite short. Follow the line of least resistance, passing a large, striking pinnacle near the top. Next, descend down to the scree gully mentioned above and up to the ridge.

This ridge separates two of the major gullies on the west face. Follow the ridge easily to a minor high point on Barnaby Ridge, north of the summit, for a scenic panorama. Hike south to the summit. There are three summits in the area. The middle is the highest, but the lower, westernmost summit is only 5 minutes away and is worth a quick visit. After taking in good views of Haig, Rainy Ridge and several unnamed summits, return to the middle and then continue over to the east summit. Here, the view to the Front Range peaks of the Castle is excellent.

If you've had enough at this point, either return the way you came or descend to the low point north of Barnaby's summit and then turn west down scree slopes back to the original ascent slope.

45A. SOUTHFORK MOUNTAIN

If you are up for more, the traverse up and down (mostly down) to the summit of Southfork Mountain is easy, colourful and enjoyable. Simply follow the wide ridge northwest, first to the big bump of red argillite. This summit is only about 10 vertical metres lower than that of Barnaby. Along the way, be sure to check out the impressive, steep walls of the mountain's east face – just don't go too far east!

From the red bump it's pretty much all downhill to the summit of Southfork. One section will require some easy scrambling and route-finding but is straightforward. Views toward Syncline Mountain and peaks of the Crowsnest beyond should keep you entertained.

There are a couple of options for descent from the summit of Southfork. The shortest route goes down scree slopes into the drainage immediately southwest of the summit. The scree eventually gives way to tedious rubble. Keep following the drainage down, picking the line of least resistance, until there is no option but to go into the trees. Thankfully the bushwhacking is not heavy. Head down and trend slightly left. Depending on how far left you go, you may end up back at the road or more likely at the river (creek). Follow the east bank of the river easily back to the road. It is not necessary to cross the river.

A longer but more scenic route is via the Southfork Lakes on the east side of the mountain. Note that this does require fording the West Castle River or following the east bank of it for several kilometres. In spring and early summer the river may be waist deep, and bushwhacking on the east side could be tedious and time-consuming. As well, don't expect a well-worn trail to take you all the way to the river. Some route-finding will be necessary. Now that I've completely put you off the idea, away you go!

Descend the north ridge of Southfork for about 600 m until you can take a sharp right, now heading southeast towards the upper lakes. Once there, take a look around, circling the lakes if you wish, and then take the trail that descends to the lower lake. From the lower lake, a trail goes north for about 1 km and then swings west (left), down steep, open slopes. Lower down, you may lose

Above: A close look at the vibrantly coloured lichen on the rock of the triangular face.
Below: Leaving Barnaby for Southfork Mountain. It's a colourful and easy affair. **BB**: big red-argillite bump; **SM**: Southfork Mountain; **ER**: easier descent route.

the trail. Keep heading northwest to eventually arrive at the river. If the river is not too deep, ford it. Then continue west to the main road and hike about 5 km back to your vehicle. If the river is too deep, start the long hike south to a place where you can get across. The unlucky ones will have to hike the entire 4 km through the bush until the river goes under a bridge. An excellent description of this descent (in reverse) can be found in Robert Kershaw's *Exploring the Castle*.

46. RAINY RIDGE 2469 m

(MAP 10, PAGE 455)
Rating moderate via the west ridge
Round-trip time 6.5–9 hours
Elevation gain Approximately 1000 m
Maps 82 G/8 Beaver Mines, G/1 Sage Creek

There are several routes to the summit of Rainy Ridge. All are very enjoyable and offer unique scenic opportunities. The described route is not the shortest one to the summit, but it gives you the opportunity to complete a very pleasant loop route. It ascends the west ridge and then descends to the Middlepass Lakes. The lakes are surrounded by larches and therefore an ascent in late September or early October can be extremely rewarding.

Drive to Castle Mountain Ski Resort. Instead of turning right to enter the resort, stay left on the gravel road. In several hundred metres this road trends left and immediately crosses a bridge. Drive about 2.6 km past the bridge to where the road forks. A large clearing on the right provides a place to park and is also a good bivy site if you choose to stay awhile (GR890638). The road is decent, even for low-clearance vehicles, but may have large, deep puddles. If such is the case, you may want to

back up, park at the bridge and walk or bike the 2.6 km to where the road forks.

From the parking area, it is possible to bike all the way to Middle Kootenay Pass. Just make sure your brakes are in good working order – you'll need them! Also, the amount of snow on the trail may dictate whether a bike is a good idea or not.

Take the right branch of the fork in the road and follow it over a bridge within 100 m and then another bridge a little later. The next several

Approaching the black rock, with the summit block in the distance to the left.

View to the Middlepass Lakes, with Three Lakes Ridge behind. "Mount Miles" and "Krowicki Peak" are to the right.

kilometres are easy to follow. Arriving at another major fork (GR891616), with a sign warning of avalanche danger for snowmobilers, again take the right branch (heading uphill) and keep following the wide path towards Middle Kootenay Pass. This fork is a good place to leave your bike if you are not up for a very strenuous ride up to the pass and then a "riding your brakes" trip back down. You'll eventually go through an open gate (or walk around it if it's locked) and cross two small streams. A high point is soon reached, with the slopes of Rainy Ridge to the left and "Middle Kootenay Mountain" to the right. The actual pass sits about 200 m from the point where the trail descends a small slope.

From Middle Kootenay Pass turn left (east) and scramble up the easy slopes of the far west ridge of Rainy. Route-finding is straightforward throughout – simply follow the ridge. You'll quickly notice that it is probably faster to travel on scree slopes to the right of the ridge, but staying on the ridge

definitely offers better and more interesting scrambling. Pick whichever route suits your liking.

A short stint of red argillite soon gives way to golden shales. At the first minor high point, the mountain separates into two ridges: one heading north-northeast and the other south-southeast. Turn right and follow the south-southeast-trending ridge, losing a small amount of elevation towards the more intimidating black rock band (see photo next page). Fortunately, looks are deceiving here and the black band is easily ascended straight up the middle, trending to the right as you go up. The scrambling is moderate and mildly exposed, but only for a few moves. Continue with ease to the black summit and take a break to enjoy the beautiful view of the Middlepass Lakes with Three Lakes Ridge above and also the remainder of the Rainy Ridge ascent.

From the black summit, lose a fair amount of elevation to the col and start up the red slopes of Rainy Ridge proper. Again, travel can be easy on scree slopes to the right of the ridge or more challenging directly on the ridge. The terrain is never committing, and easy slopes are always available to the right if the scrambling gets too difficult. A pleasant ridgewalk to the summit cairn completes the ascent. Views of the surrounding area are excellent from the top.

Options from the summit are plentiful:

Route 1, continue the high-level ridge traverse to the summit of Three Lakes Ridge; **Route 2,** descend to the Middlepass Lakes and follow a good trail back to Middle Kootenay Pass; **Route 3,** return the way you came.

If Three Lakes Ridge is not on the agenda, visiting the Middlepass Lakes via **Route 2** is a must-do.

Route 1: This traverse is not the best way to the summit of Three Lakes Ridge – that honour goes to the northeast face described later in the book. The main reason for doing this route is because you are already there and the traverse is very scenic, if sometimes tedious. Careful route-finding will get you past most of the difficulties, but still

expect some steep terrain and possible exposure. This traverse is *not* the pushover the Rainy Ridge ascent was.

From the summit of Rainy, continue following the ridge as it descends west. The terrain is initially easy but soon becomes a little more serious when rock bands interrupt progress. The first of these can be downclimbed via a gully slightly to the right (north) of the ridge, while the second is easily circumvented around the left side. The third rock band offers considerable challenge and must be circumvented on the south side of the ridge. This requires you to back up a few hundred metres and look for a reasonable descent route through treed terrain to the south. As mentioned, careful route-finding is necessary if you want to avoid exposed slopes. Also be ready to lose a significant amount of elevation to the valley below before sidesloping back up to the low col between Rainy Ridge and Three Lakes.

There are two routes to the summit from the col. Both start by ascending the Three Lakes east ridge

Looking back to the reddish form of Rainy Ridge. The exposed downclimb is at the right.

on slopes of rubble and scree. When a unique pinnacle appears, you have to make a decision. Staying on the ridge is the most interesting route, but it leads to a brutally exposed downclimb just before the summit. Veering off to the left (south) avoids exposed terrain altogether, allowing you to completely circumvent the dangerous step on the ridge.

The tricky step on the ridge is best descended by staying to the right on the narrow ridge, even though this exposes you to a tremendous drop on the north side. Carefully downclimb to a huge boulder sticking out of the ridge (hopefully it's still there; if not, turn around immediately) and then down to safe terrain. A slip here will most likely be fatal, so be extremely cautious. If you decide the step is too much, return the way you came, looking for an escape route down to the easy scree slopes on the south side of the ridge. You don't have to return all the way to the col.

If you have no interest in the exposed step, stay on easy slopes well to the left of the ridge. The scrambling here is no more than steep hiking. If you get onto tricky terrain, you need to be farther south. Thankfully the scree slog to the summit is not terribly long.

The summit view is excellent, especially later in the day when the sun has moved around to the west. Rainy Ridge takes on a beautiful red hue and is quite a sight above the third Middlepass Lake. For the descent route off Three Lakes Ridge and other summit possibilities, see the route description for Three Lakes Ridge on page 163.

Route 2: This way is highly recommended. It is easy and very scenic. The three Middlepass Lakes alone are worth a visit to the area. Most of the route down to the lakes can be seen from the summit.

Return along the ridge a few hundred metres to where a direct route to the lakes becomes obvious. Descend scree slopes to the upper (and most interesting) lake. Time and energy permitting, it is well worth a trek around the entire lake. Views from every angle are terrific, and especially rewarding is that from the west end. Here Rainy Ridge can be seen in its full splendor. One particularly colourful rock band is very striking due to the exposed layers of different types of rock.

The northwest side of the lake provides great camping for those who wish to stay the night. Here you will also find Middlepass Trail. Follow it, in short order, to the much smaller second lake and then down to the first lake, lying in the shadow of Three Lakes Ridge. The trail then descends and sideslopes all the way back to Middle Kootenay Pass. It is generally very easy to follow, except nearer the pass, where it fades in and out a little. Even so, it is impossible to get lost on these beautiful, open slopes.

47. THREE LAKES RIDGE 2492 m

(MAP 10, PAGE 455)
Rating moderate/difficult via the northeast face or Rainy Ridge
Round-trip time 5.5–8 hours
Elevation gain Approximately 1000 m
Maps 82 G/8 Beaver Mines, G/1 Sage Creek

Three Lakes Ridge is one of the more unique peaks in the area, courtesy of the wonderful slabs high up on the northeast face. Other routes to the summit are possible, but the northeast face is the most enjoyable and straightforward route. Three Lakes is also the launching ground for an ascent of the highest peak in the area, "Jake Smith Peak," and its westerly brother Scarpe Mountain.

Drive to Castle Mountain Ski Resort. Instead of turning right to enter the resort, stay left on the gravel road. In several hundred metres this road trends left and immediately crosses a bridge. Drive about 2.6 km past the bridge to where the road forks. A large clearing on the right provides a place to park and is also a good bivy site if you choose to stay awhile (GR890638). The road is decent, even for low-clearance vehicles, but may have large, deep puddles. If such is the case, you may want to back up, park at the bridge and walk or bike the 2.6 km to where the road forks.

From the parking area, it is possible to bike all the way to Middle Kootenay Pass. Just make sure

The northeast face of Three Lakes Ridge as seen from the shores of the third lake. **S**: summit; **RR**: steep recommended route; **ER**: easier route.

your brakes are in good working order – you'll need them! Also, the amount of snow on the trail may dictate whether a bike is a good idea or not.

Take the right branch of the fork in the road and follow it over a bridge within 100 m and then another bridge a little later. The next several kilometres are easy to follow. Arriving at another major fork (GR891616), with a sign warning of avalanche danger for snowmobilers, again take the right branch (heading uphill) and keep following the wide path towards Middle Kootenay Pass. This fork is a good place to leave your bike if you are not up for a very strenuous ride up to the pass and then a "riding your brakes" trip back down. You'll eventually go through an open gate (or walk around it if it's locked) and cross two small streams. A high point is soon reached, with the slopes of Rainy Ridge to the left and "Middle Kootenay Mountain"

to the right. The actual pass sits about 200 m from the point where the trail descends a small slope.

From Middle Kootenay Pass, descend the west side of the pass for a very short distance, looking left for another trail that branches off. Follow this new path, again for a short distance, and look for a faint track branching off to the left, marked with flagging. This is Middlepass Lakes Trail, which sideslopes the very pleasant west side of Rainy Ridge and then ascends to the Middlepass Lakes. The trail can be a little faint near the beginning, but route-finding is never an issue and flagging along the way helps. After passing through a couple of short stints of trees, the track draws close to Middlepass Creek and then ascends to the first lake.

The first lake sits directly below the northeast face of Three Lakes Ridge. The ascent can start

Typical slabby terrain on the east face. It's quite steep!

from here after crossing the lake's outlet. However, staying on the trail to visit all three Middlepass Lakes is not only very scenic but also not terribly time-consuming. If neither time nor time energy is a constraint, you won't be sorry you made the effort to see the lakes close up. Late September and early October have the special reward of seeing the larches surrounding the lakes at their peak of yellow colour.

To see the lakes, follow the trail quickly to the second lake, cross a small outlet stream and continue on to the third lake and several excellent campsites. The view towards the Three Lakes ascent route from the shore of the third lake is very good. Make special note of the slabs high up. Go to the far west end of the lake and then up and over boulder slopes towards Three Lakes. Descend to the first lake or sideslope to the scree/rubble ascent slopes above the lake.

For those who want to skip the lakes detour, once at the first lake, cross the outlet and start up the slopes above the lake.

For both routes you'll want to decide what kind of ascent you are looking for. The most interesting, but steeper, route goes up the slabs on the south (left) side of the northeast face. The farther north (right) you go, the easier the terrain. The trade-off is less slabs and more rubble.

If you take the steep route, be sure the grip on your footwear is good. Also be watching for deep fissures in the rock that may be covered in debris, much like a snow bridge over a crevasse. The slabs are never frightfully steep, but a slip would definitely be extremely unpleasant and could cause very serious injury. Once you start ascending the slabs, traversing north to easier terrain will be difficult and dangerous; better to just keep going up. The ridge is not a huge distance away.

Regardless of the route you took, once you reach the ridge turn south (left) and follow it towards the intimidating summit block. Staying on the ridge to the summit is a tricky and very exposed affair and not worth the risk. Instead, traverse to the right onto the west side of the ridge and sideslope steep terrain into an obvious gully. Go straight up the

gully and then enjoy some moderate scrambling to the summit a short distance away.

The summit view is excellent. A few notable peaks include Rainy Ridge, "Middle Kootenay Mountain" and Mount Haig. Of more interest are the two very colourful peaks to the south: the unofficially named "Jake Smith Peak" and the official Scarpe Mountain. As the highest and third-highest peaks in the area respectively, both are worth a visit, and the best way to get there is from exactly where you are standing! See the trip descriptions for each, at pages 166 and 168.

The easiest route off Three Lakes Ridge is the way you came. Once back at the slabs, it is slightly easier to traverse north along the ridge and then descend more broken terrain back to the lakes.

Another possibility is to head east to the summit of Rainy Ridge. This route may actually prove to be easier than the previously described one in the opposite direction, because route-finding *up* the tricky terrain on Rainy is easier than route-finding *down* it. Even so, the traverse is challenging and entails a fair elevation loss into the valley south of the ridge.

For this route, head east down the east ridge of Three Lakes. Very quickly you will encounter a short but very exposed upclimb. Either go straight up the rock step (very carefully!) or bypass it on the right, down much easier terrain. If you bypass, return to the ridge when feasible. For both routes, work your down to the Three Lakes/Rainy col, noting the steep rock bands on the other side of the col.

At the col, continue to lose elevation by dropping to the right (south). This is the easiest way to circumvent the steep terrain of the ridge. Don't be too tempted to try to regain the ridge, as this will lead to steep, exposed terrain. Instead look for a less steep ascent route through the trees and back up to the ridge. Upon regaining the ridge, continue up much easier ground to the summit of Rainy. Absorb the fine view back towards Three Lakes Ridge, with the Middlepass Lakes below, and then refer to the Rainy Ridge description, #40, for descent routes.

48. "JAKE SMITH PEAK" 2630 m

(MAP 10, PAGE 455)

Rating easy, with a few moderate steps, via the north ridge from Three Lakes Ridge (which is moderate/difficult)

Traverse time 2 hours one-way from the summit of Three Lakes Ridge; 9–12 hours total

Elevation gain add 500 m to Three Lakes Ridge trip; approximately 1500 m total

Maps 82 G/8 Beaver Mines, G/1 Sage Creek

"Jake Smith Peak" is the unofficial name of the highest summit in the area. The ascent from the north is little more than a scree slog, but the colours on the mountain and the surrounding scenery are wonderful and quite unique. The best route starts with an ascent of Three Lakes Ridge. Wait for clear skies and expect a very long day, especially if continuing on to Scarpe Mountain to the west. This is one of my favourite trips in the Rockies.

From the summit of Three Lakes Ridge, follow the obvious ridge south. For the most part it is possible to stay right on the ridge, but one drop-off early on will require a detour to the east (left) side to circumvent. Return to the ridge and continue on. The next minor challenge takes you to the west side. After that it should be smooth sailing for the remainder of the trip.

Upon reaching the first low point, either stay on the ridge to go up and over the next high point, or sideslope on the west side of the peak to avoid unnecessary elevation gain. If "Jake Smith" is your only objective, I would stay on the ridge and then sideslope on the return trip. The added objective of Scarpe probably means you'll want to sideslope both ways in order to save a little time and energy. Regardless which way you take, though, the route-finding is obvious and you'll end up at another low col, with "Jake Smith" ahead and the interesting and steep face of "RA Peak" to the southwest.

"RA Peak" stands for Red Argillite Peak and for that reason alone it is worth a quick visit. This minor detour adds about 100 vertical metres of elevation gain, but what's 100 more when you are already looking at close to 2000! Depending on the time of day, you may want to save this detour for the return trip when the sun is farther west. The colours and scenery on RA and the peaks seen from its summit are amazing and best viewed with the sun in that location.

From the summit of RA follow the ridge southeastward down the RA/"Jake Smith" col and then slog up "Jake's" easy northwest slopes to your third summit of the day. Hopefully, the colourful north face of "Jake" and Scarpe will be enough to keep you entertained. As one might expect from the highest peak in the area, the summit view is excellent, including a multitude of peaks in the regions of the Castle, Waterton, Glacier National Park and the Flathead. Slightly lower Scarpe Mountain lies to the southwest. See the next description, #49, for the interesting and challenging route to Scarpe.

If Scarpe isn't on the menu, **return** the same way you came, running quickly up RA Peak if you missed it on the ascent. Return to the summit of Three Lakes Ridge and then follow your up route by descending the northeast face slabs. Upon reaching the slabs, for an easier descent, go along the ridge farther north and then turn east down the mountain.

For those wanting to minimize elevation gains on the return trip, it is possible to sideslope the entire west face of Three Lakes Ridge (after passing by RA Peak), descend into the valley due south of Middle Kootenay Pass and then route-find your way northwestward back to the south side of Middle Kootenay Pass Trail. Although this route is fairly obvious, crossing Middlepass Creek can be a challenge due to bushwhacking and canyon-like features. If you choose this route, be confident in your off-trail navigation skills.

Above: RA Peak, Scarpe Mountain and "Jake Smith Peak" are clearly visible from the summit of Three Lakes Ridge.
Below: A run up RA Peak yields this terrific view, best seen when the sun is in the west. "Jake Smith" is at the left; the little hump at the right is the summit block of Scarpe.

49. SCARPE MOUNTAIN 2617 m

(MAP 10, PAGE 455)
Rating difficult via the northeast ridge/face; a climber's scramble
Traverse time 1.5–2.5 hours one way from the summit of "Jake Smith Peak"; 11–14 hours total
Elevation gain add 700 m to Three Lakes Ridge and "Jake Smith Peak"; approximately 2400 m in total
Maps 82 G/8 Beaver Mines, G/1 Sage Creek

Continuing to Scarpe Mountain from "Jake Smith" is for hardcore peak-baggers and scramblers. While the traverse route from "Jake Smith" may appear to be a simple ridgewalk, it is far from it. There are many unseen rock bands that must be circumvented on the south side of the ridge. Even the easiest route requires descending a steep, loose gully and then a gut-wrenching, sidesloping slog back up to the summit ridge. Expect challenging route-finding, tricky downclimbing, exposure and 600–800 additional metres of elevation gain. In conjunction with Three Lakes Ridge, RA Peak and "Jake Smith Peak," your total gain will be approximately 2400 metres. Having said all that, you will undoubtedly feel an enormous sense of accomplishment upon completing the task, and the scenery is absolutely delicious throughout! Take plenty of food and TONS *of water.*

From the summit of "Jake Smith," start down the southwest ridge of the peak towards Scarpe. There are a couple of mildly exposed spots on the ridge, but nothing too alarming. Look for an obvious gully on your left. If you arrive at a steep drop-off that is beyond scrambling, you have gone past the gully – back up and find it. This gully is steep, with lots of loose rubble; it is not for everyone. If descending it does not appeal to you, it may be best to call it a day and return to "Jake Smith." For those continuing down the gully, go slowly and either keep very close together or go down one at a time (not really an option for large parties, as the gully is long and will eat up a huge amount of time). There are several spots of short but tricky downclimbing.

While it is not necessary to descend all the way to the valley, the elevation loss is significant. Once down the scary stuff, start working your way farther down but more to the west. There are many cliff bands here and your route-finding skills will be put to the test. Avoid the temptation to return to the ridge, where more technical terrain awaits. When all the cliff bands have been circumvented,

you should find yourself looking west at a huge ramp of rubble and scree with cliff bands below (see photo). If this section is snow-covered, turn around immediately or get out your crampons, an ice axe and a brave face – this ascending traverse will be unnerving in a few spots. The best strategy for this section is to stay up high and hug the rock face above. In dry conditions the route is relatively easy, but it may feel mildly exposed for short periods. When feasible, gain the ridge and follow it on easier terrain to the summit. The summit view will again be impressive. Perhaps the most rewarding scene is looking back to the beautiful hues of "Jake Smith Peak."

To get back to your car, retrace your steps. Fortunately the return trip to "Jake Smith" is considerably easier and quicker than the trek there – this is because descending the scree and upclimbing the gully is far less difficult than doing the reverse. Once back at the "Jake Smith"/RA col, refer to the "Jake Smith" description, #48, for a possible sidesloping route that avoids reascending Three Lakes Ridge.

Above: The approximate route to Scarpe. There are many unseen rock bands and obstacles along the way.
Below: Fascinating rock strata on the west face of "Jake Smith Peak."

50. "MIDDLE KOOTENAY MOUNTAIN" 2512 m

(MAP 10, PAGE 455)
Rating easy via the east ridge to false summit; moderate to true summit
Round-trip time 7–10 hours
Elevation gain 1100 m to first summit; 1200 m to true summit
Maps 82 G/8 Beaver Mines

This is a great shoulder-season trip, when new snow will grant some very pleasant scenery. There are no technical difficulties and little chance of avalanche. Still, an ice axe and crampons may be necessary for the first slope west of Middle Kootenay Pass. A bike is useful for the approach.

Drive to Castle Mountain Ski Resort. Instead of turning right and entering the resort, stay left on the gravel road. In several hundred metres this road trends left and immediately crosses a bridge. Drive about 2.6 km past the bridge to where the road forks. A large clearing on the right provides a place to park and is also a good bivy site if you choose to stay awhile (GR890638). The road is decent, even for low-clearance vehicles, but may have large, deep puddles. If such is the case, you may want to back up, park at the bridge and walk or bike the 2.6 km to where the road forks.

From the parking area, it is possible to bike all the way to Middle Kootenay Pass. Just make sure your brakes are in good working order – you'll need them! Also, the amount of snow on the trail may dictate whether a bike is a good idea or not.

Take the right branch of the fork in the road and follow it over a bridge within 100 m and then another bridge a little later. The next several kilometres are easy to follow. Arriving at another major fork (GR891616), with a sign warning of avalanche danger for snowmobilers, again take the right branch (heading uphill) and keep following the wide path toward Middle Kootenay Pass. This fork is a good place to leave your bike if you are not up for a very strenuous ride up to the pass and then a "riding your brakes" trip down. You'll eventually go through an open gate (or walk around it if it's locked) and cross two small streams. As the scenery begins to open up, note the first section of your objective, which first appears directly ahead of you and then to the right. The long ridge to the left is part of Rainy Ridge.

Although it is not necessary to continue all the way to Middle Kootenay Pass, the route from the pass is the least steep option and therefore less prone to avalanche if the slopes are snow-covered. The pass sits about 200 m from the point where the trail descends a small slope. From the pass, leave the trail and head to your right (northwest), up open slopes. Use discretion if avalanches are a possibility. The southwest slopes are subject to strong winds and may be the most snow-free option. The first summit is easily reached, though the slope is a little foreshortened.

From summit one, most of the remainder of the trip can be seen. Simply follow the ridge heading west, over another high point and then on to the main section of the mountain. A couple of minor rock bands high on the mountain are easily scrambled up and over. The false summit, at GR863600, sports a terrific view and may be enough for many.

The true summit lies about 500 m to the west and is approximately 20 vertical metres higher. The view includes a good look at Tombstone Mountain and is definitely worthwhile if you have the time and inclination. Getting there requires an elevation loss. Follow the ridge down a short distance to a drop-off. Go left and find a weakness down through this rock band. Repeat this procedure several times in order to get down to the col between the false and the true summits. This loss may be tricky if snow-covered, requiring crampons and an ice axe. In that case, staying close to the ridge is the safest option but is more difficult and exposed. Beware of the cornice to your right. Trending left onto snow-covered slopes is not recommended if there is any risk of an avalanche.

From the col follow the ridge easily to the summit. A rock band just before the top is encountered, but is easily scrambled up just around the left side. The first summit is only a couple of minutes from the rock band. Take in an excellent view and then traverse about 200 m southward to the other summit (only about 5 minutes away). These two summits are of comparable height and both warrant a visit.

Return the same way. Back at the col, sidesloping on the south side of the mountain to avoid regaining all the high points again can save a fair amount of time and energy.

Above: The easy east ridge of "Middle Kootenay Mountain" as seen from the west ridge of Rainy Ridge.
Below: From the first high point, most of the route is clearly visible. The mountain and surrounding area look very different on this highly enjoyable (and strenuous!) January ascent.

51. "MOUNT MILES" 2470 m
and "KROWICKI PEAK" 2440 m

(MAP 10, PAGE 455)

Rating moderate via the southeast slope ("Miles"); moderate with one difficult and exposed step via the west ridge ("Krowicki")
Round-trip time 8–10 hours for "Miles"; 10–13 hours for both
Elevation gain 1900 m for both peaks; 1600 m for "Mount Miles" only
Maps 82 G/8 Beaver Mines, G/1 Sage Creek

"Mount Miles" and "Krowicki Peak" were both named in honour of a dear friend and one of the greatest people I have ever known, Miles Krowicki. Miles passed away in November 2011. These two distinctive but infrequently ascended peaks lie to the southwest of Middle Kootenay Pass, necessitating a 300 metre elevation loss after gaining 500 metres to the pass. Nevertheless, travel to "Miles" is generally easy. The first part of the ascent, up a water-worn drainage, is heaps of fun and the summit view is excellent. Continuing on to "Krowicki Peak" is an optional but very interesting extension of the trip and a chance to nab a second peak. The main ascent gully often retains snow far into the summer, so a late July or early August ascent may be advisable. However, the peaks can be ascended from July on.

Drive to Castle Mountain Ski Resort. Instead of turning right and entering the resort, stay left on the gravel road. In several hundred metres the road trends left and immediately crosses a bridge. Drive about 2.6 km past the bridge to where the road forks. A large clearing on the right provides a place to park and is also a good bivy site if you choose to stay awhile (GR890638). The road is decent, even for low-clearance vehicles, but may have large, deep puddles. If such is the case, you may want to back up, park at the bridge and walk or bike the 2.6 km to where the road forks.

From the parking area it is possible to bike all the way to Middle Kootenay Pass. Just make sure your brakes are in good working order – you'll need them! Also, the amount of snow on the trail may dictate whether a bike is a good idea or not.

Take the right branch of the fork in the road and follow it over a bridge within 100 m and then another bridge a little later. The next several kilometres are easy to follow. Arriving at another major fork (GR891616), with a sign warning of avalanche danger for snowmobilers, again take the right branch (heading uphill) and keep following the wide path towards Middle Kootenay Pass. This fork is a good place to leave your bike if you are not up for a very strenuous ride up to the pass and have a "riding your brakes" trip back down. You'll eventually go through an open gate (or walk around it if it's locked) and cross two small streams. A high point is soon reached, with

the slopes of Rainy Ridge to the left and "Middle Kootenay Mountain" to the right. The actual pass sits about 200 m from the point where the trail descends a small slope. Both peaks are clearly visible from there.

From Middle Kootenay Pass descend the good trail down the valley. Travel is easy, but you may be acutely aware of the huge amount of hard-earned elevation you are now losing. Approximately 3 km down the trail you will arrive at a gravel clearing where both peaks are just visible. Ignore the clearing and continue on the trail as it dips down to the left and then continues for another 5–10 minutes to the obvious rocky drainage around GR867569 (see photo at left). This drainage offers access to both "Miles" and "Krowicki." Assuming the drainage is snow- and water-free, start ascending it. If snow remains in the drainage, stay away from it. Very dangerous conditions can exist when the snow beneath the surface melts but the surface snow remains intact.

Often the drainage will have running water in the lower sections but will be dry a little higher up. Ascend the drainage directly or on the right side. As soon as feasible (i.e., with little or no water in the drainage), get into the drainage and ascend the beautifully colourful, water-worn rock. Wet sections of rock will be extremely slippery – stay away from them. The hands-on scrambling is a real treat and represents the most enjoyable part of the actual ascent. Be sure to turn around now and then

Above: Nicole Lisafeld and Tannis Graham descend the good trail from the pass. **MM**: "Mount Miles";
KP: "Krowicki Peak."
Below: The approximate ascent route from the rocky drainage. **S**: summit.

Nicole and Tannis ascend the fascinating drainage. Fun scrambling and seriously cool rock!

to see what you have ascended – the rock looks very different and far more impressive when looking down it.

A couple of steeper sections may prompt you to leave the drainage and circumvent them on the right side, but generally you can stay in the drainage through most of the lower section. Enjoy the striking rock features and hands-on scrambling for as long as feasible.

About a quarter of the way up, the drainage forks. The left fork leads eventually to the "Miles"/"Krowicki" col. The right goes to "Mount Miles." Route-finding your way to the summit of "Miles" from this point is not terribly difficult, the ascent consisting of a combination of steep, grassy hills and somewhat annoying scree higher up. However, there are a couple of route suggestions to consider. A rock band lining the southeast face eventually appears and is most easily ascended through weaknesses on the left side. Once above the rock band, it is advisable to work your way up and to the right. The left side of the face offers more challenging terrain, but the rock is terribly loose

and unstable. It's probably best to endure the slog up the right side.

The actual summit, with a small cairn and register (probably with only a few entries), is unremarkable but the summit view is terrific. Those who have completed the "Boot Hill"/Tombstone trip will notice the remarkably similar features of the terrain and view. "Boot Hill" and "Mount Miles" are counterparts, as are Tombstone and "Krowicki." Expect the view from "Miles" to be slightly superior to "Krowicki" simply because it has a view of the striking "Krowicki," in the same way that "Boot Hill" has a great view of the impressive Tombstone. **Return** the same way or continue on to "Krowicki Peak."

51A. "KROWICKI PEAK" FROM "MOUNT MILES"

Descend easily to the "Miles"/"Krowicki" col, losing approximately 200 metres of elevation in the process. Obviously, going straight up the northeast face is out of the question. Instead, choose the right side or the left. The left is easier and more tedious. The

right is far more interesting and has one move of difficult, exposed scrambling. Both start off with a healthy dose of sidesloping. For the most complete experience, ascend the right and descend the left. Expect to take an hour to get from "Miles" to "Krowicki."

The left side

From the col, start ascending the northeast ridge towards the face. The east face can be sidesloped pretty much anywhere, but you'll definitely want snow-free conditions. Even with an ice axe and crampons, traversing this slope if it is snow-covered is highly inadvisable. Sideslope the east face of the peak where you feel comfortable. You will have to go all the way around the east face and then continue sidesloping around the southeast side before finding terrain that can be easily ascended. The farther you go, the easier the ascent. Don't go up too early, as you may find yourself on uncomfortably steep terrain.

Once you can, start going up, gain some elevation and then veer far over to the right. The best place to ascend this peak is as far to the east as possible. Follow your nose up to the summit. Descend the same way you came.

Above: "Krowicki Peak" from the summit of "Mount Miles." The left and right routes around the peak are fairly obvious.
Below: The namesake of the mountain, Miles Krowicki, at the summit of Mount Kent.

The right side

This is definitely a superior route to the left side, but it's only what you would call aesthetic for a short distance. From the col, hike up to the face and start sidesloping around the right side. This traverse takes you all the way around to the southwest side of the peak. Along the way DO NOT be tempted to shortcut up to the ridge by scrambling up the northwest face. There are several easy-looking routes, but all lead to very steep terrain near the top that is definitely more than scrambling.

Once you're around the southwest side, the route becomes very obvious. Turn northeast and follow the ridge towards the summit. Surprisingly, the mountain soon drops away on the right side and the ridge narrows for a few very short sections. The exposure is not brutal, but it would be exhilarating if the notorious west wind in the southern Rockies were raging. One difficult move of scrambling is encountered shortly before the summit. The exposure here is more intense but there are solid handholds, and an easy alternative descent route means you won't have to downclimb it. Above this step, easier terrain leads quickly to the summit.

There really is no advantage to returning the way you came. Instead, to descend "Krowicki," follow the northeast side of the mountain down. Route-finding is very obvious. Staying close to the ridge offers the best footing, but eventually drop-offs abound and you will be required to veer way over to descender's right (southwest) to find an easy route.

Descent for both routes

Once at the bottom of the summit slopes of "Krowicki," work your way down and to the left to find the original ascent line and Middlepass Creek Trail. The 300 metres of elevation gain back to Middle Kootenay Pass may seem unsavoury at this point in the day, but the grade is gentle and perhaps enjoyment of the colourful tones of Rainy Ridge will alleviate some discomfort!

CROWSNEST

The areas around the Crowsnest, about 50 km west of Pincher Creek, can hardly be regarded as a mecca for scrambling, but they still provide a healthy dose of interesting peaks to ascend. Crowsnest Mountain and Turtle Mountain are must-do ascents, described in Alan Kane's book. Due south and due west of these respective peaks lies the northeast end of the Flathead Range and North York Creek.

Three of the four peaks surrounding North York Creek have scramble routes to their summits: Mount McLaren, Andy Good Peak and Mount Coulthard. The fourth, Mount Parrish, can also be done without a rope, though the descent will test the nerve and technique of even the most experienced scrambler. It is therefore not recommended as a scramble.

The rock in this area is slabby friction limestone. Handholds are minimal, so good foot placements are imperative. It is therefore strongly recommended that approach shoes be used for these slabby sections. This is especially important if you are tackling the southeast face of McLaren or the traverse from Andy Good to Coulthard. Bring good hiking boots as well, since you will probably want them for the scree and rubble. Also, crampons don't take very well to approach shoes, if you end up ascending to the Andy Good/Parrish col when snow-covered.

Separate ascent routes are described for each mountain. However, fit and competent parties will probably want to maximize the use of their time by summiting two or even all three of these peaks in a single trip. Some suggested combinations are:

- Andy Good and Coulthard – difficult; 8.5–11 hours
- McLaren, Andy Good and Coulthard – difficult; 10–13 hours
- McLaren and Coulthard via their suggested descent routes – easy; 10–12 hours
- McLaren and Andy Good – easy via McLaren's southwest ridge, difficult via McLaren's east face; 9–11 hours

Also, three mountains at the far south end of the High Rock Range are included in this edition – "Deadman Peak," "Racehorse Peak" and "Mount Racehorse." Racehorse Peak and Mount Racehorse can be combined in a single trip. Rounding out the new additions are Hillcrest Mountain and Chinook Peak.

CROWSNEST			
Hillcrest Mountain	2185 m	easy	p. 178
Andy Good Peak	2662 m	moderate/difficult	p. 180
Mount Coulthard	2624 m	easy/difficult	p. 185
Mount McLaren	2301 m	easy/difficult	p. 187
Chinook Peak	2606 m	difficult	p. 189
"Deadman Peak"	2562 m	easy/moderate	p. 191
"Racehorse Peak"	2762 m	easy/moderate	p. 195
"Mount Racehorse"	2510 m	easy/moderate	p. 197

The summit of lowly Mount McLaren provides an expansive view of the North York Creek area. From left to right: Coulthard, Andy Good, Parrish and Chinook.

52. HILLCREST MOUNTAIN 2185 m

(MAP 11, PAGE 454)
Rating easy via the south ridge
Round-trip time 3–5 hours
Elevation gain 680 m
Map 82 G/09 Blairmore

In terms of pure geological and historical interest, Hillcrest Mountain will never be able to compete with its fascinating northerly neighbour Turtle Mountain – a peak whose east face collapsed in 1903, spilling 82 million tonnes of rock onto the town of Frank and killing 70–90 people. Nevertheless, an ascent of Hillcrest is beautiful in other ways and the summit view is excellent. The trip is short and consists of mostly steep off-trail hiking. Try from June on.

Driving west on Highway 3, turn left onto East Hillcrest Drive (1.2 km west of the Leitch Collieries). Drive 2.1 km on East Hillcrest and take a very sharp left onto Adanac Road. Follow Adanac for 5.4 km (4.2 km from the "NO WINTER MAINTENANCE BEYOND THIS POINT" sign) to an open area on the right side of the road and park. Along the way there are decent views of the objective.

A good system of logging roads/ATV trails provide easy access to the south ridge. From the parking area hike the main trail for a few minutes, quickly intersecting another trail. Turn left (west)

A winter view of Hillcrest Mountain from near the parking area. The ascent route goes up the left skyline.
Photo: Vern Dewit

Looking up the ascent slope.

onto that trail and hike west for about 10 minutes to the bottom of the south ridge, at approximately GR878889 (see photo).

Hike up the south ridge. The bush is not terrible and disappears several hundred vertical metres up. Getting around or over deadfall will be the crux of this section, but even that is a relatively simple task. It is particularly interesting to see the old remnants and new growth on this slope after the 2003 fire that decimated the area.

A rock band is eventually reached and can be scrambled up or circumvented on either side.

Above the rock band, follow the south ridge for about 1.5 km to the summit (GR872906). The view of the Flathead Range, featuring Andy Good Peak, Mount Coulthard, Mount Ptolemy and Mount Darrah is excellent. The summit also grants a unique view of Turtle Mountain and the devastation left by the 1903 disaster. Crowsnest Mountain and Mount Tecumseh are two of the more familiar peaks to the northwest.

Return the same way. Alternative and/or more direct descent routes may look enticing, but they end up being more hassle than they're worth.

53. ANDY GOOD PEAK 2662 m

(MAP 12, PAGE 454)
Rating moderate; difficult and exposed slab scrambling via the north ridge
Round-trip time 7–10 hours
Elevation gain 1150 m
Maps 82 G/10 Crowsnest

Andy Good Peak is the highest of the peaks in this section and has a wonderful summit panorama. The ascent itself consists of tons of steep hiking, tons of scree and rubble and far too little hands-on scrambling, though the adventurous can seek out more challenging terrain. The crux may well be the approach to the Andy Good/Parrish col. Bring an ice axe and crampons for earlier-season attempts and be prepared to retreat if the avalanche danger is high. Approach shoes are recommended to tackle the steep, slabby terrain. Try from July on or wait until August for the snow to melt.

Drive west on Highway 3 past Blairmore and towards Coleman. Turn left at the "COLEMAN EAST ACCESS" sign and take the first immediate left after that. Cross the railway tracks, drive about 2 km and take a left at 83 St. Cross the river and turn right on 13 Ave. ("Staging Area"). The beginning of the approach road starts at the corner of 81 St. and 13 Ave. and is unmarked. Zero-set your odometer

here. Drive the approach road for 5.4 km (stay to the right at the 1.8 km mark). Park at the side of the road where the "45" ATV sign is.

Hike the "45" trail for about 20–25 minutes to where it forks (much quicker if you are biking). Take the right fork to the "Plane Crash." Continue hiking into the valley, losing some elevation down a gentle but long hill. Shortly after, the trail joins up

Approaching the upper reaches of the North York Creek Valley. **AG**: Andy Good Peak; **MP**: Mount Parrish; **MM**: Mount McLaren.

Above: The route to the upper plateau.
Below: The route to the Andy Good/Parrish col. **C**: col; **MP**: Mount Parrish.

Above: The view toward Mount Coulthard and its three summits. The route follows the connecting ridge and up the right skyline. Expect difficult, exposed scrambling.
Below: Approaching the challenging summit block.

The crux section of the ascent. The short, steep step is not visible.

with the "other" approach trail that parallels North York Creek, but on its north side. Go straight. Start to gain elevation again and hike past the interesting east face of Mount McLaren. Look for the point below the Andy Good/Parrish col (GR753940, approximately 1.5 hours on foot from the parking area). The trail turns left here, but you won't.

At GR753940 turn right and hike up grassy slopes to a small plateau below Andy Good and Mount Parrish. From the plateau, gain the col between Andy Good and Parrish up steep scree and/or snow slopes. If avalanches are a concern, don't go up this slope. If not, but the slopes are still snow-covered, crampons and an ice axe will be mandatory. Note that snow may persist well into July here.

From the col, the north ridge of Andy Good looks particularly daunting. Fortunately, most of the difficulties can be circumvented, though on annoying rubble and scree. Go around the right side of the first obstacle and sideslope the rubble.

In short order it becomes possible to scramble up to the ridge to enjoy some moderately difficult hands-on scrambling. However, a prominent rock band will soon force you down to the scree again. If you decide against gaining the ridge, continue sidesloping, staying below the slabs to your left.

Once around the aforementioned rock band, either scramble up slabs to the ridge or continue on scree around the slabs and then up to the ridge. The slabs are not terribly steep but have few good handholds. Solid foot placements and good tread on your boots or shoes are imperative on this type of terrain. When you've gained the ridge, follow it to the summit, either tackling short rock bands head-on or circumventing them on the right side.

Just before the summit there's a nasty surprise: suddenly the ridge becomes knife-edged. It is possible to bum-shuffle your way across this section, but the rock is horribly loose and may crumble underneath you. Instead, drop down to scree slopes on the left side of the ridge. Traverse a short distance and then scramble back up to the ridge as soon as possible. The scrambling here is not terribly difficult, but the exposure gives it a more serious feel. Remember that unless you are going on to ascend Coulthard, you will have to come back this way and it will invariably be more difficult.

After the crux, the summit is easily reached. Take in a splendid panorama that features terrific views of Mount Ptolemy to the southwest, Mount Coulthard to the southeast and Mount McGladrey farther south. If not continuing on to Coulthard, **return** the same way.

Andy Good Peak and Mount Coulthard

From the summit of Andy Good, hike/scramble down the southeast ridge. The left side of the ridge offers easier terrain. The connecting ridge will not be so easy. Scramble along the ridge, staying on top of it as much as possible. Occasional detours on the right side will be necessary, but don't stray too far from the ridge. One or two short but exposed downclimbs are necessary. Yet again, grippy approach shoes will be invaluable here. The ridge is longer than you might think, but it does eventually widen as you approach the west ridge of Coulthard.

Hike up the ridge to the daunting-looking summit block. If the connecting ridge was a scary experience for you, the summit block will be doubly so. At this point there is still the option to circumvent the entire west summit around the left side on scree slopes. Once you start scrambling up the summit block, you become committed to finishing it. Downclimbing some of this terrain would be very unnerving.

The best strategy for ascending the summit block is to work your way leftward into the middle, where a huge slab from the left crashes into slabs on the right at a right angle. This right angle makes enjoyable work on the ascent to the ridge. A bulge near the top is the crux of this section. Once on the ridge, look to the left for the weakness that cuts through the centre of the block (see photo).

Scramble diagonally left and up an obvious crack, and follow the natural path of the terrain as it curves to the right. The crux is reached very quickly – a short but steep (almost overhanging) step with good but small holds. Bulky hiking boots would make the ascent very unnerving if not downright dangerous on this section. Climb it and scramble easily to the west summit.

The centre summit is a short hike away. Getting to the true summit requires losing elevation on the north side of the centre summit and then circling around to the north side of the east ridge. A goat trail makes the sidesloping easy. The true summit is then easily reached. See Mount Coulthard on page 185 for the suggested descent route.

54. MOUNT COULTHARD 2624 m

(MAP 12, PAGE 454)

Rating easy via northwest slopes; difficult via the west ridge from Andy Good Peak (a climber's scramble)

Round-trip time 6–8 hours for northwest slopes

Elevation gain 1100 m

Maps 82 G/10 Crowsnest

If you are attempting Coulthard as a solo trip, the easy northwest slopes are your best bet. The difficult west ridge has only a short section of hands-on scrambling which is best wearing approach shoes.

Northwest slopes (easy)

See the driving directions for Andy Good Peak. Hike the "45" trail for about 20–25 minutes to where it forks (much quicker if you are biking). Take the right fork to the "Plane Crash." Continue hiking into the valley, losing some elevation down a gentle but long hill. Shortly after, the trail joins up with the "other" approach trail that parallels North York Creek but on its north side. Go straight. Start to gain elevation again and hike past the interesting east face of Mount McLaren and then on to the crash site (approximately 2 hours). After checking out the wreckage, continue hiking farther south up the valley on a good trail on the right side of the creek. Pass by the steep northern outlier of Coulthard on your left side and start looking left to the open slopes that go between this northern outlier and the western false summits of Coulthard.

Looking up the ascent slope. The centre summit is at the upper right.

Head up where you see fit. The farther up the valley you go, the gentler the slopes. The scree may be frustrating on the way up, but it will serve you well when coming back down.

Gain the ridge between the northern outlier and the centre summit. It is not necessary to gain either the west or the middle summit, but both are reached with little effort and do have good views towards Mount Ptolemy. Otherwise, find a decent goat trail on the north side of the east ridge that leads easily to the summit, at the far east end of the mountain. The summit view is similar to that of Andy Good Peak, though the full massif of shapely Mount Ptolemy is partially blocked. Mount McGladrey to the south and its connecting ridge look quite intriguing from this vantage point.

Return the same way. The entire descent can be completed in less than 2.5 hours at a decent pace.

West ridge (difficult)

Here is a quick description of how to get to the base of the west ridge of Coulthard's west summit (not the true summit) if you are not combining the ascent with one of Andy Good Peak. Follow the directions for the northwest slopes of Coulthard, but instead of taking a sharp left up the northwest slopes, simply trend left to the left side of the connecting ridge between Andy Good Peak and Coulthard. Refer to Andy Good Peak and Mount Coulthard on pages 180 and 185 respectively for the remainder of the description.

55. MOUNT McLAREN 2301 m

(MAP 12, PAGE 454)
Rating easy via the southwest ridge; difficult via the east face (a climber's scramble)
Round-trip time 5–7 hours
Elevation gain 800 m
Maps 82 G/10 Crowsnest

While the southwest ridge of McLaren offers an easy route to the summit, the east face is a complex scramble for experienced scramblers only. Good route-finding skills are necessary, as are good down-climbing skills on exposed terrain if you get into a bad situation. The reward is some amazing rock scenery and the thrill of finding your own way. Approach shoes are strongly recommended for this route. They will suffice for both the ascent and descent. Try from July on.

Follow the driving directions for Andy Good Peak, #53, page 180.

East face (difficult)

Hike the "45" trail for about 20–25 minutes to where it forks (much quicker if you are biking). Take the right fork to the "Plane Crash." Continue hiking into the valley, losing some elevation down a gentle but long hill. Shortly after, the trail joins up with the "other" approach trail that parallels North York Creek but on its north side. Go straight. Start to gain elevation again and hike below the interesting east face of Mount McLaren. Here, start looking for the second opening in the trees. It lies at GR766948 and has an orange ATV sign on a tree nearby (approximately 1.25–1.5 hours on foot from your vehicle). The east face looks quite intimidating from this point, but it will take on a less formidable appearance as you hike up to the face.

This face is a complex maze of rock bands, pinnacles and gullies, so a specific route is impossible to outline. A general route is described here, but many variations are possible.

Hike directly up to the face and then traverse

One route up the convoluted east face of McLaren. Many variations are possible.

Looking along the southwest ridge. From left to right: Coulthard, Andy Good and Parrish.

left below it until a weakness is visible. As you route-find your way up, you will probably find yourself getting pushed farther and farther to the left. Keep looking for ways to get back into the centre. Eventually, a route does become available, though it requires some steep, exposed scrambling on friction slabs. You'll be very happy you brought your approach shoes here!

It is then possible to cut under a very distinctive band of rock and then up again towards the ridge. You will probably top out slightly northeast of the summit. An easy walk takes you to the highest point. Again, this is a general route description and it is likely your route will differ in some or all respects. If that prospect scares you, perhaps this is not a good route choice for you. Enjoy a very pleasant view of the surrounding peaks before deciding on your return route.

The easiest way off the mountain is to descend the southwest ridge for several hundred metres until you can turn left onto easy scree slopes. They will take you down to the trail. Otherwise, continue down the southwest ridge to the McLaren/Parrish col and turn left down even easier slopes

and back to the trail. This route is a little longer but more forgiving on the knees.

Southwest ridge (easy)

Hike the "45" trail for about 20–25 minutes to where it forks (much quicker if you are biking). Take the right fork to the "Plane Crash." Continue hiking into the valley, losing some elevation down a gentle but long hill. Shortly after, the trail joins up with the "other" approach trail that parallels North York Creek but on its north side. Go straight. Start to gain elevation again and hike past the interesting east face of Mount McLaren. The goal here is to attain the Parrish/McLaren col. Keep looking to the right until you see the grassy/scree slopes that lead in that direction – approximately GR753940, 1.75–2 hours into the trip.

Take a sharp right and head up these slopes to gain the col or the ridge northeast of the col. From either of those points, the summit is easily attained by hiking up the southwest ridge. **Return** the same way or take the shortcut suggested in the above description for the east face.

56. CHINOOK PEAK 2606 m

(MAP 12, PAGE 454)
Rating difficult via the southwest face
Round-trip time 9–11 hours
Elevation gain 1250 m
Map 82 G/10 Crowsnest

Chinook Peak may be the least aesthetic of all the peaks of the north section of the Flathead Range, but it sports a terrific summit view and will introduce you to the wonderful environs of Ptolemy Creek. Scrambling is minimal; scree, rubble and creek crossings are maximal; and the loose and downsloping rock of the summit ridge render it more teeth-clenching than exhilarating (how's that for upselling!). I nevertheless thoroughly enjoyed this ascent with my good friend Raff. A bike is useful for the approach, but wear runners, as you may be carrying your bike across Ptolemy Creek six to eight times! Try from mid-July on.

Drive west on Highway 3 through the town of Coleman and on to Crowsnest Lake. About 1.8 km west of the end of the lake, turn left onto an unsigned gravel road. Drive 3.3 km to the unsigned but obvious Ptolemy Creek trailhead, on the left (south) side of the road.

Hike or bike 5 km along the trail. There are eight creek crossings along the way. Crossings 2 and 3 are avoidable by staying on a narrow trail on the left side of the creek. The rest of the crossings can be completed on strategically placed logs near the trail – no need to get your feet wet ever! Of course, it is also an option to wear runners for the approach and walk right through the creek. This may save a little time.

For those completing the approach on a bike,

The main ascent line as seen from near where you leave Ptolemy Creek Trail. **LP**: low point to aim for; **S**: summit.

using the logs is next to impossible – best to wear runners and wade across the creek, carrying or pushing your bike. Later in the season the water may be low enough to allow you to ride across most of the crossings.

The scenery finally starts to open up around the 4 km mark, the lengthy and convoluted northwest ridge of Mount Ptolemy appearing to the right side of the valley and the Sentry/Chinook/Parrish massif to the left. At 5 km you'll reach a large clearing where the trail forks. Here, Chinook Peak is visible to the left, but the true summit and route up are not.

Take the left fork, drop immediately down to Ptolemy Creek, cross it one last time and then embark on a long, uphill grind through forest. The terrain opens up suddenly, right beneath the ascent slope of Chinook Peak (see photo and note the location of the summit).

Turn left onto the rubble slope and up you go. The ascent from here is long and a little foreshortened, but the scree and rubble underneath is relatively stable. Higher up, aim for the low point between the two apparent summits. Remember that, contrary to appearance, the true summit is the

one on the right. As you gain elevation the footing becomes less stable, but persevere. It could be much worse!

An excellent view to the north waits at the low point, as well as the tenuous ridge traverse east to the summit. The terrain here is loose, downsloping and exposed. Gain the summit ridge and scramble carefully along it towards the summit, looking for an escape to easier rubble slopes to the right. As soon as it is possible, leave the ridge and traverse below on annoying but far less exposed rubble. Follow your nose to summit. Depending on your route, you'll probably go a very short distance past the summit, up to the ridge on more rubble and finally back to the left to the top.

The summit view is the best feature of this trip, so you may want to stay a while to enjoy it. Clearly visible are many of the Kane scrambles in the Crowsnest section as well as other scrambles in this edition. Although the summit register indicates that parties have traversed from Sentry Mountain and Mount Parrish to the summit of Chinook, neither of these traverses is recommended as a scramble, due to the exposed, loose and downsloping rock throughout. Return the same way.

The approximate route along the nasty summit ridge! The easiest path traverses below the ridge.

57. "DEADMAN PEAK" 2562 m

(MAP 13, PAGE 456)
Rating easy/moderate via the south ridge; options for difficult scrambling
Round-trip time 5.5–9 hours
Elevation gain 1170 m
Map 82 G/10 Crowsnest

"Deadman Peak" (named by Dave McMurray) is the southernmost high point of the Allison Peak/ Mount Ward massif. An excellent trail makes easy work of the approach, the terrain is quite varied and the ridgewalk to the summit is great. Expect the usual amount of Rockies rubble, but the views and scenery are worth that price. Biking the approach cuts about 1.5 hours off the trip time. Try from mid-June on.

Heading west on Highway 3, drive about 3 km past the west end of Coleman and turn right, onto the Allison/Chinook–Atlas Staging Area road. Drive 7.8 km and turn left (just before the yellow 5 km marker) down a short road to a large clearing. The Deadman Pass trail is at the west end of the clearing (see photo). ATVers regularly use this trail – give them a wide berth and the right-of-way.

Follow the wide trail north and slightly downhill for a few hundred metres. Turn left and cross Allison Creek using a bridge. Follow the trail to the "73" marker and take the left fork. At the next marker ("72") go straight. Soon you will pass a small tarn/pond on your left side. About 10 minutes later (much shorter if you are on a bike), start looking to the right for an opening

Deadman Peak as seen from the clearing. **DP**: Deadman Pass; **FS**: false summit; **S**: summit.

Above: The ascent up the avalanche slope, as seen from the trail. Many routes up to the ridge are possible. **S**: slabby terrain for good scrambling.
Below: The enjoyable ridgewalk and ascent to the summit, as seen from the false summit. **WR**: West Ridge; **S**: summit; **DR**: difficult route; **ER**: easier route. Photo: Dave McMurray

and a very obvious avalanche slope (GR701072, see photo).

Slog up steep rubble slopes and gain the wide ridge. From there it is just a matter of following this ridge up to a false summit and then to the true summit. Before the false summit, slabs and good, solid rock make for excellent, moderate scrambling, offering a nice respite from the unstable scree. You can avoid this more challenging terrain by going around it on the left side if desired.

At the false summit the remainder of the route is revealed. Stay on the ridge, enjoying pleasant scenery all around and mostly good footing. When you arrive at a small grassy col, the terrain ahead seemingly takes on a far more serious nature, with a significant, lichen-covered rock band barring the way. You can bypass this entire section by going around the left side on scree and rubble. However, if you are up for a challenge, you can actually scramble up and through the rock band. Some route-finding and a few moves of difficult scrambling up short sections of rock will be required, but the rock is generally solid where you need it to be. Be prepared for some exposure for brief sections.

For both routes, work your way back to the right-hand ridge as soon as possible and finish the ascent by following the ridge to the summit. While Crowsnest Mountain and Seven Sisters Mountain may draw the majority of attention, the array of ridges emanating from the summit of Deadman Peak are pretty cool too. One glance to the north and you will know immediately why traverses to the slightly higher summit in that direction are out of the question. Of more interest is the ridge to the west. It provides a terrific extension of the trip and is described below. If the west ridge is not on the agenda, return the same way, avoiding the more challenging terrain by moving to the right (west) onto scree and rubble slopes. There are other ways off the mountain, but all involve annoying scree or heavy bushwhacking – best to stick, in general, to the ascent route.

WEST RIDGE EXTENSION

This delightful extension adds an hour or two to the day and is very interesting and scenic throughout. Unfortunately, like the other return routes, it ends with tedious terrain that is somewhat less than delightful to descend!

The route is obvious at first. Descend the west ridge to a small col, where a more serious-looking rock

The first part of the West Ridge Extension. **WS**: West Summit; **RB**: rock band you can scramble directly up.

The split in the ridge. **LR**: exposed left ridge; **RR**: easy right ridge; **RD**: rocky drainage.

band rears up in front of you. Scramble directly up the rock band or bypass it by using more-exposed ledges to the left. Continue easily to the West Summit (see photo).

Returning the way you came from this point seems illogical. It is better to continue down the ridge southward to where the ridge splits at a big drop-off (see photo). Between the two ridges lies a rocky, dried-up drainage. Both suggested routes lead to here. The right (westernmost) ridge is an easy stroll and the route is straightforward. Follow it down to where it becomes easy to make your way left, down into the rocky drainage.

If you want a much bigger and exciting challenge, the left ridge is for you. For this route, back up and look for a feasible way down to the flatter terrain below on the east side. The downclimbing is a little exposed but not difficult. Once down, head over to the ridge. It looks innocuous from this vantage point, but that view is deceiving. If you choose to follow the ridge, there are a few exposed sections where you will probably decide to bum-shuffle across. As well, there are many places where you can simply descend into the aforementioned drainage to the right.

For either ridge route, once you make it down to the drainage, follow it down, in the middle or on either side. There are some animal trails that help, but this part of the descent can be slow and tedious. Upon reaching the Deadman Pass trail, turn left and return to the starting point. Don't forget to grab your bike if you cycled the approach.

58. "RACEHORSE PEAK" 2762 m

(MAP 13, PAGE 456)

Rating easy/moderate via the south ridge
Round-trip time 4.5–6 hours
Elevation gain 1030 m
Map 82 G/15 Tornado Mountain

This unofficial peak sits immediately north of Racehorse Pass. It is fairly high for mountains in the area and has a very respectable summit view. The ascent is straightforward and not as ankle-jarring as you would think – "surprisingly pleasant" best describes it. Hats off to the Southern Scramblers for doing the pioneering work on this one. Try from July on.

Heading west on Highway 3, drive about 3 km past the west end of Coleman and turn right, onto Allison/Chinook Atlas Staging Area road. Drive 18.3 km along the road, looking for an unsigned side road veering off to the left. Park to the side. This is the Racehorse Pass trail. It is 500 m after the yellow 15 km marker.

Start hiking or biking (recommended) the dirt road towards Racehorse Pass. The south ridge makes a quick appearance before the more impressive southeast ridge, characterized by its red tinge due to being covered in lichen, interrupts the tableau. Although quite scenic and very interesting, this ridge has one section of steep and very exposed climbing/scrambling on suspect rock and is therefore **not** recommended as a scramble route.

Beyond and to the left of the southeast ridge

the distinctive south ridge then appears again (see photo). It looks steep at the bottom, but this section is easily avoided. Hike past the steep rock of the ridge to the much gentler terrain to its west side (see photo). Turn right (north) and make your way up slopes of rubble and vegetation, trending right (northeast) as you ascend. Eventually gain the south ridge and it's a no-brainer from there! Stay near the edge of the ridge for the best scenery and go straight up it to the summit. There are even a few rock bands, surprisingly solid, along the way that can tackled head-on (hence the "moderate" rating). Otherwise, avoid the moderate scrambling by circumventing the rock bands on the left side.

Notable peaks in the summit view include the very distinctive forms of Seven Sisters Mountain and Crowsnest Mountain (a terrific Kane

The ridges of Racehorse Peak. The ascent route is on the other side of the south ridge. **MT**: Mount Racehorse; **SR**: south ridge; **SER**: southeast ridge.

The easy route to the south ridge.

scramble) to the southeast and Mount Ward, Window Mountain and Allison Peak (three more Kane scrambles) to the south. Farther south and slightly east sits Mount Ptolemy and other peaks around North York and Ptolemy creeks. The long ridge to the west, stretching south, is Erickson Ridge, with Mount Erickson at its south end. The higher peak to the north on the same massif as Racehorse Peak is also unnamed. The only official peaks on this massif, of no fewer than ten significant high points, are Mount Erris and Mount Domke much farther north.

Return the same way. The high point a short distance to the east may look scrumptiously inviting, but the ridge is interrupted by several unseen drop-offs and pinnacles. Negotiating this steep and severely exposed terrain is way beyond scrambling. You can avoid it by downclimbing to easier ledges below, but even this is a tenuous proposition, with exposed downclimbing and route-finding. The view from the east summit is not significantly different to warrant a traverse over there. Therefore, this traverse is recommended only for experienced scramblers with strong downclimbing abilities who just want a little more out of their day. From the east summit, downclimbing the southeast ridge is likewise fraught with difficulties. If you have ventured over to the east summit, the easiest descent is directly down into the bowl between the south ridge and southeast ridge.

59. "MOUNT RACEHORSE" 2510 m

(MAP 13, PAGE 456)
Rating easy via the northeast face; moderate for the loop route
Time 4–6 hours; add 1–2 hours for the loop route
Elevation gain 800 m
Map 82 G/15 Tornado Mountain

On the southwest side of Racehorse Pass lies another unofficial peak that has been given the delightfully comical name "Mount Racehorse" by Sonny Bou, Bob Spirko and Dinah Kruze. While this summit is really just an outlier of slightly higher Mount Ward, climbing it is enjoyable in many ways and it can be ascended in conjunction with Racehorse Peak or as an objective by itself. A loop route that grants an excellent view of Window Mountain Lake below Mount Ward is highly recommended.

Heading west on Highway 3, drive about 3 km past the west end of Coleman and turn right, onto Allison/Chinook Atlas Staging Area road. Drive 18.3 km, looking for an unsigned side road that veers off to the left, and park off to the side. This is the Racehorse Pass trail. It is 500 m after the yellow 15 km marker.

Hike or bike (recommended) about 4.5 km towards Racehorse Pass. As you approach the pass, look for a dirt ATV trail forking to the left. Hike up this trail for about 5 minutes and then turn right, into the trees, making your way through them and up to the foot of the northeast face.

Once you emerge from the trees, the route

The objective as seen from near the beginning of the ATV trail. Multiple routes to the summit are possible.

is obvious. The footing is initially tedious but improves as you gain elevation. A couple of short rock bands can be fun to scramble up if desired. With fortuitous timing you may get to enjoy a stunning array of colourful wildflowers that litter the lower slopes early in the season.

The views from this lowly summit are surprisingly gratifying, highlights of which include the window of Window Mountain in front of Crowsnest Mountain, massive Tornado Mountain to the distant north, shapely Mount Washburn far to the west, and nearby Mount Ward, Allison Peak and Racehorse Peak. Return the same way if you are not doing the loop route.

Loop route

Most of the loop route can be seen from near the summit and although it may look straightforward, there are several surprises along the way. This is a fun and interesting route to help you get the most out of your day.

The goal is to descend to the col south-southeast of the summit and then make your way up to the minor high point southeast of the col. Follow the ridge south until you arrive at a drop-off. Circumvent this impasse by backing up a little and then dropping down to the left side of the ridge. Once you get down and around, you'll see that calling this a "drop-off" was not an exaggeration. The southwest side of Mount Racehorse is a series of huge cliffs stacked atop one another.

This pattern continues all the way down to the col and should require only moderate scrambling and downclimbing. The rock scenery throughout is very impressive.

From the col, it's an easier and equally interesting grind up to the summit at GR692143, where you get a great view of dark-turquoise Window Mountain Lake and Mount Ward. If you have had enough at this point, descend to the col to the northeast and then turn left (northwest), making your way easily to the ATV trail you encountered at the beginning. Follow it out to Racehorse Pass.

To finish the loop (easy and recommended), descend to the col to the northeast and then continue up to the obvious high point at the end of the ridge. Views of the lake should keep you entertained. From this high point there are two options. The easiest and most obvious is to return to Racehorse Pass by going down, in a northwest direction. The bush is generally light if you find the easiest route.

If you have boundless energy and time, the second option (the Ultimate Loop route!) is to make your way down to Window Mountain Lake (maybe you brought fishing gear) and then follow the trail at the northeast end of the lake back to the main road. You then have to hike several kilometres up the road, back to your vehicle. The only draws for this route would be the extra exercise and a close-up look at the lake. Needless to say, the second option is not an option if you biked the approach to Racehorse Pass.

SOUTH KANANASKIS

Kananaskis Country extends from the Trans-Canada Highway in the north to Highway 532 about 100 km to the south, encompassing an area of approximately 4000 square kilometres. While there is no official distinction between the quadrants of Kananaskis, dividing the area into four sections seems appropriate for the purposes of this guidebook. Since Highway 40 is closed between the Kananaskis Road turnoff and Highwood Junction from December 1 to June 15, I've designated the Kananaskis turnoff as the starting point of South Kananaskis. All peaks south of that point are included in this section. Be aware that the annual road closure on Highway 40 renders many of these peaks inaccessible during that time.

Many of the routes in this section, specifically those on the Continental Divide, are a great distance from the highway and require lengthy approaches. Fortunately for scramblers and hikers (but unfortunately for the environment) old logging roads allow you to bike many of the approaches. That is not to say you are going to be covering 10 km in 45 minutes of super-speed pedalling. Many of the trails are rough when dry and a muddy mess when wet. In addition, streams frequently cross them, further slowing you down. Attempting to negotiate these trails too early in the season may mean you will be pushing your bike through muddy puddles more than riding it. Nevertheless, the reward of making it to the Continental Divide is clearly evident in the wild and breathtaking surroundings (see pages 19 and 24 for more information on biking the approaches and river crossings).

This entire area is thoroughly documented and described in Gillean Daffern's *Kananaskis Country Trail Guide*. This outstanding resource gives detailed descriptions of many of the approaches to scrambles in this section and should be on your bookshelf or in your backpack.

GEOLOGY

Kananaskis is all about limestone and lots of it! The quality of the rock ranges from amazing to downright atrocious. Unfortunately, much of the limestone in south Kananaskis fits into the latter category, especially the piles of rubble along the Continental Divide. Of course, there are exceptions to this rule, and certainly there are sections

of enjoyable scrambling on solid rock throughout the area. Just be prepared to hike a long way to get to them.

In contrast to the horizontally laid beds of Waterton and the Castle, the orientation of the rock in Kananaskis is more vertical. This is the result of two crustal plates colliding millions of years ago, pushing the rock upward and at the same time bending and folding it. Many of the peaks in the area display the classic northwest to southeast alignment that resulted from the collision. Mount Rundle, in Banff National Park, offers an obvious example, with its steep northeast face contrasting nicely with the more gently graded slopes on the southwest side of the peak.

CLIMATE AND WEATHER

Since this section contains mountains in the Front Ranges and those farther west along the Continental Divide, the climate varies a fair amount. Typically the Front Range peaks receive less precipitation and therefore enjoy a longer scrambling season. Once the Continental Divide peaks receive snow, usually in November, it is unlikely they will clear off until the following summer. That's okay – you can't get to them anyway because of the road closure!

ACCESS

Most of the peaks in this section lie off the south section of Highway 40. That road can be reached via the Trans-Canada from the north or via Highway 22 at Longview from the south.

In general, from Calgary, the drive via Longview is shorter. Drive south on Highway 2 and take the turnoff to Okotoks (2A). Continue through the town of Okotoks and turn right (west) onto Highway 7. Follow it to Black Diamond and turn left (south) onto Highway 22. At Longview, turn right (west) onto Highway 541, which eventually turns into Highway 40 at the 940/40 junction.

ACCOMMODATION

If you plan on spending the night in south Kananaskis, you are basically relegated to one of several campgrounds along Highway 40 or to motels or camping in Longview or Black Diamond.

SHEEP RIVER AND HIGHWAY 532			
Mount Burns East Peak	2622 m	moderate/difficult	p. 202
Mount Burns	2936 m	moderate/difficult	p. 205
Shunga-la-she	2625 m	moderate/difficult	p. 209
Junction Mountain	2682 m	moderate	p. 211
Pyriform Mountain	2770 m	moderate	p. 215
Mount Livingstone	2422 m	easy	p. 216
Coffin Mountain	2412 m	easy/difficult	p. 219
Thunder Mountain	2376 m	easy	p. 221

All four of the Sheep River peaks are accessed from the Bluerock/Junction Creek parking area, at the far end of Highway 546. From Calgary, follow the directions to Highway 7 given above. Continue westward through Black Diamond, reaching Turner Valley 3 km after that. At the west side of Turner Valley, the road becomes Highway 546. The level of the Sheep River may dictate whether Junction, Pyriform and Shunga-la-she are feasible or not.

Looking east to the Sheep River area from the summit of Gibraltar Mountain. The peak in the centre is Shunga-la-she. The taller one to the right has been given the unofficial and humorous name "Jägermeister Peak" by Rafal Kazmierczak.

60. MOUNT BURNS EAST PEAK at GR555096 2622 m

(MAP 14, PAGE 457)
Rating moderate with a few difficult sections via the east ridge; some exposure
Round-trip time 6–11 hours
Elevation gain 1000 m
Maps 82 J/10 Mount Rae; Gem Trek Highwood & Cataract Creek

GR555096 is just one of the many high points of a long and interesting ridge that culminates with Mount Burns at 2936 m. Though GR555096 is considerably lower, the ascent, while not terribly aesthetic, is interesting and not very long. A good objective for days when time and ambition may be lacking. For those with good downclimbing skills, a visit to GR565088 is a very pleasant diversion along the way. Try from June on.

Drive to Turner Valley via Highway 7 westbound and continue through town to where the road soon turns into Highway 546. Drive to the end of the road and park in the lower section of the Bluerock/Junction Creek lot, close to the Sheep River. Hike the wide Sheep River Trail (starts from the upper section of the parking lot) for about 10 minutes. The objective is on your right and your goal is to quickly gain the east ridge (treed slopes rising from right to left). Turn rightward into the bush and head directly to the ridge through light forest. Once you're on the ridge, simply follow it upwards. Above treeline, minor rock bands can be easily circumvented on the right or tackled head-on. To get

the most out of the scenery, return to the ridge as much as possible. At some points it is actually more enjoyable to traverse along the bottom of the huge cliff bands (left side of the ridge) of the upper ridge. When it becomes obvious to do so, return to the ridge and continue to the first cairn, at GR570084.

After reaching the first cairned high point, continue heading west on the ridge towards a rather daunting-looking summit block (GR565088). Upon reaching the base of the block, traverse around the right side for about 40 m, looking for a weakness to gain the first ledge. Scramble up and left to the wide ledge. There are two routes from here to the west side of the block:

Beginning of east ridge as seen from Sheep River Trail. **H**: high ridge traverse; **L**: low ridge traverse.

Above: First high point at GR570084. **L**: traverse around left; **R**: traverse around right; **C**: crux; **S**: summit at GR565088.
Below: The crux of GR565088, looking somewhat innocuous. It is in fact very steep and very exposed.

The remainder of the route from the west side of GR565088. **E**: easy route; **D**: difficult route; **S**: summit.

Route 1: Head around the right side of the band. Quickly it becomes easy to scramble up the rock band, trending left as you gain elevation. Just before the summit of GR565088, a steeper rock band rears up, guarding the summit. If you want to make a quick visit to the top, there is a weakness up and along a narrow ledge. Getting up the step is easy; getting back down it is very difficult, as there are no decent handholds and the terrain is exposed. A slip while descending the band would certainly result in a very serious fall. This downclimb is only for those who are extremely confident in their abilities. Most will want a good length of rope to set up an anchor and rappel down. If the summit of GR565088 is not on the agenda, keep traversing around the right side of the band, below the upper rock band. Quickly, you'll arrive at the west side of the band. This route is much shorter than its counterpart around the left side.

Route 2: Traverse left along the ledge around the entire band, regaining lost elevation when it is feasible. Stay high, close to the summit block. Regain the ridge at the west side of the block and continue heading west.

Stay on the ridge, circumventing the odd pinnacle on the left side. The ridge soon narrows as the terrain changes from crumbly shales to more solid limestone. A few mildly exposed moves on the right side of the ridge lead to a steeper rock band that can be ascended head-on or circumvented on grassy ledges on the right side. Atop this rock band, the remainder of the route is visible. Continue along the ridge. When steep rock bands bar the way, traverse right onto scree slopes that lead easily to the summit.

When finished admiring the very respectable summit vista, which features a head-on view of the impressive 800 m vertical face of Gibraltar Mountain's north side, **return** the same way. Though it is tempting to escape to the Sheep River Trail directly from the summit via the south slopes, cliff bands and drop-offs abound and route-finding is challenging; this route is therefore not recommended.

61. MOUNT BURNS 2936 m

(MAP 14, PAGE 457)

Rating moderate, with one or two difficult moves, via the southwest face; some exposure
Round-trip time 9–11 hours with a bike approach; add 4 hours if on foot
Elevation gain 1300 m
Maps 82 J/10 Mount Rae; Gem Trek Highwood & Cataract Creek and Bragg Creek

For the scrambler who has done everything, there is Mount Burns. Not to imply that Burns is not a worthwhile trip – the scenery is very pleasant and the summit view excellent. Just expect a long bike approach and tons of scree on the way there. Try from mid-June on. Note that access to this peak may be restricted, because part of the route crosses private land.

Follow the driving directions for the east peak of Burns and start riding along the Sheep River trail. A bridge takes you across the first river crossing, but you must ford the remainder of the crossings (7–9, depending on whether some have dried up). By July the water is below knee-deep and so running or approach shoes will do fine (hip waders may be overkill here but are certainly an option). After numerous creek crossings, the trail will suddenly curve towards Mount Burns in an S-like pattern and then continues more or less in a straight line, with Burns on your right. Watch for this, as the next creek crossing marks the end of the bike ride. This crossing sits at GR495098 (no need to actually cross the creek here). You will also be able to see the correct ascent slope as depicted in the photo. Leave your bike here. This bike approach is approximately 12.5 km long, and though strong cyclists may be able to complete it in 1.25–1.5 hours, most should expect to take 1.5–2 hours.

The view of the ascent slope from the wide, dried-up drainage.

Leave the trail and head northeast through light bush towards the mountain. Quickly you'll arrive at a wide and dried-up drainage on your left. Cross to the other side and hike alongside it for a few hundred metres. Pick any line at this point, trending up and slightly left through the trees. The terrain is initially steep but easy to negotiate. The trees soon give way to scree and rubble. Continue up to a high point at GR504111 where the upper slopes become visible. This is a good place for a break, as you are still 500 vertical metres from the summit.

The next part of the ascent to the false summit requires a little route-finding. The ridge is lined with drop-offs, some of which are overhanging and cannot be scrambled down. To save a little time and energy it is best to sideslope the left side of the ridge until past these difficulties. Start towards the false summit, losing a little elevation on scree slopes to the left. Sideslope, keeping the ridge within striking distance. Once past several drop-offs, look for a small but striking pinnacle on the ridge. Head up to the base of the pinnacle, which actually turns out to be a fin of rock. Past the fin is another rock formation that looks quite tempting. Avoid this one, as it leads to an exposed downclimb that will likely scare the pants off you (and no-one wants to arrive at the summit of a mountain in their underwear!). Circumvent this formation, obviously on the left side, and then return to the ridge for some enjoyable moderate scrambling on firm rock. Again, for expedience and ease, all can be bypassed on the left side of the ridge, though that is less enjoyable.

Continue up the ridge until the ascent takes on a more serious nature as short but steep rock bands rise up ahead. Scramble up to the base of the first band. Don't try to scramble directly up this band, though; it is hideously loose and the rock is unreliable. Instead, traverse around to the left side, where a narrow but easy scree ramp takes you above the first band. Repeat this process for the next band.

The upper slopes. Although the terrain looks fairly simple here, drop-offs are characteristic of the ridge. Sidesloping on the left side is best.

Above: Looking along the impressive east ridge of Burns.
Below: Looking down the alternative descent route.

This section may require one or two difficult moves with exposure. Things get easier after this. Return to the ridge and continue upward. As sort of a bad joke, some good rock makes another all too brief appearance right before the false summit.

From the false summit the true summit is a couple hundred metres away to the northeast and marked by a very large cairn. Skirt the first section on the left side and then follow the ridge easily to the summit. The panorama features peaks of the Elbow Valley to the north, the Highwood Range to the south and the Misty and Opal Ranges to the west.

If you just want to get off the mountain as quickly as possible, it is best to **return** the same way. If you have a little more adventure left in you and want to see more of the mountain, an alternative descent route is described below. Note, however, that this alternative descent is not trivial. It requires route-finding and has tedious scree and steep slabs. It is not an "easy" way off the mountain. The upside is the change of scenery and negotiating an interesting drainage lower down.

The alternative descent goes down south slopes into the valley below and then follows the drainage out to join up with the ascent route. From the summit, head directly south down scree slopes with slabs to the left. The idea here is to work your way down and to the left, going from one scree run to another. The slabs are quite steep and best avoided for now. Near the bottom, depending on how far you have traversed, you may end up in a water-worn drainage that is more enjoyable to descend. Boulder-hop down this drainage until it suddenly drops off. Traverse around this and another drop-off lower down, on the left side, and then make your way down to a dried-up drainage at the bottom of the valley.

Boulder-hop down the drainage as it winds and twists through the valley. It eventually becomes a water-worn gully. Continue down the gully, down-climbing a couple of steeper steps. Arrive at a unique feature where the gully turns left beneath a major overhang of rock. Descend this step. Shortly after, you'll arrive at a two-tier step where down-climbing the smooth rock is not a safe option. Ascend scree slopes to the left to grassy terrain above. Stay on the grassy and treed terrain paralleling the drainage. Eventually a drainage on the left will appear. Continue downward as both drainages converge. Just before they do, descend steep scree on the left to the left drainage. With all the route-finding behind you now, simply follow the drainage back to your bike. Even though the bike ride back has several uphills, it is still relatively fast (just over an hour at a good pace).

62. SHUNGA-LA-SHE 2625 m

(MAP 14, PAGE 457)
Rating moderate, with a few difficult sections, via the northeast ridge; some exposure
Round-trip time 6–9 hours
Elevation gain 1000 m
Maps 82 J/10 Mount Rae; Gem Trek Highwood & Cataract Creek

The oddly named Shunga-la-she has a good scramble route via its northeast ridge, with options to extend the trip to a higher peak to the west, unofficially called "Jägermeister Peak" (courtesy of Rafal Kazmierczak). As a Front Range mountain, Shunga-la-she is a good candidate for an early- or late-season trip, although there is no access to the parking lot via Highway 546 from December 1 to May 15 and the Sheep River can be running too high in the early season. Try from mid-June on.

Drive west to Turner Valley on Highway 7 and continue through the town to where the road soon turns into Highway 546. Drive to the end of the road and park on the lower section of the Bluerock/Junction Creek parking lot, close to the Sheep River. Head west on the trail paralleling the Sheep for a few minutes and look for a decent place to cross. Descend steep slopes to the river and cross.

Hip waders or runners would work well here, but if you leave them on the other side of the river and then use the alternative descent route, you'll have to cross again to retrieve them.

Keep heading west. A pleasant jaunt through thin forest leads to the northeast ridge. GPS or a compass reading could save you some unnecessary route-finding (or getting lost!). Eventually

The route up the northeast ridge, as seen from near the parking lot. **FS**: false summit.

The alternative descent route down the north ridge.

the terrain starts rising and the forest gives way to scree slopes below a significant rock band. Unless you brought your rock shoes, circumvent the rock band easily on the left side and continue up the ridge. The remainder of the route is actually very straightforward from this point, though numerous rock bands straddling the ridge complicate things a bit. Depending on your skill and comfort level, many of the bands can be tackled head-on – use good judgment and common sense. Others simply have to be circumvented, usually on the left side. Depending on how far you traverse alongside these bands, you may lose some elevation and then have to gain it back on laboriously steep scree slopes.

After gaining a couple of high points, it may be discouraging to discover that the summit is still some distance and elevation away. Persevere – the interesting rock scenery and great views of Gibraltar Mountain's daunting northeast face should be enough to keep your feet moving. Just before the summit, the ridge narrows considerably.

This may or may not be the crux (depending on the route you've taken). Regardless, use caution, as a slip here would probably be fatal. The summit is a minute beyond this step.

Enjoy a very respectable summit panorama featuring the east faces of Mist, Storm and Rae to the west as well as Bluerock and Burns to the north. Junction, Pyriform and many unnamed peaks of the Highwood Range dot the horizon to the south.

Return the same way, or take a far easier descent line down the west and northwest ridge. Continue heading west as the ridge curves down and then to the northwest. The goal is to descend into the obvious drainage to your left. Stay on the ridge until you see the easiest line down to the drainage. Once there, follow the drainage all the way down to Sheep River Trail, which leads effortlessly back to the parking lot (don't forget to retrieve your hip waders or runners if you left them on the other side of the river).

63. JUNCTION MOUNTAIN 2682 m

(MAP 14, PAGE 457)

Rating moderate, with one difficult, exposed step, via the north ridge
Round-trip time 8–10 hours
Elevation gain 1100 m
Maps 82 J/10 Mount Rae; Gem Trek Highwood & Cataract Creek

This trip involves a great deal of hiking, with a few minor sections of interesting scrambling. The scenery is pleasant throughout, and the trip's considerable length should not deter those looking to summit an infrequently ascended peak. Try from mid-June on.

From the hamlet of Turner Valley, drive to the end of Highway 546 (which becomes Twp. Rd. 194A, then 195A) and park at the far east end of the lower section of the Junction Creek parking lot. Put on your hip waders if desired and hike down to the Sheep River. If you look upstream you should be able to see Junction Creek spilling into the Sheep. The goal is to get to the southeast angle of the confluence of these two streams, i.e., the south bank of the river and the east bank of the creek. Ford the Sheep here, or go a short way west along it, past the confluence, and then ford first the river and then the creek to arrive at the same point (obviously the Sheep will have slightly less water in it before Junction Creek enters).

Start hiking southeastward, up increasingly steep forested slopes to the first of many high points of the day (GR608074). Expect to take 30–45 minutes of steep hiking to reach this point.

Once you are on the ridge, the route is obvious

A good portion of Junction's lengthy north ridge. **C** crux rock band. **S** summit.

The crux rock band. **C**: crux.

but long. Hike along the ridge (south-southeast) over open and lightly forested slopes. Farther along, the ridge sometimes abruptly ends in minor drop-offs; downclimb these or back up a little and find an easier way around.

Several hours later the ridge is interrupted by a prominent rock band – the crux. Go around to the left side, ascending slightly downsloping scree ledges with an increasing drop-off to your left. After several hundred metres you turn a corner where the scree ledge narrows and the exposure increases. Here you'll want to look to the right for a good place to ascend to the ridge. Backing up a little offers several options, but all require a few moves of difficult and exposed scrambling. Pick your line carefully in case you have to downclimb to find an easier option.

On the ridge, turn left and enjoy sections of hiking and easy to moderate scrambling all the way to the summit. As is commonly the case, the ridge is best enjoyed by remaining on it instead of taking

the faint trail below the right side of the ridge. Some sections, however, will have to be circumvented on the right. The ridge soon curves around to the right and descends to a col, where a short hike leads to the summit. The summit view takes in many of the beautiful but unnamed peaks of the Highwood Range. Pyriform and Mount Head lie to the south. The Elk Range can be seen to the west and Mount Harrison beyond that to the southwest.

If Mount Pyriform is not on the agenda (see below) **return** the same way. If you want to avoid the crux, return to the small col below the summit and descend north-facing scree slopes. Sideslope until you can regain the ridge north of the crux rock band.

An alternative descent exists via Junction Creek. Route-finding can be tricky here, so have a good map with you. This route allows you to visit the beautiful three-tiered waterfall near Junction Creek, but it is circuitous and will likely take at least 4 hours. From the top, descend tedious rubble

The alternative descent route off Junction Mountain (middle) and the straightforward but challenging ridge traverse to Pyriform Mountain (left). **P**: Pyriform Mountain; **JC**: Junction Cirque.

and scree in the middle of the slope, aiming for the meadows to the southwest. Hike down through the meadows, staying well to the left. If you're lucky, you'll find a trail that trends southwest and then turns northwest to eventually intersect Junction Creek. If not, go in those directions anyway!

At Junction Creek, turn north and follow the creek if you haven't found a good trail. Eventually, waterfalls will prevent you from staying near the creek. Ascend slopes on the left (west) side of the creek and continue north. Soon you should find a well-used trail that parallels the creek high above it. When this trail intersects a side creek coming from the west, cross it and turn left for a quick visit to the waterfalls, which are well worth a 10-minute detour. Return to Junction Creek Trail and follow it back to the parking lot. Don't forget to retrieve your hip-waders.

JUNCTION TO PYRIFORM

If there ever was a time to ascend Pyriform Mountain, this could be it. However, this is not a "skipping along a flowery ridge, singing selections from The Sound of Music" *traverse! As well as the usual glut of ankle-jarring Rockies rubble, the trip has several route-finding challenges and moderately difficult scrambling with some exposure and requires an additional 400 m of elevation gain. Expect to take 2–3 hours to get to the summit and 4–6 more to get back to your vehicle using an alternative descent route.*

The general route is easy peasy – follow the ridge south to the summit of Pyriform. There is really only one way to go.

The specifics are a different story, although they are very consistent. Descend to the col and then up to the first non-scrambling obstacle. Circumvent this on the left side and then return to the ridge. This is the pattern you will basically follow until you reach the summit. Each time you go left you should never have to lose a significant amount of elevation. Always look to your right to find a scrambling route back to the ridge. Expect a few difficult moves of scrambling and a little exposure.

The summit, at GR633990, sports a great view that is surprisingly different than that from Junction (you see the same mountains but from

The summit view to the west and the alternative descent route down to Junction Creek. Photo: Rafal Kazmierczak

different angles). Of particular interest are the noticeably tiered Dogtooth Mountains to the south.

Assuming you are not up for the epic feat of returning the way you came, use the alternative descent route as follows. From the summit, descend nasty rubble slopes in a west direction. Note that this requires you to traverse to the right as you descend, as the main slope faces southwest. There are several rock bands to get below, but each has a weakness, so that very little downclimbing is required. Keep going west and down, searching for the easiest route. Thankfully the annoying rubble eventually gives way to scree that is a little easier to descend.

The crux of the descent is finding the trail that leads down to Junction Creek. While it is not imperative that you find it, the trail does make life considerably easier. As you get closer to treeline, start heading north, traversing the west side of Pyriform. Eventually you will want to go more to the left (northwest), soon running into the unofficial Junction cirque trail (GR610006). A right turn will take you into Junction cirque, below the summit of Junction Mountain. Go left. This trail parallels a rocky drainage but high above it, then descends to the drainage, crosses it and eventually ends up at Junction Creek, around GR604016. Cross the creek and follow the trail on the other side for 7.5 km back to the intersection of Junction Creek and the Sheep River. Don't forget to retrieve your hip waders if you used them to ford the waterways.

64. PYRIFORM MOUNTAIN 2770 m

(MAP 14, PAGE 457)
Rating moderate via the west face
Round-trip time 10–13 hours
Elevation gain 1200 m
Map 82 J/10 Mount Rae; Gem Trek Highwood and Cataract Creek

Perhaps the best route to the summit of Pyriform is a moderately long ridge-scramble from the summit of Junction Mountain (page 213). However, for those who have already completed an ascent of Junction, a more direct route to Pyriform via Junction Creek is described here. Thankfully an excellent but long trail leads all the way to the base of Pyriform. At some point in history this trail was a good candidate for biking, but at present it is too deeply rutted to cycle. Hip waders are a good idea for the almost immediate crossing of the Sheep River. Note that this river can flow high and fast early in the season. Try from July on. The road is closed from December 1 to May 15.

From the hamlet of Turner Valley, drive to the end of Highway 546 and park at the west end of the lower section of the Junction Creek parking lot. Walk down to the Sheep River and ford it. Find the wide Junction Creek Trail on the other side and start hiking south, ignoring all side trails to the right.

At about the 7.5 km mark the trail descends to Junction Creek and a beautiful sinkhole (GR604016). Cross the creek to the east side and find the continuation of the trail. The path gains elevation, descends to a rocky drainage and then ascends the other side of the drainage. As you approach treeline you will notice you are now at the northwest end of Pyriform Mountain. This is where you can start trending south, traversing the northwest side of the mountain.

There are plenty of routes up the mountain from here. Most will go south to about GR623990 and then turn west and slog their way up the mountain's west side. There are several rock bands to overcome, but all have easy routes through them. Note that this route requires you to traverse to the right as you go up (not a bad thing, as it may help you negotiate the tedious scree and rubble). The summit sits at GR633990.

The summit panorama provides a pleasant contrast of rocky peaks (mostly unnamed) to the west, with foothills and prairies to the east. The noticeably tiered summits to the immediate south are the Dogtooth Mountains. Junction Mountain lies due north, and although traversing the ridge between Pyriform and Junction may look very tempting, the route is not recommended, as route-finding and downclimbing will be very tricky. The route is much better in reverse, from Junction to Pyriform. Instead, return the same way you came.

As you near treeline the main bulk of Pyriform starts to appear. The summit sits to the right. Photo: Rafal Kazmierczak

65. MOUNT LIVINGSTONE 2422 m

(MAP 15, PAGE 456)
Rating easy via the southwest ridge
Round-trip time 3–5 hours
Elevation gain 670 m
Maps 82 J/1 Langford

Mount Livingstone is possibly the easiest ascent in the book. Elevation gain is minimal and the trip can be completed in about 3 hours round trip at a good clip. If you're looking for something easy and stress-free, this is a good day out. Consider combining it with an ascent of Coffin Mountain to the south and/or Isola Peak to the west to make the most of your day. Inaccessible from December 10 to April 30.

Heading south on Highway 22, drive approximately 28 km past Longview and turn right (west) onto Highway 532. Continue for 25.7 km and turn left (south) onto Forestry Trunk Road 940. Go 8.1 km and either park at the turnoff or turn left and drive the logging road for 1.6 km to an open area with a "NO MOTORIZED VEHICLES BEYOND THIS POINT" sign. This road may not be good for low-clearance vehicles. Parking at the turnoff adds only 1.6 km of easy hiking to both ends of the trip, and you may not want to take the chance of damaging your vehicle for that paltry distance.

If you drove the 1.6 km to the parking area, hike

directly north up lightly forested slopes to gain the ridge. If you parked at the turnoff, hike the road for about 1 km, and when feasible, hike through a clear-cut and arrive at the west-facing slopes near the south end of the mountain. Gain the ridge and turn north. Both routes soon join up. Hike the ridge, enjoying good footing on solid, slabby terrain higher up. The ridge soon narrows and appears to drop off, but in fact it leads easily to a small col. While it is not necessary to ascend slopes to the northeast to gain the false summit, that is the best route.

Trend to the right as you ascend, to find yourself

The not so impressive form of Mount Livingstone as seen from the turnoff. **S**: summit.

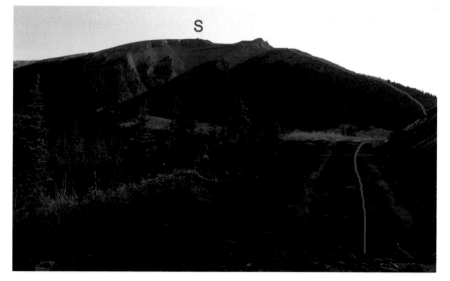

Left: Far more impressive scenery on the ridge.

Middle: The north ridge/face of Coffin Mountain as seen from the south end of Mount Livingstone. The route has plenty of hands-on scrambling.

Bottom: The unremarkable form of Isola Peak. It ain't no Assiniboine! **S**: summit.

atop a vertical cliff band. Follow the ridge easily to the false summit. The traverse north to the highest point of the trip is also easy. A couple of rock bands right before the summit add some interest and can be ascended via a variety of different routes.

The summit view features an array of shapely and distinctive peaks along the Continental Divide. Tallest is Tornado Mountain at a height just shy of 3100 m. The craggy-looking peaks north of Tornado are the Cache Creek Elevators.

Continuing farther north about 500 m to the slightly lower top is worth the effort. Undoubtedly the highlight will be the impressive cliff bands on the east side of the mountain. Not surprisingly, the view from this lower peak is very much the same as that seen from the higher one.

For descent, **return** to the high point and then back to the false summit. Going back the way you came is probably the easiest route from there, but if you want some variety, descend the south ridge all the way down to the valley floor, or start descending the south ridge and then trend to the right onto scree slopes between the two ridges. The south ridge route generally provides good footing on slabby terrain but can be tedious and slow at times. Still, it is the most interesting of the descent routes and would also make an enjoyable ascent route. Check out the north ridge/face on Coffin Mountain as you descend. It could be your next objective.

On the valley floor, hike west on a good trail back to your vehicle.

65A. ISOLA PEAK

If you want more from your day, **Isola Peak** to the west (map 15, page 456) is also an option. Be warned, however, that the ascent is very straightforward (actually almost too straightforward!) and the summit view is unremarkable. This is one ascent you would do simply for the exercise or to get another official peak under your belt.

From the turnoff to Mount Livingstone/Coffin Mountain, drive north up Highway 940 for about 700 m, turn left and go several hundred metres to where the road starts to degrade at an intersection. Park here (GR835551). The Livingstone River is about 100 m farther up this road. Ford the river. By mid-summer the water should be low and the crossing is very easy. Expect higher water in the spring. On the other side of the river, hike the wide road for several kilometres to where it opens up into a wide flat. At the far end, the trail narrows and continues down to the left and then west again. Stay on the trail for another kilometre and then leave it to head northwestward up lightly treed slopes to the right. The rest of the trip simply involves going up. The bushwhacking is light and shouldn't pose any problems. It is actually fairly pleasant at times. Eventually, trees will give way to a rocky summit expanse. Simply head up to the highest point, at GR787558.

As mentioned, the summit view is nothing to write home about and the devastation of clear-cutting in almost every direction is actually quite sobering. **Return** the same way.

66. COFFIN MOUNTAIN 2412 m

(MAP 15, PAGE 456)
Rating difficult via the north face; easy via the northwest ridge
Round-trip time 3–4 hours
Elevation gain 640 m
Maps 82 J/1 Langford

There are easier and shorter routes to the summit of Coffin Mountain, but the north face offers interesting scrambling with a minimal amount of elevation gain. The easier northwest ridge can then be used for descent. Given the shortness of the trip, it is best to combine Coffin with an ascent of Mount Livingstone immediately to the north. Total elevation gain for both will be 1310 metres. Try from May on for the easy routes or wait until mid-June to attempt the north face. Inaccessible from December 10 to April 30.

Park as for Livingstone Mountain. Before you head up, decide what kind of adventure you want. If you would like an easy and quick route to the summit, the northwest ridge is your best bet. If you want a challenging, hands-on scrambling experience, the north ridge/face offers a good dose of that. For this route, grippy approach shoes will make the experience more enjoyable, allowing you to tackle more challenging terrain.

NORTHWEST RIDGE

Hike up a slope covered in fallen logs directly above the parking area. Trend slightly left and make your way up to the first rocky high point. From there the north summit and true summit are visible. Best to hike up to the north summit first and then easily to the true summit, about 800 m away.

NORTH RIDGE/FACE

From the parking area, hike east for approximately 800 m on the narrow trail that runs between Livingstone and Coffin. A forested area soon appears on the right. Hike to a barbed wire fence with a seasonal tarn on the other side. Turn right (south) into the trees and hike uphill, trending leftward. Very quickly the trees give way to rock and scree.

Head for the solid rock immediately and up you go. Pick whatever line suits your comfort level, but try to trend left towards the centre of the north face. The rock is generally very good, with good hand- and footholds, but there are some large loose blocks. Check all holds carefully before committing to them.

When more or less in the centre of the north face, scramble directly up the ridge as the terrain allows. Most rock bands can be tackled head-on. At

The two primary routes up Coffin. Recommended is an ascent via the north ridge/face (**NR**) and descent via the northwest ridge (**NWR**).

Looking up the north face. This is where you start the ascent.

any time, it is easy to leave the solid rock and move onto one of numerous scree trails leading upward. The first large and overhanging rock band can be circumvented on either side. I chose the left (east) side. Quickly regain the ridge and continue up more interesting rock. The last rock band must also be circumvented. The right side is an easier option here, although it is not necessary to lose elevation around the entire band. There are several weaknesses on the right side. These weaknesses will probably be the crux of the trip. Be sure you are comfortable ascending them. Otherwise, lose the necessary elevation to get around the band.

Atop the last rock band, gain the southwest-trending ridge and follow it easily to the north summit. The true summit is reached shortly after. This ridgewalk may seem anticlimactic following the interesting scrambling of the north face. The summit view may also fail to impress, especially if you've been up Livingstone already.

There are many ways to get back to your vehicle. If you took the north ridge/face up, returning that way is not recommended, though quite feasible. Instead, return to the north summit and go down the northwest ridge and slopes. Expect a good deal of climbing over fallen trees lower down. Another option is to hike down the south ridge for several hundred metres and then turn right (west) down rubble and scree slopes into the dried-up drainage below. Don't expect to enjoy any decent scree surfing. It's a tedious descent but not terribly long and a pleasant change of scenery. At the bottom, trend right through the trees and find another road (trail) that leads back to the parking area.

67. THUNDER MOUNTAIN 2376 m

(MAP 16, PAGE 456)
Rating easy, mostly hiking
Round-trip time 5.5–7.5 hours
Elevation gain 1000 m
Maps 82 G/16 Maycroft

Thunder Mountain is a good choice if you are looking for an easy day out. It is also a great shoulder-season or winter trip. The reward of doing the ascent right after the first major snowfall might be some terrific scenery along the north ridge. If undertaking the trip in winter, crampons and an ice axe may be required. Be prepared to battle a fierce west wind. Try from June on.

Drive south on Highway 22 to where the road crosses the Oldman River. Right after the bridge, turn right onto Highway 517 (may be signed). Follow 517 for about 17 km as it approaches the north end of Thunder Mountain. Park on the left (west) side just before the road turns the corner. Hike to the end of the ridge and find a trail that winds its way up the north end. If you can't find the trail, just get to the north end and start heading up and south. Route-finding challenges are practically non-existent as long as you are heading south. Any obstacles are easily tackled head-on or circumvented.

The north ridge route soon becomes visible, with a false summit at the end. Follow the ridge easily to the false summit.

Again, choose a route to your liking. If you stay on the ridge, there are a few opportunities to scramble. A short walk atop the false summit reveals the remainder of the ridge to the summit.

Near treeline the route to the false summit is obvious. Raff and Ferenc enjoy the fresh snow on this beautiful day in early October.

Atop the false summit, the true summit and the route to it are revealed.

The connecting ridge from the false summit to the true summit does get narrow in a few places and may feel a little exposed, especially if the ferocious west wind, characteristic of the area, is pounding the mountain. There is a trail on the right side of the ridge to avoid some sections, but the best place to be is right on the ridge. If you are doing the ascent in winter conditions, extra care will be required to negotiate the ridge. Crampons and an ice axe may be necessary.

The ridge eventually drops a little to a col, where the final push to the summit is a short and easy affair. There are two summits within a short distance of one another, and both are worth a few minutes of your time. On a clear day, less frequently seen peaks such as Tornado Mountain, Gould Dome, Mount Erris and Mount Domke can be seen to the west. Crowsnest Mountain and the Seven Sisters are also prominent. The tremendously long ridge heading south extends all the way to the town of Bellevue on Highway 3, with Centre Peak as its high point.

Return the same way.

CATARACT CREEK AND HIGHWOOD			
Holy Cross Mountain	2685 m	easy/moderate	p. 224
Mount Head	2782 m	moderate/difficult	p. 225
Mount Armstrong	2804 m	moderate	p. 227
Patterson's Peak	2728 m	moderate	p. 229
"Lineham Creek Peaks"	2716–2775 m	moderate/difficult	p. 232
Lineham Ridge and GR593982	2698, 2807 m	moderate	p. 234
Gibraltar Mountain	2665 m	moderate	p. 237
Mount Odlum	2716 m	moderate	p. 239
Mount Loomis	2822 m	moderate/difficult	p. 241
Mount Bishop	2850 m	moderate	p. 244
Mount McPhail	2865 m	easy/moderate	p. 246
Mount Muir	2743 m	easy	p. 248
Mount Strachan	2682 m	easy	p. 249
Mount MacLaren	2840 m	easy	p. 252

These peaks lie in the southern section of Kananaskis Country, off Highway 40 (identified as Highway 541, east of the 940/40 junction at Highwood Junction). Again, the driving approach from the south via Longview is probably quicker than the one via the Trans-Canada from the north. From Calgary, drive south on Highway 2 and take the turnoff to Okotoks (2A). Continue through the town of Okotoks and turn right (west) onto Highway 7. Follow it to Black Diamond and turn left (south) onto Highway 22. At Longview turn right (west) onto Highway 541.

Only Holy Cross Mountain and Mount Head can be accessed year-round. Access to the other scrambles is restricted due to the closure of Highway 40 from Highwood Junction to the Kananaskis Lakes turnoff. As the area is an important corridor for wildlife, this road is barricaded each year from December 1 to June 15.

The trips east and north of the highway are generally shorter and benefit the most from snow-clearing chinook winds. Those west of the highway all lie on the Continental Divide. As such, their approaches are some of the longest covered in this book and they are the first to hold snow. Biking old logging roads helps to shorten the lengthy time required for many of these mountains, especially on return. These peaks also are a magnet for clouds and the formation of clouds. You may find yourself in whiteout-like conditions on Mount Armstrong while people on Mount Head at exactly the same time are enjoying clear blue skies.

Overlooking the beautiful blue waters of Carnarvon Lake from the lower slopes of Mount Strachan.

68. HOLY CROSS MOUNTAIN 2685 m

(MAP 17, PAGE 458)
Rating easy via the east face; moderate via the northeast ridge
Round-trip time 7–11 hours
Elevation gain 1225 m
Maps 82 J/7 Mount Head; Gem Trek Highwood & Cataract Creek

Depending on the level of scrambling you desire, Holy Cross offers a couple of routes to its summit, from steep hiking to moderate scrambling. With the right snow conditions, the east face grants a superb glissade. Otherwise, expect the usual fare of Rockies rubble and scree. Try from June on.

Park on the side of the road by Gunnery Creek. When heading west, this is approximately 1 km past the Sentinel Recreation turnoff. Find the trail on the right side of the creek and off you go (heading north) for several kilometres. Soon, the trail begins to drop. Follow it for several minutes and then leave the trail, heading northwest and aiming for a grassy hill. From the hill, both ascent routes are visible. The northeast route offers better and more interesting scrambling and is recommended for ascent. The east face can then be used for descent.

To tackle the northeast route, drop down to the creek from the hill, cross the stream and then head up the other side through light forest. Once above treeline, a rock band is visible which can be circumvented by trending to the right. This will put you at the lower end of the northeast ridge. Follow the ridge, enjoying various degrees of scrambling to the summit ridge. Steeper rock bands can be circumvented on the left side.

Once on the summit ridge, turn left and follow the sometimes narrow and mildly exposed ridge to the summit. If a strong west wind is blowing, this traverse may be "exciting." The summit panorama features a comprehensive view of the Continental Divide peaks of the southern Kananaskis, from Mount Odlum all the way down to Pierce and beyond. Mount Head (another worthwhile scramble) sits to the northwest and is connected to Holy Cross by a narrow ridge.

Return the same way or descend the much easier east face. If snow conditions are good and you are skilled at glissading and self-arrest, a great deal of elevation can be lost in minutes. At the bottom, follow the drainage, looking for the hill you started from. Lower down, stay on the right side of the valley to avoid unnecessary elevation loss and regain, and make your way back to the hill and then back down to Gunnery Trail.

The ascent routes from the hill. **NE**: northeast ridge; **S**: summit; **D**: east face and descent route.

69. MOUNT HEAD 2782 m

(MAP 17, PAGE 458)
Rating moderate, with one difficult step, via the east ridge; moderate via southeast slopes
Round-trip time 9–12 hours
Elevation gain 1500 m
Maps 82 J/7 Mount Head; Gem Trek Highwood & Cataract Creek

Mount Head is one of the higher peaks of the Highwood Range and is a fine objective (the highest, at GR571013, is unnamed, although it is sometimes referred to as Highwood Peak). The east ridge of Mount Head provides splendid scenery and its front-range location makes early and late season ascents possible. Try from June on.

Park at Sentinel lot on Highway 546. Hike a couple of hundred metres back up the road, heading east. Cross to the north side and find the Grass Pass trailhead. A 3.2 km hike takes you to the pass, at which point you'll start to lose elevation as you keep heading north on the wide trail. An occasional glance to the left should give you a decent view of the route you will be taking.

After several kilometres the trail suddenly drops sharply down to the left and you arrive at a meadow. Two routes exist from this point:

Route 1: difficult east ridge. Head northwest across the meadow and find the creek that originates from the valley south of the mountain. Cross the creek and hike up easy slopes to the start of the treed ridge. Once on the ridge, turn left and head directly west. The trail undulates in a couple of places, but eventually you will arrive at a clearing with the ascent route visible straight ahead (see top photo next page).

Ascend treed slopes just left of centre to circumvent the first outcrop of vertical rock. Once around the band, it is best to veer right and ascend alongside it. At the top, head straight towards the cliff bands and then traverse left around the band to find an obvious weakness. Ascend the weakness to a small plateau. Now for the crux: finding a feasible way up the second rock band. From the plateau, hike up to the face of the rock band and traverse left below its vertical walls. If snow remains here, a slip might launch you over the cliffs below unless you can self-arrest immediately. In this case, crampons and an ice axe are mandatory. Another option is to turn around and look for another route. Turn a corner and the crux step should be right in front of you: a 5 m high, nearly vertical step, with trees at the top (bottom photo next page). Initially the step may look easy, but upon starting the ascent you may find it more challenging than it appears. There

are few good holds, and more than likely, near the top, you will find yourself grabbing for tree branches and hoping they will hold your weight should you slip. Once you start up, it will be difficult to back down, so be sure of your decision to ascend this crux step. If you don't like the looks of it, there are easier places to ascend the rock band. These will, however, require you to descend back through the weakness and then traverse around the left side of the band to look for a viable route up. You may have to lose a fair amount of elevation before something becomes apparent.

After the crux, the remainder of the ascent is significantly easier and the scenery improves dramatically as you gain elevation. Though it is possible to avoid unnecessary elevation losses and gains by sidesloping the south side of the east ridge more or less directly to the summit, this route is tedious and means you will miss out on some of the more interesting scrambling and scenery that the mountain has to offer. I recommend you stay on the east ridge throughout and visit every high point along the way. The first significant high point is easily ascended and descended and doesn't require a great deal of extra time. The second will require you to head left and down to circumvent an airy drop-off on the north side of the ridge, but it is well worth a quick visit. After this second high point, regain the ridge and continue up towards the summit. At the top, enjoy the pleasant contrast of the shapely peaks to the north, south and west, with the foothills and prairies to the east.

Route 2: moderate southeast slopes. At the meadow, head northwest and find the creek that originates from the valley south of the mountain. Follow the creek on its left side for approximately 2 km. Once past the first major drainage, turn right and ascend steep, treed slopes northwestward. Once above treeline, the route becomes

clear. The summit is way over to the left and can be reached more or less in a direct line by side-sloping the south face. That said, it is preferable (and certainly more interesting) to gain the east ridge and follow it to the summit. See the route described above after the crux.

Several **return** routes exist:

Return 1: *via the east ridge.* You must be confident you can downclimb the crux (or rappel if you have the necessary equipment). Don't try this descent route if you didn't come up this way.

Return 2: *via the southeast slopes (the moderate route in reverse).* This is the recommended option for avoiding the crux. Descend the east ridge until is it feasible to turn right, then head southeastward to the treeline. You'll want to stay well to the right of a major drainage on your left. The route is fairly tedious due to the rubble. At treeline, continue down to the valley, where you will turn left and hike down the valley to rejoin the creek.

Return 3: *via the southwest slopes and Stony Creek.* This route offers a quick way off the mountain, though route-finding at the beginning can be tricky, and bushwhacking alongside Stony Creek will be tedious and very time-consuming. Recommended only if you need to escape to lower elevations very quickly.

From the summit, start down the obvious gully on the southwest side of the mountain. As you lose elevation, trend to the right over several ribs to find the gully that leads straight down to the valley bottom. Other gullies lead to drop-offs, so

Above: The ascent route from the trail. **C:** crux; **1:** 1st high point; **2:** 2nd high point; **S:** summit; **ED:** easy descent route.
Below: The crux step.

finding the correct one is imperative. Once in the valley, there is only one way to go: down and due south. Follow Stony Creek out to the highway, turn left and walk about 4 km back to your car.

70. MOUNT ARMSTRONG 2804 m

(MAP 19, PAGE 460)
Rating moderate via the south and southwest ridges; some exposure
Round-trip time 10–14 hours
Elevation gain 1200 m
Maps 82 J/7 Mount Head; Gem Trek Highwood & Cataract Creek

Mount Armstrong is a long way from the highway, but an old logging road that parallels Baril Creek makes relatively short work of the approach, especially if you ride a bike. The environs of Fording Pass are superb and the summit view is stunning. For a two-peak day, nearby Mount Bolton is an easy ascent. Summit at GR588799. Try from mid-June on.

From Longview drive west on Highway 541 and turn left onto Highway 940 at Highwood Junction. Drive 3.3 km and park on the right in a small clearing. Follow a trail on the right (north) side of the clearing, which leads to Baril Creek Trail within a few minutes. Hike or preferably bike the trail for 6.9 km until you arrive at the first of several creek crossings marked by an "ICY TRAIL AHEAD" sign. Cross Baril Creek on two logs to your left. When you reach the second "ICY TRAIL AHEAD" sign,

The route up the westerly south ridge of Armstrong. As a Continental Divide peak, Armstrong is prone to sudden whiteouts and that's exactly what we got at the summit! **S**: summit.

take a track that heads off to the right. This route bypasses a couple of the subsequent creek crossings. The trail eventually descends to an open area. Continue west until you run into the creek again. If you are riding a bike, this is a good place to ditch it and continue on foot (GR616784). Cross the creek and continue on for approximately 500 m, then cross the creek a third time. Look for a sign on the right side of the trail that reads "GDT NORTH," at GR612778. Take this path and follow it up and west. It eventually joins up with a wider trail which takes you up to the beautiful and open terrain south of Armstrong. To the south lie Baril Peak, Mount Cornwell and several outliers of those peaks. Mount Bolton is due west. U-shaped Mount Armstrong has two south ridges, and you will be ascending the more westerly one.

Continue west until the westerly south ridge becomes visible to the northwest (see photo). The trail continues to a col between Bolton and the southwest ridge of Armstrong, but it is quicker to leave it here and ascend a ridge on the right directly to the south ridge. On the way, you will be required to lose a little elevation and cross a small creek. Gain Armstrong's south ridge at about GR587782 and follow it north to a great viewpoint southwest of the true summit. This slope is foreshortened and may take longer than you think. It will, however, also net you all but 100 metres of the remaining elevation gain for the day.

Provided you are blessed with clear skies, the 1 km ridgewalk to the true summit is probably the best part of the trip. Follow the ridge throughout, carefully downclimbing several steps along the way. The ridgetop is narrow and exposed for a few short sections. After taking in the superb summit panorama, **return** the same way.

Tagging Mount Bolton to the southwest is an easy affair. Add approximately 500 metres of elevation gain and about 2.5–3.5 hours to your day. Bolton also makes a good alternative ascent if you're not up for Armstrong. Descend to the Bolton/Armstrong col and then head up the easy northeast slopes to a fine viewpoint. **Return** the same way.

71. PATTERSON'S PEAK 2728 m

(MAP 17, PAGE 458)
Rating moderate, with mild exposure
Round-trip time 9–11 hours
Elevation gain 1400 m
Maps 82 J/7 Mount Head; Gem Trek Highwood and Cataract Creek

Patterson's Peak is named after Raymond Patterson and received its title in 2000. The ascent is long and trails are almost non-existent. Seclusion is almost guaranteed. Tons of hiking and only periodic sections of hands-on scrambling. Try from July on.

The crux of this trip is to navigate up and down several kilometres of treed ridges to the start of the ascent ridge. Thankfully, the bush is light throughout and the elevation losses and gains are not as significant as they often appear. Study your topo map well before you start, and use the waypoints described below if you are so inclined.

Park on the east side of the highway, 1.3 km south of the Lineham Creek parking lot (GR597906), recognizable by a group of distinctive orange lichen-covered fins of rock a short way

upslope. Hike up to the fins, have a quick look and then continue upward. The grade soon eases as you head northeast and then east along the treed ridge (GR603917). The ridge then curves to the right and drops down before ascending to the next ridge. You will now be going slightly southeast. Aim for GR614913. At the next high point, "Serendipity Peak" (as named by Bob Spirko) will become visible in the distance.

Open, grassy slopes lie at the bottom of the ascent ridge and that's where you'll want to be.

The route from a clearing on the first ridge. **SP**: Serendipity Peak; **GR**: GR628936.

Above: The meadows below Serendipity. **SP**: summit of Serendipity Peak.
Below: Patterson's Peak as seen from Serendipity. **A**: rock arch; **S**: summit of Patterson's; **D**: Dogtooth Mountains.

Descend northeastward and start up the next ridge that leads to the start of Serendipity. The third high point lies at GR618920, and the start of the ascent ridge is at GR622926.

Once you've reached the ascent ridge, head directly up it. Several drop-offs intervene, but all are easily downclimbed or circumvented on the right side. One downclimb does feel a little exposed. Fairly low down you will run into a slab of uniquely textured rock. This slab appears steep, but the rock is fairly solid and enjoyable to ascend. This may be your only chance to get your hands dirty, so take advantage if you feel up for it. Otherwise, simply avoid the slab, again on the right side. After that, the summit of Serendipity Peak is easily reached (GR632927 at 2665 m).

From the top, Patterson's Peak is clearly visible to the northeast.

Although following the ridge north and then east to the summit appears feasible, it is exposed and requires several dangerous downclimbs and is not recommended. The best route is a more direct, though less aesthetic line. Descend the east ridge for a short distance until it becomes easy to go down scree slopes to the left, heading into the bowl between Serendipity and Patterson's. Sidesloping to avoid elevation loss is self-defeating here. It is better to lose elevation as fast as possible and then just hike across the bowl to the low point. There is a small but interesting rock arch at the low point that is worth a visit.

From the low point simply follow the ridge to the false summit, passing over one high point along the way. Stay on or near the ridge to best enjoy some cool rock scenery. Since this is a Front Range peak, the summit view features the pleasant combination of foothills and prairies to the east and rugged mountains to the west. Mount Head dominates the horizon to the south and the Dogtooth Mountains lie to the north. **Return** the same way. Though the elevation gain back to Serendipity is a little unsavoury after the hard-earned summit of Patterson's, the remainder of the gains are minor. Alternative descent routes do exist, but they will invariably cause you more route-finding grief than the effort warrants.

Summary of GPS waypoints and elevations:
Parking lot: GR597906 at 1695 m
1st high point: GR603917 at 2091 m
2nd high point: GR614913 at 2151 m
3rd high point: GR618920 at 2189 m
Start of ridge: GR622926 at 2270 m
Summit of Serendipity Peak: GR632927 at 2665 m
Low point and arch: GR636935 at 2492 m
Summit of Patterson's Peak: GR645943 at 2730 m

72. "LINEHAM CREEK PEAKS" 2716–2775 m

(MAP 17, PAGE 458)

Rating moderate via the northwest ridge to GR618951, with mild exposure; difficult to GR628936, with considerable exposure – a climber's scramble
Round-trip time 5–7 hours for GR618951; add 2 hours for GR628936
Elevation gain 1150 m to GR618951; add 200 m for GR628936
Maps 82 J/7 Mount Head; Gem Trek Highwood & Cataract Creek

Though the Highwood Range is home to more than 25 distinct peaks, only five have been named. This trip allows you to visit up to four of the ones without names. The first three are relatively straightforward, but the fourth involves difficult scrambling with plenty of significant exposure and should only be attempted by experienced scramblers. Inaccessible from December 1 to June 15. Try from June 15 on.

Park at Lineham Creek parking lot, 11.9 km north of the Highway 40/940 junction. Note that sections of the Lineham Creek trail were affected by the 2013 floods. The trail now starts near the centre of the parking lot. It gains a little elevation and then parallels Lineham Creek, but well away from

The ascent route as seen from the trail. **S**: summit of GR618951; **LS**: lower summit at GR616953; **ED**: easy descent route.

and very high above it. About 1.3 km along, the trail descends to Lineham Creek, intercepting it around GR594924. Here is where most of the damage occurred. Instead of crossing the creek, stay on the west side and work your upstream, now without a trail. Once you are a few hundred metres up the creek, you can either just stay in it for the remainder of the approach to an important intersection at GR595927, or find the remnants of the old trail, again on the west side of the creek, and follow it to that same point. Once you arrive there, the route up the mountain becomes far more obvious, though some bushwhacking and route-finding will be required (see photo).

The goal is to gain a bench that leads to the ascent slope. Cross Lineham Creek and then ascend the creek heading east, until you can turn right to gain that bench. When the terrain opens up a little and it becomes obvious to do so, trend right to gain the lower slopes of the objective. The left peak is also feasible but it is closer to steep hiking than scrambling. Once on the correct slope, take it all the way to the top, staying on the ridge throughout. Higher up, the scrambling begins. For the best scrambling, choose enjoyable slabs instead of tedious scree. The terrain does get steeper towards the top and some hikers may consider it mildly exposed.

The summit grants a comprehensive view of the Continental Divide peaks of southern Kananaskis. Mount McPhail is the noticeable triangular-shaped peak and one of seven mountains in the Rockies loosely classified as a "pyramid." The 11,000er Mount Harrison will be visible behind Mount Muir on a clear day. Abruzzi and Joffre dominate farther north and even distant King George can be picked out.

Of more immediate concern, however, are the ridges that extend from the summit in either direction. If satiated, **return** the same way, though the northwest extension offers an easier descent. The northwest extension to GR616953 is a simple ridge-walk with a narrow exposed section right before

the summit. The rock is loose here, so check all hand- and footholds carefully. From the summit, follow the easier ridge (paralleling the one you ascended to GR618951) to the valley below, where it eventually intersects the trail.

A more extensive and considerably more challenging option goes all the way to GR628936 and offers a chance to nab GR623946 on the way. GR628936 is the second-highest point of the southern section of the Highwood Range, surpassed only by Mount Head. This route is only for experienced scramblers who are comfortable with long sections of exposed scrambling on less than solid rock. Make sure the tread on your boots (or approach shoes) is in good condition – you'll need it!

Continue south over to GR623946 without difficulty. As always, stay on the ridge as much as possible. From this summit, lose a fair amount of elevation to a low point between GR623946 and your objective. The ridge starts to narrow even more and then drops down again. Before this drop, it is better to back up a little and descend in order to circumvent this entire section (see photo). Traverse easier terrain until a clear route back to the ridge becomes visible, just before a major slab on the west face. Do not regain the ridge too early, as this detour will take you around the steepest section of the ridge. Once back on the ridge, follow it to the summit. This section is longer than you may think. It is very exposed and the rock is not always solid. Go slowly and carefully, as any slip would be fatal.

At the summit, newly named Patterson's Peak lies to the east, while Mount Head sits farther south along the ridge. Assuming you have no desire to downclimb the ridge you just came up, descend the west ridge directly from the summit until you arrive at a dirt/scree slope on the right side of the ridge (dark dirt, not the light-brown scree slope). Descend this easy but tedious slope all the way down to the valley. Keep going down and to the right, towards the creek. Follow the creek out to where it joins up with the trail and head home.

73. LINEHAM RIDGE 2698 m
and EAST PEAK at GR593982 2807 m

(MAP 17, PAGE 458)
Rating moderate via the northwest ridge; some exposure
Round-trip time 4.5–6 hours for Lineham; 6–8 hours for GR593982
Elevation gain 950 m to Lineham; add 280 m for GR593982
Maps 82 J/7 Mount Head, 82 J/10 Mount Rae; Gem Trek Highwood & Cataract Creek

The summit of Lineham Ridge can be easily reached via a good hiking trail along its southeast ridge. The northwest ridge of the mountain, however, provides interesting scrambling on good rock. As well, a higher summit to the east can be added on to the day, with an easy descent route that takes you alongside all four of the popular and scenic Picklejar Lakes. A good candidate for the use of approach shoes, on ascent anyway. Inaccessible from December 1 to June 15. Try from June 15 on.

Park in the Lantern Creek parking lot, 17 km north of the Highway 40/940 junction. Hike north on the road for 50 m or so and find Picklejar Lakes Trail on the east side. Hike the trail for 4 km (about 50–60 minutes at a fast pace). Lineham Ridge appears in front of you and the route ascends the left skyline. As soon as the first Picklejar Lake becomes visible, leave the trail to your right and easily gain the ridge.

From here to the summit, for the best scrambling experience, you'll want to stay on the ridge throughout, even when it becomes steeper and appears to end in drop-offs. All are easily downclimbed or simply don't exist. Lower down, it is possible to circumvent steeper sections on either side of the ridge, but eventually that option disappears, so you may as well get used to the terrain. The rock is surprisingly solid and easy to grip in most sections. Approach shoes lend themselves very well to this terrain, though boots with good tread are fine too.

The ridge is deceptively long, and a cairn at a false summit may be somewhat of an annoyance. Continue past this cairn and make your way to the obvious high point. If you've had enough, enjoy the panorama and **return** the same way. Alternatively, for an easier descent, head south to the next (and much lower) high point (one exposed section). A trail then heads down northwestward, eventually joining up with Picklejar Lakes Trail.

The ascent route. **S**: summit of Lineham Ridge.

Above: Typical terrain on the ridge.
Below: The route to GR593982 and the alternative descent route. The descent is less steep than it looks from this angle, although it remains a tedious rubble-slog. **S**: summit.

73A. GR593982

The extension to a higher summit at GR593982 to the east is worthwhile for several reasons:

1. it affords the added view of the Dogtooth Mountains to the east;

2. it allows for an easier descent route and a chance to visit the scenic Picklejar Lakes; and

3. it's higher!

The actual scrambling falls short of that which you've just come up and mostly amounts to a rubble ascent. Head east, losing 80 metres of elevation to a grassy col, and start up the other side. Again, stay close to the edge to get the best experience. As with Lineham, there are a few false summits. The high point has a cairn and the best view. The alternative descent is far from aesthetic, but it is shorter, easier and more scenic. Continue along the ridge for a short distance, looking for an obvious ramp to the left. Here the scree is a light shade of brown. Unfortunately, this slope is all rubble and offers little in terms of good scree surfing. If you're wearing approach shoes, you'll be hating life for the next 45 minutes. At the bottom, work your way over to the south shore of the fourth Picklejar Lake and find the trail that takes you effortlessly past all of the lakes and back to the parking lot.

74. GIBRALTAR MOUNTAIN 2665 m

(MAP 14, PAGE 457)
Rating moderate via Mist Ridge and west slopes
Round-trip time 12–15 hours
Elevation gain 1700–2000 m (depending on return route)
Maps 82 J/10 Mount Rae; Gem Trek Highwood & Cataract Creek

A long but enjoyable scramble in beautiful surroundings. Be prepared for approximately 2000 metres of elevation gain by the time you have negotiated the ups and downs of Mist Ridge. Try between June 15 and November 30 in dry years.

Start from Mist Creek parking lot on the west side of Highway 40. Find the trail at the north end of the parking lot and follow it across the highway, continuing along the trail on the other side. After 50 m, take a right, then a left, and hike the wide trail for 2 km. At the Mist Creek intersection, take the right-hand trail, which eventually leads to the south summit of Mist Ridge. Follow the undulating ridge to the north summit, raking in beautiful views of Mist Mountain and Storm Mountain to the west and your destination ahead and to the right.

From the north summit, descend east-facing slopes to the Mist Ridge/Gibraltar Mountain col and start up the other side. Travel a little to the left as you ascend, in order to gain the ridge as soon as possible. Once on the ridge, stay there and traverse enjoyable terrain towards the summit, which

Mist Ridge and Gibraltar Mountain as seen from the south summit of Mist Ridge. **MS**: summit of Mist Ridge; **S**: summit of Gibraltar.

Kevin Barton enjoying some typical scrambling on the ridge.

is incorrectly identified on some maps. The tilted orientation of the rock leads to a few drop-offs, which may or may not be downclimbable, depending on whether there is any snow or ice remaining on the rock. If not downclimbable, lose elevation to the right and traverse around these obstacles. One obstacle may require a fair loss of elevation to circumvent.

From the true summit it looks awfully tempting to continue east, down the ridge to the lower summit. The northeast face of this peak boasts a remarkable 800 metre vertical climb, completed in eight gruelling days by Bill Davidson and Jim White in 1971. In the equally remarkable event that you have both the time and the energy to complete the descent, head down the ridge, traversing right when needed. Just remember, once you get there, it's a long, long way back to your car, and the return trip will involve several significant elevation gains. **Return** the same way.

75. MOUNT ODLUM 2716 m

(MAP 18, PAGE 459)
Rating moderate via the north ridge
Round-trip time 6–8 hours
Elevation gain 840 m
Maps 82 J/10 Mount Rae, 82 J/7 Mount Head; Gem Trek Highwood & Cataract Creek

Mount Odlum will not be winning the "Scramble of the Year" award, but it is relatively short when compared to its neighbours to the south and it grants a good view of the valley to the west and the Italian Group. The route described below is best if you intend to summit Odlum only. If Loomis is also in your plans, use the Loomis/Odlum description (#76, route 2, page 243). Inaccessible from December 1 to June 15. Try from late July on.

Park on the south side of Highway 40 just after a guardrail at 28.9 km south of the Kananaskis Lakes Trail turnoff or 12 km south of the Highwood Pass sign. Odlum is visible to the southwest, between two treed ridges. The object is to ascend the valley between these ridges to the northeast side of Odlum. From the road, descend to Storm Creek and cross (ford) it. The crux of the trip follows, which is to find the trail. As long as you are heading southwestward, you'll run into the trail or an abundance of flagging sooner or later. If you find the flagging first, follow it to where it runs into the unmaintained but distinct trail. Upon reaching the trail, hike it southwestward for several kilometres and cross a small stream. Stay to the right after the stream and follow another trail to more-open

The ascent from the meadows northeast of the summit. **R**: rubble ramp.

meadows. The trail disappears in long grass here. Wade through the grass to another meadow, where the entire ascent route should be visible (see photo on previous page).

The key to gaining the col northwest of Odlum is an obvious rubble ramp far to the right. It may look steep from the meadow, and in fact it is in places, but it still requires only easy to moderate scrambling to ascend. Work your way over to the ramp and start upward. Getting up the ramp is very tedious. Sticking to the right side allows you to use the rock walls to help, but it is still a grunt. A snow-patch just before the col may persist well into July. Move onto the rock on the right if this is the case, or kick steps up the snow if you have an ice axe.

From the col, head southeast and follow the ridge to the summit of Odlum. There are a couple of mildly exposed moves right near the beginning, but it's mostly easy ridgewalking after that. Be careful when walking on the west side of the ridge – you'll be in BC there and may be subject to their provincial sales tax. If anyone tries to sell you something up there, just hop over to the east side of the ridge, back into Alberta! Just before the summit the terrain gets steeper. Either scramble straight up the ridge or avoid the steep part by going around it on the right side.

If you've completed other scrambles of the southern section of the Elk Range, the summit view here may be a little repetitive, but it is satisfying nonetheless. Rather than retracing your steps, a much easier **return** route exists on the southeast side of the peak in the form of rubble slopes. Head down the south ridge for a few minutes until the slope becomes clear. Follow it down to the valley, trending left to find a trail heading northeast at the bottom. You now have to swing around the east side of the mountain to get back into the correct valley. Be careful you don't descend into the valley directly east of Odlum. It will take you back to the road but more than 8 km away from your vehicle. Once in the correct valley, return the way you came.

76. MOUNT LOOMIS 2822 m

(MAP 18, PAGE 459)
Rating moderate from the north; difficult from the south
Round-trip time 9–12 hours, depending on route; add 5 hours if also ascending Odlum
Elevation gain 1200–1400 m
Maps 82 J/7 Mount Head; Gem Trek Highwood & Cataract Creek

There are at least three feasible routes to this summit. The most challenging and interesting of the three (Route 1) goes first to Loomis Lake and then to the southern outlier of Loomis before reaching the true summit. Route 2 is best if you also plan to summit Mount Odlum on the same trip and gives you the choice of both or either of the two summits. See the preceding description of Mount Odlum, #75, for the third route. Expect at least a 14-hour day to do both mountains. Inaccessible from December 1 to June 15. Try from July on.

Route 1: difficult, via Loomis Creek Trail. This is a climber's scramble; a bike approach is recommended. Park on the east side of Highway 40, 1.2 km north of the Lineham Creek parking lot. Cross the road, hop the guardrail and descend grassy slopes to a wide trail heading north and arriving at the Highwood River within a few minutes. Hip waders are highly recommended, not only for the ford of the Highwood but also for the numerous creek crossings after. Ford the river and find the wide Loomis Creek Trail on the other side. Bike (or hike) the trail for approximately 1 km to where it crosses Loomis Creek. Cross the creek and take the trail on the left as it heads uphill. Follow the trail for another 6.2 km, leaving your bike at the end of an open meadow. Allow 1.5–2 hours by bike from your car to the meadow. The trail starts to degrade here and is often muddy. Eventually it runs

Difficult route: the southern outlier of Loomis from Loomis Lake. Ascent route is approximate.

Above: Moderate route, to GR468932 from Odlum Pond.
O: Odlum Pond;
GR: GR468932.
Left: At GR468932, checking out the ascent route to Loomis and a miraculous layer of dense cloud in the valley to the west (a very rare phenomenon – please don't expect this exact view if you go there!).

right into Loomis Creek and then ascends alongside it. Follow it into more-open terrain (popular campsite) and trend left, either following the trail as it weaves its way uphill or heading more directly west to the lake.

You'll certainly want to take a break at beautiful Loomis Lake to enjoy the wonderful surroundings. Take special note of the prominent outlier northwest of the lake – that's where you'll be going. The route basically ascends steep rubble slopes above the lake towards several rows of striking pinnacles and rock formations. Though it is not necessary to ascend all the way to the ridge, this route does give you the best scenery. It also gives you a chance to bail on the difficult route by taking an easier one on the other side of the outlier, and maximizes your options up the southeast face of the outlier.

Depending on where you top out on the ridge, you will have to hike a few metres or a few hundred metres up the ridge before you arrive at a steep rock band that is not within the realm of scrambling. Lose elevation on the left to circumvent this and then gain it all back while traversing up and across. This is the pattern you will be following to reach the 2743 m summit of the outlier. A detailed description here would be too complicated. Route-find your way up and across the face, looking for the path of least resistance. Even the easiest route will require some intense and exposed scrambling. Again, this is a route for experienced scramblers/ climbers with good route-finding abilities. If you are not confident about ascending steep, loose, exposed terrain with the occasional lower class 5 move (and downclimbing that same terrain), this is not a good route choice for you.

At the summit of the outlier, the route to Loomis is clear. Descend one of a few gullies to the northwest for about 50 metres and then traverse back east to the ridge. Descending the ridge is easy, though you wouldn't want to slip to the right! From the low col, a 250 vertical metre and 25 minute slog takes you easily to the summit. Hug the ridge for the best scenery. Just above the col, take note of the cairn that marks the optional and easy descent route.

If you didn't bike Loomis Creek Trail, you have the option to continue north to a couple of outliers between Loomis and Odlum and then on to the summit of the latter. This makes for a very long day and will leave you a great distance from your car (see optional route descriptions for Loomis and

Odlum to investigate routes for return). Most people will **return** via Little Loomis Lake. Descend the way you came, almost to the col, and then work your way down onto steep scree slopes east of the col. Unfortunately the terrain here is hard and not good for scree surfing, but it leads easily to the valley below and Little Loomis Lake. Find a trail on the right (south) side of the lake and follow it down to where it intersects with Loomis Creek Trail. If you lose the trail, just go southeast and down, through the bush. Eventually you'll run into Loomis Creek Trail. Turn left onto it and head home.

Route 2: moderate, via Odlum Creek Trail. Park at Lantern Creek parking lot, 17 km north of the Highway 40/940 junction. Hike a few hundred metres north up the highway, looking for a large boulder that marks the start of Odlum Creek Trail. Follow the trail as it drops down to the Highwood River. Carefully cross the river (runners or hip waders) and find the cutline (trail) on the other side. The cutline parallels Odlum Creek for the next 7.5 km (go straight at all intersections), eventually leading to Odlum Pond. Mount Loomis towers above you, while the summit of Odlum is, for now, blocked by its slightly lower southern outlier.

From Odlum Pond the objective is to gain the outlier immediately north of Loomis (GR468932). Circle around the south side of the pond and cross the creek, aiming for the right side of the watercourse – the least steep route. Above a waterfall, cross the creek again and continue up towards the col between Loomis and GR468932. Pass under the steep walls of GR468932, looking to the right to ascend the first gully, a route that leads to the east ridge. Scramble up the ridge to the first of four possible summits you may achieve in the day.

After enjoying views of Sir Douglas and Joffre to the northwest and Mount Abruzzi due west, turn south and follow the easy to moderate ridge to the summit of Loomis. If Loomis is your only goal, return the same way. If you miraculously have the energy to also bag Odlum, return to the col and continue north along the ridge, first to the southern outlier of Odlum and then to Odlum itself. Use the easier descent route outlined in the Mount Odlum description or return the same way. The former means avoiding additional elevation gains, but this descent may be trickier, since you didn't come up this way, and it will also leave you about 8 km from your car once you reach the highway.

77. MOUNT BISHOP 2850 m

(MAP 18, PAGE 459)
Rating moderate via southeast slopes
Round-trip time 7–10 hours
Elevation gain 1200 m
Maps 82 J/7 Mount Head; Gem Trek Highwood & Cataract Creek

Bishop is a little closer to the road than its neighbours to the north and south (Loomis and McPhail respectively), but it still requires a lengthy approach. Old logging roads and good trails make the approach an easy one, and if you are unable to summit Mount Bishop, Bishop's Ridge makes for a fine alternative. Inaccessible from December 1 to June 15. Try from July on.

Park on the east side of Highway 40, 1.2 km north of the Lineham Creek parking lot. Cross the road, hop the guardrail and descend grassy slopes to a wide trail heading north and arriving at the Highwood River within a few minutes. Hip waders are highly recommended, not only for the ford of the Highwood but also for the numerous creek crossings after. Ford the river and find the wide Loomis Creek Trail on the other side. Bike or hike the trail for approximately 1 km to where it crosses Loomis Creek, the first of five such crossings. Cross the creek and take the trail on the left as it heads uphill. About 100 m after the fourth crossing, the grassy and unsigned Bishop Creek Trail veers off to the left. Leave your bike here and start along Bishop Creek Trail, which almost immediately crosses Loomis Creek yet again (the last crossing of the day).

Follow the trail as it slowly gains elevation above Bishop Creek. Soon the view begins to open up, with Bishop Ridge in front and Mount Bishop to its left. Stay on the trail as it traverses the south slopes of Bishop Ridge. Before you know it, the daunting east face of Mount Bishop is right in front of you. Now you must swing left (south), over to the southeast side of the mountain. Lose a little elevation and then trudge up scree slopes to the shoulder. Now, looking at the southeast face of the mountain, it may appear that you can go straight up the ridge. Beware: much of the terrain on this slope is much steeper than it looks from afar and the rock is loose and downsloping. Therefore an easier route farther south and then west along the face is recommended.

Traverse scree slopes to the left around the south side of the mountain, looking up to your right for a distinctive band of rock that is the key to the ascent (see photo next page). After several hundred metres of traversing, head up to the left side of the rock band and an obvious weakness. Scramble easily up the weakness, arriving at a steeper band that doesn't look too bad but is more challenging than you might think. Descend left alongside the band to find a more feasible route up.

Once above this band, the terrain and route-finding become a little easier. Ascend the face, trending to the right as you go, always looking for the path of least resistance (moderate scrambling at most). If the rock is dry, more challenging routes with steep, hands-on scrambling are certainly feasible. Arrive at the ridge and plod to the summit a short distance away.

The view is splendid, even if you have completed nearby ascents of McPhail or Loomis, which lie respectively to the south and north. **Return** the same way. If by any chance you have 400 vertical metres of elevation left in you, head up scenic Bishop Ridge, directly east of Mount Bishop, on the way back. The ridge is home to some wonderful rock scenery and is a terrific viewpoint in itself.

Above: The southeast slopes and ascent route of Bishop from Loomis Creek Trail.
Below: The key rock band to look for: **R**.

78. MOUNT McPHAIL 2865 m

(MAP 19, PAGE 460)
Rating easy via the southeast ridge; moderate via south slopes
Round-trip time 8–11 hours, with bike approach; add 4 hours if also ascending Mount Muir
Elevation gain 1290 m
Maps 82 J/7 Mount Head; Gem Trek Highwood & Cataract Creek

Don't let a long bike approach deter you from attempting this beautiful mountain in wonderful sur-
roundings. Success may depend on the condition of the lengthy McPhail Creek trail and the water
level of the Highwood River, so don't try it too early. Inaccessible from December 1 to June 15. Try
from July on.

Park at the Cat Creek parking lot, 5.5 km north of the Highway 40/940 junction. Start from the northwest end of the lot, following a wide trail that parallels the Highwood River. Cross the Highwood at about the 2.3 km mark (hip waders are a luxury here, but runners will do) and continue on. Stay on the trail throughout or take the regular shortcuts to the left on more narrow trails to avoid excess elevation gains and losses. Hopefully, the trail will be dry and relatively easy to negotiate. If it is wet and muddy, though, the 10 km ride may well be the crux of the trip. After going more or less northwest, the trail eventually turns west, heading towards Mount McPhail. Don't change your footwear yet, as several streams interrupt the trail.

Eventually you will arrive at a headwall, with Mount McPhail to the right and Mount Muir to the left. Ditch your bike and start ascending the headwall to the right of the waterfall. If you have lost the trail, don't despair – you'll run into it as long as you are going up. At the top of the headwall is a shallow tarn, backdropped beautifully by Mount McPhail. If you're doing an overnighter, this would provide a great bivy site. The route up McPhail starts to be become obvious at this point and more so as you head farther west.

The fastest way up ascends scree slopes on the east side of the south face. Staying near the edge provides great views to the east. If you are looking for a more challenging route with hands-on scrambling, keep heading west and ascend the centre gully of the south face up numerous rock bands. If you arrive at a section that is too difficult, traverse right (east) towards easier terrain. The summit is at the top of the gully.

Hopefully you'll be blessed with clear skies to enjoy a magnificent summit panorama: Bishop and Loomis to the north, the Highwood Range to the east, the 11,000ers Joffre, King George and Harrison and a beautiful sea of Continental Divide peaks to the south. The entire route up Mount Muir is also plainly visible. The east side of the south face provides the fastest descent, and if snow conditions are good (assuming there is any snow) a long and exhilarating glissade may be possible. **Return** the same way.

The beautifully pyramidal form of Mount McPhail and the long route to get there via McPhail Creek.

Above: Approaching the headwall. **H**: headwall; **S**: summit.
Below: The south and southeast slopes. **S**: scramble route; **SE**: easier southeast route.

79. MOUNT MUIR 2743 m

(MAP 19, PAGE 460)
Rating easy via west slopes
Round-trip time 8–11 hours, with bike approach; add 4 hours if also ascending Mount McPhail
Elevation gain 1170 m
Maps 82 J/7 Mount Head; Gem Trek Highwood & Cataract Creek

Given the long approach, it is best to try and summit both McPhail and Muir in a single trip. This does make for a very long and strenuous day, and success may also depend on the negotiability of McPhail Creek Trail. Leave early. Inaccessible from December 1 to June 15. Try from July on.

Park at the Cat Creek parking lot and follow the approach directions for Mount McPhail (#78, page 246). At the tarn above the headwall, continue on the trail, heading southwest to the high point at Weary Creek Gap. Turn 90 degrees to the left and head up the wide and easy west ridge. The route curves a little to the south as you reach the false summit and then heads northeast to the true summit. **Return** the same way.

The west ridge ascent route of Muir as seen from the lower slope of McPhail. **S**: summit.

80. MOUNT STRACHAN 2682 m

(MAP 19, PAGE 460)
Rating easy via the south ridge
Round-trip time 8–11 hours (with bike approach)
Elevation gain 1120 m
Maps 82 J/7 Mount Head; Gem Trek Highwood & Cataract Creek

Even if you come up short of Mount Strachan's summit, this trip takes you, in exciting fashion, to the gorgeous blue waters of Carnarvon Lake. Consider the summit as icing on the cake. Strachan is a little lower than its neighbours but still sports a terrific view. Again the ascent involves a lengthy bike approach. Inaccessible from December 1 to June 15. Try from July on.

Park at the Cat Creek parking lot, 5.5 km north of the Highway 40/940 junction. Starting from the northwest end of the parking lot, bike or hike the wide trail that parallels the Highwood River. Cross

Approaching the headwall.

the Highwood at about the 2.3 km mark (hip waders keep you dry here, but runners will do) and continue on. Several hundred metres after crossing the river, take the left branch where the trail forks (the unmarked Carnarvon Lake Trail). The track goes down a hill, crosses a stream and then continues on a little to the right. This trail is popular with people on horseback, so please remember to get off your bike to pass or be passed; you never know when somebody's steed may be skittish about fast-moving bikes.

The trail forks again 2.9 km later. Take the right fork (marked with a cairn) and continue southwest for 4.5 km to the headwall. For cyclists, this part of the trail starts off okay, but several kilometres from the headwall it becomes steep and rocky. When this happens, it is best to ditch your bike and continue on foot.

Around the lake and up the southwest ridge.

The southwest ridge route.

At the headwall, enjoy the beautiful upper waterfall cascading down, and then ascend the headwall using the chains to the right of the fall. Continue easily to reach stunning Carnarvon Lake in minutes. Strachan is to your right, and the ascent route goes up the left skyline starting at the west end of the lake (see photo next page). From here, turn right and embark on an easy scree slog to the summit (hiking poles are useful here). Any route will do, but staying to the right will at least keep the lake within your field of vision for the longest amount of time. Also, the east face does have a few interesting pinnacles to admire. Near the top, the ridge turns to the west and the summit is reached shortly after.

On a clear day, the view boasts a couple of 11,000ers (Harrison and the southeast side of Joffre), plus Mount Abruzzi to the west and an unrestricted view of the entire Highwood Range.

Mount MacLaren lies to the south, while Muir and McPhail are immediately north. A quick stroll to the north summit of Strachan gives an even better view of Muir.

While it is tempting to continue north to Mount Muir, this requires a steep descent to the col on dangerously loose rubble. It also involves a very steep downclimb with few good holds. This route is not recommended. Another option is to descend almost all the way back to Carnarvon Lake, then turn north to gain the southwest ridge of Muir and continue to the summit. This route is not difficult, but it is lengthy and tedious and, again, is not recommended. The summit of Muir is best reached via the McPhail Creek approach. **Return** the same way, or head down rubble slopes towards the valley to the southwest pretty much at any place from the summit ridge. There are a few large towers of rock that are worth checking out on the southwest side of the mountain.

81. MOUNT MacLAREN 2840 m

(MAP 19, PAGE 460)
Rating easy via the northwest slopes and/or the northwest ridge
Round-trip time 8–11 hours
Elevation gain 1380 m
Maps 82 J/7 Mount Head; Gem Trek Highwood & Cataract Creek

Mount MacLaren shares a great deal in common with Mount Strachan. Notably the long approach, a scenic walk around stunning Carnarvon Lake, a tedious scree slog to the top and a similar summit view. Nevertheless, the trip is still very enjoyable and the comprehensive panorama from the 2840 m summit is excellent. Use a bike for the approach. Inaccessible from December 1 to June 15. Try from July on.

Follow the directions to Mount Strachan, #80, page 249. Upon reaching Carnarvon Lake, follow the trail around the north side of the lake and gain the upper bench above the west end of the lake. Two routes become very obvious from there.

Route 1: Easiest and quickest is to hike up the centre of the huge scree slope that trends southeastward. Put it in cruise control and follow the natural line of the slope to a small col between the

two unnamed peaks northwest of MacLaren. From the col the pyramid-shaped summit is visible to the southeast. Though it may be tempting to sideslope in order to avoid unnecessary elevation gains, the terrain is steeper than it looks and very tedious to traverse. In the end it is actually more work to sideslope than to gain the high point immediately above. Instead, follow the ridge to the unnamed high point immediately to the east.

At the east end of Carnarvon Lake, looking to the west end and the start of MacLaren's ascent route.

Top: The two ascent routes.
Bottom: Approaching the third high point. **HS**: higher, unnamed summit; **MS**: Mount Shankland.

Route 2: More scenic is to follow the ridge to the left (east) of the scree slope. The ridge is tedious at times, but the improving view will hopefully take your mind off that. Follow the ridge all the way up to the unnamed high point northwest of MacLaren's true summit.

For both routes: The unnamed high point is of comparable height to the summit of MacLaren, so take in the view here too. The remainder of the route is obvious. Hike southeast down to the col and then easily up to the summit. A minor rock band can be easily circumvented on the left side.

The view to the east, north and west is very similar to that of Mount Strachan. However, the interesting array of peaks immediately to the south really makes this a unique viewpoint. The pyramid-shaped forms of Cornwell and Courcelette, with rounded Mount Bolton in the foreground, are especially eye-catching. Unless you plan to head over to Mount Shankland, **return** the same way. Again, avoid the urge to sideslope to avoid the elevation gain back to the unnamed high point. If you ascended via the ridge, going down the centre may be a pleasant change. There is also another alternative descent route outlined in the Mount Shankland description just next, for those who wish to extend their day and enjoy more of this interesting area.

Mount Shankland
(difficult scrambling along the ridge)

The naming of this peak defies all logic, but an ascent route is given here for the sake of completeness and for those who are looking to add to their list of official peaks. Other than some interesting scrambling at the beginning, this mountain has very little to offer.

Return to the summit of the unnamed high point northwest of MacLaren and then head down to the next col to the west. Here's where the actual hands-on scrambling lies. Scramble directly up the ridge, tackling the first few rock bands head-on. You will encounter one or two difficult moves on each and a little exposure. One rock band requires a small traverse to the left, then up a weakness and back right, along a ledge. The next rock band after this is far more serious and again will require a traverse left around the side of the band until an easier route becomes visible. Scramble back up to the ridge and continue without much difficulty to the summit of this third high point of the day (so far!).

The ridge now splits, curving to the northwest and to the south. The alternative descent route mentioned above follows the northwest ridge. If, at this point, you decide to go home, hike along this ridge as Carnarvon Lake slowly comes into view again, beautifully backdropped by Mount Strachan. At the northwest end of the ridge, descend scree slopes to the left, and when possible curve back around to the right and make your way back to Carnarvon Lake.

If you've still got Shankland on the brain, from the third high point follow the ridge south and then up to what should be the official summit of Shankland but is not. As you gain elevation on an increasing variety of colourful rock, you may find it easier to swing out a little onto the west side of the mountain. Several times the top may appear to be near, but it's not. At the summit, rejoice in the sobering fact that this is not the summit! That honour goes to the lower peak to the southwest. What's more, you may not be too impressed by the summit view, although you do get a slightly different perspective of the group of mountains to the south.

Getting over to the true summit is the unpleasant crux of the trip. Descend large, loose boulders towards the col. **Extreme caution** is required here, as the rocks are unstable and can shift when you step on them. Drag yourself up to the summit and a somewhat anticlimactic view.

There are three options for getting back to Carnarvon Lake:

Route 1: *return the way you came.* This option is long and strenuous and will require extra care to reascend the false summit of Shankland and then go down to the col northwest of the unnamed high point northwest of MacLaren. In other words, it is not recommended.

Route 2: *return to the higher summit of Shankland and then go north towards the next high point.* Instead of going all the way to the high point, sideslope and gain the ridge northwest of the high point. Follow the ridge overlooking Carnarvon Lake to its end and then descend scree slopes to the left. When possible, curve back around to the right and make your way back to the lake. You can sideslope some of this route, but watch the stability of the rock underfoot.

Route 3: *the recommended route.* This way is mostly visible from the summit and makes a pleasant loop through the valley northwest of Shankland. Descend the northwest ridge of Shankland. Do not try to descend scree slopes to the right into the valley – there is an unseen cliff band below. Instead, keep following the ridge downward until you see a good trail coming from the left and leading down through trees to the right. This trail takes you into the valley, where you can follow the stream northwestward. Before getting too far down into the trees, turn north and hike through thin forest. If you are lucky, you will find another good trail that ascends the valley to a point west of Carnarvon Lake. The trail eventually crosses a creek, but you'll want to stay on the east side of the creek and make

The recommended descent route from Shankland. A scenic alternative, but it does have route-finding challenges.

your way north and then east to the lake. If you don't find the trail, the route is fairly obvious, as outlined above: north, then east.

For all routes, once you are back at Carnarvon Lake, **return** the same way you came.

NORTH KANANASKIS

The northern section of Kananaskis extends as far north as Canmore. Many of the peaks in this section are much closer to the road (primarily Highways 1, 40, 742 and Powderface Trail) and are therefore shorter and do not require the lengthy approaches of their southern counterparts. As well, these peaks are the most likely to be snow-free early in the season and benefit from chinooks at any time throughout the winter.

Again, the northern section of Kananaskis Country is thoroughly documented and described in the new volumes of Gillean Daffern's *Kananaskis Country Trail Guide*.

GEOLOGY

Not surprisingly, the geology of the north end of Kananaskis is very similar to that of south Kananaskis as described in the previous section. Though samples of good-quality limestone may be more prevalent in the north, the rock remains loose and largely unreliable. The west ridge of Mount Baldy's west peak is a notable exception, offering a difficult but very worthwhile scrambling experience on beautifully solid friction slabs. North Kananaskis is also home to one of the most striking and noticeable examples of rock folding in the Canadian Rockies. I imagine there are very few who have not looked with amazement at the obvious syncline (where the rock has been folded in a trough-like shape) on Mount Kidd's south face. This specific geological phenomenon is readily viewed when driving north on Highway 40.

ACCESS

From Calgary drive west on the Trans-Canada Highway. For access to peaks along the southern section of Powderface Trail and the Elbow Valley (Bryant, Howard, Seven Peaks, Threepoint and Rose), turn south onto Highway 22 and follow it to the town of Bragg Creek. Turn left at the four-way stop and then right onto Highway 66 when Highway 22 hits a T-intersection.

"Tiara Peak" is better accessed from the north section of Powderface Trail. From the Trans-Canada take the Sibbald Flats turnoff onto Highway 68. Drive west and turn left onto Powderface Trail.

As you continue along the Trans-Canada, the Highway 40 turnoff appears next and offers access to all the peaks along that road.

Shortly after the Highway 40 turnoff, the Highway 1x turnoff provides access to Wendell Mountain and the East Peak of Wendell Mountain.

For the remainder of the peaks along the Smith-Dorrien Trail (Highway 742), access is via Canmore for peaks at the north end of the road and via Highway 40 and the Kananaskis Lakes Trail turnoff for peaks at the south end.

ACCOMMODATION

The northern section of Kananaskis offers considerably more options for accommodation than south Kananaskis. Canmore is rife with motels, hotels and lodges. Deeper into the mountains, the three lodges at Kananaskis Village appeal to those who may be looking for a more luxurious place to stay. Of course, as hearty scramblers, you and your party may be searching for the best campground in the best location. There are several right around Canmore, and the Mount Kidd RV park, south on Highway 40, is very popular. Lakeshore campsites along the west side of Spray Lake take you away from the bustle of Canmore. Campgrounds at the Kananaskis Lakes lie in wonderful surroundings and seem more secluded, even though they are often relatively busy.

ELBOW VALLEY			
"Tiara Peak"	2533 m	easy/difficult	p. 258
Seven Peaks	2304–2626 m	easy/difficult	p. 260
Mount Bryant	2629 m	easy/difficult	p. 263
Mount Howard	2777 m	easy	p. 265
Threepoint Mountain	2595 m	easy/moderate	p. 268
Mount Rose	2550 m	easy	p. 271

A snowy descent on Threepoint Mountain.

These six peaks stand almost at the front of the Front Ranges and make great early or late season objectives. Four of them require a drive along Powderface Trail. When dry, this gravel road is easily negotiated, but it can be treacherous when icy. In those circumstances, a couple of steep hills may prove to be problematic, so the Powderface is best avoided. While the quickest driving route to "Tiara Peak" approaches from the north, Bryant, Howard, Seven Peaks, Threepoint and Rose are all accessed from Bragg Creek and Highway 66. The access roads to all four peaks are closed from December 1 to May 15.

82. "TIARA PEAK" 2533 m

(MAP 20, PAGE 461)

Rating easy via the north ridge and southwest slopes; very difficult shortcut is optional
Round-trip time 5–7 hours
Elevation gain 800 m
Maps 82 J/15 Bragg Creek; Gem Trek Canmore

Tiara Peak is the unofficial and descriptive name given to this summit that appropriately resembles a tiara when viewed from the north. There are plenty of routes to the summit, ranging from easy scrambling to class 4 climbing. The easiest route is recommended but the difficult shortcut is also included. Tiara can easily be combined with an ascent of Belmore Browne Peak. Inaccessible from December 1 to May 15. Try from mid-May on. Note that the trailhead is near a "14" marker and new logging roads have made the approach easier.

Drive to the Sibbald Flats turnoff and head south on Highway 68. At roughly the 23 km mark, turn left onto Powderface Trail and follow it for 14.7 km before parking at the side of the road. Hike back along the road about 200 m, looking for a trail on the west side. Follow the obvious path along a cutline and past a large cutblock. Eventually the trail crosses a creek and then parallels it on the left side. Hike alongside the creek for about 10 minutes and then move into the middle and boulder-hop your way up the creek until it forks. Both forks will eventually take you to Tiara Peak, but the right-hand one is best for ascent. The left one is a good option for a quick and easy descent.

Follow the right-hand fork until you get above treeline and the scree slopes of Belmore Browne become visible. At this point, if Belmore Browne is your destination, keep following the creek and up scree slopes to the ridge. Turn right and head up to the summit of Belmore. To get directly to Tiara, look to your left for steepish but easy slopes and head up to the ridge north of the peak. Ascend these slopes and turn left when you reach the ridge. A scenic ridgewalk follows and soon you'll arrive at the crown of Tiara Peak – a steep and daunting-looking rock band.

Traverse along the base of the east (left) side of the summit block, around its south end and then

The view from Powderface Trail. **BB**: Belmore Browne; **S**: summit of Tiara; **AD**: alternative descent.

Starting up the difficult route to the summit.

along the southwest side of the block. An easy route up soon reveals itself, though care should be exercised on the scree-on-slabs sections. Several cairns mark the route. **Return** the same way. Once back around the east side of the summit block, it is possible to descend east-facing slopes to a drainage below. Follow the drainage back to the original route.

Difficult route

This route provides direct access to the summit up a gully of about 70 vertical metres. The scrambling is at the difficult end of difficult and recommended only for those who are very confident on loose, exposed terrain that has very little in terms of good handholds. **Do not attempt** *this route if it is wet or snowy.*

From the summit block, traverse the base on the left side about 50 m to an obvious gully. This gully looks straightforward from below but is deceptively steep (see photo). As mentioned, good handholds are almost non-existent and therefore solid foot placements are essential, especially for the first 10 m. Getting up the first step is the crux of the gully. It can be tackled by going straight up or by ascending the left side and traversing right on very small ledges to a point above the step. For either route you are likely to feel uneasy on the precarious terrain. Above the first step, the terrain does improve marginally and handholds are readily available, although they should all be tested before committing any weight to them. Trend left as you ascend the gully and then go straight up to finish the ascent. The summit is metres away from the top of the gully. Descend via the easy route. Follow a trail that goes down and slightly left, looking for a cairn far below. Don't go too far left or you'll get cliffed out. At the cairn, the route starts curving around the base of the summit block on the west side. Gain elevation to the south end of the block; then either use the alternative descent route described below or continue to circumvent the summit block and return the way you came.

83. SEVEN PEAKS 2304–2626 m

(MAP 20, PAGE 461)
Rating mostly ridgewalking, with a few difficult steps
Round-trip time 10–12 hours for full loop; 4–10 hours for portion
Elevation gain 1400 m for full loop
Maps 82 J/14 Spray Lakes Reservoir, 82 J/15 Bragg Creek; Gem Trek Canmore

The seven peaks described here are those surrounding Upper Canyon Creek and Mount Bryant. The first four are clearly outlined in Mike Potter's terrific guidebook Ridgewalks in the Canadian Rockies. *The description below includes those summits and the remaining three. The trip is included here because of a few short sections of difficult scrambling necessary to complete the traverse of all seven summits. The scenery is interesting and the views change enough along the way to keep you entertained. The nice thing about this route is that at any part of the trip you can bail down easy scree slopes, choosing to ascend anywhere from one to seven high points. Try from June on.*

From Calgary, drive west on Trans-Canada (Highway 1) and turn south onto Highway 22. Follow the highway to Bragg Creek and turn left at the four-way stop (continuation of Highway 22). The highway ends in about 4 km and intersects Highway 66. Drive west on Highway 66 and turn off (actually the road just goes straight) onto

Powderface Trail. Continue for about 14 km and park in an open area where wide Canyon Creek meets the road (GR458419).

Hike along the wide, dried-up riverbed for about 25 minutes, looking for an obvious tributary coming in from the right. Follow this tributary for about 10 minutes. A steep rock band can

From the first summit, much of the first part of the loop is visible. **TP**: "Tiara Peak".

Some of the interesting rock formations. Note the one that looks like a dinosaur head.

be seen high on the slopes to your right. The goal is to bypass this band, going below it where it peters out. Ascend treed slopes towards the bottom of the band, go around it on the left side and continue up to reach the ridge. Follow the ridge to the first summit of the day, at GR435427, 2308 m.

The remainder of the trip simply involves following the ridge as it circles counterclockwise around Upper Canyon Creek and Bryant Lake. At almost any point, it is easy to descend scree slopes to your left and then follow drainages out to Canyon Creek.

Between peaks 2 and 3 there are some very interesting rock formations.

The ridge also gets interesting here, requiring route-finding and elevation losses on either side – first on the right side of the ridge, then on the left. If things get dicey, it is best to descend the left side to easier ground to circumvent the difficulties on the ridge itself. Gain the ridge at the low point between peaks 2 and 3 and continue to the top. Just before the summit, slabs appear and offer one of very few opportunities to actually scramble. Stay on the ridge and don't venture to the left onto more exposed terrain. Arriving at a short, steep step, downclimb the left side to scree and continue easily to the summit. It is possible to scramble directly up the step and avoid the scree, but most people will find this option too exposed and risky. A slip would send you hurtling down the mountain all the way to the bottom. Above this step, it's a pleasant scramble to the summit of 3.

There are no difficulties between peaks 3 and 4; it is from 4 to 5 that is the most challenging. Two rock bands bar the route. Both are circumvented around the left side. The first is easy and obvious, but the second requires more elevation loss. Scramble to the right up to the face of the steep band and then lose elevation to the left until it becomes easy to scramble over the ledgy terrain to scree slopes. Slog back up to the ridge and continue on to peak 5. There are cairns at two locations on 5. The cairns at the southernmost point designate the summit for the purposes of this description (GR396418, 2612 m).

From the summit of peak 5, Bryant Lake is

visible, and if you have never been to this beautiful tarn, it is worth a visit. But not before completing the rest of the traverse! If you've come this far, you might as well finish it off. The traverse to peak 6 is easy until a rock band rears up right before the summit. Scramble steep rock up the centre of the band. Terrain to the left is a little easier. This summit is the highest point of the trip. A slightly lower top a few hundred metres to the west is reached with minimal effort if you so choose.

Back at peak 6, decide whether you want to tag peak 7 and which descent route you wish to take. If you want to visit Bryant Lake, peak 7 is a mere formality and not really worth the effort unless you really want to. Return to the col between 5 and 6 and descend scree slopes to Bryant Lake, where you've definitely earned a relaxing rest beside the clear waters. Go around to the northeast side of the lake and follow a trail north, paralleling the creek emanating from the lake. The trail eventually leaves the creek and goes through forest before returning to the creek after it turns the corner heading northeast. Back at the creek, follow it out to Canyon Creek and back to your vehicle. Expect the return trip from peak 6 to your car to take 2.5–3.5 hours.

If you are on the slightly lower summit west of peak 6 and want to visit 7, sideslope on the south side of the ridge to the col between 6 and 7. If you are on summit of 6, downclimb the rock band you came up and then head down to the col. Easy scree slopes lead quickly to the summit of 7. For descent, either return to the col between 5 and 6 and follow the instructions above via Bryant Lake, or use the following alternative descent route.

From the summit of peak 7, head southwest down good scree slopes, staying relatively close to the ridge. Keep following these slopes as they gently curve to the right towards the drainage. Drop down into the drainage and follow it out. Several detours are required on the left side of the drainage as waterfalls and other steep sections come up. When the drainage intersects Canyon Creek, turn left (east) and walk about 5.5 km back to the parking lot. Again, expect to take 2.5–3.5 hours to complete this descent.

For reference, here are the GR numbers and heights of the Seven Peaks:

435427: 2308 m
430436: 2334 m
411445: 2501 m
409437: 2571 m
396418: 2612 m
394404: 2626 m
401402: 2613 m

The second half, and more challenging part, of the Seven Peaks loop. **BL**: Bryant Lake.

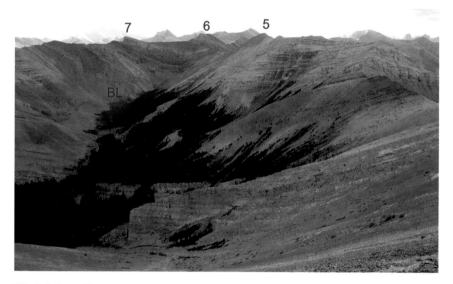

84. MOUNT BRYANT 2629 m

(MAP 20, PAGE 461)

Rating easy via northwest slopes; difficult traverse to the lower east summit
Round-trip time 6.5–8 hours
Elevation gain 900 m
Maps 82 J/14 Spray Lakes Reservoir, 82 J/15 Bragg Creek; Gem Trek Canmore and Bragg Creek

This mountain is the only one for which I recommend an easy route up and a more challenging way down. The day includes a visit to a beautiful tarn, a terrific summit view, a challenging traverse to the lower east summit and a very entertaining alternative descent route. As such, it's strongly recommended you wait for a clear day to make the attempt. Inaccessible from December 1 to May 15. Try from June on. Summit at GR412407.

From Calgary, drive west on Trans-Canada (Highway 1) and turn south onto Highway 22. Follow the highway to Bragg Creek and turn left at the four-way stop (continuation of Highway 22). The highway ends in about 4 km and intersects Highway 66. Drive west on Highway 66 and turn off (actually the road just goes straight) onto Powderface Trail. Continue for about 14 km and park in an open area where wide Canyon Creek meets the road (GR458419).

Hike along the wide, dried-up riverbed for about 25 minutes. Bryant is in front of you to the right. Look for an obvious tributary coming in from the right. This drainage wraps around Bryant and takes you to a tarn, from which the ascent is made. Hike up the tributary on the creekbed or on the trails alongside it. Stay left at all intersections. At GR412423 (marked with two large cairns and flagging on the left side of the creek), the trail ascends the steep left bank and then wanders through light forest before emerging on the open slopes of Bryant's northwest side. Continue traversing the slopes, eventually arriving at the clear and colourful waters of an unnamed tarn, referred to by some as Bryant Lake, for obvious reasons. Allow 2.5 hours to this point.

The remainder of the ascent is a less than inspiring slog up scree slopes on the east side of the tarn. Walk around the left side of the tarn for 100 m and turn left,

The east side of Mount Bryant as seen from Canyon Creek. **E**: east summit; **S**: true summit.

The east ridge descent route. **C**: scenic cliff bands; **P**: parking area; **M**: Moose Mountain.

aiming for the only rock band that stands in your way. Either go around the left side of the band or tackle it head-on to enjoy a few moves of hands-on scrambling. Unfortunately, the scrambling is over before it has begun and then it's loose scree and rubble all the way to the top – 500 vertical metres of it! The bright side is that, higher up, the view starts to open up with each step and suddenly an ocean of familiar peaks stands before you (actually behind you).

If you arrive at the summit under cloudy skies, you may start to wonder what prompted you to undertake this trip. If the weather is clear, though, enjoy a wonderful, peak-filled panorama. A fresh sprinkling of snow all around adds to the scenery dramatically.

Returning the same way is fine, but traversing over to the east summit and then down the east ridge makes for a very satisfying loop route and allows you to explore more of this interesting peak. Continue along the ridge heading east. There are a couple of narrow and mildly exposed sections. After ascending a wide ramp, the terrain suddenly becomes more serious. Here, either continue along the ridge, carefully downclimbing the exposed ridge, or downclimb to scree slopes on the right (easier, but still requiring care).

Unfortunately, regaining the ridge at this point quickly leads to additional steep terrain that will require a rope. Instead, descend a scree gully on the south side of the mountain until you can take a sharp left, traversing below vertical walls of rock on wide, scree-covered ledges. Continue below the cliffs but stay high. Circle around the impressive summit block and then gain the summit easily.

There are numerous descent options on the south side of the mountain from this summit, but the best one (though not the shortest) follows the east/northeast ridge most of the way. Head down the ridge, circumventing steeper sections or drop-offs on the right. Stay on the ridge as much as possible. You're aiming for the very obvious reddish-brown scree slopes that lead south to Canyon Creek. Once you hit the brown scree, continue almost to the end of it and then turn right and bomb down the scree, losing elevation at a tremendous rate. The scree soon runs out, but the terrain is still easy and enjoyable to descend. Aim for the drainage in the middle, but do not go into it. The last stunning piece of scenery will soon appear to your left, in the form of an enormous cliff band. After a quick visit, continue down, again on the left side of the drainage. Arrive back down at Canyon Creek, turn left and follow the creek for about 2.5 km back to your vehicle.

85. MOUNT HOWARD 2777 m

(MAP 20, PAGE 461)
Rating easy via the north ridge
Round-trip time 8–10 hours
Elevation gain 1040 m; more if you visit all the high points
Maps 82 J/15 Bragg Creek; Gem Trek Canmore and Bragg Creek

Mount Howard is an easy ascent from the north and a good late-season objective. The north ridge allows you to gain elevation quickly and then enjoy a terrific ridgewalk to the summit. Inaccessible from December 1 to May 15. Try from June on. Summit at GR419350.

From Calgary, drive west on the Trans-Canada (Highway 1) and turn south onto Highway 22. Follow 22 to Bragg Creek and turn left at the four-way stop (continuation of Highway 22). The highway ends in about 4 km and intersects Highway 66. Drive west on Highway 66 and turn off (actually the road just goes straight) onto Powderface Trail.

Hike southwest up Canyon Creek, passing Compression Ridge on your left and Mount Bryant on your right. At a leisurely pace you'll reach the start of Howard's north ridge in about 1.25–1.5 hours, beginning at GR422388 (see photo). The ridge rises immediately from the left side of Canyon Creek, gaining elevation through light

A beautiful, wintry day on Mount Bryant yields an excellent view of the north ridge ascent of Howard. **S**: summit; **G**: Mount Glasgow; **AD**: alternative descent.

Above: Start of the north ridge from Canyon Creek.
Below: The upper ridge. **S**: summit.

The recommended descent route is the rib at the lower right, **R**. Photo: Bob Spirko

forest. The terrain soon opens up and you'll arrive at the first of many high points along this scenic ridge.

You really can't go wrong once on the ridge. Follow it as it trends southwestward over a couple of high points and first turns southeast, then south and finally southeast to the summit. Staying on the ridge throughout and visiting every high point provides the best scenery and views, even though it entails more elevation gain and the requisite losses. Save the sidesloping for the descent.

The ridge is fairly long. Expect to take 4–5 hours from car to summit. Though higher than Mount Bryant to the north, the summit view from Howard is not as far-reaching. Nevertheless, it is nothing to sneeze at and includes great views towards the Twins (mounts Remus and Romulus), Glasgow, Fisher Peak and The Wedge, to name a few.

For the descent, start by **return**ing the same way. When you reach the high point north of the summit, either descend scree slopes into the valley and drainage to the northeast (the fastest route) or start heading east along the ridge that connects Howard to Compression Ridge. When you reach the last rib (ridge) before Compression Ridge (GR428363), turn left and descend the rib easily all the way to the valley bottom. This option allows you to stay high up and enjoy a little more of the beautiful surroundings. Both routes join up at a drainage that leads you back to Canyon Creek.

For those who have not completed the very enjoyable traverse of Compression Ridge, here's your chance to complete a long loop route and get two summits in one trip. Continue east along the connecting ridge to Compression Ridge. Alan Kane's *Scrambles in the Canadian Rockies* contains an excellent detailed description. Note that Compression Ridge is a difficult scramble and far more involved than the easy ascent of Mount Howard.

86. THREEPOINT MOUNTAIN 2595 m

(MAP 21, PAGE 461)
Rating easy/moderate via west slopes and northwest ridge
Round-trip time 9–13 hours
Elevation gain 1000 m
Maps 82 J/10 Mount Rae, 82 J/15 Bragg Creek; Gem Trek Bragg Creek

Visiting the three high points of Threepoint Mountain is a surprisingly enjoyable trip, with lots of scenic ridgewalking. A bike approach saves time, and an alternative descent route makes for a pleasant loop route. A terrific late season outing. Inaccessible from December 1 to May 15. Try from June on. Summit at GR534194.

From Calgary, drive west on the Trans-Canada (Highway 1) and turn south onto Highway 22. Follow 22 to Bragg Creek and turn left at the four-way stop (continuation of Highway 22). The highway ends in about 4 km and intersects Highway 66. Drive west on Highway 66 and turn left into the Elbow recreation area. Park at the second trailhead parking area, across from the big suspension bridge. Sometimes this road is closed, in which case park at the first trailhead parking area and hike west alongside the Elbow River a few hundred metres to the bridge. Cross the bridge and

hike or preferably bike Big Elbow Trail for 8.3 km to Big Elbow Campground. Continue along Big Elbow Trail for another 1 km or so, looking for a small drainage that comes down from the right (GR509207). This is where you'll want to head east to the Elbow River and find a place to cross.

Either boulder-hop or ford the river and continue east through the trees towards the right side of the west-facing ascent slopes (see photo). Pretty much any line of ascent will do here, but quickly you'll arrive at a rock band of crumbling shale. Ascend the band through one of numerous

The west side of Threepoint Mountain as seen from Cougar Mountain.

The ascent route from the Elbow River. There are several ways to get across the river and this is not one of them – I fell in while trying to place logs over the water!

weaknesses and continue up to a second and more vertical band. This one may require some route-finding to circumvent and a few steps of moderate scrambling. Traverse right for easier terrain.

Above the second band, a quick stint through trees followed by a longish scree slog leads easily to the ridge. Aim for the left side of the very prominent buttress at the top. This slope gets fairly steep higher up and would not be safe when the avalanche danger is above a rating of "low." Fortunately, its west-facing orientation means it will frequently get wind-blown free of snow.

At the impressive buttress, hike around to the left and then scramble up steeper rock to gain the ridge. An easier and faster (but less interesting route) traverses well below the ridge. Gain the ridge after circumventing the first major section. Once on the ridge, the route is straightforward, easy and scenic. Follow the ridge to the first of Threepoint's three high points and then continue south over the second and finally to the true summit at an elevation of 2595 m. Stay on the ridge throughout.

Needless to say, Threepoint is dwarfed by its neighbours to the west and south, but the view is satisfying nonetheless. Mount Rose is the slightly lower mountain connected to Threepoint. Unfortunately, a vertical rock band below the south-facing slopes of Threepoint renders a direct traverse to Rose impossible. Farther south,

Heading down the west ridge descent route. The snowy conditions made this a little trickier than it normally would be.

Bluerock Mountain and Mount Burns dominate the view. A route to Bluerock's summit is described in the fourth edition of Gillean Daffern's *Kananaskis Country Trail Guide, Volume 4*. Three Alan Kane scrambles from *Scrambling in the Canadian Rockies* (Cougar, Banded and Glasgow) line the southwest and west horizon.

The most enjoyable way off the mountain is the west ridge, though **return**ing the way you came does not present any difficulties. If snow remains on the west ridge, an ice axe, crampons and even a rope may be necessary. There are a couple of sections where the ridge is narrow and slipping down snow slopes on either side would have serious consequences. If the ridge is snow-free, it is a pleasant and easy hike. Simply follow the ridge down, taking the ridge on the right when it splits (see photo). One small rock band interrupts the ridge and can be carefully downclimbed head-on or circumvented on the left side.

Much lower down, stay near the edge as the ridge starts to curve left with an increasingly steep drop-off on your right. Hike through light forest down to the creek far below. Follow the creek out (easier above the bank on the right side) as it joins up with the Elbow River. Ford the river and continue west to find Big Elbow Trail and the easy route back to your vehicle.

87. MOUNT ROSE 2550 m

(MAP 21, PAGE 461)
Rating easy via the west ridge
Round-trip time 7–10 hours
Elevation gain 900 m
Maps 82 J/15 Bragg Creek, J/10 Mount Rae; Gem Trek Bragg Creek and Elbow Falls

This is an easy and relaxing day out, with pleasant scenery along the way. You won't get your name in the Canadian Alpine Journal *upon completing an ascent of Mount Rose, but it does make a great jaunt when a stress-free day is appealing. Definitely a trip where a bike approach is preferable. Try from June on.*

From Calgary, drive west on the Trans-Canada (Highway 1) and turn south onto Highway 22. Follow 22 to Bragg Creek and turn left at the four-way stop (continuation of Highway 22). The highway ends in about 4 km and intersects Highway 66. Drive west on Highway 66 and turn left into the Elbow recreation area. Park at the second trailhead parking area, across from the big suspension bridge. Sometimes this road is closed, in which

case park at the first trailhead parking area and hike west alongside the Elbow River a few hundred metres to the bridge. Cross the bridge and hike or preferably bike Big Elbow Trail for 9.9 km in total.

About 1.6 km after passing Big Elbow Campground, you cross the Elbow River on a bridge. Leave your bike after crossing the bridge. The crux of the trip now follows: finding the horse trail that runs alongside Cougar Creek. Bushwhack

Above the creek, the west ridge of Mount Rose is visible.

due east up and over small hills. You'll quickly arrive at a dried-up rocky drainage. Do NOT go up this drainage. Continue past it, still going east (northeast will get you there too) until you run into a well-defined trail on the west side of Cougar. If you have problems finding the trail, it starts at GR513201.

Turn right (southeast) and hike the trail up Cougar Creek. The trail, which stays in the trees for the first section, eventually descends to the creek. Follow along the right side of the creek until you are forced to cross it. Very shortly after, you will have to recross the creek back to the right (west) side to find the trail again. The trail then reenters the trees and soon descends again to the creek. Hike along the creek for several hundred metres until you see another creek coming down from the left (may be dry at certain times of the year). The intersection of these creeks lies at GR522181, 1822 m. It's this second creek, running east–west between Threepoint and Rose, that you'll be ascending alongside. Cross Cougar Creek.

The right (south) side of the second creek leads to the west ridge Mount Rose. From the intersection you can either follow the creekbed up interesting, slabby rock for several hundred metres and then gain the ridge above the right side of the creek, or simply cross to the right side immediately and ascend treed slopes paralleling the creek below. Either way, you'll eventually end up high above the creek with an open view to the east. The route soon becomes obvious. Follow the ridge and then bushwhack up through trees to the west ridge, characterized by orange-coloured shale. Follow the ridge easily to the summit.

The view probably won't knock your socks off, but the contrast of mountains to the west and green, rolling hills to the east is charming and serene. If satiated for the day, **return** the same way.

Potential extensions of the day are limited. A direct traverse to Threepoint is blocked by a vertical cliff band. Nevertheless, if you are in the mood for a little more, you can traverse the connecting ridge for a fair distance before being repelled. This requires you to lose elevation towards the drainage between the two peaks (Rose and Threepoint) and then swing around to the right to the connecting ridge. Follow it up to a high point and then towards the vertical cliff band. You'll have to **return** the same way, so turn around when you feel like it. This extension is simply for the exercise and to enjoy the scenery along the ridge. There really is no specific objective here. Do not try to descend into the drainage and follow it out – it leads to a dropoff. Instead, tramp back up to the summit of Rose, or sideslope to avoid too much elevation gain (this is usually self-defeating) and **return** the same way you came up.

EAST KANANASKIS

Good scrambling on Ribbon Peak.

The peaks in this section are definitely your best bet for year-round scrambling. Of course, any winter attempt at one of these will depend on having "no" or "low" avalanche potential, and crampons and an ice axe may be necessary. Approaches are generally short, which makes these summits ideal for the shorter days of the winter months. Wind Mountain and Ribbon Peak are the exceptions here, as they both have long approaches that would be extremely arduous in deep snow. Naturally, all the peaks in this section also make great summer objectives as well.

EAST KANANASKIS AND HIGHWAY 40			
Wendell Mountain East Peak	2294 m	easy/difficult	p. 275
Wendell Mountain	2360 m	moderate	p. 278
Mount McGillivray	2450 m	difficult	p. 280
Mount Baldy West Peak via West Ridge	2192 m	difficult	p. 282
"Mary Barclay's Mountain"	2250 m	moderate	p. 284
Mount Lorette	2487 m	moderate	p. 285
"Skogan Peak"	2662 m	moderate	p. 287

EAST KANANASKIS AND HIGHWAY 40

"Wasootch Peak"	2352 m	easy	p. 289
"Kananaskis Peak"	2419 m	difficult	p. 291
GR338442	2283 m	easy/moderate	p. 293
Old Baldy Mountain	2728 m	easy/moderate	p. 295
Mount McDougall	2726 m	moderate/difficult	p. 298
Wind Mountain	3108 m	moderate	p. 301
Ribbon Peak	2880 m	difficult	p. 303
"Mount Lillian" (via Upper Galatea Lake)	2890 m	moderate/difficult	p. 306
Limestone Mountain	2173 m	moderate	p. 309
Mount Denny	3000 m	moderate	p. 312
Mount Evan-Thomas	3090 m	difficult	p. 314
"Packenham Junior"	2300 m	easy	p. 316
"Mount Roberta"	2460 m	easy	p. 319
Mount Schlee	2850 m	moderate	p. 321

88. WENDELL MOUNTAIN EAST PEAK 2294 m

(MAP 22, PAGE 461)
Rating easy via the south ridge; difficult via col and the west ridge
Round-trip time 6–8 hours
Elevation gain 1200 m
Maps 82 O/3 Canmore

Many climbers will be quite familiar with this peak, as it is home to numerous rock routes. Fortunately for those without a technical-climbing background, there is an easy scramble route to the summit. To best enjoy the terrific rock scenery this trip has to offer, the "scenic" route is recommended. The "direct" route is ideal for the return trip. A far more challenging ascent route also exists and can be combined with the south ridge to complete a loop. Try from May on.

From the Highway 1X/1A intersection, drive 2 km east and turn left onto a gravel road that leads quickly to the Yamnuska parking lot. Starting at the far end of the parking lot, hike the trail as it crosses the maintenance road and then winds its way slowly up the hillside. At the sign, turn right and follow the hikers trail until it reaches the east ridge of Mount Yamnuska (about 1 hour). Decide which route you want to take.

Scenic route: Upon reaching the ridge, look for a clear spot to the right where you can see the objective to the northwest. Head downhill directly to the right side of the mountain. At the low point, continue uphill to the base of the stunning vertical walls of rock. Turn left and start a lengthy but thoroughly enjoyable traverse of the mountain's south face on a good scree trail.

Direct route: Upon reaching the ridge, continue heading west on the trail, looking through the trees for open slopes to your right. Once out in the open, descend grassy slopes heading directly for the west side of the objective.

East peak of Wendell from the east ridge of Mount Yamnuska. Note the location of the fascinating pinnacles, well worth a few extra metres of elevation gain. **SR**: scenic route; **DR**: direct route; **P**: pinnacles; **S**: summit.

Both routes join up at the west side of the east peak. Ascend scree slopes on the south ridge. Slabs to the right provide some relief from the scree. The route looks to be tricky and guarded by steep rock bands, but such is not the case and the scrambling should never be difficult. Route-find your way through the upper rock bands (trending left as necessary) and gain the upper south ridge. Turn left and hike easily to the summit. After taking in the beautiful contrast of rugged peaks to the west

Above: The south ridge of the east peak.
Below: Difficult route from the west side of the east peak. **C**: Wendell/East Peak col.

The tricky summit block from the west ridge of the east peak. Expect some route-finding and exposure.
C: crux; **S**: summit.

and flat prairies to the east, **return** the same way. Do not attempt to downclimb the west ridge and return via the "difficult" route. The downclimb is very steep and exposed, and route-finding will be extremely tricky throughout.

Difficult route via col and west ridge: This is a terrific route that, when combined with the easy descent via the south ridge, provides the most comprehensive experience of this interesting peak and outstanding area. Gain the west side of the peak via the "scenic" or "direct" route. Instead of going up the south ridge, traverse the west side of the mountain on an obvious scree trail. Eventually this trail ends as the steep walls of Wendell Mountain rear up to block the way. Look for the path of least resistance to the right, evident through a maze of rock bands and gullies. Moderate scrambling with a little route-finding will take you in short order to a scree slope that goes all the way to the col of Wendell Mountain and its east peak. As you make your way through the gullies and up the scree slopes, make sure to look back at your ascent route,

as it will appear quite different if you choose to return via this route.

At the col, turn right and follow the west ridge to the summit. The first pinnacle is obviously circumvented on the right side. After that, stay on the ridge until you arrive at steeper terrain that, again, must be circumvented. Lose elevation on the right, traverse south a little and then look for a way back to the ridge on the left side of the summit block. Choose your route carefully, as you may have to retreat this way if the crux is not to your liking. Back on the ridge, you are now confronted with the crux. Scramble very carefully up the steep and then narrow ridge. The rock is loose, so check all hand- and footholds carefully. If snow remains on any part of the ridge, a rope and climbing protection may be necessary – a slip down either side of the ridge would be fatal. Either **return** the same way (provided you feel comfortable downclimbing the crux) or descend the easy south ridge (do the south ridge route in reverse).

89. WENDELL MOUNTAIN 2360 m

(MAP 22, PAGE 461)
Rating moderate via west slopes
Round-trip time 7–10 hours
Elevation gain 1400 m (includes necessary losses)
Maps 82 O/3 Canmore

Wendell Mountain benefits from warm, chinook weather, and its Front Range location makes it an ideal "off-season" candidate. The west slopes can offer a snow-free ascent during any given month, though snow may persist in the sheltered valley. Try from April on or any time when reduced amounts of snow permit easy access and an easy ascent.

Park in the Yamnuska parking lot and follow the directions for the direct route for the east peak of Wendell Mountain. Upon reaching the valley bottom, turn left (west) and follow the open, grassy meadows and lightly forested terrain towards the west end of the valley. It is important to look up the valley to spot the correct drainage, which lies on the right side of the valley, below a distinctive cliff band coming down from the southwest side of Wendell (see top photo on next page).

Follow Old Fort Creek up the valley until you reach a drainage coming down from the right just below the cliff band. Turn up the drainage and follow it northwestward. Stay to the right when another tributary comes down from the left. Once out of the trees, the drainage widens and the scenery improves significantly. The beautiful friction slabs on the right look inviting but are quite steep and would best be ascended with a rope and protection. Continue up the drainage towards the obvious col in the distance. From this point on, it's a battle with treadmill scree all the way to the ridge.

The easiest route stays on the scree and then trends to the right to avoid a couple of pinnacles on the ridge. A slightly more interesting route goes more directly to the ridge and then heads east along the ridge to the summit. It is also possible to ascend slabby terrain to the right once you have gained some elevation. If you are going to tackle a more challenging line of ascent, be sure the terrain requires scrambling only, not technical climbing. Depending on where you reach the ridge, you may encounter a few moves of difficult scrambling with exposure along the ridge. Regardless of the route you take to the ridge, the final scree slog to the summit is short and easy.

The summit view includes the north side of Yamnuska to the south, Goat Mountain farther west, a host of unnamed summits to the west, northwest and north and Association Peak to the northeast. If you have already ascended it, the slightly lower east peak of Wendell to the east will be a familiar sight. **Return** the same way.

If you have the energy, a run up the east peak of Wendell Mountain will save you a return trip to the area to summit that peak. Take note, however, that this will bring your total elevation gain for the day close to 2000 metres. The final 200 metres of elevation back up to the Yamnuska shoulder, right near the end of the day, will more than likely be excruciating!

Above: The route up the valley. **C**: cliff band to watch for; **S**: summit.
Below: The route up the ascent drainage.

90. MOUNT McGILLIVRAY 2450 m

(MAP 23, PAGE 462)
Rating difficult via the west side
Round-trip time 8–11 hours
Elevation gain 1200 m
Maps 82 O/3 Canmore; Gem Trek Canmore

Lying immediately west of popular Heart Mountain, Mount McGillivray is a familiar peak when seen from the Trans-Canada Highway. Its prominent and distinctive north buttress is the key to this ascent. As a Front Range peak, McGillivray can be snow-free quite early in the season, but snow lining the exposed and narrow upper ridge can put a quick stop to a summit bid. Expect tons of annoying, sidesloping rubble on this trip. It will not win any awards for aesthetic trip of the year! Try from mid-May on.

Park in a small lot on the south side of the Trans-Canada Highway 3.4 km east of the Dead Man's Flats turnoff. Hike the old road for several hundred metres, looking a little to the left for the "hump" that starts the ascent. Turn left onto the Trans Canada Trail, arriving at a clearing on your right in a few minutes. Turn right, aiming for the treed hump in front and to the left of the visible and steep rock face. Initially, the slope is steep but eases soon after. Heading southeast, a long and gradual ascent through the trees follows. As long as you are going up, you can't go wrong.

Eventually, the terrain opens up and the north buttress becomes visible. Simply aim for the base of this buttress, climbing up open, shaley scree slopes through another stint of tress and then onto more scree. Allow 1.5–2 hours to get to this point. It is not necessary to ascend all the way to the base of the buttress. When feasible, start sidesloping the scree bowl towards a break in the far side. When far enough over, it is possible to scramble directly to the ridge, though the rock is very loose and caution is recommended. Probably better to simply go all the way to the far end, where only easy to moderate scrambling is involved.

Upon reaching the far end, decide whether you want to take the easy route to the summit ridge or the difficult one. Unless you are familiar with the easy route, it will be hard to find the easy way down if you take the difficult way up, so make sure you are comfortable downclimbing what you will upclimb via the difficult route. Regardless of which way you take, both will join up for the final push

to the summit, which is narrow and exposed and therefore rated difficult.

Easy route: Continue traversing west, below cliff bands of the second bowl, until an easy route to your left becomes visible. Turn left and ascend scree slopes, taking the path of least resistance. The route neatly works its way above a significant cliff band to the right. As you ascend, take careful note of the route and look back frequently to see how it looks from above; on descent, the route can be difficult to see. Once above the cliff band, the summit is visible to the right. Head directly for the summit ridge or up and to the right for a more direct line.

Difficult route: This route traverses a scree ledge between the two cliff bands of the second bowl. The crux is getting up to the ledge. Once around the south side of the first bowl, turn left and hike east to the base of the buttress. Scramble up an obvious, steep gully and then traverse right to gain the ledge. Traverse the ledge along the base of the upper rock band until you reach the end, where the rock band starts to breakdown. Look for a place to scramble up – some difficult scrambling here. Gain the upper slopes and head up to the ridge.

Summit ridge: Follow the ridge towards the summit. Take extra care on the narrow and exposed final 50 metres. Enjoy the front-row view of the four peaks of Mount Lougheed and Collembola before **returning** the same way you came up. Again, trying to find the easy route down (if you took the difficult one up) may prove to be arduous and time-consuming.

Above: Approaching the north buttress.
Below: The two routes to the ridge, along the second bowl. **D**: difficult route; **E**: easy route; **S**: summit.

91. MOUNT BALDY WEST PEAK via WEST RIDGE
2192 m

(MAP 23, PAGE 462)

Rating difficult and exposed; a climber's scramble (approach shoes recommended)
Round-trip time 4.5–6 hours
Elevation gain 825 m
Maps 82 J/14 Spray Lakes Reservoir, 82 O/3 Canmore; Gem Trek Canmore

If you've done Mount Baldy by the normal route, or you're looking for a shorter and more challeng-ing route to Baldy's west summit, you're in luck. The west ridge offers a short approach with difficult and interesting scrambling and some fairly intense exposure. This route must be snow- and ice-free. Try from mid-May on.

Drive about 14.1 km south on Highway 40 and park on the side of the road by an obvious, rubble-filled drainage (about 300 m south of O'Shaughnessy Falls). Although it is feasible to ascend treed slopes directly below the ridge, a well-worn trail farther north runs along the left side of the drainage and takes all the guesswork out of the first section. Follow this trail to treeline. If you really want to get your money's worth on the trip, ascend the actual drainage from the road, enjoying interest-ing scenery and moderate scrambling up a variety of good-quality rock. When the canyon gets too

difficult, find an escape route by ascending steep slopes on the left to gain the west ridge. Follow the ridge to treeline.

When the scrambling begins, the most excit-ing route follows the ridge throughout, though the first section circles to the left around a very steep slab. Often the ridge may appear to lead to steep drop-offs, but this is a facade and easier ter-rain awaits at the top of each section. The crux is a very steep-looking and narrow section that, again, appears to lead to a drop-off. That is not the case. Scramble carefully up the centre of the very

The ascent route from Highway 40. **D**: drainage; **S**: summit; **SD**: south ridge descent route.

exposed ridge onto a small plateau. A shorter, less steep section follows, but still a slip anywhere on the crux section would most likely be fatal. If the crux is not to your liking, downclimb to scree on the right side of the ridge just before the crux and then continue up scree or slabs to avoid the crux. After the crux, more enjoyable (and easier) scrambling leads to the summit ridge and then a pleasant stroll to the top.

Several options exist for descent. Avoid the tempting west-facing slopes immediately south of the ascent route. This terrain is steep and rubbly and requires much route-finding and detouring around steep drop-offs. Instead choose one of three options, from easiest to hardest:

1. Take the south and then southwest ridge of Baldy's west peak (recommended): From the summit, continue south down the ridge on a noticeable trail. The most exciting route stays on the sometimes airy ridgecrest throughout, but if you're not in the mood, a few mildly exposed sections can be avoided by dropping down to scree slopes to the right. Just before a multi-cairned high point of the south ridge, the ridge narrows considerably. If you're up for a little challenge (be ready for some serious exposure on the left side!), ascend a short but steep rock-step and then traverse the very narrow ridge. All but the most courageous and sure of balance will probably choose to bum-shuffle across this short section.

At the high point, trend to the right on a trail down towards the treed bump of the southwest ridge. Once past the rock outcrops, follow the treed ridge for about 15 minutes and then either turn left and descend slopes towards Baldy Pass Trail or turn right and descend slightly steeper slopes directly to the highway. If you go left, then upon reaching the trail, turn right and follow it out to the road. Then turn right again and walk along the highway for about 1 km to your vehicle. The route to the right of the ridge is shorter, but it is steeper at the top and not that much faster.

2. Use Alan Kane's route in reverse: Carefully downclimb the east face of the west peak and then continue down to the col between the west and south peaks. Turn left, descend scree slopes (possible glissade if there's enough snow) and follow the drainage out to the highway about 1 km north of your car.

3. Return the way you came: If at all uneasy about downclimbing what you have upclimbed, use one of the other alternative routes. Downclimbing the crux presents a considerable challenge and is not recommended.

Mark approaches the crux.

A close-up of the narrow and exposed crux.

92. "MARY BARCLAY'S MOUNTAIN" 2250 m

(MAP 23, PAGE 462)

Rating moderate via the south ridge, with mild exposure near top
Round-trip time 4.5–6 hours
Elevation gain 850 m
Maps 82 J/14 Spray Lakes Reservoir, 82 O/3 Canmore; Gem Trek Canmore

Provided the Kananaskis River is low enough to ford, the south ridge of unofficial "Mary Barclay's Mountain" is a scenic and interesting scramble. This trip makes for a great early-season warm-up. Try from May on.

Drive 17.5 km south on Highway 40 and park at the pull-off on the east side of the road right after the Wasootch Creek Bridge. Check out the ascent route as you hike along the mostly dried-up creekbed to the Kananaskis River. The objective is to gain the south ridge as soon as possible. Wade the river, provided it is low enough. If not, pick another trip or see the Mount Lorette description to find out how to circumvent the river crossing. After crossing the river, scramble up the steep embankment on the other side and hike through light forest to the start of the south ridge.

Follow the ridge in its entirety to the summit. Near the top the ridge gets steeper and narrows for a short section; use care on this mildly exposed terrain. The summit panorama is quite respectable, highlighting many familiar scrambles and other peaks.

For your descent, **return** the same way or, for a little variety, continue heading down the northwest ridge to a col and then left down easy slopes to the drainage. Follow the drainage out to the river.

The ascent and descent routes as seen from near Highway 40. **KR**: Kananaskis River; **S**: summit.

93. MOUNT LORETTE 2487 m

(MAP 23, PAGE 462)
Rating moderate via the south gully and the northeast ridge
Round-trip time 6–8 hours
Elevation gain 1100 m
Maps 82 J/14 Spray Lakes Reservoir; Gem Trek Canmore

The normal route up Mount Lorette is an airy and exposed class 5.4 climb via the south ridge. Although climbers sometimes do this route without a rope, several deaths have occurred there and it is therefore not recommended as a scramble. For experienced hikers and scramblers, the climber's descent route offers a much safer and easier route to the summit. Although this is little more than a steep hike, the scenery and summit view are enough to make it a worthwhile excursion. As well, the trip can be extended to a higher and unnamed peak to the north ("Skogan Peak") for a long but very rewarding day. Try from mid-May on.

Park on the west side of Highway 40, 19 km south of the Trans-Canada. From here, the initial part of the ascent route is very obvious and should be noted. Wade the frigid Kananaskis River, provided it is low enough to do so. Hip-waders are ideal for this trip, as you can put them on at your vehicle and then leave them on the other side of the river for the return ford. If the river is too high, pick another trip or continue driving south on Highway 40 and turn right at the Kananaskis Village turnoff. About 1 km along the road take your first right to a parking area. Hike or bike the Stoney Trail, heading north, for approximately 5 km. The ascent route will quickly become visible and obvious.

Back to the river crossing: once across, head west through light forest, eventually arriving at the wide open Stoney Trail, where you will be able to clearly see the ascent gully (take note of this gully,

The ascent route as seen from Highway 40. **KR**: Kananaskis River; **H**: first high point; **S**: summit.

in case you lose the trail). Hike north along the trail until you arrive at the top of a steep embankment. Turn left and continue on another trail that parallels the drainage. In a short time it becomes possible to head left through light forest to the ascent drainage or continue north until you reach the point where the drainage crosses Stoney Trail. Turn left up the drainage and look for a trail that runs along its left side. It will take you, without difficulty, all the way to a col that leads to the summit of Lorette (stay to the right when the grade becomes steeper before the col). Be patient – this gully is fairly foreshortened.

At the col, turn left (west) and make your way to a minor summit where you will be able to view the remainder of the route and another route towards the highest mount of the range, "Skogan Peak," at GR302516. At the high point, continue heading in a westerly direction and follow the ridge easily to the summit. The ridge is mildly exposed in a couple of sections, but these can be avoided on the right if necessary. On the way, the impressive, vertical east face of Lorette and a higher, unnamed peak to the north should be enough to keep you interested. After enjoying a very pleasant summit panorama, **return** the same way. Back at the first high point there is the option to continue on to "Skogan Peak" to the north (see the next trip).

94. "SKOGAN PEAK" 2662 m

(MAP 23, PAGE 462)
Rating moderate via the southeast ridge; some exposure
Round-trip time 9–11 hours
Elevation gain 1250 m
Maps 82 J/14 Spray Lakes Reservoir, 82 O/3 Canmore; Gem Trek Canmore

This is the highest point of the Lorette/McGillivray traverse, surpassing both mountains in height by a fair margin. It is also a terrific scramble. Though the scrambling is never too difficult, it is fairly exposed in places. Any snow remaining on the ridge would add considerable danger and push the ascent into the realm of mountaineering. Try from June on. Summit at GR302516.

See the route description for Mount Lorette, #93, page 285, and follow it up to the first high point. Continue north along the easy ridge, down and then up to the next high point. Here, the connecting ridge to the summit will be more clearly visible for assessment. Again, if snow remains on the ridge, this may be the end of the line. If not, start along the ridge, which soon narrows and becomes exposed on both sides. The first section of exposed scrambling can be avoided by dropping down to the left and traversing below it. Return to the ridge and continue on until the next narrow section. This one cannot be circumvented unless you lose a great amount of elevation. The best strategy for

this section is to traverse on small ledges on the left side of the ridge, just below it. This serves a dual purpose, as it will prevent you from seeing the butt-clenching drop on the right side!

Once across, scramble up the steeper rock face near the ridge and continue for a short while. Angled bands of rock now line the ridge, preventing further access along it. Start traversing left, going across successive gullies until the summit (actually a false summit) is in view. Be prepared for a few short but necessary elevation losses. Do not regain the ridge too early – you may be forced to retreat. When the false summit is visible, scramble up slabs and/or scree towards it.

The ascent route as seen from the first high point. **DS**: double summit.

Above: The ridge and upper slopes. **B**: bypass of first narrow section; **FS**: false summit; **TS**: true summit.
Below: On the ridge between Lorette and "Skogan." The Nakiska ski hill can be seen in the background, to the right.

At the false summit, descend to a col between it and the true summit and then continue easily up to the top. As the highest point of the massif, the summit offers a wonderful view. Looking down on Lorette to the south and McGillivray to the north should make you feel good about completing this trip, the longest and perhaps most challenging of the three. **Return** the same way. Tagging Mount Lorette on return will add about 1.5–2 hours and approximately 100 metres of elevation, but it will save you another ford of the Kananaskis River and the long trudge up the ascent gully.

95. "WASOOTCH PEAK" 2352 m

(MAP 24, PAGE 463)
Rating easy via southwest slopes
Round-trip time 3.5–5 hours
Elevation gain 900 m
Maps 82 J/14 Spray Lakes Reservoir; Gem Trek Canmore

There are at least four distinct routes to the summit of the unofficially named "Wasootch Peak": two from the Wasootch Creek side and two from the Highway 40 side. The route described below is the easiest one to the summit and is best combined with an ascent of "Kananaskis Peak" at GR345444. While "Wasootch Peak" is mostly a steep hike, "Kananaskis Peak" is a considerably more challenging undertaking, requiring steep and exposed scrambling. Given its easterly location, "Wasootch Peak" makes for a good early-season objective.

Park on the east side of Highway 40 a few hundred metres north of the Kananaskis Village turn-off. The wide swath of rock spilling down from the forest, courtesy of the 2013 floods, is a logical place to start. Ascend the easy terrain for about 5 minutes, staying near the left side. Look to the left for a large cairn (as of 2016) that marks the trail. Once you have found the trail, it is very easy to follow, paralleling the drainage for a while and then going up steeper terrain, high above the drainage. This trail pretty much leads all the way to the summit via the south ridge. Take an easy line up scree slopes or

The route to the south summit of "Wasootch Peak" from Highway 40.

Nicole Lisafeld and Michelle Marche enjoying the rewards of an early-season ascent: beautiful, snowy views in all directions.

explore the rock for a little hands-on scrambling. Enjoy the pleasant view and then decide where you want to go next. If home, **return** the same way. You can extend the trip slightly by following the ridge to the north to a slightly lower summit at GR333458, and given its close proximity, it is worth the minimal effort. A more serious and rewarding extension exists by heading south to "Kananaskis Peak" at GR345444 (see next trip).

96. "KANANASKIS PEAK" 2419 m

(MAP 24, PAGE 463)
Rating difficult via the north/northwest ridge; some exposure
Round-trip time 7–11 hours
Elevation gain 1290 m
Maps 82 J/14 Spray Lakes Reservoir; Gem Trek Canmore

Lying immediately south of "Wasootch Peak" at GR334455, "Kananaskis Peak," at GR345444, does not appear to be a significant summit when seen from the road. It is, however, the highest point of the north end of the Mount McDougall massif and has a beautifully scenic ridgewalk. An alternative descent route offers a very easy way off the mountain, although the 2013 flood may have rendered the lower part of the descent a little more difficult. Try from mid-May on.

Follow the directions to the summit of "Wasootch Peak," #95, page 289.

From the summit of "Wasootch," downclimb a short section to where a small rock outcrop blocks the route. Climb up and over the outcrop (there is some exposure, so use care), continue down to the low point and then up. The route is obvious. The crux follows shortly after. Upon arriving at a steep rock band that guards the upper slopes, trend right to find a weakness where the rock is the least steep. Even here, the rock is loose, downsloping and steep. If the scrambling exceeds your comfort level, turn back. Also consider that you must downclimb this section if you fail to reach the summit.

Continue up easier terrain, taking the path of least resistance. At one point you will come to

Ascent and descent routes from "Wasootch Peak." **S**: summit; **D**: descent route; **ED**: easy descent route.

Above: The crux.
Below: A terrific view to the north from the summit. The highest mountain in the distant centre is "Skogan Peak."

another outcrop barring the route. Circumvent this obstacle on the left side. The first summit follows shortly. Perhaps the most enjoyable section is the traverse from the first summit to the highest point of the trip, at GR345444. Stay on the ridge throughout and enjoy the beautiful scenery of slabby, vertical rock on your right. There are a couple of exposed sections you may want to bum-shuffle over. Expect approximately 30 minutes for the traverse.

At the summit, look back to see the long route you have just completed and get ready for a much easier descent. Continue heading north along the ridge (including one short, mildly exposed section) and then drop down to a small col on the right. From there, scree surf down the easy, north-facing slopes. At the bottom, follow the creek right back to your car. Again, note that the 2013 flood may have changed the landscape around the creek.

97. GR338442 2283 m

(MAP 24, PAGE 463)
Rating easy to moderate via west slopes
Round-trip time 6–10 hours
Elevation gain 830 m
Maps 82 J/14 Spray Lakes Reservoir; Gem Trek Canmore

An easy trip that won't get you to a significant summit but does offer magnificent rock scenery and the option to continue on to "Kananaskis Peak," at GR345444, where a loop route is possible. A good early-season trip to get you back in shape. An hour of gruelling bushwhacking is the crux of the route. In warm years, the ascent may be possible from mid-April on.

Start at the Highway 40 sign just north of the Kananaskis Village turnoff at a dry creekbed (GR316442). The peak is directly east; head straight for it. The bushwhacking ranges from moderate to downright nasty – persist; the effort will be worth it. A compass or GPS may be useful.

Once above treeline (approximately 1 hour), you are rewarded with the terrific and somewhat intimidating views of the peak's huge and nearly vertical walls. Not to worry – you won't have to climb any of them. Continue up to the first rock outcrop and go around it to the left. The route is quite obvious. With the exception of a short, steeper section right before the summit, the scrambling should never be too difficult. If you have the time, take the opportunity to explore some of the fascinating terrain on your way up (or down).

Just before the summit, the terrain becomes a little steeper but it never demands more than moderate scrambling. After enjoying the summit panorama, **return** the same way or continue eastward towards "Kananaskis Peak." This traverse requires a little more route-finding and scrambling than the ascent to GR338442, but it is enjoyable and quite easy. For the most part, it is possible to stay on the ridge. One steeper rock band about halfway across can be circumvented on the right, though this does require some elevation loss. The final push to the summit of GR345444 requires you to descend a little to a brown scree col and then follow the ridge as it curves up and to the left. The summit of GR345444 is only a few minutes away, but the ridge does narrow significantly right before the top.

The brown scree is also the key to the alternative

The ascent route from Highway 40.

descent and loop route. **Return** to the col and start down the scree slopes in a northerly direction. The scree is great for surfing and you should be able to lose a significant amount of elevation in a very short time. Once at the bottom, follow the creek back to your vehicle. Bear in mind that the 2013 flood may have changed the landscape around the creek, making the descent more difficult that it previously was.

Left: A small taste of the fantastic, vertically tilted rock characteristic of the ascent.
Below: The summit cairn at GR338442 and the first part of the route to the summit of "Kananaskis Peak," at GR345444.

98. OLD BALDY MOUNTAIN 2728 m

(MAP 24, PAGE 463)
Rating easy/moderate via the west ridge
Round-trip time 7–10 hours
Elevation gain 1280 m
Maps 82 J/14 Spray Lakes Reservoir; Gem Trek Canmore

One would think this peak, as the highest point of the massif, would deserve an official name. Such is not the case (at the time of writing anyway). Don't let this stop you from enjoying this easy and very scenic ascent. Problems are few and even if you don't make it all the way to the summit, Old Baldy ridge is a fine destination in itself. Try from June on.

There are two approaches to Old Baldy Ridge, where the ascent to the summit of Old Baldy Mountain starts:

Approach 1 (longer): Park in the Evan-Thomas lot on Highway 40 some 28 km south of the Trans-Canada Highway. Hike or bike approximately 1.8 km to a "TRAIL NOT MAINTAINED…" sign. Continue up the trail for several hundred metres to a path branching off to the left. Ignore this and continue down the main track for another 50 m to another left-branching trail. This is the one you want (GR325385). Follow this as it parallels McDougall Creek for about 10–15 minutes to where it forks (GR330384). Take the left fork, going uphill.

This trail gains some elevation above McDougall Creek, parallels it for a while, and then goes steeply uphill to the south end of Old Baldy Ridge. Keep following the trail to a huge boulder field. A string

The approximate ascent route as seen from Highway 40 at the Boundary Ranch turnoff.

Above: The west ridge as seen from Old Baldy ridge.
Below: The scenic jaunt along Old Baldy Ridge. **S**: summit of Old Baldy Mountain.

of cairns leads you to one end of the boulder field and up through it back to the ridge. Continue following the crest all the way to the top of Old Baldy Ridge. It's a long trudge, but views of the surrounding peaks and the lichen-covered vertical rock on the east side of the ridge keep you entertained.

Approach 2 (moderate): Park at Boundary Ranch, 25.8 km south of the Trans-Canada on Highway 40. Hike along a dirt road (horse trail) heading east until it curves south and eventually runs into Flat Creek. Turn left and follow the trail that parallels the creek on its north side. The trail may be overgrown and hard to find. It takes you up steep, treed slopes to the wonderful viewpoint of Old Baldy Ridge. From here you can see the remainder of the west ridge leading to the summit of Old Baldy Mountain.

From Old Baldy Ridge or the col, the route up Old Baldy Mountain is as easy and obvious as it looks. Gain the west ridge and stay on it until you get to the summit. Staying on or near the edge of the ridge offers the most scenic views, especially an impressive, nearly vertical slab about a third of the way up. Though initially steep, the grade eases in a short time, providing an easy and enjoyable ascent to the top.

The summit offers a splendid panorama in all directions. Of special note are the ridgewalks heading both north and south from the summit. If you are looking to nab the two highest peaks of the range, head south to Mount McDougall, again staying on the ridge throughout. It will take about an hour to get to McDougall's summit (see the Mount McDougall description, #99, next page, for descents off this peak). For the descent from "Old Baldy Mountain," **return** the same way you came up.

99. MOUNT McDOUGALL 2726 m

(MAP 24, PAGE 463)
Rating moderate/difficult via the southwest ridge
Round-trip time 7–11 hours
Elevation gain 1200 m
Maps 82 J/14 Spray Lakes Reservoir; Gem Trek Canmore

Mount McDougall is the only official peak of this massif, yet still sees very few visitors. The fairly lengthy approach and tedious slog to the ridge may have something to do with that. Once you get above treeline, however, the southwest ridge offers an interesting and enjoyable route to the summit. If snow remains on the route, an ice axe and crampons may be needed. Try from June on.

Park at the Evan-Thomas parking lot on Highway 40, 28 km south of the Trans-Canada highway. Hike Evan-Thomas Trail for approximately 1.8 km (take a left at the "TRAIL NOT MAINTAINED" sign). Several hundred metres after the sign, look for a small cairn on the left, just before a drainage crosses the trail. Turn left on the trail by the cairn – this is the unsigned Old Baldy Trail. Follow the trail through light forest for approximately 30 minutes as it parallels McDougall Creek. The ascent route is now to your right – look for

an open avalanche slope. At GR337388 (approximately), cross McDougall Creek and start up easy slopes, heading for the open area. Look for a boulder field. Ascend these tedious and foreshortened slopes to the ridge and turn left towards the volcano-shaped western outlier of McDougall. It is not necessary to ascend this outlier, but it does give you an excellent view of the remainder of the route and requires minimal effort. Besides, you may decide against completing the entire route, and the outlier does make a satisfying objective in itself. If you

Mount McDougall from Highway 40. **VP**: "Volcano Peak"; **S**: summit.

don't want to ascend the outlier, traverse around the peak on the south (right) side.

The summit of the outlier is a good place to take a break and survey the rest of the route as well as enjoy views of the surrounding peaks. The ascent up McDougall is quite obvious from this vantage point, although unseen are several drop-offs and narrow sections that add a little excitement. Also, the true summit is the peak on the left. Descend easily to the col and then make your way along the crest of the ridge, taking care on several narrow and mildly exposed sections. Most of the exposure can be avoided by dropping down to the right side of the ridge and traversing below.

Soon you arrive at another low col and the ridge widens considerably. Slog up the ridge until once again it narrows and you arrive at a steep drop-off. This is the crux. Though it is only about 5 m in height, downclimbing this crux will probably be beyond the comfort level of most people. It is much safer to descend slopes to your left and downclimb through one of several weaknesses in the rock band. Regain the ridge and continue on. A similar situation occurs a little farther on but is far less severe, so downclimbing that one should be

manageable. If not, again drop down to the left and find an easier route.

The lower, south summit is now only minutes away. An enjoyable ridgewalk leads easily to the true summit, farther north. If you have completed the Alan Kane scrambles in the area, the surrounding peaks should be very familiar. Mount Kidd dominates to the west, with Bogart and Sparrowhawk beyond. Also clearly visible are The Tower, Galatea, Gusty and The Fortress. Immediately north is the slightly higher "Old Baldy Mountain," at GR356417.

There are several options for descent:

Route 1: Return the same way.

Route 2: The easiest descent is to head down west-facing slopes directly below the summit. Trend left, aiming for the gully in the centre of the slope. Initially the grade is quite gentle, but it does get steeper lower down. At the bottom of the slope, follow McDougall Creek back to Old Baldy Trail;

Route 3: Continue heading northwest down the ridge. This route is entirely visible from the summit and curves around to the west before dropping down to McDougall Creek and out. Along the way you will encounter a small but exposed step that must be carefully downclimbed.

The upper slopes from just beyond "Volcano Peak." **S**: summit; **D**: suggested descent route.

100. THE BIG TRAVERSE
("WASOOTCH PEAK" to MOUNT McDOUGALL)

(MAP 24, PAGE 463)
Rating difficult
Round-trip time 12–16 hours
Elevation gain 1600 m
Maps 82 J/14 Spray Lakes Reservoir; Gem Trek Canmore

Instead of picking off the many high points of the Mount McDougall massif one or two at a time, as my brother and I did, it is possible to get them all in a single day. This is a very long and strenuous trip, though, entailing approximately 1600 metres of elevation gain and a tremendous amount of horizontal distance. As well, completing the entire circuit will leave you about 6 km from your car, so taking two cars or having a bike stashed at the other end will save you time and energy.

The traverse can be done in either direction, but north to south is preferable because most of the difficult sections will then be upclimbed and not downclimbed. A detailed description is pointless, as the ridge allows only one route. Basically, follow the route for "Wasootch Peak" and "Kananaskis Peak," then continue south along the ridge up to Old Baldy Mountain and then over to Mount McDougall. There are several exposed situations and you'll want snow-free conditions. If you decide to bail out somewhere along the line, the best bet is down the west ridge from Old Baldy Mountain or descend west-facing slopes just before reaching the top of Old Baldy. This second option means you'll have to reascend the east side of Old Baldy ridge, which probably defeats the purpose of bailing out!

Other suggested routes for the McDougall range:

"Wasootch Peak" and "Kananaskis Peak"
GR338442 and "Kananaskis Peak"
Mount McDougall and Old Baldy Mountain

From the summit of Old Baldy Mountain, the northern section of The Big Traverse. Photo: Zeljko Kozomara

101. WIND MOUNTAIN 3108 m

(MAP 25, PAGE 464)
Rating moderate via southwest slopes
Round-trip time 9–12 hours
Elevation gain 1630 m
Maps 82 J/14 Spray Lakes Reservoir; Gem Trek Canmore

Often referred to as the fourth peak of Mount Lougheed, Wind Mountain has an almost identical elevation to the summit of Lougheed, and, like its northern brother, rewards those who can handle the long approach and 1600+ m of elevation gain with a magnificent view. Try from July on. Summit at GR232462.

Note: The peak identified as Wind Mountain on the Gem-Trek map (2819 m) is the lower eastern outlier of the mountain described here.

Drive 23.4 km south on Highway 40 and turn right at the Kananaskis Village turn-off. Some 800 m farther, turn left, again towards Kananaskis Village, and then make a quick right into the Ribbon Creek parking lot. Drive to the end.

The 2013 floods radically changed the terrain around Ribbon Creek, completely destroying huge sections of the trail. Fortunately Alberta Parks has done a magnificent job of rebuilding the route and it is still easy to follow.

Hike the trail for 2.2 km, staying to the right at that point (the left fork goes down to the creek). About 10 minutes later (GR272432), look for a narrow but obvious trail that branches off to the right. Turn right onto the trail, paralleling North Ribbon Creek. In about an hour the track suddenly becomes very steep as it ascends alongside a nearby waterfall. Near the top of this steep section, a side trail appears on your right. Take this right fork as it gains elevation on the hillside and then turns north up the valley high above a creek. The trail eventually peters out but the route is obvious as you continue up the valley, with the imposing walls of

The two routes up Wind as seen from the south ridge. **S**: summit; **DR**: direct route; **SR**: scenic route.

Mount Sparrowhawk's east face to your left and the shapely form of Wind Mountain on the right.

Soon the terrain opens up and you have a decision to make: whether to take the direct route (moderate difficulty) or the scenic route (difficult). Most will want to take the direct route. The scenic route offers more variety and a better view, as well as more interesting, challenging and exposed scrambling. It does, however, require a fairly big elevation loss and will likely add at least an hour to your overall trip time. This route also offers other potentially more challenging routes up the face, but although the terrain may look straightforward, it is often deceptively steep and exposed and is therefore not recommended.

Direct route: Continue up the valley, aiming for the scree slopes in the middle of the southwest face of Wind Mountain. Ascend the left side of the scree ramp and make your way up easy terrain through the lower rock bands (moderate scrambling up one). Scenic and more significant rock bands soon rear up in front of you. Start angling right, following the line of scree towards the west ridge. Gain the west ridge and follow first a scree trail, then slabs to the summit.

Scenic route: Turn right (east) and make your way up to the south ridge of Wind Mountain. Follow the ridge, enjoying a few sections of scrambling on the way. When you arrive at a large and vertical rock band (clearly not scrambling terrain), traverse around its right side to find a steep, exposed upclimb that angles slightly left. Ascend this step carefully and then continue along the ridge to the next rock band, which again would require technical climbing. At this point, you have to lose elevation on the left side of the band, down scree and steep slabs. There are numerous points along the way where it appears to be feasible to ascend the band to easier terrain, though these only lead to steep and difficult terrain that most people would want a rope and protection for. To play it safe, descend all the way down to the scree slopes that join up with the direct route and then follow that way up. After losing all this elevation, you may question why you bothered with this diversion in the first place, but at least you got some good scrambling in and saw a good deal more of the mountain.

Return down the direct route.

102. RIBBON PEAK 2880 m

(MAP 25, PAGE 464)
Rating difficult, exposed scrambling via the south ridge
Round-trip time 9–13 hours
Elevation gain 1400 m
Maps 82 J/14 Spray Lakes Reservoir; Gem Trek Canmore

Ribbon Peak lives figuratively and literally in the shadow of much taller Mount Bogart. The two peaks blend so well together, one might have to look twice to discern the outline of Ribbon Peak when seen from Highway 40. The south ridge involves a lengthy and considerably exposed knife-edge ridge traverse. Though much of the exposure can be avoided, this trip is included only for experienced scramblers. Snow may persist in the sheltered valley of the Memorial Lakes. Try from mid-July on.

Note: Ribbon Peak is actually the summit identified as Mount Bogart on the old NTS maps (see map 25 on page 464).

Drive 23.4 km south on Highway 40 and turn right at the Kananaskis Village turn-off. Some 800 m farther, turn left, again towards Kananaskis Village, and then make a quick right into the Ribbon Creek parking lot. Drive to the end.

The 2013 floods radically changed the terrain around Ribbon Creek, completely destroying huge sections of the trail. Fortunately Alberta Parks has done a magnificent job of rebuilding the route and it is still easy to follow.

Hike the trail for 2.2 km, staying to the right at

that point (the left fork goes down to the creek). About 10 minutes later (GR272432), look for a narrow but obvious trail that branches off to the right. Turn right onto this trail, which soon parallels North Ribbon Creek. Hike the well-used track for 4.6 km, past the two lower Memorial Lakes and up to the third. Scope out Bogart's Tower looking down over the third lake as you pass by – you may want to run up it on the return trip.

From a scenic vantage point above the third lake, Mount Bogart dominates to the southwest and Ribbon Peak to the southeast. The first goal is to ascend the headwall. Traverse rubble slopes coming off Bogart towards the obvious rubble/

Ribbon Peak from above Third Memorial Lake. **S**: summit.

scree slope at the end of the valley. Once on this slope, you'll find the terrain to be steep and very unstable – be careful. At the top, work your way left onto a wide, downsloping scree ledge and continue traversing left. There are many places to overcome the first rock band above you, but the farther left you go, the easier it becomes. Still, you will be required to make a few steep moves, so you may as

well pick a challenging line. The premise of "difficult up, easy down" fits very well here. This will also grant you more hands-on scrambling, as opposed to the scree bashing farther left.

At the top of the headwall, hike south. The summit is actually directly to your left, and the huge slab that separates you from it may look tempting but it is far too steep near the top to

Top: Above the headwall, looking at the ascent/descent routes. **D**: difficult route; **E**: easier route.
Right: A closer look at the easier route up and down.

The striking form of Bogart Tower above the beautiful third Memorial Lake. Equally striking Ribbon Peak is at the right. **W**: west ridge; **S**: south ridge. Photo: Vern Dewit

scramble up. The most exciting (and recommended) route gains the ridge near its south end. Hike south, and when the terrain begins to drop, traverse left and up to gain the ridge. Turn north and follow the ridge to the summit. Along the way there are several sections where the ridge narrows to a knife-edge and exposure is considerable on both sides. Other sections can be avoided by dropping down to scree ledges on the left, but don't stray too far down and away from the ridge. Near the summit, the ridge widens, although you'll still want to tread carefully on a couple of short sections.

A shorter and easier (but less exciting) route gains the ridge earlier and hence avoids most of the exposed situations. Again, hike south from the top of the headwall, but don't go all the way to the end. Once past the major slab, look for a moderate route up to the ridge (see photo on previous page). You can zigzag your way up on scree ledges or tackle the slabs directly, but either way they are quite steep. On the ridge, turn north and follow the ridge to the summit (some exposure).

Even with Mount Bogart blocking almost the entire view to the west, the summit panorama is respectable, with unique views of Sparrowhawk, Wind, Kidd and little Bogart Tower below. **Return** the same way. If you took the "exciting" route up, the easier route down is the way to go. Descend the easy part of the ridge until you can see a way down to the right alongside a rock outcrop. Work your way down on scree ledges to the bottom and then back to the headwall.

Tagging Bogart Tower on the return trip requires minimal effort and is an interesting ascent. The summit view, however, is anticlimactic given that you can't see the Memorial Lakes below. Ascent routes exist via the south face, then the west ridge, or simply up the west ridge. Both involve moderate scrambling. Once back at Ribbon Creek Trail, head back to your car. If you biked the first part of the trip, you'll love the exhilarating ride back.

103. "MOUNT LILLIAN" (VIA UPPER GALATEA LAKE) 2890 m

(MAP 26, PAGE 464)
Rating moderate/difficult via the southwest face and west ridge, with some exposure
Round-trip time 9–12 hours
Elevation gain 1450 m (add 250 m to the GR)
Maps 82 J/14 Spray Lakes Reservoir; Gem Trek Canmore and Kananaskis Village

You are probably not alone if you have never heard of Mount Lillian. A brief description appears in David P. Jones's Rockies Central, *Volume 2, with John Martin having recorded the first ascent. You can ascend this peak from Buller Pass or via the Galatea Lakes. Both routes are described in this edition of* More Scrambles. *The Buller Pass route is shorter and easier. The Galatea Lakes route is quite long, but it is super scenic, especially on a clear day when the sun lights up the brilliant lakes. Although this route earns a rating of moderate because of the nature of the actual scrambling, it may "feel" difficult due to its length, steep scree and some narrow sections on the summit ridge. The reward is a mind-blowing summit view. Try from July on.*

Drive 33 km south on Highway 40 South and park at the Galatea parking lot, on the west side of the road. Hike down to the suspension bridge, cross the Kananaskis River and follow the trail signs to Lillian Lake (1.5–2 hours). From near the Lillian Lake campground, follow the signs to the Galatea lakes. As you approach Lower Galatea Lake, Mount Lillian appears in front and to the right. Hike around either side of the lower lake (the north side is slightly easier) and continue on the trail to Upper Galatea Lake. Allow 2.5–3 hours from the car to reach the upper lake.

Upon reaching the first viewpoint of the upper lake, leave the trail and gain the ridge to the right.

The two routes to the ridge. The summit is off to the right. **DRF**: distinctive rock formation – stay to the right of it.

Hike north to a point where the ascent route should become visible (see photo opposite). There are two ways to reach the ridge about 700 vertical metres above. Both will at some point involve steep, tiresome rubble and scree. The left route has better footing lower down but requires more traversing. The route on the right has some cool rock and water scenery and there are some fairly solid ribs you can scramble up to take a break from the rubble. However, the footing is generally more challenging and this line feels steeper. Pick your route and up you go. Perseverance is the key, as both routes are quite foreshortened. Expect to take 2 hours from Upper Galatea Lake to the ridge. At least the views of the lakes and surrounding mountains get better and better as you gain elevation.

If you chose the left-hand route, do not stay on the ridge when it forms higher up. Instead, go to the right side, below the ridge. Then traverse right, below a distinctive rock formation on the ridge. If you go to the left of this formation, you will get cliffed out and have to lose elevation to get around it.

For both routes the good news awaits at the ridge. Not only is the summit now only 10–15 minutes away, but the view completely opens up to the north and it is a fine one! Turn east and scramble towards the summit. The ridge feels narrow in places but is easy to negotiate when snow-free. If there is snow, an ice axe will definitely be handy.

Although the final push to the summit may look tricky, it's only a few moves of moderate scrambling, with some exposure. The summit is small, with room for only one or two people, but the view is outstanding – far better than you would think for a relatively obscure peak. A couple of the "giants," Assiniboine and Sir Douglas, are clearly visible. Closer at hand The Tower and Mount Galatea look awesome from this viewpoint, as does Red Peak to the north and Mount Bogart more northeast. Many other sights will hopefully impress. If you want to see both Galatea lakes, scramble carefully over the narrow ridge to the south (it's only a few metres, but very exposed on the right side). Return the same way. If you took the left route up, you could choose to take the right-hand (more easterly) one back down – it's scree all the way.

The scree ascent route up GR224359 and the return route back to Lillian Lake. **S**: summit.

Galatea Lakes

Once down the scree, circling both Galatea lakes is a great way to make the most of your trip, time and energy permitting. There is actually a sandy beach at the west end of the upper lake, as well as other interesting features. The south side of the lower lake offers fantastic views of the lake and Mount Lillian above.

GR224359, 2485 m

If you are *really* looking for the full-meal deal, run up this minor peak for a bird's-eye view of Lillian Lake to the east and Lost Lake to the south. The route is obvious (see photo on previous page), up a scree gully that lies to the right (west) of the high point. Use the rock on the left side of the gully for better footing in some sections. Like Mount Lillian, the scree is steepest near the top. Turn left (east) upon reaching the ridge and hike to the summit within minutes.

It does look possible to scramble up to the higher points to the west. Unfortunately, an untimely September blizzard while I was at the summit of the GR prevented me from checking this out. Return the way you came. The scree run down is excellent once you have descended past the steeper upper section. Follow one of several trails past the Lower Lake and then back down to Lillian Lake. Fortunately the long hike back to the car is mercifully easy.

104. LIMESTONE MOUNTAIN 2173 m

(MAP 24, PAGE 463)

Rating moderate via the south ridge; mild exposure
Round-trip time 3–7 hours
Elevation gain 580 m to Limestone; ~300 m for the extension
Maps 82 J/14 Spray Lakes Reservoir; Gem Trek Canmore

Limestone Mountain could very well be the least impressive-looking lump of rock called a summit in the area. However, if time and/or energy are lacking, or you are simply looking for a quick and easy ascent, the trip is worth the minimal effort required. Some enjoyable hands-on scrambling. Try from May on.

On Highway 40 some 34.6 km south of the Trans-Canada, park at the pull-off on the west side of the road immediately after the Rocky Creek bridge. The summit and ascent route (the right-hand skyline) are both visible from the road. Hike along the left side of the creek for a few hundred metres and then head up and into the trees on a decent trail. It is a good idea to take note of the creek's water level in case you want to use the alternative descent route, which will require low water. Continue heading northeast through light forest until you arrive at the south ridge.

Upon reaching the ridge, turn north and stay on the ridge for the remainder of the ascent, enjoying easy to moderate hands-on scrambling on good rock. The dramatic view of The Wedge improves

The south ridge. It may not look exciting from this angle, but there is some very pleasant scrambling about halfway up. **S**: summit of Limestone; **E**: extension.

Above: Nicole Lisafeld starts up a section of fun scrambling on the upper section of the ridge. Speedy Grant Colijn waits at the top for us.
Below: The extension.

as you gain elevation. Considering the very modest height of the mountain, the summit view is quite respectable: Mount Kidd, The Fortress, Opal Ridge and more are visible. Of particular interest, however, is the higher ridge to the east that leads to the impressively steep walls of the west face of The Wedge. Gaining that ridge is the logical extension of this trip.

If the extension isn't in your plans, **return** the same way. Though it is tempting to descend alongside a rock band that lies immediately west of the summit, the terrain is fairly steep and loose and is therefore not recommended.

The crux of the extension is getting down to the col. Go down the ascent route for a few metres, looking to your left for a weakness that can be downclimbed. Carefully downclimb and then continue heading east to the next rock band. Search for an obvious weakness through the rock band and descend (never more than moderate scrambling).

At the col, keep going in the same direction and aim for the ridge at its most northern point. Hike/scramble up scree-covered, slabby terrain, avoiding steeper sections by traversing right. When you reach the cairn, enjoy another pleasant view and then either **return** the same way or, better yet, start heading south along the ridge towards The Wedge. This ridge starts off tame, but it soon narrows and is fairly exposed in a couple of sections. Some of the exposure can be avoided by dropping down to the right side of the ridge, but staying on the ridge is definitely the most enjoyable route. One short downclimb is unavoidable and is seriously exposed for two or three moves. The ridge goes up and down for a fair distance before it widens under the steep north walls of The Wedge. Continuing up this formidable-looking rock band is possible, but the rock is extremely loose and the route is not recommended.

Depending on how far you get, it is possible to descend one of several gullies on your right (west) for a fast and more direct descent. Be sure of your intended route before you commit to it. If uncertain, **return** the way you came. It is not necessary to reascend Limestone Mountain, as the south slopes in between Limestone and the ridge you just ascended lead easily down to Rocky Creek and then back to Highway 40. Again, be sure you have checked the level of the creek on the way up before you take this alternative descent. On one occasion we almost had to reascend Limestone when we arrived at the creek to find it a raging torrent and completely unfordable – a fortuitously fallen tree allowed us to escape over to the other side of the creek.

105. MOUNT DENNY 3000 m

(MAP 27, PAGE 465)
Rating moderate via southwest slopes
Round-trip time 9–11 hours
Elevation gain 1340 m
Maps 82 J/14 Spray Lakes Reservoir; Gem Trek Kananaskis Lakes

Mount Denny is 100 vertical metres lower than nearby Evan-Thomas to the south but still has a wonderful summit panorama. The relatively easy-to-follow approach trail takes you into the beautiful and infrequently visited valley between Opal Ridge and the long, north-trending massif to the east. The slabby southwest face offers a decent dose of hands-on scrambling. Try from July on.

About 44 km south of the Trans-Canada on Highway 40 (2.5 km south of a gas station), park on the east side of the road where Grizzly Creek flows under it. A good trail heads up the valley on the north (left) bank of the creek. Follow it to some power lines and turn right. Follow that trail a short distance and then go left onto another that continues eastward up the valley. This trail takes you all the way into the scenic valley between Mount Potts and Mount Denny to the east and Opal Ridge to the west. The track generally stays high above the creek and is at times indistinct. Should you lose the trail, just ascend slopes until you find it again. Expect some minor scrambling to get over gullies. There are several animal trails that take you to the same place. Along the way enjoy some stunning examples of rock-folding on the north side of Grizzly Peak to the south.

Mount Potts soon becomes visible at the east end of the valley, with the rounded summit block of Mount Evan-Thomas farther south. Continue around the south side of Opal Ridge (a wonderful destination in itself if you don't feel like continuing on to Mount Denny) as it starts to curve north. Head up to the grassy plateau that marks the highest point of the valley. From this high point, the west ridge of Mount Denny is visible to the north, with the south summit just barely sticking over the top. Hike north down the valley towards the southwest side of the peak. A pleasant hike down the right side of the valley takes you there in no time. The double summit of the peak and another interesting display of rock-folding at the base of the mountain are good visual confirmations that you are in the right place (see top photo opposite). Allow 1.5–2 hours to reach this point.

Lose a little elevation and head up to the right side of the rock band that seems to bar access to the southwest slopes but doesn't really. Simply scramble up the first gully to the right of the band. Above the band, it's really up to you which route you take. The southwest slopes consist of slabby, often scree-covered terrain with a small drainage running down the middle. The best routes avoid the scree and seek out the sections of slab that are clean. Many of these slabs, however, are quite steep and you should be very careful in deciding which ones to tackle and which ones to avoid. The suggested route stays on the right side of the slopes. Here, the terrain is a little steeper but there is less scree. Still, thin layers of scree hide some of the slabs and care should be taken.

The two summits are within a couple of vertical metres of one another and both are worth a visit. Since the summit register is at the south peak, it is logical to head there first. Route-find your way towards the south summit or the col between the summits, depending on where you are ascending. From the bottom of the southwest slopes to the summit is about 600 vertical metres, so be prepared for a fairly lengthy ascent. Any snow on the slopes may increase your time a fair amount. If you top out on the ridge between the summits, turn south to reach the south summit in short order. Although this is not the highest peak in the area, the panorama still packs a real punch. On a clear day, the views in all directions are wonderful.

Once satiated, either return the same way or continue north to the second summit. The round-trip time to this peak is less than an hour and arguably the view is slightly better, so do your best to make the effort. It is possible to follow the ridge, but it does get exposed. Most people will want to drop down to the left side of the ridge on easier terrain. Descend to the low point and then traverse towards the scree ramp that leads easily to the summit. Highlights of the north summit panorama include Fisher Peak to the northeast, summits of

Elbow valley farther south, the north-trending continuation of the long ridge you're presently on, and of course several 11,000ers to the west.

To descend from the north summit, go down the scree ramp and then trend down and left towards your original ascent line. It is not really necessary to gain elevation back to where you came up unless no easy lines of descent are visible. Resist the urge to attempt alternative descent routes down obvious gullies on the south side of the peak. These gullies are filled with loose scree and rubble and they get dangerously steep near the bottom.

Left: The troops (Dan, Andrew and Troy) put on extra layers before starting the main ascent of Denny. **R:** rock band that only seems to bar the way; **N:** north summit; **S:** south summit. **Below:** Two routes to the north summit are possible from the south summit.

106. MOUNT EVAN-THOMAS 3090 m

(MAP 27, PAGE 465)
Rating difficult via southwest slopes and the west ridge
Round-trip time 8–11 hours
Elevation gain 1430 m
Maps 82 J/14 Spray Lakes Reservoir; Gem Trek Kananaskis Lakes

Even though it is the highest summit of the Opal Range, this mountain receives very little atten-
tion. The approach is scenic, the scrambling is straightforward and the summit view is fantastic. The
upper slopes and west ridge must be snow-free or else you may be in for a mountaineering trip. Try
from July on or whenever the upper slopes are snow-free.

This approach is the same as that for Grizzly Peak in Alan Kane's *Scrambles in the Canadian Rockies*. Park on the side of the road at Ripple Rock Creek (unsigned), 46 km south of the Trans-Canada on Highway 40 (1 km south of Grizzly Creek). On the north side of the creek, an obvious trail gains elevation before gently turning to parallel the creek, high above it. Gain elevation on the southwest side of Grizzly Peak. Stay on the well-trodden trail as it levels out and curves around Grizzly Peak. Soon Mount Evan-Thomas and shapely Mount Packenham, to the right of Evan-Thomas, appear at the east end of the valley. You now have to lose a little elevation down grassy slopes towards the usually dried-up creek below. Cross the creek and head up more grassy slopes up into the valley between Evan-Thomas and Packenham.

When the grassy slopes start to give way to rubble, it is best to move more to the right towards the centre of the valley instead of sidesloping. The ascent slope, on the left (north) side of the valley, is fairly obvious, as it is very wide and not terribly steep-looking. It is not the gully at the far end of the valley, but rather the one before that at GR341247, right before a buttress that sticks out of the southwest face. The wavy lines of rock created by geological folding are also a key visual clue (see photo next page).

Start the long trek up the face on scree slopes. Ascending scree-free ribs along the way helps ease the tedium. Be warned: this slope is very foreshortened. Aim for the low point on the west ridge. Also be aware that this crumbly face is subject to rockfall, especially when snow on the upper slopes is melting. A helmet is a good idea here.

Upon gaining the west ridge, check out the condition of the upper slopes and summit block to the east. Any snow may quickly turn this pleasant scramble into full-on mountaineering. Turn around if such is the case. If the summit block is dry, problems will be few, though the scrambling is steep and exposed in a few places.

Scramble east along the ridge. You may encounter some narrow sections, depending on where you gained the ridge. The terrain suddenly becomes steeper as you reach the summit block. Scramble up the centre or slightly left of centre, eventually arriving at even steeper terrain to your right. Fortunately, the scrambling to the left is much easier, and following an obvious gully in that direction leads to the summit ridge and a very short walk to the summit.

As this is the highest point in the general area, the summit panorama is, needless to say, impressive, including a great view of the west slopes of Mount Romulus and Fisher Peak, an intimidating look at the striking Mount Packenham and the connecting ridge to Evan-Thomas immediately south, and 11,000ers Assiniboine, King George, Joffre and Mount Harrison far to the south. Enjoy the view and then **return** the same way.

Above: The key ascent line to gain the west ridge. Missing this line may eventually put you on some very serious terrain!

Below: Starting up the west ridge to the summit block. Even the small amount of snow present on this October day turned the ascent into a fairly intense mountaineering trip.

107. "PACKENHAM JUNIOR" 2300 m

(MAP 27, PAGE 465)

Rating easy via the west face
Round-trip time 2–4 hours
Elevation gain 630 m (add about 200 m for the extension)
Maps 82 J/11 Kananaskis Lakes; Gem Trek Kananaskis Lakes

I was first introduced to this little gem of a peak by Calvin Damen, who also named it. It's a great trip for beginners and/or those looking for something quick and easy. Elevation gain is minimal, route-finding is straightforward, the trip amounts mostly to steep hiking, and the terrific summit view is a real bargain for the effort required to see it. The peak can also be a good off-season objective, although avalanche hazard may be a concern. Snowshoes, crampons, an ice axe and avalanche gear may be necessary for early season ascents. Try from June on.

Drive about 47 km south on Highway 40 to the Hood Creek bridge (1.9 km south of the Grizzly Creek turn-off). Park on the west side of the road, north of the newly installed guardrail, or on the east side of the road, south of the guardrail. From the bridge the summit of Packenham Junior is clearly visible, as should be much of the route. It's as easy as it looks – hug the south (right) side of the peak all the way to the summit.

Start the ascent on the north side of the Hood Creek bridge. Find the obvious trail that quickly rises above the canyon-like features of Hood Creek

The approximate ascent route as seen from near the bridge. **PJ**: "Packenham Junior"; **MP**: Mount Packenham.

Looking at the extension and the route up Mount Evan-Thomas (a separate trip, page 314), from the summit of Packenham Junior. **ET**: Mount Evan-Thomas; **E**: approximate end of the line for the extension; **MP**: Mount Packenham.

but generally parallels the creek. The track fades to nothing and then resumes, but even without a trail, route-finding is generally easy. There are a couple of places where faint paths split off to the right. Some of them lead down to Hood Creek – **not** where you want to go!

Continue up the side of the mountain, through stints of forested slopes and then more open terrain. Views start to improve as mounts Packenham and Hood suddenly become visible. Closer to the summit the terrain does get a little steeper, but it still amounts more to steep hiking than actual scrambling.

The summit is great, considering how little energy is required to get there. This is largely thanks to the wildly jagged contours of the fantastic Opal Range in front of you (east), stretching out to both north and south. Most distinctive is Mount Packenham to the east. The next peak to the north

is the "monarch" of the Opal Range – Mount Evan-Thomas, reaching to a superior height of 3097 m. The view to the south and southwest is likewise fantastic, highlights of which include the impressive multitude of peaks around the two Kananaskis Lakes and peaks of the Spray Range farther north.

Return the same way or, for more fun, complete the extension described below.

Extension

For those wanting a little more out of the day and an opportunity to get up close to Mount Packenham, this extension to the east is short, relatively easy and pleasantly scenic, adding a couple hundred metres of elevation gain.

Getting down to the col between Packenham Junior and the main bulk of Mount Packenham is the crux of the extension, but it still only amounts to easy/moderate scrambling with a wee bit of

An early-season ascent has snowy, scenic rewards of its own.

exposure (excuse my Scottish!). Start heading east and find a path that neatly winds its way down through the rock band. If you encounter any difficult and/or exposed scrambling, you are off route. Once below the rock band, continue east along the ridge towards Packenham, perhaps enjoying some exciting cornice scenery if it's early in the season.

You can go all the way to the first rock band, gaining a little elevation en route, where clearly the terrain moves into the "serious climbing" category. The steep gully off to the left (north) may look very tempting for continued progress up the peak, but it is steep and prone to rockfall and leads to dead ends – not recommended! Instead, enjoy the elevated views from the ridge and then return the way you came. **Do not** descend into Hood Creek. It is impassable and you will forced to reascend steep slopes back onto Packenham Junior.

108. "MOUNT ROBERTA" 2460 m

(MAP 28, PAGE 465)
Rating easy via the west face and south ridge
Round-trip time 3.5–5 hours; add 1.5–2 hours for the extension
Elevation gain 650 m; add approximately 100 m for the extension
Maps 82 J/11 Kananaskis Lakes; Gem Trek Kananaskis Lakes

"Mount Roberta" is merely the north end of Mount Pocaterra and hardly deserving of an official title (strangely, even Mount Pocaterra, the highest peak on the range, has yet to be officially named!). However, the ascent of Roberta is interesting and the summit view is fantastic and therefore the peak certainly deserves a few ascents. It's a relatively short trip with minimal elevation gain and good for days when time or energy may be in short supply. As with many peaks in the area, an ascent during larch season can make for a very visually rewarding day. Try from mid-June on. The peak is inaccessible from December 1 to June 15.

On Highway 40 South, drive approximately 9.5 km past the Kananaskis Lakes turn-off and take the unsigned but very obvious road on the west (right) side of the highway. Park off to the side, without blocking the usually locked barricade. Roberta is right in front of you.

Finding the correct ascent gully is fairly important. The gully eliminates a long and steep uphill bushwhack. Hike down the road and over the bridge spanning Pocaterra Creek. Continue following the wide road (ski trail in the winter), ignoring the signed hiking trail that branches off to the right. The road quickly turns south. About 15–20 minutes from your vehicle, look for a large drainage pipe going under the trail. Continue past the pipe for another 350 m or so, looking for a boulder about the size of a large microwave oven on the right side

of the trail (at approximately GR367108). The summit is barely visible through the trees, to the east. Also just visible is a significant wall of rock lying south of the summit. The col you are aiming for sits between the summit and the rock wall.

The boulder is as good a place as any to turn left (east) into the forest and bushwhack to the ascent gully. Trend slightly to the right as you go up. There is a fair amount of deadfall to climb over but nothing too challenging. You should reach the start of the ascent gully in about 15–20 minutes (approximately GR370106). Of course, you may have a search around a little for it. Just keep going up, looking for the open terrain around the gully.

Once you find the gully, route-finding should not be an issue. Simply follow the gully upward. Up high the aforementioned colourful rock wall

The objective as seen from the parking area. **RW**: important rock wall to aim for; **S**: summit.

Some of the ridgewalk to GR379101. **HP**: high point.

acts as a guide. You should be to the left (north) of the rock as you gain elevation. Another impressive landmark is a large triangular slab of rock protruding from the grassy slopes. From afar it doesn't look like much, but up close it is quite spectacular. Continue upward on increasingly steep slopes, past the triangular rock and then up even steeper, forested terrain to the col.

A lone tree sits at the col. Turn left (north) and hike/scramble easily to the summit, a few hundred horizontal and about 90 vertical metres away. For a peak that doesn't reach the 2500 m mark, this summit boasts a surprisingly excellent view, perhaps even better than several higher (and named) peaks in the area. The Kananaskis Lakes and surrounding mountains to the west are sublime, as is the magical form of Elpoca Mountain to the northeast. Peaks of the Misty Range (Kane scrambles all) stretch out to the southeast. The long crest directly southeast is Pocaterra Ridge, an excellent hike described by Gillean Daffern in volume 1 of her *Kananaskis Country Trail Guide* (4th ed.). Early in the season you'll see Rockfall Lake nestled between

Pocaterra Ridge and the steep east face of Mount Pocaterra; the lake usually dries up later in the year.

When satiated, return the same way or, for some extra exercise and even better views, consider completing the extension to the south as described next.

Extension to GR379101

A route description is hardly required here. Simply return to the col and then continue south along the ridge until you've had enough or you reach the high point at GR379101, 2520 m (see photo). As mentioned earlier, the view from this location is outstanding. Note how far below you to the southwest the Kananaskis fire lookout is.

Travelling farther south from this point gets pretty dicey and is not recommended. Furthermore, the true summit of Mount Pocaterra is a very long way off. That peak is best accessed via a traverse from Mount Tyrwhitt (Kane) or the east face of the actual mountain (also Kane). Return the same way.

109. MOUNT SCHLEE 2850 m

(MAP 28, PAGE 465)

Rating moderate via southeast slopes
Round-trip time 9–12 hours
Elevation gain Approximately 1000 m
Maps 82 J/11 Kananaskis Lakes; Gem Trek Kananaskis Lakes

Don't let the obscure nature of this peak deter you from making the trip. The approach is long but very scenic in places and the summit view is tremendous. Given that most of the surrounding peaks are technical, Schlee is a great way for scramblers to experience the south end of the magnificent Opal Range. The trailhead is far enough north that accessing it from the Trans-Canada and Highway 40 southbound may be a faster drive than coming up from the south. The area is inaccessible from December 1 to June 15. Try from June 16 on.

Drive south on Highway 40 to the Elbow Lake parking lot (12.3 km south of the Kananaskis Lakes/Kananaskis Trail junction). From the parking lot, hike or bike the wide, steep trail to Elbow Lake. Continue around the west side of the picturesque lake and cross its outlet over a small log bridge to another prominent, gravel trail (former road). Hike this trail north for about 2 km – it parallels the Elbow River and is therefore slightly downhill all the way. The strikingly beautiful form of Elpoca Mountain to the left is good company along the way.

The approximate route up as seen from near where you leave Little Elbow Trail to cross the Elbow River. **S**: summit of Schlee; **CE**: Cat's Ears.

Above: The route from near the point where you leave Piper Pass Trail.
Below: Not too far up the valley from the starting point for Mount Schlee lie the sublime meadows below Piper Pass. Rafal Kazmierczak and Kevin Barton hike towards Piper Pass en route to the north summit of Tombstone Mountain.

The goal (and sometimes crux of the trip) then becomes finding the terrific trail on the southwest side of Tombstone Mountain South. The water levels in the Elbow River and Piper Creek may dictate how difficult this is. If the Elbow is low (late in the season), it is best to leave Little Elbow Trail around GR413140, heading west, down to the river.

Cross the river and then turn north. Hike approximately 800 m over hills and through light forest to Piper Creek and find a place to cross. Continue north to eventually intercept the unofficial but prominent Piper Creek Trail. Once on this trail, follow it northwest towards Piper Pass (unseen at this point). Again, the impressive features of Elpoca Mountain will hopefully keep you entertained. Also impressive is the unique form of "Cat's Ears" at the end of the valley. The inconspicuous hump of rock to the left (southwest) of Cat's Ears is Mount Schlee (see photo on page 321) and the route up is obvious.

Hike up the valley until the trees start to clear around GR395163 (see top photo on facing page). At this point it becomes very easy to descend to and cross Piper Creek (see **Note** below). Do so and start going up Schlee, angling to the left to get around a buttress of rock right away. The route graciously reveals itself, providing a line of least resistance that initially trends to the left and then goes straight up. Pick a line that's to your liking and away you go. Slabs sometimes provide a better alternative to the loose scree. Higher up, the terrain does get a little steeper and a conservative line should be taken. Nevertheless, the scrambling should never break the moderate rating.

Contrary to appearances from below, the summit actually sits over to the right, and a short traverse to that point may be needed once you reach the ridge. The summit view is outstanding. If the daunting forms of Elpoca Mountain to the south and Mount Jerram to the north fail to impress, perhaps the Kananaskis Lakes to the west will. **Return** the same way.

Note: If you have never visited the open meadows immediately south of Piper Pass, this is one of the premier destinations in the southern Kananaskis. The colours and scenery on a clear summer day are absolutely wonderful and should not be missed. If time and energy permit, hike past Mount Schlee to take in the spectacle. Add an extra hour or two to the trip for this "must-do" diversion.

WEST KANANASKIS

Amid the exquisite environs west of Smuts Pass, the Birdwood Lakes lie below Mount Smuts on the way to "Smutwood Peak."

The mountains along Highway 742, also called the Smith-Dorrien Road, receive more snow than the peaks a little farther east along Highway 40. The scrambling season for these objectives is therefore likely to be shorter. These peaks also include some of the more "statuesque" ones in the book and offer outstanding summit panoramas. An easy, more direct and very scenic route up Mount Lougheed is the most significant addition to this section and is likely to become quite popular. "Smutwood Peak" does not boast Lougheed's lofty elevation but it more than makes up for that with incredible scenery and views.

WEST KANANASKIS AND HIGHWAY 742				
Mount Lougheed direct		3107 m	easy/moderate	p. 326
Mount Lougheed traverse		3107 m	difficult	p. 328
"Little Lougheed"		2483 m	moderate	p. 330
Mount Bogart (via west ridge)		3144 m	moderate/difficult	p. 333
"Buller Creek Peak"		2680 m	easy	p. 335
"Mount Lillian" (via Buller Pass)		2890 m	moderate/difficult	p. 337
Mount Fortune		2350 m	easy	p. 339
	"Fortulent Peak"	2520 m	easy	p. 340
Mount Turbulent		2850 m	easy	p. 341
"Smutwood Peak"		2690 m	easy	p. 343
"Headwall Peak"		3030 m	moderate/difficult	p. 345
Mount James Walker		3035 m	moderate	p. 347

WEST KANANASKIS AND HIGHWAY 742				
Kent Ridge – North Summit		2914 m	easy	p. 350
Mount Kent		2635 m	moderate	p. 352
Snow Peak		2789 m	easy	p. 355
"Piggy Plus"		2730 m	difficult	p. 357
Mount Worthington		2915 m	moderate	p. 359
"Rawson Lake Ridge"		2444 m	easy/difficult	p. 361

Mount Lougheed

The four peaks of Mount Lougheed are a classic Bow Valley landmark to those who regularly drive into the mountains. The summits of the first three can be reached from the west side of the mountain, while the fourth (Wind Mountain) is ascended from Ribbon Creek off Highway 40 south. The true summit of the massif is the second peak from the north. The views from the first and second peaks are tremendous, making this a must-do mountain in the area.

The first route described will probably become the most popular and it goes directly to the true summit. The ascent involves only easy to moderate scrambling and starts with a scenic hike into the sublime surroundings of upper Spencer Creek, a more than worthwhile destination in itself. Once at the top, there is the option to traverse over to the third peak.

The second route ascends the first peak and then traverses over to the second, with again the possibility of nabbing the third. This is a very difficult trek, with challenging route-finding and exposed scrambling on very steep terrain. It is a climber's scramble. This route will likely only appeal to those wanting to visit the impressive first peak.

110. MOUNT LOUGHEED DIRECT 3107 m

(MAP 25, PAGE 464)

Rating easy/moderate scrambling directly to the second peak (true summit) via south slopes
Round-trip time 6–9 hours
Elevation gain 1400 m
Maps 82 J/14 Spray Lakes Reservoir; Gem Trek Canmore

A terrific route up one of the most prominent mountains in Kananaskis. Try from July on.

On Highway 742, drive about 4.4 km south of the Driftwood turnoff to unsigned Spencer Creek (approximately 2.75 km north of the Sparrowhawk day use parking lot). A good trail near the north side of the creek heads east. Moss soon lines the trail and a very scenic brook springs suddenly from the ground. This is the first point of interest on this trip.

Continue on the trail as it parallels Spencer Creek, first at about the same level as the creek and then high above it for all but the last part of the approach. A brisk pace will get you into the upper valley in about 45 minutes to an hour. Escaping the forested slopes, the trail disappears and the scene opens up to a stunning valley: the huge vertical walls of Mount Sparrowhawk's north face to the right, the equally impressive and massive summit block of Lougheed to the left and Wind Mountain at the head of the valley.

At this point it is best to continue hiking up the valley, at the same time making your way to the right into Spencer Creek. The boulder-laden creek-bed soon gives way to a short section of fantastic water-worn slabs, the second point of interest and perhaps my favourite part of the trip (tied with the awesome summit view!). Farther up, a branch of the creek swings down from the left. This is the key to the ascent and you should turn left and go upslope (north) just before reaching the branch. At the top of this slope, the main ascent line comes into full view (see top photo next page).

Tramp up the scree, staying over to the left side. A decent trail makes travel a little easier if you can find it. At the top of the scree cone, the trail swings over to the right to get above most of the difficulties with ease. Atop this first section, keep going right to an obvious notch. The route here is easy throughout and should involve only a few moves of easy hands-on scrambling. Anything more and you are off route.

Above the notch, the rest of the route is visible. The easiest route ascends the ridge (north) for a few hundred metres before traversing rightward to the other ridge (east). Follow that ridge to a false summit, turn right and head easily over to the true summit.

Back to the notch, a more moderate route goes straight up the ridge to the westernmost point of the summit ridge. Some route-finding and scrambling are required, but the view over Spray Lake is fantastic at the top. Turn east and follow the ridge to the summit. The first part of this traverse has some exposure but is easily avoided on the right side if desired.

The summit view is comprehensive to say the least! A clear sky will grant you stellar views of pretty much everything in the Fisher Range, Kananaskis Range, Goat Range and the northern end of the Spray Mountains. A handful of 11,000ers are also easily spotted.

To **return**, descend the easy route described above (if you ascended the moderate route) and then the same way you came up. Alternatively, if you have extra time and energy, traverse over to the third peak of Lougheed and then use the descent route via the third/fourth (Wind Mountain) col. That route is described on page 328.

Above: The super-scenic upper section of Spencer Creek. **WM**: Wind Mountain.
Below: The main section of the ascent route. **MR**: moderate route; **ER**: easy route; **WE**: western end of the summit ridge; **FS**: false summit.

111. MOUNT LOUGHEED TRAVERSE 3107 m

(MAP 25, PAGE 464)
Rating difficult to the first peak; even more difficult to the true summit; a climber's scramble
Round-trip time 8–14 hours
Elevation gain 1400–1675 m
Maps 82 J/14 Spray Lakes Reservoir; Gem Trek Canmore

A very challenging route, for experienced scramblers only. Try from mid-July on if the slopes are snow-free.

On Highway 742, drive about 2 km south of the Driftwood turnoff to an obvious drainage about 4 km north of the Sparrowhawk day use parking lot. Hike up the drainage for about 45 minutes. When it splits, take the right fork and continue up the drainage. Eventually the drainage becomes overgrown with bush. Either circumvent this section on the right and then make your way back into the drainage, or ascend steepish slopes on the left, working your way up and to the right. Both routes end up in a bowl directly south of Lougheed's first peak.

The key to the ascent is the south ramp system. Ascend scree slopes heading north between two sets of cliff bands, staying left. Curve around the upper band. There is a more difficult but interesting route in between two prominent pinnacles (steep and exposed). Ascend this gully to a ledge, where an exposed traverse across a narrow ledge takes you to the top of a gully. An easier route goes around this pinnacle and then up an obvious gully on the right. Scramble up the ledges on the steep rock band to easier terrain.

Both routes then follow a string of cairns and the path of least resistance. A shorter rock band is the last obstacle before a scree trail leads you to the right, around to the upper west slopes. At this point the best route gains the west ridge as soon as possible and then follows it east to the summit. There is some mild exposure along the ridge.

If going up to the second peak (true summit) is not in your plans, **return** the same way. The route to the second peak simply follows the ridge until you approach the upper slopes, where it is easier to ascend the ones to the right of the ridge. Just before

the summit, a 4–5 m vertical rock band provides the crux. Ascend an easy gully to the base of the band (characterized by a scree ledge that runs up and to the east), and then climb up one of several weaknesses. All of these involve some lower class 5 moves and some people may feel a rope is necessary. A less steep but longer and more hazardous route descends the scree ledge to an obvious gully on the left. This gully appears to be quite gentle in grade, but it is long and extremely loose and gets steeper and more exposed near the top. Though time-consuming, it is strongly recommended that only one person be in this gully at a time due to the potential for serious rockfall. The summit is easily reached to the left of the top of the gully.

Enjoy a magnificent summit panorama. It is possible to descend southwest slopes from the true summit to the creek below, but a better option is to continue over to the third peak. Nothing but scree separates peak 2 from peak 3. Once at the lower third peak, which quite surprisingly also sports a terrific view, descend to the col between 3 and 4, staying near the ridge on the way there. Tramp down rubble slopes into the valley below. Head to the right side of the valley, where a watercourse soon becomes an interesting canyon. Follow easy slopes down to the valley floor and Spencer Creek. This valley, lying in the shadow of the incredible north face of Mount Sparrowhawk, is pristine and wild – do your best to keep it that way. Follow Spencer Creek out on the right side. Approximately 2 km from the highway, you will be able to ascend slopes to the right of the creek onto a good trail which takes you out to the road. Turn right and hike another 2 km back to your car.

Above: Ascent route from the upper bowl. **D**: difficult route; **E**: easier route.
Below: Route up second peak. **D**: two short, difficult routes; **G**: long, loose, steep gully.

112. "LITTLE LOUGHEED" 2483 m

(MAP 25, PAGE 464)
Rating moderate via the southwest ridge/slopes
Round-trip time 3.5–5 hours
Elevation gain 780 m
Maps 82 J /14 Spray Lakes Reservoir; Gem Trek Canmore

Little mountain, big views – if you are looking for a short, interesting trip with outstanding views, this is it! If you're lacking time or energy, this is a good consolation for Mount Lougheed. An alternative descent, with the potential to explore the upper reaches of extraordinary Spencer Creek, gives you options to extend the day. On a clear, calm day the view of Old Goat Mountain and Mount Nestor reflected in Spray Lake can be super cool. Try from June on.

The trip starts at Spencer Creek (not identified on some maps), about 2.8 km south of Spurling Creek, or 1.5 km north of the Sparrowhawk parking lot on the Smith-Dorrien Highway (see photo below). Hike east, up the trail on the north side of Spencer Creek. You will quickly arrive in a magical area where an underground stream appears, surrounded by vibrant green moss.

Continue past this section to a bridge that spans

Spencer Creek. Turn left onto the main trail, now called the High Rockies trail (watch for bikers). Follow this for about 5 minutes, gaining a little elevation. When the trail curves more dramatically to the north, leave it and go northeastward and up. Bushwhacking for the next stretch is fairly light, but the terrain does start to get steeper. Be sure you are going northeast and not just paralleling Spencer Creek in an easterly direction.

Several routes up Little Lougheed, as seen from the road. **BF**: Boulder field; **1ML**: first peak of Mount Lougheed; **LL**: Little Lougheed; **ML**: true summit of Mount Lougheed.

Above: A stunning view of Spray Lake. Perfect reflections in the lake are uncommon, but spectacular when they occur.

Below: Nicole Lisafeld checks out the airy terrain of the alternative descent route. Thankfully there is an easy way down this!

Depending on your specific route you will soon arrive at a huge boulder field or on slopes to the south (right) of the field. Either go straight up the boulders or gain the ridge on the right side. Both routes are fun and interesting. Above the boulder field, gain the ridge to the right (airy on the right side in some places) and simply follow it towards the summit block.

Nearing the summit, you can swing around to the left for the least steep route and then turn back to the right once on the ridge, or scramble more or less straight up to the summit, making a slight detour to the left along the way. The top lies at GR199469 and sports a fantastic view of mounts Lougheed and Sparrowhawk and of Spray Lake and the peaks surrounding it. Return the same way or take the alternative descent route described next.

The alternative descent is not a shortcut and it is not a cakewalk. However, it gives you opportunities to experience the cool rock scenery on the southwest side of the summit block and take a side trip up Spencer Creek if desired.

The route is steep and mildly exposed in a couple of places but obvious. Descend the west ridge towards the Little Lougheed/Mount Lougheed col until the terrain suddenly drops off. Take a sharp right and descend steep scree and loose rubble alongside the impressive and nearly vertical walls of the summit block. Be careful not to knock rocks down. Route-find your way down toward the valley below and Spencer Creek. The easiest route is consistently steep but should not require downclimbing or be exposed.

The Spencer Creek trail is relatively close to Spencer Creek, so keep an eye out for it as you near the stream. Turn right and follow the trail easily back to the highway. If you want to explore the upper section of Spencer Creek, turn left. It's up to you how far you go, but try to make it at least to the very interesting slabby terrain of the creekbed. Note that this valley is also the launching point for an ascent of Mount Lougheed (direct route, see page 326). Turn around when desired and hike back to the highway along Spencer Creek trail.

113. MOUNT BOGART 3144 m

(MAP 25, PAGE 464)
Rating moderate/difficult, depending on route, via the west ridge
Round-trip time 7–11 hours
Elevation gain 1400 m
Maps 82 J/14 Spray Lakes Reservoir; Gem Trek Canmore

The sheer height of Mount Bogart makes its summit one of the finest viewpoints in the north Kananaskis. The mountain is accessible from both east and west. The ascent from the west is shorter and has less elevation gain than the east route, but it still involves a good deal of annoying rubble. The ascent starting from Highway 742 via the mountain's west ridge is described here. Try from July on.

Note: Mount Bogart is incorrectly identified on the old NTS maps (see map 25 on page 464).

Park in the Sparrowhawk parking lot, approximately 26 km south of Canmore on Highway 742. Cross the highway and find the well-worn Sparrowhawk Tarns Trail. Hike the trail for 5.4 km to the Sparrowhawk Tarns (take the left fork at the

second intersection, about 20–25 minutes in). A couple of interesting boulder fields are thrown in for fun.

Upon reaching the tarns, work your way around them on the left side and head up the scree slope slightly to the left. Gain the ramp that leads to the col between Bogart's west ridge and an outlier of the unofficially named "Red Ridge" (see photo

The ascent route as seen when approaching Sparrowhawk Tarns. **T**: tarns; **C**: col; **S**: summit.

The ridge route to the top. **C**: crux; **ER**: easier route.

on page 333). Work your way up the ramp to the col, where the remainder of the route is visible (see photo above). Start up the ridge. Don't try to avoid elevation gains and losses by sidesloping on the right side of the ridge – the rubble is loose and unstable. Drop down to another col and then start up the ridge again, staying near the edge as much as possible.

Soon a very steep rock band blocks the way. The objective here is to head around the right side of the block and look for easier terrain to gain the ridge again. Depending on where you ascend, this may involve steep scrambling on exposed terrain. Use extreme caution here, as the slopes are often deceptively steep (especially near the top), and the holds are often loose. Double-check all holds and be sure you can downclimb what you go up. You will also want to take careful note of your route for the return journey; build a couple of cairns if necessary and dismantle them on return.

If gaining the ridge right away isn't to your liking, continue around the base of the block until you arrive at less steep terrain and ascend from there. Once back on the ridge, follow it easily to the summit. As well as taking in the far-reaching panorama, be sure to follow the northeast leg of the ridge for a few metres, where the beautiful Memorial Lakes become visible far below. **Return** the same way. If time permits, stop at the colourful upper Sparrowhawk Tarns for a well-deserved, relaxing and scenic break.

114. "BULLER CREEK PEAK" 2680 m

(MAP 26, PAGE 464)
Rating easy via the east ridge or south face
Round-trip time 5–7 hours
Elevation gain 1100 m
Maps 82 J/14 Spray Lakes Reservoir; Gem Trek Canmore and Kananaskis Village

If you have never experienced the pristine environs of Buller Creek and Buller Pass, then a trip up Buller Creek Peak is a terrific and easy way to do so. Though not as quite as eye-popping as the view from nearby "Mount Lillian" (next description), the summit vista here is still excellent. This trip can be done in conjunction with Mount Lillian, as a stand-alone trip or as a consolation if Mount Lillian is not in shape. Try from July on.

Drive south on Highway 742 and park at the Buller Mountain lot on the west side of the road, near the south end of Spray Lake. Hike back to the road, cross it and find the Buller Pass trailhead on the east side of the road. Within 10 minutes the trail drops down to Buller Creek and crosses to the north side of the creek. Right after the bridge, take a sharp right turn uphill to continue on Buller Pass Trail. The new trail going north is the multi-purpose High Rockies Trail.

About 3 km farther up the valley, around GR191382, right after the fourth bridge crossing of the day, the trail forks. Take the right-hand fork to Buller Pass. The left one goes to North Buller Pass.

Some of the interesting scenery along the Buller Pass trail. **BC**: route up Buller Creek Peak; **U**: unnamed peak; **BP**: Buller Pass; **ML**: route up Mount Lillian.

The route to the col from Buller Pass Trail. **C**: col; **U**: unnamed peak.

The scenery soon starts to open up. Buller Pass will eventually appear, due east, while Buller Creek Peak is the huge mass right in front of you to the north. Mount Lillian lines the valley on its south side. There are many ways to get to the top of Buller Creek Peak, but the suggested route, though a little longer, takes full advantage of the awesome trail.

Continue up the valley, passing by Buller Creek Peak to your left. The col between the objective and the unnamed peak to the east soon becomes obvious. When the trail starts to swing to the right towards Buller Pass, leave it and make your way up to the col (see photo).

From the col, ascend the east ridge to the summit. There are two summits of approximately equal height and both are worth a visit. The second requires a few scrambling moves but nothing serious. The summit view is surprisingly good, given the relatively low elevation of the summit. Highlights include Bogart, Red Peak, the two Kidd summits, Lillian, Galatea, The Tower, Engadine, Mount Buller and Mount Assiniboine in the distance.

After enjoying the summit view, return the same way or take a more direct route back down to the trail by descending south from the summit. Get back on the Buller Pass trail and return to the highway.

115. "MOUNT LILLIAN" (via BULLER PASS) 2890 m

(MAP 26, PAGE 464)
Rating moderate/difficult via the north face, with some exposure
Round-trip time 6–9 hours
Elevation gain 1100 m
Maps 82 J/14 Spray Lakes Reservoir; Gem Trek Canmore and Kananaskis Village

This is the shorter and easier but no less scenic route up Mount Lillian. See Mount Lillian via the Galatea Lakes on page 306. The first part of the scramble, along Buller Pass Trail, makes this a win-win trip: an easy and scenic approach followed by a spectacular summit view. The only challenges will be the 420 vertical metres of rubble and scree that separate Buller Pass from the ridge, plus a few moves of steep, exposed scrambling right before the summit. Try from July on.

Drive south on Highway 742 and park in the Buller Mountain lot on the west side of the road, near the south end of Spray Lake. Hike back to the road, cross it and find the Buller Pass trailhead on the east side of the road. Within 10 minutes the trail drops down to Buller Creek and crosses to the north side. Right after the bridge, take a sharp right turn uphill to continue on Buller Pass Trail. The new trail going north is the High Rockies Trail.

About 3 km farther up the valley, around GR191382, right after the fourth bridge crossing of the day, the trail forks. Take the right-hand fork to Buller Pass. The left one goes to North Buller Pass.

The scenery soon starts to open up. Buller Pass

The ascent ridge of Lillian as seen from Buller Pass. The early-season snow made the summit block (not visible here) feel quite challenging, but the descent was almost effortless! **S**: summit.

Just before tackling the summit block, you get this stunning view. The two Galatea Lakes are far below. The shapely, snowy ridge on the right is part of the Mount Lillian route from Upper Galatea Lake. Mount Galatea (centre) and The Tower (right) frame distant Mount Sir Douglas.

will eventually appear, due east, while Mount Lillian lines the valley on its south side. The summit on the north side is the unofficial "Buller Creek Peak," which can be ascended separately as part of this trip (see photo in previous trip, page 335). From the intersection it is 2.6 km of scenic hiking to Buller Pass, where a stunning view to the east awaits. Be sure to go far enough eastward to see Ribbon Lake, tucked in below South Kidd.

From Buller Pass the route to the summit of Mount Lillian is clear. Turn south and hike/grovel up about 400 vertical metres of steep rubble and scree towards the summit block (see photo). For the best views along the way, stay to the left side, near the edge. Once you reach the ridge the summit is only a few minutes away to the east. The only scrambling occurs right near the top, with a couple of moderate but exposed moves. When snowy this section will likely require crampons and an ice axe and may feel "exhilarating"!

Expect to be floored by the summit view. The Tower and Mount Galatea are awe-inspiring from this angle, as are the two peaks of Mount Kidd to the east and Mount Bogart to the northeast. If you want to see both of the gorgeous Galatea Lakes, a very short but exposed traverse onto an outcrop of rock to the south is required. Return the same way.

"BULLER CREEK PEAK" 2680 M

If you want to nab this minor but interesting summit on the way down, it's only a few hundred metres of extra elevation gain. Needless to say, the summit view is not quite as breathtaking as that from Mount Lillian, but it is unique and very satisfying nonetheless.

Again the route is obvious and straightforward. From Buller Pass, sideslope to the col between Buller Creek Peak and the unnamed peak east of the objective. Ascend the east ridge to the summit. A few scrambling moves are required but nothing serious.

After enjoying the summit view, return the same way or take a more direct route back down to the trail by descending south from the summit. Get back on the Buller Pass trail and return to the highway.

116. MOUNT FORTUNE 2350 m
and "FORTULENT PEAK" 2520 m

(MAP 29, PAGE 465)
Rating easy; mostly hiking
Round-trip time 8–11 hours
Elevation gain 700 m to Fortune, add 250 m for "Fortulent"
Maps 82 J/14 Spray Lake Reservoir; Gem Trek Canmore

Mount Fortune and "Fortulent Peak" are probably best done in the winter, when you can ski, snow-shoe or walk across a frozen Spray Lake. Nevertheless, the view from both is excellent and therefore worthy of ascent at any time of year, and the bike approach around the lake is actually faster than skiing across it. Expect a fairly long day with minimal scrambling. A bike approach is strongly recommended and in fact essential if you plan on continuing over to Mount Turbulent. Try from July on.

Drive south on Highway 742 and turn right at the Mount Shark/Engadine Lodge turnoff. Continue to the end of the road and park in the Mount Shark lot. Follow the signs to Watridge Lake, but instead of turning left down to the lake, keep going straight. Shortly after, you will start losing a significant amount of elevation – great on the way there, but you won't be smiling on the return trip! Bike over a bridge that crosses the Spray River, continue for a short distance and then bike over another bridge crossing Bryant Creek. Right after the second bridge, the trail forks at a sign. Take the right (Canyon Dam) fork and bike approximately 3.5 km to a bridge over Turbulent Creek. Cross the bridge

and continue for about another 800 m, looking left for a good place to start the ascent of the south/southwest face.

Head up the south/southwest face through light bush to more-open slopes. Continue upward, either taking the line of least resistance (steep hiking) or going farther right to some interesting rock bands. There is an opportunity here to do some hands-on scrambling, but most people will just gain the south ridge as soon as possible. Atop the ridge, it is an easy and scenic walk to the summit of Mount Fortune. The massive form of Cone Mountain lies to the west.

For a peak with a lowly elevation of 2350 m, the

The south side of Mount Fortune and ascent route up the southwest side. **S**: summit.

The straightforward route to "Fortulent" and its twin peak. **S**: summit of Fortulent; **TP**: twin peak.

summit view here is quite remarkable in all directions. The British Military Group is a particularly impressive backdrop for Spray Lake.

116A. "FORTULENT PEAK"

The extension to "Fortulent Peak" is easy and relatively short, and it boasts an even better summit view. You may regret not going, so try to make the effort. The route is obvious. Follow the ridge north down to a low col and then continue up to the first of "Fortulent's" two summits. Trend left to easier terrain as you approach the top. A few moves of hands-on scrambling will be required. Be sure to visit both summits, separated by only a couple of

hundred metres. You'll notice that the next high point is not too far away, if you are so motivated. When finished taking in the splendid views, **return** the same way. Alternative descent routes down the west side of the mountain to Turbulent Creek are possible but offer no advantages over following the ridge back. You might as well enjoy the view for the maximum amount of time. Once back at your bike, expect to take about an hour to get back to your car.

For those who really want to make the most of their day, continuing north to the summit of Mount Turbulent is highly recommended (see next trip).

117. MOUNT TURBULENT 2850 m

(MAP 29, PAGE 465)
Rating easy but long; mostly steep hiking
Round-trip time 10–13 hours via Mount Fortune
Elevation gain 700 m to Fortune; add 250 m for "Fortulent"; add 750 m for Turbulent
Maps 82 J/14 Spray Lake Reservoir; Gem Trek Canmore

The shortest route to the summit of Mount Turbulent follows Turbulent Creek for 4 km before gaining the upper valley, SSE of the summit. This route is uninspiring, however, and not the recommended way to go up. Save it for the descent. A far more enjoyable line traverses the long ridge from Mount Fortune, over "Fortulent Peak" and then on to Turbulent. Be prepared for about 1800 metres of elevation gain in total and a very long day. A bike approach is essential. Try from July on.

Follow the directions for Mount Fortune and "Fortulent Peak." From "Fortulent," continue to follow the ridge north to the next high point a short distance away, and then to the next a much greater distance away. The elevation of this last high point before Mount Turbulent is about 2610 m and, like "Fortulent," the view is excellent.

Now comes a significant elevation loss. Go down to the col, and then, instead of following the ridge back up, turn west, continuing to lose elevation into the hanging valley SSE of the summit of Turbulent. Once in the valley, turn north and hike to the first of two scenic lakes. The lakes can be circumvented on either side, but the west is probably easier. Past the lakes, the route to the summit is obvious and the scree quite tolerable by Rockies standards. The slope is somewhat foreshortened and the true summit lies to the left once you reach the ridge.

The summit block of Turbulent and the daunting ridge. The route goes down to the valley first. **V**: valley; **ER**: exposed ridge (avoid); **S**: summit.

The route down to the valley.

Pat yourself on the back for completing this long, strenuous trip, and rest up before the descent. Yet again the summit panorama is very pleasant, even though Spray Lake is no longer visible.

It is unlikely that anyone completing the ascent of Turbulent from Fortune will want to return the same way. This would put your total elevation gain well over 2000 metres! If that doesn't appeal to you, return as follows. Descend the way you came, but instead of reascending to the ridge, follow the natural lay of the valley as it curves around and down to the right. This simply takes you down to Turbulent Creek. Expect a good stint of bushwhacking in a southwest direction to reach the creek. Upon arriving there, follow the creek out on the east side. Look for game trails to make the job easier, and expect some minor

stream crossings and swampy areas. Sometimes you will be close to the creek and at other times a fair distance from it. As you near Spray Lake, stay high on the east slopes. The creek eventually narrows into a deep canyon and you want to be high above it here. You'll probably end up near the bridge over Turbulent Creek. Hike back up the trail to your bike. Expect the bike ride back to your car to take about an hour.

Note: It may be possible to follow the ridge the entire way to the summit without dropping down into the valley. The author has not completed this route. If you are confident in your scrambling skills and your ability to assess the feasibility of an unknown route, the ridge may be worth a try. Be prepared to back down if the route becomes technical.

118. "SMUTWOOD PEAK" 2690 m

(MAP 30, PAGE 466)
Rating easy via the south ridge
Round-trip time 6–8 hours
Elevation gain 800 m
Maps 82 J/14 Spray Lakes Reservoir; Gem Trek Kananaskis Lakes

Those who have completed the exciting south ridge of Mount Smuts in Alan Kane's book may find little appeal in an ascent of nearby and very unofficially named "Smutwood Peak." However, the outstanding scenery around the Birdwood Lakes and the stunning views of Mount Birdwood should be ample motivation to make the trek up to Smuts Pass and beyond. Wait for a clear day. Try from July on.

Drive south on Highway 724 and turn right (west) at the Engadine Lodge turnoff (about 40 km south of Canmore). Follow the road for 900 m and turn left into a parking area, which is where the hiking trail starts. Take the trail south for about 2 km to a fork. Take the right branch. Quickly this new trail narrows to a single track. It eventually arrives at a scenic waterfall of Commonwealth Creek. Follow the trail along the right (north) side of the creek

Right: The summit block as seen from the first high point.
Below: Routes to "Smutwood Peak." **S**: summit.

The awesome view you came to see! Photo: Doug Lutz

up to the beautiful hanging valley below Mount Birdwood. The trail leads west through the valley, which is frequented by moose. Make noise to avoid a surprise encounter with one. Follow the trail along the valley and then up to Smuts Pass. Enjoy good views of The Fist, Smuts and Birdwood throughout the ascent to the pass.

From Smuts Pass, the objective is the obvious high point above the right side of the lower Birdwood Lake. A closer look at the lakes is worth a couple of extra metres of elevation loss. Drop down to the first lake and circle around it on the left (south) side. The small waterfall that connects the upper lake to the lower lake also warrants a visit. After admiring the beautiful scenery, scramble up the left side of the waterfall to the equally beautiful upper lake.

The route to the summit is as straightforward as it appears. Follow the ridge above the lake as it curves to the right and then heads north towards the summit. Stay near the edge for the best views. The faint trail to the left can be used on descent.

Fairly quickly the only rock band of any consequence appears. Traverse left and down alongside the band for about 20 m, then up an easy weakness. Ascend immediately back to the ridge. The next rock band looks more daunting, but it's just a walk-up if you are back on the ridge. Follow the ridge to the first high point.

A small elevation loss ensues and then it's just a scree slog to the summit. Again, stay near the edge, though it may feel mildly exposed for some people. The trail to the left is always a slightly easier option.

Enjoy an outstanding summit panorama for such a small peak. The view of Mount Birdwood, with the lakes below, is simply jaw-dropping! Mount Sir Douglas lies to the right of Birdwood. The small high point about 100 m to the west is slightly lower and not worth a visit. The rock is hideously loose and the exposure down the north side is shocking to say the least. **Return** the same way. Using faint trails does make things a little easier. If time is not a concern, circling around the north sides of both Birdwood Lakes makes an enjoyable end to the day.

119. "HEADWALL PEAK" 3030 m

(MAP 30, PAGE 466)

Rating mostly moderate via the southeast face, with a short, difficult summit ridge
Round-trip time 6.5–9 hours
Elevation gain 1200 m
Maps 82 J/14 Spray Lakes Reservoir, 82 J/11 Kananaskis Lakes; Gem Trek Kananaskis Lakes

If you enjoyed making your way to the foot of Mount James Walker, an ascent of Headwall Peak is the perfect excuse to make another foray into the serene James Walker Creek valley, as both peaks share the same approach. While the actual ascent from the valley to the summit is not terribly aesthetic, the summit view is well worth a minor battle with some steep rubble and slabs. Legendary climber John Martin and company claimed the first recorded ascent in July of 1981. Try from July on. The ascent is not recommended when the slopes are plastered with snow.

Park in the Sawmill lot near the south end of Highway 742, 6.1 km south of the Chester Lake parking lot or 5.7 km north of the Black Prince one. The approach starts on the snowshoe trail. Biking this section is a good idea. There are several trails that leave the parking lot – take the one behind the outhouse, heading east and uphill. Within minutes you'll reach a trail map and snowshoe sign. Take the left fork, labelled as the "1.5" section, and follow the wide trail 1.5 km to another trail sign. Turn left and continue northwestward for about 350–400 m, looking for an unsigned and narrower trail that branches off to the right and goes uphill (GR233250). There is an identical-looking trail doing exactly the same thing a few hundred metres before – ignore that one. Go to the right and up onto this narrow, mostly single-track trail, unofficially called "James Walker Creek Trail." Most of this route is also bikeable, but doing so can be dangerous for others, since the trail is narrow and bushy on both sides. If you do decide to continue up on your bike, it is imperative that on the return ride you make tons of noise and ring your bike bell to warn others you are coming down.

Amélie Stavric hikes toward the base of the south ridge of Mount James Walker. Go left to get to Headwall Peak. **HP**: Headwall Peak; **JW**: Mount James Walker. Photo: Marko Stavric

One of many possible routes to the summit. The slabby terrain lies to the left of the red line.

Hike or bike the James Walker Creek trail for about 2.5 km to unofficial "James Walker Lake." Note that you can only bike about two-thirds of that distance. There is a fascinating boulder field just before the lake that you may want to explore. From the lake, Mount Inflexible lies to the right, Mount James Walker is obvious straight ahead and Headwall Peak lies to the left. However, the summit of Headwall is not yet visible (see photo for Mount James Walker, next page).

Follow a faint path around the right (east) side of the lake to the north end. Floods have altered the trail here. Staying to the right, following the watercourse and rocky debris (tons of cairns as of 2016). Shortly along, look to the right for the well-worn trail which takes you up the headwall. There are a few scenic opportunities along the way to see the creek and some waterfalls running down the headwall.

Eventually you will pop out into the open beneath a steep wall of rock. Continue along the trail up into the beautiful James Walker Creek valley. The expansive south face of Mount James Walker will be staring you in the face, while Headwall Peak sits, less conspicuously, to the left (see photo previous page).

The route to the base of the peak and then up to the summit ridge is straightforward. Hike up to the right (north) side of the face and then slog your way up scree and slabs to the summit ridge (see photo above). Many routes are possible. The slabs, more in the centre of the face, can make the ascent less tedious, as it is quite foreshortened.

Reaching the summit ridge, turn right (north) and make your way up a narrowing ridge. The exposure is never nail-biting, but extra care will be required to negotiate a few steps. Some of the solid-looking rock is actually very loose and crumbly. After the exposed section, the summit is only a few minutes away.

The summit panorama is fantastic, perhaps the highlights being distant Mount Assiniboine behind close-by Mount Chester and the narrow ridges of Headwall Peak itself, extending in both directions. Mount Joffre and the British Military Group are also very striking.

Return the same way. On descent the scree may be preferable to the slabs, but be careful about knocking rocks down. You will be loving life if you have a bike waiting for you to finish the trip!

120. MOUNT JAMES WALKER 3035 m

(MAP 30, PAGE 466)
Rating moderate, with some exposure, via southwest slopes and the south ridge
Round-trip time 8–11 hours
Elevation gain 1200 m
Maps 82 J/14 Spray Lakes Reservoir, 82 J/11 Kananaskis Lakes; Gem Trek Kananaskis Lakes

From Highway 40, the summit of Mount James Walker appears as a series of nondescript uplifts and is overshadowed by the lower but more striking form of The Fortress to the north. From Highway 742 the mountain isn't even visible. Perhaps that is why it undeservedly gets little attention. The ascent takes you through rugged and interesting terrain, past a small lake, and ends with an exciting ridge-walk. Try from July on.

Park in the Sawmill lot near the south end of Highway 742, 6.1 km south of the Chester Lake parking lot or 5.7 km north of the Black Prince one. The approach starts on the snowshoe trail. Biking this section is a good idea. There are several trails that leave the parking lot – take the one behind the outhouse, heading east and uphill. Within minutes you'll reach a trail map and snowshoe sign. Take the left fork, labelled as the "1.5" section, and

follow the wide path 1.5 km to another trail sign. Turn left and continue northwestward for about 350–400 m, looking for an unsigned and narrower trail that branches off to the right and goes uphill (GR233250). There is an identical-looking trail doing exactly the same thing a few hundred metres before – ignore that one. Go to the right and up onto this narrow, mostly single-track trail, unofficially called "James Walker Creek Trail." Most

Marko Stavric beautifully captures the extraordinary environs of James Walker Lake as Amélie explores the lakeshore (sorry to redline it to death, Marko!). **I**: Mount Inflexible; **JW**: Mount James Walker; **HP**: route to Headwall Peak.

Above: An overnight snowstorm made this mid-September ascent a little more challenging.
Below: Amélie starts down the alternative descent route. **I**: Mount Inflexible. Photo: Marko Stavric

of this route is also bikeable, but doing so can be dangerous for others, since the trail is narrow and bushy on both sides. If you do decide to continue up on your bike, it is imperative that on the return ride you make tons of noise and ring your bike bell to warn others that you are coming down.

Hike or bike the James Walker Creek trail for about 2.5 km to unofficial "James Walker Lake." Note that you can only bike about two-thirds of that distance. There is a fascinating boulder field just before the lake that you may want to explore. From the lake Mount Inflexible lies to the right, while Mount James Walker is obvious and straight ahead.

Follow a faint path around the right (east) side of the lake to the north end. Floods have altered the trail here. Staying to the right, following the watercourse and rocky debris (tons of cairns as of 2016). Shortly in, look to the right for the well-worn trail which takes you up the headwall. There are a few scenic opportunities along the way to see the creek and some waterfalls running down the headwall.

Eventually you will pop out into the open beneath a steep wall of rock. Continue along the trail up into the beautiful James Walker Creek valley. The expansive south face of Mount James Walker will be staring you in the face, while Headwall Peak sits, less conspicuously, to the left

(see photo in Headwall Peak trip, page 345). The route to the base of James Walker is obvious. Hike across the valley to the base of the southwest slopes, then scramble up the slopes on a mixture of slabs and scree. It is steepest near the bottom and then the angle eases a little. This slope is foreshortened and can be tedious; trending right to gain the ridge earlier may be your best bet.

The route is obvious and straightforward once you've gained the ridge. Basically, follow it to the summit. A rock step early on is easily overcome by going right over the top of it or by circumventing it on the right side. After that, there is one short section of exposed scrambling if you stay on the ridge. The drop on the left side of the ridge is wonderfully vertiginous (as long as you don't fall down it!). Past the exposed section, easier terrain leads to the summit and a spectacular view. With the Fisher and Opal ranges to the east and the British Military Group and the Spray Range to the west, you could spend all afternoon picking out familiar peaks.

Either **return** the same way or, for something different, descend southeast directly from the summit. The slopes eventually curve to the right and you'll end up at the head of the valley. Hike southwest back to the ascent route and then out the same way you came.

121. KENT RIDGE NORTH SUMMIT 2914 m

(MAP 30, PAGE 466)
Rating easy via south and west ridges
Round-trip time 6–9 hours
Elevation gain 1200 m
Maps 82 J/14 Spray Lakes Reservoir, 82 J/11 Kananaskis Lakes; Gem Trek Kananaskis Lakes

The northernmost summit of Kent Ridge is not an official peak, but it is the highest point of the lengthy ridge and offers easy scrambling (steep hiking) to a pretty decent viewpoint. If comfortable with snow travel and competent at assessing avalanche conditions, this makes a great winter ascent with a potentially long glissade on descent. Try from July on or earlier as a winter or spring ascent. Be wary of avalanche danger.

From the Sawmill parking lot, take a good look to the northeast to scout out the ascent route. You'll want to gain the ridge as soon as possible to minimize the bushwhacking. Hike the red/yellow/green trail for about 15 minutes and then turn 90 degrees and head right into the bush. Go straight uphill until the trees give way to open slopes and the ridge above.

Upon gaining the ridge, turn left and hike to the high point at GR244254. Once there the remainder of the route becomes obvious. Drop down to the col between GR244254 and Kent Ridge north. In winter this may involve losing elevation to the left in order to find a safe spot to descend towards the col.

From the col a long and foreshortened scree (or snow) slog ensues. No route-finding is necessary here – just go up! On a clear day, the summit view is surprisingly eye-catching: the length of the Opal Range to the east, Chester and James Walker to the north, Birdwood and many others to the west and a good portion of the Kananaskis Lakes area to the south. Throw in a few 11,000ers (Assiniboine, Joffre and King George) and you're guaranteed to be impressed.

Return the same way. When you reach the col, if you don't feel like reascending GR244254, turn right and follow the drainage to the north down to where it eventually joins up with a cutline. Turn left and follow the cutline back down to the trail.

The very much approximated route to the outlier of Kent Ridge North. **O**: Outlier; **S**: Summit of Kent Ridge North.

Above: Mark traverses steep snow slopes to the low col before the summit. Ice axe mandatory!
Below: Mark and Kevin slogging their way up to the summit in mid-December.

122. MOUNT KENT 2635 m

(MAP 30, PAGE 466)
Rating moderate via west slopes
Round-trip time 5–7 hours
Elevation gain 950 m
Maps 82 J/11 Kananaskis Lakes; Gem Trek Kananaskis Lakes

Mount Kent is a rather nondescript peak that can be reached quickly and easily via a direct ascent from a point on Highway 742 just southwest of the summit. While its elevation pales in comparison to the surrounding mountains, its strategic location between the Spray Mountains and the Opal Range ensures a magnificent view. In addition, the route boasts some terrific slab scrambling when the slopes are snow-free. In fact, it's one of my favourite mountains in Kananaskis. A much longer route traverses the length of the southeast ridge. Try from July on. Summit at GR275217.

Park 10.3 km north of the Kananaskis Lakes Road/ Highway 742 junction (about 2 km north of the Black Prince parking lot turn-off) at the overgrown drainage coming down from Mount Kent. The 2013 floods have made the approach up the drainage a little more challenging and tedious, but nothing

The west ascent slopes from the upper section of the drainage. Brad Richens and Dan Cote descend the drainage.

Above: Four of my favourite people in the world get in the way of the terrific view to the north. Left to right, three members of the rock band Talking Dog: David Sparks, Jeff Kushner, Miles Krowicki; the guy at the end is my brother Mark. Photo by the fourth member of the band

Right: An impressive feature of the recommended descent route. Chris Taylor and Mike Exner flirt with death while Nicole Lisafeld takes a saner route!

too extreme. Follow the drainage up and north-eastward. A faint animal trail has developed on the right (south) side of the drainage and will make travel a little faster. Always stay near the drainage. Slabs soon appear in the drainage and can be fun to scramble up when dry.

A set of steeper and longer slabs is eventually reached. Here you can tackle them head-on or bypass them on the right side. You may see some orange flagging directing you to cross to the left side, but it is easier to stay on the right side of the drainage and then go right into the drainage once above the slabs. Staying in the drainage is best from that point on.

Eventually the terrain opens up and the drainage splits. Take the right fork. Shortly after, the drainage splits again. Take the left fork, arriving at a slab about 100 m up. Scramble directly up the slab. Enjoy a variety of slab scrambling straight up the west-facing slope from here on in. Sometimes the slabs provide good friction and sometimes big holds, but at other times they are smooth with very small holds. Use good judgment as you decide which slabs to tackle head-on and which to avoid by moving to easier terrain on either side. A good compromise is to ascend the slabs near their edge, where an escape to easier terrain is feasible at all times.

Higher up, the terrain becomes a little more challenging. Some of the slabs here are dangerously steep and smooth and should be avoided. Continue straight up the face to the ridge. Depending on where you top out, a short hike north with a little moderate scrambling may be required in order to reach the summit.

On a clear day the view is an absolute bargain, considering the minimal effort spent getting to the top. The entire Opal Range is stretched out to the east, with mountains of the Highwood farther south. To the west, most of the British Military Group are visible, highlighted by the wonderfully curved contours of Mount Smith-Dorrien. To the north lies the highest point of the ridge (a separate trip), which then turns east and connects to Mount Inflexible and then south to Mount Lawson. The south ridge of James Walker is just visible to the left of Inflexible.

There are three options for the **return** trip. The first is to descend the same way you came up. There are no advantages or disadvantages to this route, although downclimbing the slabs will certainly be trickier than upclimbing them.

The second and **recommended** route is to aim for the small col far below to the northwest of the summit. Follow the summit ridge northwest. The mountain soon drops off, forcing you down and to the left, with a great view of an impressive rock face (make sure you turn around to see it!).

Shortly after, you can start to trend left (west) and down, descending grassy and sometimes tedious slopes towards the col. From near the col turn left (south) and descend easier slopes back to the original descent drainage. Follow that one back to the road. Stay in the drainage for most of the descent, but when possible it is a little easier to use the forested slopes on the left (south) side of the drainage.

The third option is similar to the second, except you make your way to the small col to the south of the summit. From the summit descend the same slopes you came up. When you are past the scree, trend left (south) and descend grassy slopes to the small col. At the col, turn right and descend the drainage, which eventually joins up with your ascent route. Stay in the drainage for most of the descent, but when possible it is a little easier to use the forested slopes on the left (south) side of the drainage.

123. SNOW PEAK 2789 m

(MAP 30, PAGE 466)
Rating easy via Burstall Pass and south slopes
Round-trip time 6–8 hours
Elevation gain 900 m
Maps 82 J/14 Spray Lakes Reservoir; Gem Trek Kananaskis Lakes

The strategic location of this peak guarantees a superb summit panorama. While you may not have the 8 km hike along the popular Burstall Pass Trail to yourself, solitude and an easy ascent are almost guaranteed once you leave the trail. Try from July on.

Park at the Burstall Pass parking lot on Highway 742, located 44 km south of Canmore or 20 km north of the Kananaskis Trail/Highway 742 junction. Hike Burstall Pass Trail a full 8 km to the pass. Basically the trail parallels the marshy valley, crosses the flats (often convoluted with braided streams), enters trees at the far side (look for the trail sign) and ascends to a higher valley which then leads easily to the pass. Along the way, enjoy the shapely form of Mount Birdwood to the north and eventually the impressive form of 11,000er Mount Sir Douglas to the south.

Snow Peak from the flats along Burstall Pass Trail. Nicole trying to get cell reception! **BP**: Burstall Pass; **S**: summit

Bob Spirko heads to the south ridge of Snow Peak. The infamous Mount Smuts is in the distant right. Photo: Dinah Kruze

At the pass, leave the trail and turn to the right towards Snow Peak. Ascending the south slopes is an easy and stress-free affair. Rock bands can be circumvented on the left side. Otherwise, follow the ridge all the way to the summit. At the top, close-up views of Birdwood and Sir Douglas will likely garner most of your attention, but the panorama in every direction is splendid. **Return** the same way.

124. "PIGGY PLUS" 2730 m

(MAP 30, PAGE 466)
Rating difficult, steep, exposed and loose
Round-trip time 6–8 hours
Elevation gain 880 m
Maps 82 J/11 Kananaskis Lakes; Gem Trek Kananaskis Lakes

"Piggy Plus" is the unofficial peak west of Mount Burstall and the northern extension of Mount Robertson. It is not terribly high, but it offers a scenic approach and terrific views of mounts French, Robertson and Sir Douglas. The origin of the unusual name remains unclear. Try from July on.

Park in the Burstall Pass lot on Highway 742, located 44 km south of Canmore or 20 km north of the Kananaskis Trail/Highway 742 junction. Hike or bike Burstall Pass Trail for 3.4 km, looking for an open area (the remnants of a clear-cut) on the left side. This opening, at GR171264, comes after you have passed Mount Burstall on the left. If you reach the bike lock-up, you've gone about 120 m too far.

Hike up the overgrown clear-cut a good distance until you reach a stream coming down from the valley. Follow this stream south into a pristine valley between Mount Burstall (left) and "Piggy Plus." This valley is relatively untouched and very fragile. Remember to avoid trampling the plant life, and use faint trails where they exist.

Higher up you are bound to encounter large

The route from the pass to the ridge. **EG**: easier ascent gully (and descent route); **D**: more difficult route.

The summit ridge, looking far more intimidating than it really is. The 11,000er Mount Sir Douglas sits proudly to the right.

snow patches, even into August. Be wary of walking on top of patches that hide streams underneath and may collapse. Eventually the greenery gives way to glacial rubble. Ascend the rubble to a pass with a beautiful view of mounts Murray, French and Robertson. At the pass, turn right (west) and ascend steep slopes to the ridge. The easiest route (see photo on preceding page) starts in the middle and then swings to the left side and up a narrow gully of rubble (best ascended by straddling the gully). A more challenging route goes up to the right alongside a wall. Here the terrain is steep and loose and you may need the odd class 4 move near the top.

Once on the ridge, turn south and follow the ridge to the summit. There are a couple of exposed sections but nothing too alarming. With the exception of one steep pinnacle that may require climbing gear to negotiate (circumvent it on the left side), the ridge can be maintained throughout, though some may choose to use easier terrain on the left side of the ridge.

Needless to say, the front-row view of French, Robertson and Sir Douglas is fantastic. As well, two-thirds of the popular French–Haig–Robertson glacier traverse can be seen. Haig Glacier hides behind Mount Robertson. **Return** the same way. To go from the ridge back down to the pass, the aforementioned gully provides the easiest route. Remember to work your way over to the left (north) side near the bottom.

125. MOUNT WORTHINGTON 2915 m

(MAP 31, PAGE 467)

Rating moderate, with one difficult rock band, via the east face
Round-trip time 10–12 hours as day trip; 4–6 hours from Three Isle Lake
Elevation gain 1200 m
Maps 82 J/11 Kananaskis Lakes; Gem Trek Kananaskis Lakes

As a day trip, Mount Worthington is a long affair. The actual ascent is preceded by a 10 km hike to Three Isle Lake. Leave early, travel light and fast and wait for a clear day, as the summit view of Mount King George and the Royal Group is unbeatable. Spending the night at the Three Isle Lake campground may enable you to also ascend nearby Mount Putnik (not described in this book). Try from mid-July on.

From the Trans-Canada, turn south onto Highway 40 and follow it for about 50 km to the Kananaskis Lakes Trail turnoff. Turn right onto the Trail and follow the road to the end. Park in the Upper Kananaskis Lakes parking lot.

From the parking area, walk over the dam to the start of Three Isle Lake Trail, which parallels the north shore of the Upper Lake. Follow this 10.2 km trail to Three Isle Lake, taking the left fork at the 7.2 km mark. Upon reaching the east tip of Three

The ascent route from Three Isle Lake. **S**: summit; **E**: easier route; **SC**: south col.

A closer look at the east face of Mount Worthington. The route shown is approximate.

Isle Lake, hike around the south side of the lake on a good trail. Soon the path turns south onto open plains. Go south for several hundred metres, looking to your right for the easiest route onto the east face (see photo next page). Turn right, cross the flats and make your way up onto the east face.

Aim for the lower rock bands to get some relief from the scree. After the first band, more scree follows, then more solid rock. Work your way straight up the face (on easy to moderate terrain) to the brown-coloured rock that tops the mountain. The stratum of brown rock rises from left to right, making this a logical direction to scramble to the ridge. Choose your line carefully, as the going does get quite a bit steeper near the top. Expect about 10–15 metres of steep, mildly exposed scrambling before the terrain levels off right before the ridge. Thankfully, the rock is solid and holds are plentiful. You'll probably top out on the ridge close to the summit.

The view is first rate: four 11,000ers (Joffre, King George, Assiniboine and Sir Douglas) stand like sentinels around you. The entire Royal Group looks to be only a stone's throw away to the west,

though of course the awesome drop down into the Palliser Valley would render this a very long throw! Enjoy the view and then head southwest to Mount McHarg.

Mount McHarg

Bagging McHarg after Worthington is by far the single easiest double summit day you'll ever complete. One wonders why McHarg has earned official status, but in fact it was named in 1918, 38 years before Worthington received a title. Though missing on many maps, a glacier presently resides on the north and northeast sides of McHarg. It's unlikely you'll find yourself at the bottom of a gaping crevasse, but if the peak is completely snow-covered, it is best to swing around to the left side of the summit and then northwest to the top – a 10-minute walk from Worthington's summit.

Returning the same way poses few problems, though it is much easier to descend easy scree slopes from McHarg (southeast) down to the col south of Worthington. From the col, pick your way down and north back to the flats. Following one of the several drainages makes travel easy.

126. "RAWSON LAKE RIDGE" 2444 m

(MAP 31, PAGE 467)
Rating mostly easy, but one difficult rock band with exposure before the true summit
Round-trip time 5–7 hours
Elevation gain 665 m
Maps 82 J/11 Kananaskis Lakes; Gem Trek Kananaskis Lakes

Rawson Lake Ridge sits quietly in the shadow of statuesque Mount Sarrail, yet still offers one of most sublime views of the Kananaskis Lakes in the park. The short, difficult step of scrambling just before the summit may stop some from making it to the high point, but it won't prevent them from experiencing the view. The trip is relatively short, and to sit on the shores of beautiful Rawson Lake is alone worth the effort. Try from July on.

Drive south on Highway 40 South for about 50 km and make a right turn onto Kananaskis Lakes Trail. Follow that road for about 12.4 km and turn left into the Upper Kananaskis Lakes parking lot. Find the Rawson Lake trailhead and follow the signs to Rawson Lake, which is 3.9 km and 300 vertical metres away. At 1.2 km along the lakeshore, turn left at a trail sign and head 2.7 km up to Rawson Lake.

After taking in the amazing view of Mount Sarrail towering above the lake (and possibly also reflected in it), hike around the south side of the lake all the way to the northwest side. The route up to the ridge is obvious, going up and alongside the major drainage (see photo).

Reaching Rawson Lake Ridge on a clear day and looking over the other side is one of the better experiences the Canadian Rockies has to offer. The

Kelly Wood, Joanne Francis and Shelley Skelton approach the west end of Rawson Lake. The ascent route goes up the obvious drainage at the far right. Photo: Sonny Bou

view of the Kananaskis Lakes is simply unbeatable. Great place to take a lunch break and decide if the true summit is part of your future! If not, return the same way you came.

The rock band that guards the true summit has way more bark than bite (i.e., it looks harder than it is). There are still several moves of difficult, exposed scrambling, however. Hike along the ridge to the rock band and scramble up the least steep route. Enjoy another fine view from the top. A summit of equal height lies to the east and is only a few minutes away.

There are several ways to get back to Rawson Lake:

- The same way you came, provided you are comfortable downclimbing the rock band.
- Down one of two avalanche paths. The first basically parallels the crux rock band. The second is to the east of the east summit. Both routes lead to the north side of the lake and will require some bushwhacking. Once you reach the lake, turn left (northeast) and follow the lakeshore to the lake outlet. Cross the outlet using logs and find Rawson Lake Trail on the other side.
- **Recommended:** Continue following the ridge in an easterly direction. Once you get into the trees, turn right (south) and bushwhack down to the lake outlet. Cross the outlet using logs and find Rawson Lake Trail on the other side.

Left: Joanne hikes towards the crux rock band and summit. Photo: Sonny Bou
Below: Sonny Bou (circled) ascends the crux. Photo: Kelly Wood

BANFF

In terms of scrambles, there is little left in the Banff area that hasn't already been covered in Alan Kane's and other guidebooks, but a few little gems are described here. Chimper and Ochre Spring peaks, down Highway 93 South, are technically not in Banff National Park, but definitely considered to be in the Banff vicinity. Both of those peaks not only sport incredible summit views, but also offer exciting glissades down, for earlier season trips.

Climate and weather

In regards to good weather, Banff sits in the centre – more sunshine than Lake Louise but less than Kananaskis. Precipitation follows a similar pattern.

Access

The Banff townsite is about 1.5 hours west of Calgary along the Trans-Canada Highway or 30 minutes east of Lake Louise.

Accommodations

Your best bets for camping around Banff are the Tunnel Mountain campground, Two Jack Lake or Castle Mountain. The townsite has tons of lodges and hotels if you are looking for something a little more upscale.

BANFF				
Citadel Peak		2607 m	easy	p. 364
	Fatigue Mountain	2958 m	easy	p. 366
	"Little Fatigue"	2920 m	moderate	p. 366
Eagle Mountain		2820 m	easy	p. 367
Mount Howard Douglas		2877 m	easy/moderate	p. 368
"Chimper Peak"		2874 m	moderate	p. 370
"Ochre Spring Peak"		2777 m	moderate	p. 372

Marta Wojnarowska makes her way up the snowy slopes of "Chimper Peak." Glissading down this slope was a riot!

127. CITADEL PEAK 2607 m; FATIGUE MOUNTAIN 2958 m; and "LITTLE FATIGUE" 2920 m

(MAP 32, PAGE 467)
Rating easy via southwest slopes
Round-trip time 8–14 hours
Elevation gain 760 m–1400 m
Maps 82 O/4 Banff; Gem Trek Banff and Mount Assiniboine

Checking out the environs of Citadel Pass and experiencing a terrific summit view will be the only motivation for an ascent of Fatigue Mountain and company. The approach is very long and the ascent itself is a laborious scree slog. Options include Citadel Peak, "Little Fatigue" and Quartz Hill. Wait for a clear day and take plenty of water (at least 3–5 litres). Try from July on.

From mid-June to the end of September, a shuttle bus service is offered to reach Sunshine Meadows from the Sunshine ski hill parking lot. Using the service is almost mandatory, as walking up and down the ski-out adds 13 km and 500 m of elevation gain to the day. Fast parties will be able to take the 8 a.m. bus (advance booking required), complete an ascent of Fatigue and then hike back to catch the last bus at 5:30 p.m. Adding any of the aforementioned options to the trip means you will have to hike down the ski-out. Therefore, it is best to purchase a one-way ticket.

Drive to the ski hill parking lot and take the shuttle bus to Sunshine Meadows. Start hiking the wide trail (to the left) to Citadel Pass. Follow the trail signs, staying left. Quickly you'll arrive at

flatter terrain. The double summit of Quartz Hill appears to the right. Continue hiking past Howard Douglas Lake and onto Citadel Pass. All objectives are now visible. Citadel Peak is to the right (west) and Fatigue Mountain to the left. If you are going only for Fatigue, skip the following section on Citadel Peak.

CITADEL PEAK

Citadel can be ascended from the northwest or the northeast from the pass. A loop route is recommended, going up the northwest ridge and down the northeast slopes. To complete this route, leave the Citadel Pass hiking trail about 1 km before reaching the pass. Hike southwest to the peaceful shores of Citadel Lake. Go around the north side

The pleasant and extensive environs of Citadel Pass. Note the routes up and down Citadel and Fatigue. **FM**: Fatigue Mountain; **CP**: Citadel Peak; **MA**: Mount Assiniboine; **HDL**: Howard Douglas Lake. Photo: Amber Kunimoto

LF

FM

Above: From near the shores Citadel Lake, the route up Fatigue (**FM**) is very obvious, as is the traverse to Little Fatigue (**LF**). Note the shortcut descent route if you are going to Little Fatigue. Photo: Amber Kunimoto

Left: Amber Kunimoto leads the way to the lower outlier of Little Fatigue.

of the lake to intercept the northwest ridge. The summit (only 250 vertical metres above you) can be reached in many ways.

To avoid any hands-on scrambling, go around the first major obstacle on the right side and then grovel up one of many steep gullies to the left, up to the wide ridge. The remainder of the route is obvious, as it swings around to the left and then up to the summit on easy ground.

If you are craving to get your hands dirty, go straight up the ridge, route-finding your way up short steps. The northwest ridge has some pretty solid rock, but lots of loose stuff in between. Check holds carefully. Atop the first step, keep going straight. The rock band guarding the summit looks daunting but has many easier routes (moderate scrambling) through weaknesses in it. Above this step, hike easily to the summit within minutes.

Descending Citadel is as simple as it gets. Although the mountain is lined by an impressive cliff band, the band has many easy routes through it. Descend easy slopes as you head northeastward. Lose elevation on grass or scree slopes until you arrive on the top of the cliff band. Find an easy route through the band in either direction (never more than moderate scrambling). Below the cliff band, continue easily to Citadel Pass Trail. Sidesloping to avoid elevation gain back to Citadel Pass is self-defeating – just go down and then hike back up to the pass. Hike easily back to Sunshine Meadows if you've had enough. With a decent pace you should be able to get back to Sunshine Meadows before the last bus leaves at 5:30.

On the way out, tagging the summit of Quartz Hill (2566 m) is an easy affair, but it offers little reward except another official peak to check off your list. From the high point of the trail, northwest of Howard Douglas Lake, turn southwest and hike to the summit at GR869545 (the southeast of the Hill's double summit). **Return** the same way.

127A. FATIGUE MOUNTAIN

Hike all the way to Citadel Pass (approximately 2.5 hours from the bus). The ascent route is brutally obvious from the pass, hardly requiring a description. Simply slog up the southwest slopes, taking the easiest line possible. In general the scree and rubble are fairly stable and the ascent probably won't be as bad as it looks from the pass. Intercept

the northwest ridge and then hike to the summit. At a decent pace you can reach the summit in less than 1.5 hours from the pass.

As mentioned, the view is the primary motivation for this ascent. If you arrive at the summit in gloomy or whiteout conditions, you will be very disappointed. If clear skies prevail, the summit panorama is terrific, especially towards the Assiniboine area. Either **return** the same way or continue the trip to Little Fatigue.

127B. "LITTLE FATIGUE"

This extension is a worthwhile endeavour, but like the high-level traverse of Victoria Peak to Victoria Ridge, beginning on page 96, it *will* leave you "dead on your feet." Make sure you still have plenty of food and water – you'll need it!

Again, the route is a simple one. From the summit of Fatigue, follow the ridge northwest down to the col and then northward up the other side. A small rock band is eventually reached, but it has an obvious weakness in it. Continue up to the false summit. At the false summit, the terrain suddenly looks more serious, with a series of drop-offs. All are easily bypassed on the right side of the ridge. The ridge then widens again and it's an easy plod to the top. From the 2920 m summit, a lower outlier is visible to the northeast and it warrants a quick visit. The ridge narrows significantly just before the summit of this outlier. It's only a few steps, but go slowly across this crumbling and loose terrain. From the outlier, look across to some very impressive vertical walls on the east side of Little Fatigue.

Unfortunately there is no direct route back to Sunshine Meadows and you must return basically the way you came. However, you need not return all the way to the low col between Fatigue and Little Fatigue. Instead, go back to the base of the aforementioned rock band with the weakness in it and then turn southwest down straightforward scree and grass slopes. Stay right to avoid steeper, more challenging terrain. When it becomes obvious to do so, start hiking more southward, back to Citadel Pass Trail. Trying to shortcut directly to the trail is self-defeating. Once on the trail, it's about 8 km to Sunshine Meadows and then another 6.5 km down to the parking lot. Again, a reminder that this extension is very long and tiring and is recommended only for very fit people.

128. EAGLE MOUNTAIN 2820 m

(MAP 32, PAGE 467)
Rating easy via west slopes
Round-trip time 4–6 hours
Elevation gain 1160 m
Maps 82 O/4 Banff; Gem Trek Banff and Mount Assiniboine

This trip starts with hiking on a wide road, followed by a ski run, and ends with an easy hike to the summit – it's almost embarrassingly easy! Most will want to save this ascent for winter and complete it on skis using skins. However, it does make a good objective in the summer months too, when combined with Howard Douglas or by itself if time or energy are lacking. And there's certainly nothing wrong with an easy day once in a while. Wait for clear weather, when the pleasant summit views will make up for the overall lack of scrambling. Try from July on.

After passing the Banff turnoffs on the Trans-Canada, take the turnoff to the Sunshine ski resort and drive 7 km to the parking lot. The ski-out road is at the back left of the lot. Hike up the ski-out for approximately 3 km to the Goat's Eye Express ski lift (GR860611). You may want to consider biking up this road, as the ride down will be fast and exhilarating. It is consistently steep, however, and you may find yourself pushing the bike uphill a fair distance. Pick one of two ski runs to the immediate right of the lift path and hike up. At the top keep following the path of the ski lift. Once past the terminus of the lift, trend a little to the left and hike straight to the top of the mountain (GR879614).

Enjoy a respectable summit view and then **return** the same way or continue on to the summit of Mount Howard Douglas.

The trip to Howard Douglas requires a 550 metre elevation loss followed by a 600 metre gain. Most topo maps indicate you can do this via the south slopes, but this is not the case, as they are riddled with cliffs. Instead, head more southwesterly down easy slopes towards a larch-filled cirque due west of Howard Douglas (GR875600). From the cirque follow the instructions for #129, Mount Howard Douglas, starting from the paragraph that begins with "Prepare yourself…" (on page 368).

Two ski runs to pick from as an ascent line. Photo: Bob Spirko

129. MOUNT HOWARD DOUGLAS 2877 m

(MAP 32, PAGE 467)
Rating easy, with a couple of moderate steps
Round-trip time 6–8 hours
Elevation gain 1210 m
Maps 82 O/4 Banff; Gem Trek Banff and Mount Assiniboine

Mount Howard Douglas sports an excellent summit panorama. The price of this view is a scree slog of biblical proportions. It's not actually that bad, but don't expect too much in the way of hands-on scrambling. Hiking poles are almost essential on this trip, as is a helmet. Combining this route with an ascent of Eagle Mountain is a great way to spend your day. Try from July on.

After passing the Banff turnoffs on the Trans-Canada Highway, take the turnoff to Sunshine ski resort and drive 7 km to the parking lot. The ski-out road is at the back left of the lot. Hike up the ski-out to the Goat's Eye Express ski lift (approximately 3 km). You may want to consider biking up this road, as the ride down will be fast and exhilarating. It is consistently steep, though, and you may find yourself pushing the bike uphill a fair distance. From the lift looking south you will see several ski runs and smaller open areas that connect runs to the lift. Hike south to the connector that parallels a small rocky drainage. Find the trail here and follow it alongside the drainage. Quickly it forks and at this point you should go left onto another trail, again paralleling the drainage. There is a maze of ski run connectors in this area and it is easy to follow the wrong one. In the distance you will see a significant summit leading down to a smaller hump. This summit lies west of Howard Douglas and therefore you need to be at the left (east) side of it.

The trail moves away from the drainage at times but eventually returns to it as you enter a beautiful, larch-filled cirque at GR875600. The objective is now finally visible at the end of the cirque (see photo next page).

Prepare yourself for 600 vertical metres of scree-bashing on foreshortened slopes. Some of the scree and rubble is quite unstable, so use caution. Ascend scree slopes that eventually curve left toward a significant rock face with a large pinnacle on the right side. Aim for the left side, where it is feasible to gain a scree ledge below the face and then traverse to the right to get around the face. More scree slopes follow as you traverse below a noticeable cave in the upper rock bands. Gain the ridge well to the right of the cave. You are now between the significant summit to the southwest mentioned earlier and the summit of Howard Douglas to the northeast. Go northeast up the ridge, circumventing the first obstacle on the right side. The final rock band is ascended easily through a weakness on the left side – possibly the only time you may have to use your hands on this ascent.

Most prominent from the summit is the view towards Mount Assiniboine and the area around it. The glaciated southeast side of Mount Ball also stands out, as does a striking peak in the Sundance Range that, at the time of writing, is unnamed. **Return** the same way. Some sections of scree provide a fairly fast descent, although other sections are tedious. Back at the cirque, if you haven't already done so, an ascent of Eagle Mountain will cost you an additional 550 metres of elevation gain. The view from Eagle is a little less comprehensive than that from Howard Douglas, but if you've ever planned to ascend Eagle, this is the time. Almost the entire route can be seen from the cirque (see photo below).

Simply follow your nose up southwest slopes towards the terminal of the Goat's Eye Express chair and then easily to the summit. For descent from the summit of Eagle Mountain, head back towards the chairlift and then follow one of the ski runs down to the bottom of the lift and then back to the parking lot via the ski-out.

Above: The ascent route from the cirque. **C**: cirque; **T**: traverse on scree ledge below rock face; **S**: summit.
Below: The route up Eagle Mountain from the cirque. **S**: summit.

130. "CHIMPER PEAK" 2874 m

(MAP 33, PAGE 468)
Rating moderate via the south face
Round-trip time 7–10 hours
Elevation gain 1400 m
Maps 82 N/01 Mount Goodsir; Gem Trek Kootenay National Park

This objective is one of several unnamed peaks between Chimney Peak and Mount Whymper (hence the awesome unofficial name, coined by Fabrice Carrara!). Like "Ochre Spring Peak" across the valley, Chimper sports a phenomenal summit panorama and should only be attempted when the skies are clear. Early-season ascents are strongly recommended for those comfortable on steep snow slopes and who know how to use an ice axe. Kick-stepping with or without crampons up snow is by far preferable to the scree and rubble slog of late summer ascents. Also, the glissade down can be a fast and wild ride! Do be wary of avalanche potential, however. Without snow, the ascent of the upper part of the route can be very tedious. Still, the summit view makes the grind worthwhile.

Drive 17 km south on Highway 93s and park in the Marble Canyon lot. Hike the Tokumm Creek trail for about an hour to the very obvious avalanche slope coming down from the right side of the valley at GR591741 (see photo). The route to the summit from here is obvious. Ascend the avalanche slope

Connor Young, Marta Wojnarowska, Raff Kazmierczak, Josée Ménard and Fabrice Carrara at the base of the obvious avalanche slope.

The magnificent upper cirque and obvious route towards the summit. Josée enjoys the last vestiges of snow on descent.

and trend left at the top (see photo), taking the line of least resistance to the summit at GR602762. There are some rock bands to overcome but nothing too difficult. The upper slopes can feel quite steep. Views improve dramatically as you gain elevation.

At the summit, enjoy a tremendous 360° panorama, highlights of which include almost all the Kane scrambles along Highway 93 (Boom, Whymper, Storm, Stanley, Ball and Vermilion), and the south faces of many of the mountain that make up the Valley of the Ten Peaks. The airy drop on the northeast side of the peak down to a small glacier below is also quite a treat.

Return the same way. With enough snow the glissade can be fantastic, but watch for steeper sections where it might be easy to lose control. If you haven't seen Marble Canyon, it is well worth a visit on the way back or on the way there and only adds a very small amount of distance.

131. "OCHRE SPRING PEAK" 2777 m

(MAP 33, PAGE 468)
Rating moderate via the south face
Round-trip time 6–8 hours
Elevation gain 1350 m
Maps 82 N/1 Mount Goodsir; Gem Trek Kootenay National Park

I first learned about "Ochre Spring Peak" from the website of So Nakagawa (soistheman.com). The peak is unofficial but has a magnificent summit panorama that is superior to many official peaks in the area. Ochre Spring and Chimper (see previous trip) are remarkably similar and both can grant awesome glissades given the right snow conditions. Visiting the colourful Paint Pots is a great way to start this trip. Wait for a clear day to see the amazing view, and bring a Crazy Carpet for the lower slopes if they are snow-covered. Try from May on if you want snow on the ascent slopes. Wait until July if you prefer a snow-free ascent.

Drive 20 km on Highway 93 South and turn right, into the Paint Pots parking lot. It is actually best to drive about 1.7 km past the lot, where you can check out how much snow the upper slopes of the mountain are holding. If there is any snow at all, an ice axe will be mandatory and crampons or even snowshoes an asset.

Drive back to the parking lot and hike Paint Pots Trail. Upon reaching the end of the Paint Pots, resume travel on the signed Ochre Creek Trail.

The amazing colours of the last section of the Paint Pots, with the far southeast end of Ochre Spring Peak behind.

Follow this good trail for approximately 3 km to an obvious and open avalanche path at GR571698 (35–45 minutes from the parking lot).

The route is obvious from here (see photo). Don't be deceived by the view from the bottom of the slope. It is quite foreshortened and you still have about 1200 m of elevation to gain. Also, the upper slopes are steeper than they look.

Several routes to the summit are possible once you have gained about half the elevation. Follow your nose to the top. Snow on the upper slopes will most likely make the ascent easier.

I can't rave enough about the view from the top. I was totally taken off guard by its magnificence. In addition to the Goodsirs and The Rockwall, you are now treated to an unreal view of most of the mountains of the Valley of the Ten Peaks, with Deltaform being the most prominent. Other 11,000ers include Hungabee and Mount Temple. Mount Assiniboine sits in the opposite direction, some distance away. Closer at hand, Stanley Peak dominates the view to the east, although a sliver of icy Mount Ball can be made out behind Stanley. Vermilion Peak appears quite small. Due south, Foster Peak is the tallest and most dramatic mountain in the immediate vicinity. Even the very distant three summits of the Howser Towers in the Bugaboos can be seen on a clear day.

As tempting as continuing northwest along the ridge to other points is, that traverse is fraught with difficulties, including extremely poor rock quality and a big drop-off about 100 m along. Instead, stay at the summit and soak in the sweet view.

For descent, you don't necessarily have to retrace your steps exactly for the upper third. Variations are possible, but the least steep line is

Josée Ménard finishes the descent on foot after a great glissade. Also showing possible ascent routes. **S**: summit. Photo: Rafal Kazmierczak

A small and snowy section of a most incredible view. **B**: Mount Biddle; **H**: Hungabee Mountain; **D**: Deltaform Mountain; **A**: Mount Allen; **P**: Mount Perren; **T**: Mount Temple; **F**: Mount Fay; **Q**: Quadra Mountain; **C**: Chimper Peak.

recommended. The descent can be a riot if you glissade it! However, know your comfort level and limitations on steep slopes and assess the danger (i.e., potential to lose control of the glissade). Many will decide to plunge-step, or kick-step (facing in), the first hundred metres or so and then glissade when the slope eases to a more manageable angle. My mid-May ascent in 2015 granted me a thrilling 600 vertical metre glissade!

LAKE LOUISE AND YOHO

It doesn't take along to figure out why Lake Louise is a world-renowned tourist destination and a post-card and calendar favourite. The picture-perfect views of both Louise and nearby Moraine Lake and their surrounding mountains are but a drop in the bucket of innumerable scenic treasures in the area. The price of such wealth is a dramatic increase in the number of visitors to the area, accompanied by traffic woes. On summer weekends the public parking lot at the Chateau is full by 9:30 a.m. and traffic can be chaotic. Plans are in the works to address this issue, but until then the best strategy to avoid them is to get there early! At present a shuttle from the overflow parking lot is available if you can't park in one of the lots.

Most of the scrambles around Lake Louise are well described in Alan Kane's scrambles book. Three new trips appear here, though all three are already popular in the hiking/scrambling community.

Another strategy to get away from the crowds of Lake Louise is to drive farther west into Yoho, where you will find mountain scenery very much on par with that at Lake Louise. Yoho Peak remains as one my favourite hikes/scrambles of all time.

Climate and weather

As expected, Lake Louise and Yoho do not see the sun as much as Kananaskis or Banff. Cloudy conditions often prevail in both areas while Kananaskis basks in the sunshine. Both Louise and Yoho also receive more precipitation than their easterly counterparts. As a result, the scrambling season for peaks in Lake Louise is generally a little shorter. But given the relatively low elevations of the trips described in this book, early- and late-season ascents still may be a possibility.

Access

Lake Louise sits just off the Trans-Canada Highway about two hours west of Calgary or 35 minutes northwest of Banff.

Accommodations

Staying overnight at one of the hotels or lodges in Lake Louise can be a fairly expensive proposition. There is a campground just east of the townsite. Yoho, especially in the town of Field, offers a number of slightly less expensive bed and breakfasts, cabins and guest houses. Other options include the campgrounds and hostels along the south end of Highway 93 North.

It's less than three hours from the parking lot to this incredible view of Lake Agnes (left), Lake Louise (right) and the surrounding mountains. Photo: Matthew Hobbs

LAKE LOUISE AND YOHO			
"Little Temple"	2650 m	easy	p. 377
Wasatch Mountain	2845 m	moderate	p. 380
"Devil's Thumb"	2466 m	easy/difficult	p. 382
Yoho Peak	2760 m	easy	p. 384
Mount Ogden	2703 m	difficult	p. 387
Emerald Peak	2566 m	moderate	p. 389
"Top Hat"	2590 m	moderate	p. 391

132. "LITTLE TEMPLE" 2650 m

(MAP 34, PAGE 468)
Rating easy from Lake Annette or Temple Lake
Round-trip time 5–7 hours
Elevation gain 940 m
Maps 82 N/08 Lake Louise; Gem Trek Lake Louise and Yoho

The major draws for this trip are the "in your face" views of Mount Temple's awesome north face and the beautiful mountain scenery around Temple Lake and Lake Annette. There are numerous route options, from 6.5 to 16 km round-trip, including a highly recommended loop route that takes it all in! Early season is great if you want to see interesting snow and ice scenery at Temple Lake and late season (September into October) is amazing for larches. For early-season ascents, make sure Moraine Lake road is open.

Lake Annette Loop

Drive towards Chateau Lake Louise and turn left onto Moraine Lake Road. Drive 2.5 km and turn right, into the Paradise Creek parking lot. Follow the signs for 6.7 km to Lake Annette. Along the way there are occasional views of Mount Temple to whet your appetite, as well as terrific scenery around Paradise Creek.

The scenery at the outlet of Lake Annette may seem a little anticlimactic, but it improves dramatically as you circle around to the right and gain some elevation above the southwest and south sides of the lake (see photo). Of course, Mount Temple is constantly looming over you, but now the often snowy forms of Hungabee, Lefroy, Aberdeen and Haddo can be seen across the valley to the southwest, west and northwest.

From the west end of the lake, go up rubble slopes to the south and then head southeast into the obvious valley between Little Temple on your left and Mount Temple on your right. Although you can gain the west ridge of Little Temple from

Lake Annette, Mount Temple and the start of the route up Little Temple. **SV:** scenic viewpoint.

here, it is simpler to follow a faint trail in the rubble up towards the Little Temple/Mount Temple col.

The grade eventually gets steeper but only for a short time. Above the steep section, the summit becomes visible to the left. Rather than heading straight for the summit, it is easier to stay to the right, away from the trees, and make your way to the Little Temple/Mount Temple col, at GR566904. Note the very steep, usually snow-filled gully on the northeast side of Mount Temple. This is called the Aemmer Couloir and is routinely kick-stepped up and skied down by very proficient skiers – impressive!

On a much smaller scale, the route to the summit of Little Temple is obvious from the col. Follow the wide ridge all the way to the top. There is a trail over to the left if you want to go that way. As well as the aforementioned peaks, the summit panorama now includes the four-pronged form of Mount Quadra and Mount Fay to the south, with the awesome and vertical east face of Mount Babel in front of them, plus a good portion of the Bow Valley, with lengthy Castle Mountain, much of the Skoki area to the northeast and Mount Hector to the north. A slightly lower peak, with an almost identical summit, lies a few hundred metres to the northeast. See **Northeast summit** int the next column for a description. Return the same way or complete the loop route via Temple Lake as follows.

Return via Temple Lake

From the summit, start returning the way you came, staying near the left (east) side of the ridge. When it becomes obvious (before reaching the Little Temple/Mount Temple col) veer left, down easy slopes towards the west end of Temple Lake. Once at the lake, make your way to its east end, choosing either side of the lake to get there. The views of Mount Temple towering above its namesake lake are terrific throughout. At the lake outlet, find the trail on the north side of the stream and start following it downstream. You may see some of the best scenery of the day here, in the form of vibrant green moss, larches and of course Mount Temple.

For the most part the trail stays near the stream but does move away from it occasionally. Eventually you will reach an important junction with a small log bridge spanning the stream and a major trail running northwest/southeast. At this point there are two options:

- Cross the stream and continue downstream on the other side until you reach Moraine Lake Road. Turn left onto the road and hike or maybe even hitchhike about 4 km back to the Paradise Creek parking lot.
- Turn left (northwest) onto the major trail and follow it easily back to the Paradise Creek parking lot. This trail is gently graded and downhill all the way. It is also a popular mountain-bike route, so give bikers the right-of-way. On hot summer days this trail through the forest offers good shade from the sun.

Northeast summit

This summit is best reached from the east end of Temple Lake. From there it's just a steep hike to the top and then you can upclimb the steep, exposed terrain between the northeast summit and the true summit. Downclimbing this terrain is significantly more challenging. However, for those at the true summit and craving that challenge, here's how.

Follow the ridge northeast until the terrain steepens dramatically on all sides. You must eventually choose to go left or right and descend steep rock down to the col. Early in the season, snow conditions may be a determining factor here. The steep gully on the right side may be your best bet. For either route, long limbs really help! At the col it's a short and easy walk to the summit.

Either retrace your steps back to the true summit or descend scree and grassy slopes down to the east end of Temple Lake. Follow the return directions from Temple Lake described previously.

Shortest route via Temple Lake
This way may eventually become the route of choice. It's the shortest (approximately 6.5 km round trip) and easiest, yet still has a more than healthy dose of fantastic scenery.

Drive towards Chateau Lake Louise and turn left onto Moraine Lake Road. Drive 6 km and park at the second obvious pullout on the east side of the road. Cross the road, find the trail on the left (south) side of the stream and start upward. In approximately 700 m (and the odd 150 m of vertical) you will arrive at an important junction. Here, a small log bridge spans the stream and a major bike trail crosses it. Cross the creek and continue up the lesser trail along the north bank, ignoring the bike trail. There is a trail on the other side of the creek, but it has more deadfall to climb over.

A big chunk of elevation is now to be gained as you make your way upward and southwestward to Temple Lake, sometimes right alongside the stream and sometimes a short distance away. Nearing the lake you may get some terrific moss and larch scenery and of course the awesome form of Mount Temple above.

From the east end of Temple Lake, hike around to the southwest end (either side of the lake will do) and then turn northwest, up easy, grassy slopes towards a point just above the Mount Temple/ Little Temple col. The summit, to the north, is easily reached from there. Refer to the information above for a summit view description and all the possible descent routes. Most will just return the way they came.

Left: Approaching Temple Lake, with the awesome east side of Mount Temple as a backdrop. **Below:** From near the west end of Temple Lake the route to the summit of Little Temple is obvious. **LT**: Little Temple.

133. WASATCH MOUNTAIN 2845 m

(MAP 34, PAGE 468)
Rating moderate via the east face
Round-trip time 6–8 hours
Elevation gain 965 m
Maps 82 N/08 Lake Louise; Gem Trek Lake Louise and Yoho

If you have ascended Mount Temple and Eiffel Peak but are looking for another excuse to return to the magnificent environs of Larch Valley, Wasatch Mountain is a great way to do so. Though considerably smaller than the aforementioned peaks, Wasatch still offers an outstanding summit view. Try from July on, though larch season ascents are very much recommended.

Reminder: On a weekend you will have to arrive at the parking lot very early to get a spot.

Drive towards Chateau Lake Louise and turn left onto Moraine Lake Road. Drive 14 km to the parking lot. The trailhead is just beyond Moraine Lake Lodge. Usually from July 12 on, the summer trail has a four-person restriction on it. If you are

not in a group of four or more, wait at the trailhead and join up with other groups.

Follow the Eiffel Lake/Larch Valley trail up endless switchbacks for 2.3 km. At the signed intersection, take the left fork towards Eiffel Lake. Hike another 3 km as the Eiffel Lake trail traverses around the south side of Eiffel Peak (an excellent

Dinah Kruze and other hikers on Eiffel Lake trail, with Wasatch Mountain looming in front of them. Photo: Bob Spirko

Dinah, Taras Kurylo and Francisco Bobadilla start up the ascent gully. Photo: Bob Spirko

scramble, described in Alan Kane's book). Views of the several of the Ten Peaks are outstanding.

As you approach Eiffel Lake, Wasatch Mountain will suddenly come into your field of vision (see photo). Hike to the point exactly north of Eiffel Lake and then turn right (north) and ascend the obvious gully of loose scree and muddy slopes towards Wasatch Pass. There are several faint trails to follow here. Grind your way up to the pass and turn west up steep, rubbly slopes. Higher up, the terrain gets steeper, with large blocks underfoot. Use care to avoid knocking rocks down. Many lines

are possible but they all lead to the obvious summit around GR552868.

Sweeping views of Paradise Valley and the Valley of the Ten Peaks greet you at the summit, highlights of which are too numerous to describe. Besides the impressive array of 11,000-foot mountains, rock-flour-filled, pale-turquoise Horseshoe Glacier Lake is certainly eye-catching.

It is worth exploring the summit area and ridge to the west a little, to experience different views, before returning the same way you came up.

134. "DEVIL'S THUMB" 2466 m

(MAP 34, PAGE 468)
Rating easy via the south side, difficult via the east ridge
Round-trip time 4–6 hours
Elevation gain 720 m
Maps 82 N/08 Lake Louise; Gem Trek Lake Louise and Yoho

Though just a small part of much loftier Mount Whyte, "Devil's Thumb" offers extraordinary scenery and views. There is also a "difficult" way up and "easy" way down for those looking for a more challenging route to the top, or just take the easy way up and down. Even if you have completed the nearby Kane scrambles (Niblock and Whyte), you will hopefully find this trip to be very rewarding. Try from July on and wait for a bluebird day.

Reminder: On a weekend you will have to arrive at the parking lot very early to get a parking spot. Alternatively, as of 2016 there is a shuttle that runs from the Lake Louise overflow parking lot, a few kilometres east of Lake Louise Village on Highway 1.

Drive to Chateau Lake Louise and park in the public lot. Hike over to the lake and then around the right side of it for a few hundred metres, looking for the Lake Agnes trail sign. Follow the signs for about 3.4 km to Lake Agnes. A quick stop along the way to see Mirror Lake is recommended.

Devil's Thumb, Mount Whyte and The Beehive are all clearly visible from the tea house at Lake Agnes. Hike all the way along the right (north) side of Lake Agnes to the southwest side and follow the obvious switchbacking trail to a col between Devil's Thumb and The Beehive. A quick visit to the summit of The Beehive is a pleasant diversion, but the view is quite inferior to what you can see from Devil's Thumb.

From the col, make sure to check out the approximate ascent line, especially if you are doing the difficult route (see photo). Follow the obvious trail going west towards Devil's Thumb. About 5 minutes up, the trail goes to the right (ignore the continuation going left), arriving at a 3 m high rock band. Climb the steps of the band to the top (easy scrambling). Time to make a route choice.

Easy via south side

From the top of the rock band, turn left and continue on the obvious trail, going around the south side of the objective. This trail may feel mildly exposed in a couple of spots – it's definitely single file all the way! Eventually the trail veers to the right and up. This could be considered the crux of

the trip, as you grind your way up very steep dirt slopes to the ridge. Turn east and hike up to the huge summit cairn.

Difficult via east ridge

From the top of the rock band, head straight up the east ridge, route-finding your way up to a steep rock band that is clearly beyond scrambling (see top photo opposite). To get past this, you will have to traverse around to the right side of the ridge for about 30 m. And although that will only bring you to a second impasse, you'll also discover a previously unseen (and even now not so obvious) ledge above you that provides good access back to the ridge. Scramble up a couple of metres of rock to the narrow ledge and then work your way carefully back to the ridge. Although the quartzite you are on is remarkably solid and doesn't get slippery when wet, the lichen on top of that quartzite does – go very slowly if the rock is wet.

Once back to the middle of the ridge, continue straight up. Expect a few moves of moderate to difficult scrambling, but always on solid rock. Easier and fun terrain leads to the first summit. The true summit of Devil's Thumb is above and easy to get to by swinging around to the left and up. An immense chasm lies to the right.

Summit and descent

To best experience the summit panorama, go all the way to the end of the east ridge. Here, you can see the exquisite waters of both lakes: the beautiful blue-greens of Lake Agnes and the silty pale turquoise of Lake Louise. Views of mounts Victoria, Lefroy, The Mitre and Aberdeen are stunning. Whyte, Niblock and St. Piran complete the spectacle in the

1S TS

Above: The objective as seen from the col. **ER**: easy route; **DR**: difficult route; **T**: traverse; **D**: difficult scrambling section; **1S**: first summit; **TS**: true summit.

Left: Mel, Hanna and Izzy enjoy the summit of Devil's Thumb. They immediately identified Mount Victoria (left), named in honour of England's second-longest-reigning monarch! Behind the UK trio are mounts Whyte and Niblock.

immediate area. And of course, there is also plenty to see to the east.

Return the same way. If you ascended via the difficult route, then descend as follows. Go west down to a small col. Turn southeast and descend steep dirt slopes to the trail below. Follow the narrow trail eastward back to the top of the rock band and back to the col between Devil's Thumb and The Beehive.

You have three descent options from the col: 1. the way you came via Lake Agnes; 2. the alternative route to Mirror Lake (not as scenic, just different); 3. via the Plain of Six Glaciers (highly recommended if you haven't done that trip and have some extra time and energy).

135. YOHO PEAK 2760 m

(MAP 35, PAGE 468)
Rating easy via the north ridge
Round-trip time 10–14 hours
Elevation gain 1200 m
Maps 82 N/10 Blaeberry River, 82 N/9 Hector Lake, 82 N/8 Lake Louise; Gem Trek Lake Louise and Yoho

Graeme Pole describes this trip as "about as fine a one-day outing as you'll find in the Rockies" and he is absolutely correct. Once you are out into the Yoho Valley, the scenery is amazing and, as such, demands clear skies. Snow is slow to melt here. Take at least an ice axe and maybe crampons too, just in case. Try from late July on. Note that the access road is closed from October to mid-June.

Drive towards Field and turn right onto the Yoho Valley Road (Takakkaw Falls). Follow the road for 14 km to the Takakkaw Falls parking lot and trailhead. Find the trailhead (depends what part of the multi-sectioned parking lot you parked in) and start hiking north, going through the Takakkaw campground within 500 m. Follow the signs for Yoho Valley Trail to Laughing Falls (4.8 km from the parking lot). At the Laughing Falls campground, stay left and continue north, still on Yoho Valley Trail. In 2 km you'll reach a major intersection. Take the right fork to Yoho Glacier.

The Yoho Glacier trail winds through forest for a fair distance and then suddenly pops out into the open and stunning terrain of Yoho Valley (see photo below). Follow the heavily cairned trail up the valley towards and then up a low-angled headwall to the left. Hopefully the headwall will have

several significant waterfalls for your visual enjoyment. If it is safe to do so, checking out these falls close up is well worth a few minutes of your time. You may also choose to ascend solid rock alongside the falls, as opposed to staying on the trail. The actual Yoho Glacier trail continues past the headwall and may require many stream crossings. Do not take this route.

Ascend the headwall. Up top, you can either follow the stream along its left side or, to avoid the bush, stay high on the slopes to the left (see photo page 386). Either way, when feasible you'll want to return to the glacial stream that bisects the upper valley and follow it. At this point Yoho Peak is directly to your left. Ignore the widely spaced topo lines on many maps. It's clear to see that the southeast side of Yoho is very steep.

The goal now is to hike around the east side of

Finally out of the forest, the first of many beautiful scenes you will see throughout the remainder of the trip. The peak in front is the infrequently seen south end of Mount Gordon.

Scrambling alongside these waterfalls can be fun and quite spectacular.

the peak and then around to the west to reach the north ridge. Simply follow the valley as it does just that. It is a longer journey than you might think. Lingering steep snow patches may require an ice axe. Gain the north ridge and then follow it south to the summit. Note that the col north of Yoho Peak is now home to the Louise and Richard Guy Hut. The hut is open only in the winter.

If you want to escape the confines of the valley and also enjoy some wonderful views of the Yoho Glacier and Wapta Icefield, it is possible (and quite enjoyable) to gain the ridge to the right (east) of the ascent valley. This leads to the high point (approximately GR297155) that could actually be considered part of Mount Collie's long southeast ridge. Gain the ridge as follows. Again, start by following the rocky valley around the east side of the peak, but as soon as possible, go right (east) to gain the ridge. Follow the ridge northwestward to the cairned summit. Some moderate scrambling will be required. Take in the unique view to Mont des

Poilus to the west and Mount Balfour to the southeast and then go south to Yoho Peak and another superb summit panorama.

For the return trip, although descending the way you came is perfectly fine, going west into Waterfall Valley is a highly recommended alternative. Follow the ridge south and descend it towards the col between Yoho and its southern outlier. Just before you reach the low col, look to your right (west) for any of the numerous shale scree slopes you may feel comfortable descending. There is nothing difficult here, but the scree is slippery and has a tendency to try to pull you down the mountain – use care.

Descend all the way to the valley floor, reaching a small stream at the bottom (may be dry at certain times of the year). On your way down, look south to locate a shallow lake near the south end of Waterfall Valley. This lake is the key to finding a good trail that takes you easily down.

At the bottom of the scree slope, follow the stream south on either side, making your way towards the lake. At some points it is easier to descend terrain 100 m or so to the west of the stream, but don't stray too far west. Upon reaching the lake, go to its southeast corner, where the lake drains to the south, and find the trail on the east side of the drainage. Follow this trail south for about 2 km until you arrive at a major intersection that has a big cairn. You should hear the roar of Twin Falls nearby. Turn left at the intersection. This is Twin Falls Trail, which will head north

(and unfortunately upward too) for a fair distance before turning south and switchbacking down towards the base of Twin Falls. If you haven't seen the falls, it is a "must-do" and will give you a few minutes to rest your feet.

Continue down Twin Falls Trail, passing the campground and then going up and over a small ridge to reach the intersection you probably stood at about 8 hours earlier. Turn right. It's 6.8 long kilometres back to the parking lot.

Left: Above the headwall, a stream shows the way up the valley, around the east side of the objective.
Below: The easy north ridge of Yoho Peak, from near GR297122. Note the glacier on the east side of the peak and The Presidents to the right of Yoho Peak.

136. MOUNT OGDEN 2703 m

(MAP 36, PAGE 468)
Rating difficult via the southeast ridge; one short section with serious exposure
Round-trip time 5–7 hours
Elevation gain 1200 m
Maps 82 N/8 Lake Louise; Gem Trek Lake Louise and Yoho

An ascent of Mount Ogden is a short trip with a nasty surprise right at the end in the form of an exposed ledge traverse. The bushwhacking is tolerable, the ridgewalk is enjoyable and the summit views are fantastic. Any snow or ice on the crux would render it impassable, so try from mid-July on just to be sure.

Park on the south side of the road at a large pullout 4.6 km west of the Lake O'Hara turnoff (700 m west of the sign for Sherbrooke Creek). Cross the road, hike back up it for a few metres past a rock wall and then turn left up a forested slope. The bushwhacking here is not too bad. The slope is steep but easy to ascend. A strong and steady pace will net you about 600 vertical metres of elevation gain in one hour. Eventually you will top out onto a beautiful larch-filled plateau (1 to 1.5 hours). Continue north across the plateau and work your way over to the right side. At the north end enjoy

a lovely view of the milky-green, glacial waters of Sherbrooke Lake, with mounts Niles and Daly farther north. You will also notice a striking array of different-coloured rock, perhaps the best feature of the mountain.

The route from here is obvious, as there is only one way to go (see photo below). The shale ridge undulates a fair bit but there are no big elevation losses. Stay on the ridge as much as possible. Only one or two sections require circumventing by dropping down to scree on the left side.

The summit block soon rears up and obviously

The route follows the ridge. **S**: summit.

Approaching the summit block. **SS**: scary section; **S**: summit.

is a much more serious endeavour. Scrambling straight up the block is not an option. Instead, traverse along the base of the west side of the block. At the end, turn to the right around the corner and you'll quickly realize why this scramble earns a rating of "difficult." The mountain suddenly drops away and you must traverse a narrow and very exposed ledge to reach the summit. The ledge is not very long, but a slip would be devastating. I'm sure, like me, you'll be exerting a veritable death-grip on all handholds! Increased traffic over this ledge may clean off the loose rocks, but it may also loosen rocks that once may have been reliable foot- or handholds. Go slowly and carefully. Also note

that returning this way will be a little more difficult, as you will be going slightly down. Ten metres of rope and belaying one another across the ledge would also be a viable option. Beyond the ledge, the summit is only a minute away.

The summit features outstanding views of Mount Stephen and Cathedral Mountain to the south and mounts Niles and Balfour to the north. Of course, there are innumerable other peaks to see, and hopefully clear skies and warm temperatures will allow you an extended summit stay. **Return** the same way. Do not be tempted by the easy scree slopes on the west side of the peak, as they lead to cliffs.

137. EMERALD PEAK 2566 m

(MAP 37, PAGE 469)

Rating moderate via the south ridge; difficult from "Top Hat" via the northwest ridge
Round-trip time 5.5–7 hours for Emerald only; add 2–3 hours for Top Hat
Elevation gain 1200 m for Emerald only; add approximately 200 m for Top Hat
Maps 82 N/07 Golden; Gem Trek Lake Louise and Yoho

Though substantially inferior in height to its neighbour Mount Carnarvon, Emerald Peak has a terrific summit view, courtesy of the exquisite colour of Emerald Lake far below and a host of shapely peaks in all directions. The approach is easy, netting most of the day's elevation, and drops you at the shores of scenic Hamilton Lake. Scrambling across the interesting summit ridge, comprised of pinnacles and chasms, finishes the ascent in fine fashion. Try from mid-June on.

Drive to Emerald Lake and find the Hamilton Lake trailhead at the south end of the parking lot. Hike about 6 km to Hamilton Lake. A moderate pace will get you there in approximately 2 hours and will also account for most of the elevation gain of the trip. The picturesque lake is a perfect place to take a break and admire the surroundings: bulky Mount Carnarvon towering over the lake to the northwest, the distinctively square form of "Top Hat" to the north and Emerald Peak immediately northeast.

It's decision time here: Emerald Peak, Top Hat or both? If you want to nab both, the recommended route is to do Top Hat first via its northwest face and then Emerald by way of its northwest

ridge. Weather may also dictate your decision. The superior view is atop Emerald Peak. If the weather is less than stellar but may improve later in the day, go for Top Hat first (see following description).

To get to the south ridge of Emerald Peak, follow the trail on the east side of the lake for a very short distance until it splits. Take the right fork. The trail quickly gains elevation above the lake and offers terrific views of the colourful waters. Within minutes a high point is reached and the south ridge appears before you (see photo).

Lose a small amount of elevation and then grovel up steep slopes to the ridge. An easier slog, up far less steep terrain follows, and soon enough you'll

The route to the south ridge.

reach a false summit. The terrain from here gets far more interesting. Try to stay on the ridge throughout, although bypassing on the left side is possible (if it is snow-free). A short but moderate downclimb is reached quickly and then it's on to the cave.

The route soon becomes a little tricky, at least in appearance. A section of pinnacles and convoluted terrain seems to end progress, but there is a solution to get past these obstacles: a cave-like feature to the right. Enter this fascinating chasm and follow it to its end. Here, you can scramble up steep terrain back onto the ridge. Jump across a gap in the ridge and proceed to the summit, only a few minutes away.

Needless to say, the highlight of the summit view is the vibrant colour of Emerald Lake, looking surprisingly close. Although Mount Burgess stands guard over the southeast side of the lake, massive Mount Stephen, behind Burgess, appears far more impressive (for now). The glaciated forms of The Presidents, to the north, will likely be the next point of attention, with a host of other familiar peaks to follow. More distant but quite breathtaking is Mount Vaux, due south, with Hanbury Glacier hanging tenaciously on its northeast face.

The fastest and best descent route takes a direct line to the peaceful shores of Emerald Lake. In the winter months this can an amazing ski run down, but it's classic avalanche terrain. The route has been accurately named "The Emerald Slide Path." Start by retracing the way you came for a short distance. Right before the "chasm," turn left onto rubble and scree slopes that lead down to the main descent line. Pick your way down steepish slopes to the centre of the slide path and easier terrain. Follow the slide path down, enjoying increasingly impressive views of Mount Burgess and Emerald Lake.

The slope eventually turns left and narrows into a drainage. Follow the drainage down to Emerald Lake. On a calm, clear day the waters can beautifully reflect the image of Mount Burgess. Stop by the lakeshore to check it out before returning within minutes to the parking lot.

From the summit of Emerald, of course, there is also the option to return via Hamilton Lake.

If not satiated you can continue on to Top Hat from the summit of Emerald. This is not the recommended route, though, as downclimbing Emerald's northwest ridge will be far more challenging than upclimbing it if coming from Top Hat. However, once down to the Emerald/Top Hat col, most of the difficulties are behind you. You can also descend the way you came, back to Hamilton Lake, and then tackle Top Hat from there.

On return, Amélie Doucet, Parry Loeffler, Maria MacAulay and Allana Fantin negotiate the cave section near the summit. Photo: Marko Stavric

138. "TOP HAT" 2590 m

(MAP 37, PAGE 469)
Rating moderate via the northwest ridge
Round-trip time 5.5–7 hours for Emerald only; add 2–3 hours for Top Hat
Elevation gain approximately 450 m from Hamilton Lake
Maps 82 N/07 Golden; Gem Trek Lake Louise and Yoho

From the south end of Hamilton Lake the steep walls of descriptively, if unofficially, named "Top Hat" appear impregnable. However, a weakness in the northwest face offers relatively easy access to the summit. Unfortunately the summit view, though still enjoyable, pales in comparison to its neighbours Emerald Peak and Mount Carnarvon. Getting to the top entails a scenic jaunt around Hamilton Lake, a fantastic trudge up surprisingly colourful and interesting rock that has peeled off the east face of Carnarvon, and a very short but potentially exhilarating ascent up a steep gully of chockstones.

Drive to Emerald Lake and find the Hamilton Lake trailhead at the south end of the parking lot. Hike about 6 km to Hamilton Lake. A moderate pace will get you there in approximately 2 hours and will also account for most of the elevation gain of the trip. The picturesque lake is a perfect place to take a break and admire the surroundings: bulky Mount Carnarvon towering over the lake to the northwest, the distinctively square form of Top Hat to the north and Emerald Peak immediately northeast.

Hike around the west side of the lake on a good trail. When the slopes leading down to the lake start to get steeper, trend left on easier terrain. You may soon notice the wide variety of colourful shattered rock underfoot – one of the best features of this ascent. Continue heading around the lake and towards the Top Hat/Carnarvon col in the distance. It takes a little longer than you think to reach that point, but travel is relatively easy, the rock is awesome to look at and views back towards Hamilton

Amélie, Maria, Parry and Allana hike around Hamilton Lake towards Top Hat. **MC**: Mount Carnarvon; **C**: Carnarvon/Top Hat col; **TH**: Top Hat. Photo: Marko Stavric

Lake are very pleasant. Expect to take 1–1.5 hours to reach the col. There you can enjoy good views of "CarMar" (the unofficially named peak north of Carnarvon), Mount Marpole and the glaciated Presidents.

From the col, the remainder of the ascent is short and obvious. Hike southeast up steep slopes to the only weakness in the face. The weakness is a chimney-like feature full of precariously balanced chockstones. Scrambling up it is relatively easy (moderate at best), but you should go one step at a time and check all handholds and foot placements carefully before committing to them.

From atop the chimney, the large summit cairn is 5 minutes away. Disappointingly, neither Hamilton nor Emerald lake is visible from the cairn. To get a good view of Hamilton, make your way over to the south side of the large summit expanse. In fact the best way to enjoy this summit is to go to the edge of the "Hat" and circle around the whole summit, though it is time-consuming.

Return the same way. Once again, use extreme caution when descending the chockstone chimney. If Emerald Peak is your next destination, circle around the southwest side of Top Hat to the Top Hat/Emerald Peak col. The route, again, is obvious and hopefully the rock scenery will continue to impress.

Scrambling up the northwest ridge of Emerald will be the most challenging part of your day. Head up the ridge, taking the scree ramp on the left side that curves right, back onto the ridge. Continue up the ridge until a steep pinnacle of rock appears ahead (clearly not scrambling). Circumvent this on ledges on the left side of the ridge.

A second "scary" section is soon encountered and must also be circumvented. This time, go around the right side for a short distance and then scramble up a steep gully, to your left, leading back up to the ridge. This is the last significant obstacle, and a short scramble leads easily to the summit. Enjoy the wonderful view and then return via the "Slide Path" or Hamilton Lake (see Emerald Peak for both routes).

If the northwest ridge sounds a little too intense, go towards the ridge and then hike across the west face below the ridge until easier terrain to the left (east) will lead to the south ridge. Follow the ridge north to the summit.

Amélie approaches the challenging northwest ridge. The easier route goes around to the right (west face). **NR:** northwest ridge; **ER:** approximate easier route. Photo: Marko Stavric

HIGHWAY 93 NORTH

There are few roads in Canada, or on the entire planet for that matter, whose scenery and views match the sheer beauty, magnificence and grandeur of Highway 93 North, more commonly referred to as the Icefields Parkway. And for those who are impressed with the roadside views, wait until you get up high and experience a few Parkway panoramas – they are simply jaw-dropping!

This road is pure magic for hikers, scramblers and climbers. Good access trails abound, but there is a feeling of remoteness for most of the ascents along the highway. As well, mountains on the west side of the road are either heavily glaciated or offer stupendous views of the glaciers in the area, further adding to the "wildness" and sheer magnificence of these scrambles.

If you are new to the Parkway, I would highly recommend a few of the shorter and easier ascents such as Bow Peak, Mount Jimmy Simpson, "The Onion" and "Boundary Peak." Cirque Peak and Wilcox Peak, from the 3rd edition of Alan Kane's *Scrambles in the Canadian Rockies*, are also easy ascents that are not to be missed.

Climate and weather

In short, the Icefields Parkway gets a lot of snow! The white stuff accumulates early in the season and stays late. This is due to its location on the Continental Divide and the numerous glaciers and Icefields to the west side of the road. Early-season ascents often will require crampons and an ice axe and are generally not recommended, because of avalanche potential.

Given the intense scenic potential, I try to wait for a high pressure system to roll in before heading to this area. The payoff is incredible!

Access

Highway 93 North intersects the Trans-Canada Highway about 2 km west of Lake Louise and heads generally northwestward for 232 km to Jasper. The highway can also be accessed via Highway 11 from Red Deer or Highway 16 from Edmonton. Note that the road is not maintained regularly during the winter months and can get quite slippery after a snowfall.

Accommodations

Given the significant driving distance from any major city, spending a few days or more along the Parkway is a great idea. Here are some accommodation options.

Luxury

- Num Ti Jah Lodge
- Crossing Resort
- Icefields Chalet

Hostels

- Mosquito Creek
- Rampart Creek
- Hilda Creek

Campgrounds

- Mosquito Creek
- Silverhorn Creek
- Waterfowl Lakes
- Rampart Creek
- Wilcox Creek
- Columbia Icefield

I imagine one could devote their entire hiking/climbing life to this single road and still never fully experience all it has to offer. Enjoy!

HIGHWAY 93 NORTH			
Pulpit Peak	2727 m	moderate/difficult	p. 395
Molar Mountain	3022 m	moderate	p. 400
"Noseeum Peak"	3000 m	moderate/difficult	p. 404
Mosquito Mountain	2970 m	easy/moderate/difficult	p. 408
"Molarstone Mountain"	2880 m	easy/moderate/difficult	p. 411
Bow Peak	2880 m	easy	p. 414

HIGHWAY 93 NORTH			
Crowfoot Mountain	3055 m	easy/moderate	p. 418
"The Onion"	2680 m	easy	p. 422
Mount Jimmy Simpson	2970 m	easy	p. 424
"Jimmy Junior"	2770 m	moderate	p. 427
Silverhorn Mountain	2911 m	moderate	p. 430
Mount Noyes	3084 m	moderate	p. 433
"Buffalo (Bison) Peak"	2925 m	moderate/difficult	p. 436
"Big Bend Peak"	2814 m	easy	p. 439
"Mount Saskatchewan Junior I"	2840 m	easy	p. 441
"North Towers of Mount Saskatchewan"	2970 m	moderate/difficult	p. 444
"Boundary Peak"	2870 m	easy	p. 446

Above: Phil Richards ascends the final few hundred metres of Molar Mountain. A 2400 m elevation gain is a small price to pay for these kinds of views – right?! Photo: Vern Dewit
Left: Pulpit Peak can be one of the more challenging routes in this book, but the scenic rewards are incredible! Marko Stavric captures a great shot of one the pinnacles on the ridge, high above appropriately named Turquoise Lake.

139. PULPIT PEAK 2727 m

(MAP 38, PAGE 469)

Rating difficult, exposed scrambling via Lake Margaret, Turquoise Lake and the west slopes; moderate via the south slopes

Round-trip time 11–14 hours

Elevation gain 960 m

Maps 82 N/09 Hector Lake; Gem Trek Lake Louise and Yoho, Bow Lake and Saskatchewan Crossing

An ascent of Pulpit Peak is not for the faint of heart. The scenic rewards are magnificent, but there is a price: deep river fords, exposed scrambling, steep scree and a long day. The most visually spectacular route visits three beautiful lakes along the way. A shorter trek, pioneered by Josée Ménard and Fabrice Carrara, offers an easier descent or ascent but has a long section of bushwhacking. Both routes are described. Try from mid-July on, although late summer/early fall ascents are strongly recommended, to make the river crossings a little easier. Take runners and perhaps a change of clothes or swimsuit for the river crossings.

Difficult route via Lake Margaret: Long, exposed, strenuous, but intensely scenic – you get the picture!

Drive 17.8 km north on Highway 93 North (1 km south of the Hector Lake viewpoint) and park on the west side of the road at the unsigned Hector Lake Campground trailhead. This isn't even a paved pullout, just an open grassy space. Hike

Marta Wojnarowska at the east end of Margaret Lake. The route up the headwall is approximate.

north to the trail sign and follow the path down to the Bow River. Don't cross the river. Instead, hike south on a lesser trail. All starts well (stay left, following more open terrain as opposed to the riverbank), but eventually the track disappears into a quagmire of streams, foliage and fallen trees. Persevere through this section and make your way southwest to the Bow River/Hector Lake outlet.

Ford the river here. Fortunately the water is very slow-moving at this point, but it can be waist deep, especially earlier in the season. If that's the case, runners and a swimsuit are a good idea and you should keep all electronic devices high on your body. Once across, you'll have a 3.5 km hike around the lake to the point where a stream drains from Margaret Lake into Hector Lake. There is a faint trail near the lakeshore, but it is often easier to simply boulder-hop right along the edge of the lake. Again, your chances for an easier hike here are better later in the season, when the lake may be slightly lower.

Around GR441147 you will see hear and see a stream coming down from the left. Leave the lake and head uphill, angling towards the stream, where you will find a good trail that leads easily to the east end of beautiful Lake Margaret. From the Margaret shore, look across the lake and check out the headwall and the way up (see photo). It appears daunting and it is! Note the huge rock high on the slopes – it's the key to the ascent.

Cross the lake outlet on logs and find the faint trail that goes around the north side of the lake. I call it a bushwhacking trail, as there is brush, trees and foliage in your face much of the time. It's still better than no track at all. Follow the trail onto a rocky platform at the west end of the lake. Slog up the rubble, traversing left as you go up to and past the huge rock.

The route up the headwall is about to get very interesting. If you are not comfortable on narrow and very exposed ledges, this is not the route for you. The actual scrambling is never difficult, but any slip while on the headwall would be fatal. You must also be okay with downclimbing this unnerving terrain. Don't be afraid to back down if it's not to your liking.

Once past the huge rock, look for a stony gully that goes up to the right. It's the only feasible route at this point. Start to look for flagging in small bushes and green paint on the rock to guide you. Eventually the route turns left and diagonally upward. A faint, left-pointing green arrow marks this spot and is the last marking you'll see. Go up and left until the ledge ends and then zigzag your

Marta and Raff hike towards the start of the upcoming slog up Pulpit. **P**: interesting pinnacles.

Moderate ascent route. Once you are down in the valley, the marshy area appears in front. Go around the north side. **S**: summit.

way up the headwall, generally trending to the left. A 20-foot length of old rusty chain marks the end of the ascent. The chain was still there as of summer 2015, but it may have been subsequently removed or replaced. If it's still there, use it as a last resort of protection, but try to avoid committing your entire body weight to it. Hopefully the chain will be replaced with something more reliable and/or permanent.

Ascend the chain all the way up to the wall and then start traversing left (south) along it. Don't let your guard down yet, as there is plenty more exposure for the next few minutes. Keep traversing, soon reaching far less extreme terrain. There will be another headwall to your right. Look for a place to easily scramble up it. Once on top, you can breathe again – the exposure is all done!

Even though the summit is not visible yet, the route up Pulpit Peak can now be seen to the southeast (see photo). Turquoise Lake quickly appears to the right. It is very close and a great place to take a break and refuel for the upcoming slog.

Leave the lake and work your way left, into the wide main ascent gully. The terrain in the gully starts off poorly and gets worse as you ascend. Higher up, aim for the rocks on the left side of the gully for more solid footing. There is lots of potential to knock rocks down – use care.

It's a gruelling ascent, but the reward is soon to come. When stopping to catch your breath, turn around to take in the remarkable spectacle of Turquoise Lake and its surrounding peaks.

Several striking pinnacles high up on the summit ridge act as a guide. As you near these it becomes clear that the summit lies to the left (east). Either go all the way up to the pinnacles and then traverse left under a black rock band and then onto the summit or angle left as soon as it is possible, taking a more direct route to the top. (Go to **Both routes**, next page.)

Moderate route via south slopes: This trek is not for the "bushwhacking faint of heart"! Use GPS and waypoints to help steer you in the right direction. Again a deep ford of the Bow River is required. Take runners. If you don't mind bushwhacking in runners, put them on at the car, as you will encounter wet terrain even before you get to the river.

It makes sense to start the trip a little farther south of the Hector Lake viewpoint, thus decreasing the travel distance by several kilometres. Drive 17 km north on Highway 93 and park at a pull-out with guardrails, on the west side of the road at GR481134. Start bushwhacking west and slightly south towards a bend in the Bow River where a log-jam existed as of 2015. En route you may run into an open but very marshy area. It is best to avoid going directly through the marsh and instead skirt around it through trees to the north. Even then, watch for innumerable water-filled holes underfoot. Aim for the logjam at GR470131. Cross the Bow either over the logjam or about 20 m north of it. We started at the logjam and then went to the northwest to find a place where the water was only mid-thigh. Regardless, you are going to get wet, as the logjam only bridges half of the river.

A long and sometimes challenging bushwhack now begins. You will be aiming for Pulpit Tarn at GR448120. The easiest strategy is to hike southwest to the stream that drains Pulpit and follow that up to the tarn. Expect a fair amount of deadfall, thick brush and some steep, bushy terrain as you near the objective.

At the tarn you are faced with an impressive headwall guarding the upper slopes of Pulpit Peak. However, a weakness, trending to the right, through the headwall is obvious and easy to follow (see photo). Hike northwest to the weakness and scramble up it to a point just north of another tarn. Depending where you top out you may or may not see this tarn.

The route to the summit now becomes quite clear (see photo). Hike northwest to the ascent slopes and then grovel up scree and rubble to a group of striking pinnacles. Cross to the north side of the ridge and make your way up to the summit, to the right.

Both routes: Pat yourself and your companions on the back when you reach the summit – you've earned it! The view is outstanding. Glaciated Mount Balfour, Mount Hector and Hector Lake, and Mount Daly will be but a few of the highlights competing for your attention. Also, if you walk north along the ridge you can get to a point where you can see all three lakes. Award-winning adventure photographer Paul Zizka (author of *Summits and Starlight – The Canadian Rockies* (RMB, 2015)) did just that, with amazing results.

For descent, if you came up by the moderate route, your only option is to retrace those steps. If you took the hard way up, you can either descend the same way or take the moderate option. The latter is easier and shorter but has way more bushwhacking and route-finding. Pick your poison!

To descend the moderate route, return to the pinnacles on the summit ridge. Go down scree and rubble on the southeast side of the ridge, aiming for the tarn below. As you near the tarn go more to the left, up and over glacial rubble, in search of the weakness through the headwall that grants easy access to the other tarn below (Pulpit Tarn). This route should be steep hiking/easy scrambling – anything tougher and you are off route.

Make your way down to the tarn and its outlet. The bushwhack begins. Using the stream as a guide, follow it down to more level terrain. The stream will eventually turn southeast, but you will want to keep going northeast, back to the outlet at Hector Lake (GR466143). Distance-wise it's only about 2 to 2.5 km in a straight line from the tarn to the river outlet, but expect to take at least 1.5 hours as you navigate your way through the bush. Ford the river and follow the trail back to the Hector Lake viewpoint.

Fabrice Carrara and Charles Lepage enjoy easier and more scenic terrain just before reaching Pulpit Tarn. The route through the headwall is marked. Photo: Josée Ménard

P

Above: The obvious route to the pinnacles. **Left**: From near the pinnacles, the start of the "easier" descent route. Photo: Marko Stavric

140. MOLAR MOUNTAIN 3022 m

(MAP 39, PAGE 469)
Rating moderate via southwest slopes
Round-trip time 11–15 hours
Elevation gain 2400 m
Maps 82 N/9 Hector Lake; Gem Trek Bow Lake and Saskatchewan Crossing

Molar Mountain is a wonderfully striking peak when viewed from Hector Pass. The ascent has a remote feel to it, though it is not terribly far from the road. What makes this trip stand out is the huge amount of elevation gain necessary to complete it in a day. Travelling fast is imperative. Though the scrambling mostly amounts to slogging up annoying scree, the scenery and views make this a more than worthwhile trip. If the ascent slopes are snow-covered, an ice axe and crampons will be needed. Try from August on.

Park on the west side of the Icefields Parkway, at a pull-out 20 km north of the Trans-Canada Highway. Cross the road and find a good trail on the right side of a creek. Follow the trail to the remnants of an old bridge, but stay on the right side of the creek. Soon the trail crosses the creek and winds its way up the left side of a waterfall. It splits in a couple of directions here, one crossing the fall, the other staying to the left. Take either route, though the trail that crosses the fall may be slightly easier. Above the falls, find the trail that ascends the left side of this hanging valley and follow it all the way to Hector Pass (GR508170), about 1.5 to 2 hours.

The objective and route as seen from Hector Pass. **MC**: Molar Creek; **MM**: Molar Mountain; **MT**: Molar Tower.

Above: The Molar ascent route. **B**: break in lower cliff band; **MM**: Molar Mountain; **MT**: Molar Tower.
Below: Ascent routes for the upper cliff band. Easier lines go to the right.

Below: The descent route to Molar Creek and the alternative ascent route back to Hector Pass. **H**: Mount Hector; **LH**: Little Hector; **HP**: Hector Pass.

At the pass, Molar Mountain and Molar Tower are clearly visible, as is the line of ascent.

Now comes the fun part: losing almost all the elevation you've fought so hard to gain. Descend the left side, first on wonderful limestone karst pavement, then grassy and treed slopes. Stay well left to avoid minor cliff bands. You are aiming for Molar Creek far below. Eventually trend to the right and pick the easiest line down, on the west side of the creek. Hike alongside the creek until you find a convenient place to ford or boulder-hop across it. Pick your location carefully, as the creek does flow fast. There is a trail on the other side. Depending where you have crossed the creek, this trail may be easy to find or you may have to hike southeast downstream until you find it. At approximately GR551160 you should be able to see Molar Mountain (left) and Molar Tower (right) to the north. Leave the trail here and make your way towards the Molars. The bush is light here and should not pose a problem. Higher up the slope a dried-up drainage appears and provides a decent route to the upper slopes.

Once the grass and trees give way to scree, trend left towards an obvious break in the first set of cliff bands near the left side of Molar Mountain (not Tower). Unfortunately the scree here is not fun to ascend and you will be provided little relief from it all the way up. Route-find your way easily through the cliffs and continue up. Staying close to the ridge to the left is more scenic, but it may require minor backtracking in places and the scree is still annoying. Another option is to traverse to the right into the middle of the ascent slope and go straight up it. The scree in the middle is better for descent, so I would save this route for coming down. Regardless, you may want to build a big cairn to mark the place where you came up, for the return trip.

The upper cliff band requires a little searching to find the easiest route up. Generally, easier lines lie to the far right of the band.

The summit is only few minutes away once you're atop the band. Having already completed 1800 metres of elevation gain, you'll probably want to enjoy an extended summit break to recuperate. The wonderful panorama should make that an enjoyable stay. Needless to say, an array of 11,000ers and other formidable peaks are present to the southwest, west and northwest. However, this is a good opportunity to see the more remote and less recognizable mountains to the east. Most of these peaks are unnamed. At 3333 m, Cataract Peak dominates the horizon to the northeast; Willingdon is directly north and the distinctive forms of Douglas and St. Bride lie to the southeast.

Return the same way. Once you're below the upper cliff bands, descending the middle of the slope is a little easier. Just remember to swing back to the right to find the easy route through the lower cliff band. Back into the trees, don't try to shortcut directly west, as you'll end up in more dense forest. When you arrive back at Molar Creek there is an excellent alternative route back to Hector Pass. This route will not save you time or energy, but it offers a change of scenery and a good look at the lower Hector glacier – anything to take your mind off the 620 m of elevation gain back to Hector Pass!

Hike back up Molar Creek and cross it as you pass by the headwall of lower Mount Hector. Look for an obvious right-to-left-rising ramp (just before the trees) that cuts through the headwall and offers an easy route up. The scrambling here is at most moderate and should never be exposed. If it becomes so, backtrack and find the easy route. Atop the headwall, go far left and then up, eventually aiming for lighter-coloured, glacially scoured slabs above. Walking up these smooth slabs is a wonderful alternative to scree bashing. Follow the contour of the slope as it starts to curve around to the right. Glacial ice will soon appear. Of course, you should never step onto the glacier and always be aware of potential rock- and sérac-fall from above. The glacier will eventually force you to go back to the right towards Hector Pass. From the pass retrace your path back to your vehicle.

141. "NOSEEUM PEAK" 3000 m

(MAP 39, PAGE 469)
Rating moderate via the southwest ridge; difficult via the southeast ridge
Round-trip time 7–10 hours
Elevation gain 1200 m
Maps 82 N/09 Hector Lake; Gem Trek Bow Lake and Saskatchewan River Crossing

Dedicated to and in loving memory of a tough scrambler and a terrific person, Becky Mansour.

If this mountain had an official name, it undoubtedly would have become a classic scramble long, long ago. The scenery and views are breathtaking throughout – in fact, far superior to many a named peak along the Icefields Parkway. There is a moderate route and a difficult one (pioneered by Graeme Pole) – take your pick and definitely wait for a bluebird day. Try from mid-July on.

Drive 23 km north on Highway 93 North and park on the east side of the road at an obvious pullout on the west side of Noseeum Creek (unsigned). Using the road, cross to the right (east) side of the creek. A good trail has developed on this side a short way up the creek.

Follow this trail and the creek all the way to a headwall that sports three beautiful waterfalls (four if you count the smaller one way over to the right on Mount Andromache). There are multiple ways up the headwall, perhaps the most interesting and exciting route being along the left side of

Approaching the headwall and the approximate route up. There are actually six people in this photo by Bob Spirko. Can you no see 'um? Jonathan Chui (grey), Zora Knezevic (yellow), Sonny Bou (black), Bernadette Cadden (green), Becky Mansour (blue) and Hanna Yanglou (pink).

Above Noseeum Lake both routes are visible. **M**: moderate route; **R**: scree ramp; **D**: difficult route; **23**: col between second and third summits; **3**: third summit; **C**: crux; **TS**: true summit. Photo: Zeljko Kozomara

the leftmost waterfall. Early in the season this cataract is usually gushing. The rock alongside it is solid and makes for fun scrambling. If you are in an adventurous mood, this is the way to go.

However, the easiest route up the headwall is a winding path that starts immediately to the left of the rightmost fall. Hike up to the base of the fall. Just before you arrive there, look left and find the steep but obvious path starting around GR486201. Follow this as it winds neatly up the headwall. At the top, take note of your surroundings and perhaps make a GPS waypoint, as it is important to return the same way.

Atop the headwall it becomes clear that there are a few more headwalls to overcome before you reach beautiful Noseeum Lake. Open terrain sits to the right, but you will want to continue upward for a short distance and then find a trail to the left that goes into a wooded area. This trail quickly joins up with a creek. Follow the creek up to a second group of waterfalls. With a couple of moves of moderate scrambling you can sneak up between these falls. However, if wet, the rock can be slick here. An easier option is to cross the main creek and find a faint trail that takes you up and around the waterfall on its left side.

Above this fall, route-finding is significantly easier. Following the streams is a great strategy here, as there are multiple opportunities to experience

exquisite mountain scenery. Eventually you will end up above Noseeum Lake, where you can take a break, enjoy the incredible view and contemplate the route you want to take to the top (see photo).

Moderate route

This route is straightforward and relatively easy, though steep in places. Be prepared for a lengthy stretch of annoying treadmill scree. Look to the northwest and spot the fairly obvious scree ramp that goes right through the cliff bands (see photo). Make your way to the ramp, over undulating and interesting terrain. It's a steep grind up the ramp, but no hands-on scrambling is required – just perseverance and a good set of hiking poles!

At the top of the ramp, turn right (northeast) and follow the ridge to the summit (GR489225). Staying right along the edge will allow you to see the fantastic contours of the ridge and the precipitous drop down the left side.

Difficult route

From Noseeum Lake this is a terrific loop with challenging route-finding and terrain for the last section. Thankfully the described moderate route provides an easy descent. Although you can take in all the high points along the ridge by going far to the southeast, the route described here misses the two southerly summits and goes to the col between

Above: Marko Stavric soaks in the sweet view to the east. Molarstone Mountain (next trip) is the colourful peak in front and The Fang of the Molarstone trip can just be seen to the right. The near-11,000er at the far right is Cataract Peak. Photo: Amélie Doucet

Below: Amélie Doucet at the north end of Noseeum Lake, checking out the lake and the north glacier of Mount Andromache – two of many reasons to explore this extraordinary area. Photo: Marko Stavric

the second and third summits (the fourth is the true summit).

The first part of the route is easy, scenic and fun. Go around the right (south) side of the lake, either right along the lakeshore or on the plateau above the lake, and then make your way to the col between the two peaks in front of you. Pick a line that keeps you on the solid rock, as opposed to the scree and rubble. From the col (GR497214), turn left (northwest) and slog up to the top. This is the most unpleasant part of the trip, the firm rock degrading to loose rubble. However, the views really start to improve.

Catch your breath at the top and then continue the ridge traverse, down to the 3/4 col and then up towards the true summit. Suddenly the terrain becomes far more complicated, and careful route-finding up challenging terrain is going to be required. Note the permanent snow/glacier on the right side of the ridge. The snow can be used to get past the first obstacle, but return to the ridge as soon as possible. An easy route that circumvents the second steep section of ridge is found on the left side. This pattern continues all the way up. Always try to return to the ridge. There should only be a few difficult moves of scrambling if the easiest route is found. Don't be shy about searching for that route, and backtrack if necessary. Past the difficulties the summit is only a few minutes away.

The summit and descent

Upon reaching the summit in July of 2011, Rafal Kazmierczak almost immediately commented to me that this summit view was better than that of many of the 40-plus 11,000ers he had ascended! As spectacular as the more familiar mountains to the south, west and northwest are, the lesser-known but more colourful peaks to the northeast and east may be the highlight of the panorama – check out the three summits of Mount Willingdon behind the quartet of "Quartzite," "Ramp," Mosquito and "Molarstone." And nearby, of course, the massive, glaciated Mount Hector is also bound to impress.

For return, if you ascended the moderate route, go back the same way. If you took the difficult route up, either return the same way or complete the scenic loop as follows. Descend the ridge in a west, then southwest direction. Go all the way to the low col at GR482219, right before a massive wall of steep rock blocks the route. It will take about 35–45 minutes to get there. Look left, down an obvious scree ramp and head that way. The route is easy and obvious. Once down the ramp, make your way back to your original ascent route, above Noseeum Lake. (If you have the time and energy, circling around Noseeum Lake provides more outstanding scenery and views.) The rest of the descent is the way you came up. It can be surprisingly easy to get disoriented when trying to relocate the top of the lower headwall. That point lies at GR487201.

142. MOSQUITO MOUNTAIN 2970 m

(MAP 39, PAGE 469)

Rating easy, with one short moderate step, via southwest slopes; moderate/difficult for the extension
Round-trip time 6–10 hours
Elevation gain 1130 m
Maps 82 N/9 Hector Lake; Gem Trek Bow Lake and Saskatchewan Crossing

This is a gem of a mountain in a spectacular area. Thanks go to Graeme Pole for opening my eyes to this peak. The ascent is nothing more than a steep hike with one moderate step if you choose, but it grants outstanding scenery once you're above treeline. Clear skies are an absolute must to fully appreciate this trip. An extension exists for those who really want to get their money's worth. Try from July on.

Park at Mosquito Creek Campground on the west side of Highway 93 (north), about 24 km north of the turnoff from the Trans-Canada. Cross the road and find the trailhead by the northeast side of the bridge. Hike approximately 6 km to the Mo5 campground – about an hour at a brisk pace. Along the way look for good views of the objective once the trail descends to Mosquito Creek (see photo below). Three uniquely shaped peaks will appear.

From left to right, they are the unofficially named "Quartzite Peak" and "Ramp Peak," along with Mosquito Mountain. Mosquito is obviously the highest. The route is quite evident from here and worth noting.

From the campground, leave the trail (GR480241) and head northeastward into the bush. Initially you can more or less follow the creek for a short distance, but then start heading up and to the

The first good view of the distinctive trio and the approximate route up Mosquito.

A taste of some of the phenomenal rock scenery lining the ridge.

left. The terrain gets steeper but the bush is light and easy to negotiate. Aim for treeline at GR487250, 2330 m. Hopefully you will soon run into a wall of quartzite slabs. If so, scramble straight up these – it may be your only opportunity to use your hands throughout the day. The slabs can also be circumvented on either side.

At GR487250 the trees suddenly disappear and the remainder of the route comes into full view. Head up the open slopes until the left side of the mountain starts to fall away. At this point the most scenic route goes over to the left and follows the vertiginous ridgeline. Of course, it is possible to stay in the middle of the peak, but you may miss some interesting rock scenery. Soon the right side of the mountain also starts to fade away. A short downclimb on the left side is eventually required. You can always back up to circumvent this step on the right side if desired. After the step, continue without difficulty to the summit.

The summit panorama features the three peaks of Mount Willingdon to the northeast as well as Cataract Peak farther south. To the south the glaciated north face of Mount Hector is quite a spectacle. Molar Mountain and Noseeum Mountain are also prominent, as are the lengths of the Pipestone and Molar valleys.

Return the same way if you've had enough. Hopefully that won't be the case and you'll have

the energy to continue the trip. The beauty of this extension is that, at any point, it is very easy to go down the south slopes of the mountain, back to Mosquito Creek. Thus, you control how much of an extension you feel like doing.

From the summit, continue southeastward along the ridge. As is almost always the case, the most scenic and interesting route sticks to the edge of the mountain, even though this requires extra elevation gains. Downclimbing the occasional step is not difficult but it is quite exposed in a couple of places. If not to your liking, circumvent these steps/drop-offs by going to the right. Some may require a fair elevation loss, after which you'll want to work your way back to the ridge. Two sections are not downclimbable and will require circumventing in the manner mentioned above (go right).

Follow the ridge all the way to GR513261, 2858 m, where the ridge splits. This is another point where it is easy to head straight for Mosquito Creek and the well-worn trail. Try to resist that temptation, though, as the last section of the trip is arguably the best bit. The ridge splits into two parts, one heading east, the other southeast. Take the southeast (right) fork. Quickly a beautiful blue-green lake becomes visible between the two ridges – the primary reason for continuing the trip. Follow the ridge down, going around the left side of any obstacles, and then scramble straight up the centre fin

This view to the north provides pretty good motivation to complete the extension. Three notable mountains in the vista are Cataract Peak at the far left, Molar Mountain in the centre and the glaciated form of Mount Hector to the right.

of rock to the next high point. This section looks more difficult than it really is and even has a few minutes of fun hands-on scrambling. The ridge then widens considerably. Follow it on its left side to get the best view of the lake. Eventually it starts to drop down to the valley below. If you want to visit the tranquil shores of the lake, follow the ridge until it is feasible to descend to the southwest side of the lake. Depending on your route, you may have to backtrack up to the lake. For the **return** trip, follow a stream that leaves the lake in a southwest direction, across the meadows and then through the trees down to the trail on the north side of Mosquito Creek.

If the lakeshore visit doesn't appeal to you, simply descend easy slopes southwestward. For both return routes, don't stray too far west. You'll want to intersect the Mosquito Creek trail when it's on the north side of the creek. If you go too far west, some bushwhacking may be required before the trail crosses back to the north side, at the campground.

143. "MOLARSTONE MOUNTAIN" 2880 m

(MAP 39, PAGE 469)

Rating easy to moderate for Molarstone; moderate to difficult for the extension
Round-trip time 7–12 hours, depending on route
Elevation gain 1050–1250 m, depending on route
Maps 82 N/09 Hector Lake; Gem Trek Bow Lake

If you have completed and enjoyed ascents of nearby Mosquito Mountain and "Noseeum Peak," "Molarstone" HAS to be on your agenda at some point. Once you get up into the valley, the scenery is sublime and views from the summit are as good if not better than the aforementioned peaks. An extension to a nearby summit makes for a long day but exposes you to some very unique scenery and scrambling. Don't go if there is any chance of foul or even cloudy weather. Save this one for a bluebird day. Try from July on.

Drive about 24 km north on Highway 93 North and park in the small lot on the west side of the road, just before the turn-off to Mosquito Creek Campground. Cross the road and find the Molar Pass trailhead on the north side of the bridge. Hike approximately 6 km to the Mosquito Creek backcountry campground. Staying on the trail, cross Mosquito Creek on a log bridge at the far end of the campsite. Continue hiking for approximately 2.25 km, arriving at two trail signs (GR497234). Take the left fork to North Molar Pass. The impressive mountain overlooking the trail is Noseeum Peak (see page 404).

Follow the North Molar Pass trail into one of the most beautiful valleys in the Rockies. In addition to the plethora of stunning but unnamed peaks that surround the valley, take note of the very small but very distinctive "Fang" to the southeast. This cool little summit is part of the extension described below (see photo next page).

The trail eventually intersects a picturesque stream that drains a big but shallow tarn farther up the valley. Just before the tarn, cross to the other side of the stream and continue on the trail. You must now make a decision whether to continue to North Molar Pass and then ascend directly to the summit, or gain the northwest end of the ridge and complete a scenic ridgewalk to the top. If you intend to complete the highly recommended extension to GR528227, then gaining the northwest ridge immediately is also recommended. If the extension is not in your plans, the North Molar Pass route is recommended – you can always do the ridgewalk on return.

Northwest ridge route

From just past the stream crossing, the route to the ridge is obvious (see photo), but many variations are possible. Work your way northeastward to the base of the ascent slope. A group of interesting pinnacles and lichen-covered rocks lie more to the right if you wish to check them out. Slog your way up steep scree and rubble slopes to the northwest summit at GR528246. This is miserable terrain to ascend, but the same is true for an ascent from North Molar Pass.

From the cairned northwest summit follow the ridge southeast to the summit at GR540234. Views are magnificent throughout and earlier-season ascents will no doubt be rewarded with amazing cornice and snow scenery. In general you can stay on the ridge, though minor detours may be necessary. There is one rock band to overcome close to the summit, but a weakness through it is easily found.

After enjoying the incredible summit view, descend steep slopes to the southwest, going down to North Molar Pass. There is a window in the rock to see a short ways down, but you'll have to turn around to see it. Once down to North Molar Pass, turn right (northwest) and follow the trail all the back to the highway.

North Molar Pass route

This is the most straightforward way to the summit. Follow the North Molar Pass trail all the way to the pass at GR536231. Slog about 280 vertical metres up steep treadmill scree in a northeast direction to the summit at GR540234. Higher up you will want to go more to the right to see an interesting window framed by a chockstone.

Above: Nearing the stream, with a comprehensive view Molarstone and possible ascent routes. **NS**: north summit; **P**: interesting pinnacles to potentially check out; **S**: summit; **NMP**: North Molar Pass; **TF**: extension to The Fang.
Below: One of innumerable scenic rewards of the extension, the summit of Molarstone is to the far right.

Return the same way or follow the ridge northwestward to the cairned north summit at GR528246. Only a few moves of moderate scrambling and a little route-finding will be required and the views and scenery are wonderful throughout the traverse. From the north summit descend scree slopes generally southwestward and then make your way back to the North Molar Pass Trail.

The summit and extension to The Fang (GR528227)

The panorama from the summit of Molarstone is one of my favourites in all of the Canadian Rockies. Parts of the Lake Louise group, Skoki mountains, the Wapta Icefield and peaks of Highway 93 North are all proudly on display. The Willingdons, Cataract Peak and so many others to the northeast, east and southeast are stunning. And to top it all off (actually, bottom!) are the gorgeous Fish Lakes to the southeast. Hopefully, you'll have clear, calm weather to enjoy a longer summit stay to take it all in.

The extension to the lower summit to the southwest is super interesting and super worthwhile. It also stretches the duration of the trip into double digits and may leave you super "dead on your feet!"

You can see much of the route from the summit of Molarstone. Descend steep slopes to the southwest, going down to North Molar Pass. There is a window in the rock to see a short ways down, but you'll have to turn around to see it.

From North Molar Pass simply continue up the other side. The conglomerate and quartzite rock is fascinating. Scramble up it or find easy routes around it. Before reaching a large cairn at the top of the ridge, you will encounter a group of absolutely striking pinnacles of rock that have been exposed to oxygen (hence the brilliant red colour).

From the cairn (GR530226), the obvious high point to the west (The Fang) looks daunting, but there is a weakness on the west side of it. To get there, scramble carefully through an amazing field of huge white quartzite boulders and work your way around to the other side of the pointed summit pyramid. There you will find a staircase of solid quartzite blocks leading to the summit. Any scrambling moves that normally would be difficult seem moderate on this awesome rock. The summit is so small that only one person will fit at a time.

There are two logical descent routes. If you have really had enough at this point, the fastest way out is to descend the summit block and then go west down the ridge. The tarn you passed earlier acts as a guide. Find the North Molar Pass trail and return the way you came.

To make more of a loop and really experience this outstanding environment to its fullest, the recommended route is to descend the summit block and then go southwest to South Molar Pass, at GR513214. The route is pretty straightforward and you can choose to visit the cairned summit at GR512220 along the way (a minor hump that provides one last look at the surrounding landscape). From South Molar Pass head north and follow the good trail all the way back to the highway. A speedy pace can have you back in about 2 hours, by which time I'm sure you will want to soak your aching feet in chilly but soothing Mosquito Creek!

144. BOW PEAK 2880 m

(MAP 40, PAGE 470)
Rating easy via the west face
Round-trip time 5.5–7.5 hours
Elevation gain 940 m
Maps 82 N/09 Hector Lake; Gem Trek Bow Lake and Saskatchewan Crossing

*Bow Peak is a sensational trip from beginning to end. A terrific trail takes you all the way to beautiful Crowfoot Pass, with a ford of the Bow River en route, and then it's a boulder and scree ascent to a spectacular view at the summit. Late-season ascents are recommended, when the river is lower – hip waders are an option for the crossing. Also, **do not** attempt this trip on a rainy day, as the lichen-covered boulders that make up the ascent slopes become slippery and very treacherous when wet. Lastly, if, like some, you have already completed a winter ascent of Bow Peak, don't be shy about repeating the trip in the summer – it's a completely different experience and you will be amazed by the colours of the lakes and tarns.*

Drive 32 km north on Highway 93 North and park at a gravel pullout on the west side of the road (8.1 km north of the Mosquito Creek bridge or 900 m south of the Crowfoot Glacier viewpoint). Hike 400 m south along the road to the unsigned but obvious trailhead immediately descending to the west.

Follow the trail for 10–15 minutes to the Bow Lake outlet. Ford the outlet and continue along the trail as it parallels the Bow River. Cross a few small creeks, eventually arriving at the bigger stream about 1 km after the river ford. Cross this and keep following the trail it as turns to the right and uphill.

Bow Peak as seen from the other side of the highway, near the trailhead. **MH**: Mount Hector; **S**: summit of Bow Peak; **CP**: Crowfoot Pass. Photo: Bob Spirko

Above: From Crowfoot Pass Dinah Kruze heads toward the ascent slopes for Bow Peak. There are many potential routes up to the ridge besides the ones depicted. **1**: direct route to the ridge; **2**: scree gully; **3**: challenging route; **C**: col on the south ridge. Photo: Bob Spirko

Below: Bob Spirko approaches the false summit of Bow Peak. The view to the north includes the crowd favourite, Bow Lake. Photo: Dinah Kruze

Eventually the pleasant scenery of stream and forest gives way to more rugged and rocky terrain. You'll go by two small tarns as you approach Crowfoot Pass. From the high point of the pass, a look to the east reveals the ascent slopes (see photo). Most people will choose the most direct line, followed by a longer ridgewalk (route 1 in the photo). The scree gully leading more directly to the false summit is also an option, but better for descent (route 2 in the photo).

If you want more of a hands-on scrambling and route-finding experience, head up and to the right to a small col on the south ridge and then turn north, scrambling up ledgy quartzite blocks (route 3 in the photo) to the false summit. Many lines are possible, but expect moderate to difficult scrambling with some exposure, for this third route.

Pick a line and make your way up to the ridge. The boulder fields at the bottom should be negotiated with care, as the rocks may move. Numerous scree trails help along the way. Atop the ridge, turn right (south) and scramble up interesting, blocky terrain to the false summit and then onto the true summit (large cairn at GR430196).

While the view of Bow Lake has been terrific throughout, that of Hector Lake is sensational on a clear day. Having the stunning, heavily glaciated form of Mount Balfour above certainly works in the lake's favour! A sliver of Margaret Lake (see Pulpit Peak on page 395) is visible above Hector Lake.

Other notable summits in the panorama include Dolomite Peak, Mount Willingdon, "Noseeum Peak," Mount Hector and the super-long ridge of Crowfoot Mountain to the northwest.

To get down, return to the false summit and then head down a scree gully and back to the trail. Of course, it is also possible to simply retrace your route up.

South ridge extension

If you are craving more, there are a couple of options. Follow Mike Potter's ridgewalk down the southeast ridge to the shores of Hector Lake and back to the highway (refer to *Ridgewalks in the Canadian Rockies*). Note that this leaves you 14 km from your car.

A less strenuous but still quite challenging route is the south ridge. Return to the false summit and then follow the ridge down as it curves south, then southeast. It starts off easy but eventually requires some route-finding and downclimbing, with potential exposure. The easiest route would be considered moderate by scrambling standards, so don't go downclimbing any 30 metre vertical cliffs!

Go as far as you like (it is possible to go all the way to Hector Lake, but not recommended), taking in the great views towards the lake, and then turn west and descend to one of the streams below. Follow the stream north back to Crowfoot Pass and out.

BOW LAKE

At present there are at least four amazing scrambles around Bow Lake: "The Onion," Mount Jimmy Simpson, "Jimmy Junior" and Crowfoot Mountain. Unfortunately (or fortunately, depending on your perspective) glacial recession may increase that number by the mid-21st century if not sooner. One reason why these scrambles earn the adjective "amazing" is Bow Lake itself. The lake is, without argument, one of the most beautiful in the Rockies. A terrific trail takes you around its north shore and then to equally stunning Bow Glacier Falls in the valley above. Bring your camera, as perfect reflections in the deep, turquoise waters are commonplace here.

The waters of Bow Lake reflect the surrounding summits. **CM**: Crowfoot Mountain; **SN**: St. Nicholas Peak; **TO**: The Onion; **PP**: Portal Peak; **MT**: Mount Thompson; **JS**: Mount Jimmy Simpson; **JJ**: Jimmy Junior.

145. CROWFOOT MOUNTAIN 3055 m

(MAP 40, PAGE 470)

Rating easy for the North Peak; moderate for all other routes
Round-trip time 4–6 hours for the North Peak; 8–10 for the North Summit; 10–12 for the direct route; 13–16 for the full traverse
Elevation gain see individual route descriptions
Maps 82 N/09 Hector Lake; Gem Trek Bow Lake and Saskatchewan Crossing

Although more popular as a ski ascent (the run down is apparently fantastic), this huge mountain, towering directly above Bow Lake, is also a great summer trip. You won't get the speedy descent, but you will see outstanding scenery at every turn and enjoy a stunning summit panorama. There are many options and variations to ascend this multi-summit peak – from a relatively short round trip to the North Peak to a full traverse of the mountain from north to south. Four routes are described here, starting with the most direct way to the true summit. Wait until at least mid-July for an attempt so that you are able, with some degree of certainty, to avoid the glacier that still remains on the ascent slope.

Drive approximately 36 km north on Highway 93 North and turn left (west) into the Num-Ti-Jah Lodge parking lot. Hike past the lodge and find the Bow Glacier Falls hiking trail. Hike around the lake, then alongside the creek draining into the lake and then start up the wooden stairs on the right side of a canyon. A short ways up, turn left at the sign for the Bow Hut alpine route and cross to the other side of the canyon on a huge boulder (chockstone).

Direct route to the true summit (3055 m)
This is the fastest and most straightforward route to the true summit, with the least amount of elevation gain, which amounts to 1135 m.

After the chockstone, follow the trail up and then south, paralleling the creek. The trail soon goes into the trees for an extended distance. About 30–40 minutes from the chockstone you will come out into the open, around GR356219 (see photo on page 419). To your left, up high, is a significant rock band. Turn hard left and ascend rubble slopes, making your way up and around the left side of the rock band. The goal is to gain a bunch of elevation and then circle around the rock band, eventually turning south again, to reach a pristine and beautiful tarn (GR362218). The green grass and foliage around the tarn, backdropped by rugged mountains and glaciers, are fantastic. Be gentle to this delicate environment.

Go to the south end of the tarn and follow its outlet stream south and gently down into the more

hostile-looking environs of rock and ice. Turn southeast (left) and start ascending the valley, basically following the main stream coming down from the glacier on the west side of Crowfoot Mountain. As a general rule, stay left from here on in. Initially you will be right alongside the stream, but soon you can move left of it, ascending smooth slabs.

Higher up, when a large buttress of rock appears, stay to the left of that too. Eventually the false summit will appear above, with a sliver of the glacier below. Even though the glacier on this part of the mountain is in its last stages of life and generally not heavily crevassed, there still may be hidden dangers and unstable terrain. It is best not to use the glacier as an ascent route or shortcut. There are several routes around it (see top photo on page 420). Note that the main bulk of the glacier is off to the right. You will see it as you gain elevation.

Pick one of the ascent routes. If you have the time and energy, I recommended going to the col north of the false summit and then south to the false and the true summits. Otherwise, take the direct route. Both routes are foreshortened and will require some stamina, patience and perseverance to reach the true summit at GR392195.

If you were expecting a mind-boggling summit panorama, you won't be disappointed in the least. Crowfoot's significant height and great location on the edge of the Wapta Icefield guarantee a comprehensive view of everything in the immediate area and many distant surprises. Mount Balfour to the south-southwest is stunning from this angle, and much farther in the distant south you can make

This is where you leave the trail and go up and around the left side of the rock band. **RB**: rock band; **NP**: North Peak; **NS**: North Summit.

out the distinctive profile of the three Goodsirs. Recondite Peak, the Willingdons, Cataract Peak and Mount Hector are a few of the more prominent summits visible to the northeast, east and southeast.

Return the way you came. Of course, it is possible to traverse the ridge and go all the way to the slightly lower north summit, but the terrain gets complicated after the summit and route-finding your way down can be very difficult. Not recommended.

North Peak (2730 m)

If your goals are a little more modest than the true summit, the North Peak offers amazing views of Bow Lake, Iceberg Lake and sections of the Wapta Icefield. This route is also the launching point to the much higher North Summit and a full traverse of the mountain to its true summit. Elevation gain for the North Peak is 810 m from the parking lot.

From the chockstone crossing of the canyon, continue up the trail for another 5 minutes until it turns south, above the junction of the two major streams. Continue on the trail for another couple of minutes and then turn left (southeast) into the bush. A short section of bushwhacking takes you to rocky terrain below a significant rock band. Hike/scramble up to the rock band and then traverse below it towards open terrain to the east. The route to the North Peak becomes very obvious very quickly. The goal is simply to avoid the stands of trees and make your way east-northeastward to the summit(s) (see bottom photo on page 420). Be warned that the final slope to either summit is quite foreshortened.

Be sure to go all the way to the north end of the ridge, at GR368236 (GV in the photo), where you can see Bow Lake's delta, directly below Mount Jimmy Simpson and Jimmy Junior. Then go south to the large cairn marking the North Peak (GR370232). A couple of scrambling moves on the left (east) side of the ridge get you there without having to lose elevation right before the summit.

Above: Direct route, the false summit and several routes around the glacier. **FS**: false summit; **SR**: steeper, more direct route to the false summit; **DR**: direct route to the summit; **G**: glacier.
Below: North Peak and North Summit routes. The obvious routes to the summits. **NS**: North Summit; **NP**: North Peak; **GV**: great view!

Enjoy the view and then return the same way or continue to the North Summit.

NORTH SUMMIT (3040 M)

If you don't mind losing about 100 m of elevation and then regaining all of it plus another 300 m, the North Summit offers a tremendous summit panorama. The total elevation gain for this trip is approximately 1220 m.

From the North Peak, continue south along the ridge, losing some elevation on the light-brown shale before gaining it back on grey limestone. It quickly becomes obvious that a glacier existed here, perhaps not too long ago, and left things in rough shape. Approaching the huge rock wall that guards the north summit, there appear to be a couple of weaknesses through it. Unfortunately those are deceivingly steep, up hardened dirt that offers little in the way of good footing and traction. Resist the urge to attempt one of these treacherous routes; instead descend the obvious scree gully alongside the wall.

Lose a fair amount of elevation and then look to the left for an easy and obvious break in the wall (easy scrambling). Cut left across the break (note the location for your return trip) and traverse south for a short distance before turning directly up the mountain. Head up one of several gullies, where you will find some pretty decent hands-on scrambling on solid rock. The gullies eventually peter out and it's a long, rubbly slog up to the ridge and then south to the summit at GR373223.

The north summit is only 15 m lower than the true summit, which is still 3.5 km away in a straight line, so the view is just as good as from the true summit – perhaps even better, since you can see Bow Lake below.

If this is the end of the line for you, start by returning the same way. Once you have traversed back into the gully where you lost elevation earlier, just go straight down that gully and traverse to the right to get back on your ascent route when feasible. The rest of the return route is the same.

Full traverse

For true masochists there is the full traverse. With all the additional elevation losses and gains your total gain for the day will be approximately 1450 m. Although this pales in comparison to the 2400 m for Molar Mountain, when combined with the significant horizontal distance required for the Crowfoot traverse, the elevation gain will feel like much more.

The route is very simple: follow the ridge south-southeastward for about 4 km until you reach the true summit, at GR392195. For the best views and footing, it is preferable to stick to the ridge throughout and avoid sidesloping, even though this will require additional elevation gains. There will be some route-finding and moderate scrambling towards the end of the traverse. Views of the Crowfoot Glacier on the east side of the ridge get better and better throughout and Bow Lake is a constant companion almost all the way, though disappointingly it disappears from sight as you near the summit. You may even be spotted by the hordes of people at the Crowfoot Glacier pullout, more than 1 vertical kilometre below you. Expect the traverse to take a solid 2 hours.

You will probably have plenty of time to enjoy the phenomenal summit panorama, because you will need it to recuperate for the return trip! Returning the same way will likely have about as much appeal as pizza without cheese, so it is recommended that you reverse the **Direct** ascent route to get down as follows.

Return along the ridge to the false summit to the north, then turn left (west) and descend rubble slopes towards the glacier below. The goal is to avoid stepping onto the glacier completely. The easiest way to do this is to go to the left side of the glacier and then traverse over to its right side much lower down, where there are only a few snow patches. (Note that in years to come the glacier and snow here may completely disappear.) Keep going down the valley, staying to the right side.

In general, follow the main stream down to a small stream that comes down from the right side of the valley. It will be obvious because the new stream is grassy on both sides (GR364213). Follow that stream up to a beautiful tarn. Continue going north, past the tarn and then down to the right. You are atop a big rock band, and circling around it on its right (east) side is the easiest way to get down. Eventually you can start going more to the left (west). Route-find your way down rubble slopes to the main trail (GR356219) that goes to Bow Hut. No bushwhacking necessary. Turn right (north) and hike back to the parking lot.

146. "THE ONION" 2680 m

(MAP 40, PAGE 470)
Rating easy, with optional moderate scrambling
Round-trip time 7–10 hours
Elevation gain 700 m
Maps 82 N/09 Hector Lake, N/10 Blaeberry River; Gem Trek Bow Lake and Saskatchewan Crossing

*"The Onion" is an unofficial hump of rock on the eastern edge of the Wapta Icefield. During the snow months the peak routinely becomes a consolation prize when whiteouts or other unfavourable conditions on the Wapta render ascents of the more ambitious peaks sketchy. So, what is this "after-thought" of a peak like as a scramble? In two words – totally awesome! First the standard phenomenal jaunt around Bow Lake, then a scenic hike above the approach canyon, and then it's glacier heaven! This is one of the few scrambles that allows you to get right up against a glacier. **Note** that going onto the glacier is not scrambling – stay off the ice unless you have the proper training and gear. Wait until midsummer and pick a clear day for this unique and visually stunning trip.*

Drive approximately 36 km north on Highway 93 North and turn left (west) into the Num-Ti-Jah Lodge parking lot. Hike past the lodge and find the Bow Glacier Falls hiking trail. The Onion can be seen right from the start (see photo on page 417). Hike around the lake to the creek draining into it. Walk along the creek and then start up the wooden stairs on the right side of a canyon. A short ways up, turn left at the sign for the Bow Hut alpine route and cross to the other side of the canyon on a huge boulder (chockstone).

Follow the trail on the other side up to Bow Hut, several kilometres away. The trail is very easy to follow. There are a couple of sections where boulder fields interrupt it, but it's always easy to find the continuation on the other side of those fields. Above treeline Bow Hut is clearly visible up and to the right (see photo). Follow the trail to the end of the valley and then around and up towards the hut. The improving and impressive scenery is but a small taste of what is to come.

It is not necessary to go to the hut. The recommended route (most scenic) stays to the left, following the headwall and eventually intercepting the edge of Bow Glacier, around GR349205. Follow the glacier (alongside it, **never** on it), enjoying the spectacular scenery those giant slabs of ice have to offer. You will have to lose a little elevation at one point, but nothing too

severe. The Onion is the obvious, rounded peak to the northeast.

At any point, you can choose to follow one of several faint trails towards the summit (GR345213) or find your own route. There is some pleasant scrambling on the glacially eroded and very colourful rock. Be sure to wander over to the northeast side of the summit to see Iceberg Lake.

If you have the time and energy, a great way to fully experience the area is to stay relatively close to the glacier and circle around to the north side of The Onion. Here you will be treated to a phenomenal view of Iceberg Lake and Bow Lake. There is some route-finding along the way and a few up and downs. Views of the Wapta Icefield and the mountains that are part of it are magnificent. Once again, you can pretty much make your way to the summit at any time (GR345213).

Sitting right on the edge of the Wapta Icefield, the summit panorama from The Onion is "A Tale of Two Cities" – everything to the west is glaciated and everything to the east is not. The contrast is striking and remarkably beautiful.

You can either return exactly the same way or take a more direct route towards Bow Hut and then down the same way you came. Route-finding is straightforward, and taking a slightly different route back gives you a little more to see and experience.

Above: The approximate route up to the glacier. **BH**: Bow Hut; **TO**: The Onion.
Below: A couple of options to the summit from a small glacial tarn. **ER**: exploratory route; **DR**: direct route;
S: summit.

147. MOUNT JIMMY SIMPSON 2970 m

(MAP 40, PAGE 470)
Rating easy via the south face and southwest slopes
Round-trip time 6–9 hours
Elevation gain 1050 m
Maps 82 N/09 Hector Lake, N/10 Blaeberry River; Gem Trek Bow Lake and Saskatchewan Crossing

The view from the summit of Mount Jimmy Simpson is one of my favourites in all of the Rockies – glaciers, beautiful peaks in every direction and the entire length of Bow Lake's stunning, turquoise-tinted waters are but a few of the many highlights. Although not the shortest path to the summit, the route described here involves the least amount of bushwhacking and keeps the scree bashing to a minimum. Try from July on. Take an ice axe and maybe crampons for early season ascents

Drive approximately 36 km north on Highway 93 North and turn left (west) into the Num-Ti-Jah Lodge parking lot. Hike past the lodge and find the Bow Glacier Falls hiking trail. Go about 4.2 km around the lake and up to the valley above, following the signs to Bow Glacier Falls. Several hundred metres before the falls, you will arrive at a flatter, open area (GR351233) with Bow Falls in front of you to the left and the far south end of Mount Jimmy Simpson to the right (see photo). Examine the route photo carefully. It is not the only line that is possible, but probably the easiest.

Gain a little elevation to above the first set of trees, and then turn right, ascending the sloping ramp near treeline. No need to go up into the rubble yet. A trail is starting to develop here and the route was heavily cairned as of 2016. About 5 minutes up the ramp, turn left and go up steep dirt slopes, aiming for the left side of a noticeable patch of low trees and foliage. This takes you to a second ramp (bench), where you can turn right and ascend the ramp.

It's now just a matter of following the ramp to the upper valley. There are a couple of very mildly exposed situations. Although the rock to the left is generally awesome for scrambling, do not be tempted to gain elevation all the way to the ridge – you will just end up having to lose that elevation on potentially tricky terrain. Also, make waypoints or take photos or mental notes of your route up. You will want to retrace your steps on descent and it is very easy to end up on a different track without knowing it.

Eventually the remainder of the route will appear. As long as you stay on that bench, elevation losses and regains will be minimal and the

The approximate ascent route as seen from above the canyon.

Above: The remainder of the route from the upper bench. **C**: col; **S**: summit; **GR**: GR347251.
Below: Two ways to go from near the col. **JJ**: route to GR347251 and then Jimmy Junior; **SD**: standard descent route.

terrain underfoot is easy to ascend. Make your way towards the col of the true summit and an outlier to the west. The grade leading up to the col is very steep, with unstable rubble and scree underfoot. Snow may help, but in that case you will probably appreciate an ice axe and possibly crampons. From the col, turn right (northeast) and hike up easy scree to the summit in about 20 minutes.

With clear skies above and all around, most would agree that this is one of the premier views in the Canadian Rockies. There is nothing but incredible mountain splendour in every direction. The contrast of glaciated peaks on one side and non-glaciated ones on the other, with stunning Bow Lake separating them, is truly remarkable. Almost every peak on the Wapta Icefield is clearly visible.

When satiated, return the same way. To help find the correct descent route, the start of the descent bench lies around GR342250.

"Jimmy Junior"

If you are interested in making this a two-peak day, Jimmy Junior is certainly within striking distance. Personally, I would prefer to climb Jimmy Junior as a separate trip so as to not miss the cool ascent route up a scenic drainage, but a description is provided anyway for those not wanting to make the extra journey. The trip will require an additional 450 m of elevation gain.

Return to the col and start descending the steep scree into the valley below. Once below the steep terrain, instead of going to the right (west) side of the valley, go to the left side, where the lighter-coloured brown rock lies. The goal is to gain the far end of Jimmy Simpson's south ridge (GR347251), then descend to the unnamed tarn on the east side of that.

Continue to lose elevation down into the valley. Sidesloping directly to the ridge can be excruciating because of the terrible terrain and will not save time or energy. It is better to descend to around GR345251 and then slog up more ankle-friendly slopes to the high point at GR347251. From there, descend scree slopes to the picturesque, unnamed tarn below. Refer to the Jimmy Junior description on page 427 for the remainder of the trip.

148. "JIMMY JUNIOR" 2770 m

(MAP 40, PAGE 470)
Rating moderate via the southeast drainage and south face, with mild exposure
Round-trip time 5.5–8 hours
Elevation gain 850 m
Maps 82 N/09 Hector Lake; Gem Trek Bow Lake and Saskatchewan River Crossing

If you are not yet convinced that smaller and unofficial peaks are worth the effort, give "Jimmy Junior" a go. Boasting views usually reserved for bigger mountains, the little brother of Mount Jimmy Simpson is short and the scenery is enthralling throughout. Wait for a clear day to best enjoy the mesmerizing turquoise colour of three lakes that are perhaps the highlight of the trip. Try from July on. Note that this route is not the same as the winter one described in Summits and Icefields *and* Snowshoeing in the Canadian Rockies, 2nd Edition. *This route follows a drainage to a beautiful tarn lying south of the objective.*

Drive approximately 36 km north on Highway 93 North and turn left (west) into the Num-Ti-Jah Lodge parking lot. Find the Bow Glacier Falls trail west of the lodge and hike around the north side of the lake for about 10–15 minutes. As always, the views across the lake are stunning, especially when the surrounding mountains are reflected in the lake. Look to the right (north) for an obvious gap between two significant buttresses of rock around GR360250 (see photo below). This is the drainage that leads to a beautiful, unnamed tarn and provides the most interesting and scenic route to Jimmy Junior.

The two buttresses where the drainage runs, as seen from the main trail.

Above: The three routes to the summit. **DR**: direct route; **C**: Jimmy Simpson/Jimmy Junior col; **3**: third route.
Below: The recommended descent route and two of the other scrambles in the area. **TO**: The Onion;
C: Crowfoot Mountain; **LB**: left buttress; **G**: descent gully; **KD**: Kaycie Dewit. Photo: Kaycie's Dad

A short stint of easy bush leads to the rocky drainage. Follow the drainage up to the first of many waterfalls. Getting above this fall is perhaps the crux of the trip. Ascend alarmingly steep dirt on the left (west) side of the waterfall, passing around an obvious rock outcrop, and then traverse to the right, into the drainage, once you are above the waterfall.

From here it is simply a matter of following the drainage all the way to the lake. Most of time you can stay right by the water (when it is not running underground). Occasional detours up the right side will be needed to overcome several nearly vertical waterfalls, but you should return to the centre of the drainage as much as possible. There is plenty of beautiful scenery to gawk at, not the least of which is the stunning colour of Bow Lake, in all its turquoise splendour, every time you turn around!

The tarn is likewise a beautiful blue-green colour. Mount Jimmy Simpson stands majestically to the northwest and Jimmy Junior is the more modest pyramidal form due north. Ascending the slopes above the tarn will grant you excellent views of the entire area. Circling the lake also provides additional scenic opportunities.

From the tarn there are three logical routes to the summit of Jimmy Junior. We'll describe the most obvious one here, a direct line due north to the false summit and then to the true summit. Those craving a little adventure involving steep, exposed scrambling up loose terrain can go to the Jimmy Simpson/Jimmy Junior col and then route-find their way to the summit. There are only a few difficult moves, but this really is terrain for experienced scramblers. The third route is a little more circuitous and goes towards the Jimmy Simpson/Jimmy Junior col before veering to the right, up to the ridge between the false and true summit of Jimmy Junior.

Most will follow the line of least resistance (direct route) up to the false summit and then continue on to the true summit (top photo opposite). Stay to the left as you approach the summit block. An obvious trail leads easily to the top.

Along with his big brother (Mount Jimmy Simpson) Jimmy Junior sports one of my favourite views in the world! Colourful lakes, jagged peaks, glaciers – this view has everything. Hopefully, clear skies above you will prevail, as they will enhance the scene exponentially.

For the return, following the wide ridge south is highly recommended, as opposed to simply going back the way you came. There is no need to down-climb the summit block on the left side. Hike south down the ridge, back to the false summit. The route is obvious throughout.

Aim for the left buttress far below. Upon reaching the end of the buttress, go over to the left side (GR356256) and look for an obvious gully trending right to left that provides the best escape to easier terrain (see photo). Descend the gully and continue down steep, forested terrain, picking the line of least resistance, towards the main trail. With a little route-finding and a ton of luck it is possible to make it most of the way down with a minimal amount of heavy bushwhacking.

149. SILVERHORN MOUNTAIN 2911 m

(MAP 41, PAGE 471)
Rating moderate from the northwest
Round-trip time 6–8 hours
Elevation gain 1200 m
Maps 82 N/15 Mistaya Lake, 82 N/16 Siffleur River; Gem Trek Bow Lake

Sandwiched between the more lofty and distinctive forms of Observation Peak and Mount Weed, Silverhorn Mountain usually gets barely a sideward glance as you drive by. No more! Silverhorn is a great trip, with varied terrain and scenery, a section of terrific hands-on scrambling and a magnificent summit panorama, right on par with its neighbours. A snow-free summit ridge is preferable, so wait until July to make an attempt.

Drive north on Highway 93 North and park off the shoulder at 5.8 km north of the Bow Summit turn-off. This section of the highway has seen some construction, so you may have to be creative about where you park. You can also drive a little farther and park where the rocky ascent drainage intersects the road. Hike into the bush, heading northeast and quickly intercepting the wide drainage that provides access to Silverhorn's upper slopes.

Hike up the drainage until a large waterfall comes into view. Although it is possible to scramble up alongside the waterfall, the route is tricky and exposed and may not be possible when the volume of flowing water is high. Instead, around GR328349 (approximately 25–30 minutes from the start), gain elevation on the left (north) side of the drainage (see photo), in order to circumvent this obstacle. Stay high above the watercourse and then return to the drainage by descending steep, dirt slopes.

Continue up the drainage. It soon veers to

The waterfall bypass route. The fall is just around a corner and becomes clearly visible upon gaining elevation.

The upper section of the mountain. **RR**: rock route (recommended); **DR**: drainage route; **S**: summit. Photo: Kerry Vizbar

the right and this is the direction you should go. Shortly after, a good portion of the remainder of the ascent is revealed (see photo). If the drainage is snow-free you can simply follow it all the way up to the summit ridge. However, a much better option is to scramble up the rock on the north side of the drainage. Innumerable lines can be taken. Most of the rock is super solid and a blast to ascend. Unfortunately, both the rock and the drainage routes eventually turn into scree/rubble slogs to the summit ridge.

Upon reaching the summit ridge, turn south and scramble along the sometimes narrow and loose ridge to the summit. You can circumvent some of the difficulties by dropping down to the right side, although that may be more trouble than it's worth. If the summit ridge is snow-free, stay on the ridge. The exception is a spot just after the false summit where the mountain does suddenly drop away quite steeply. Back up a few metres and find

the easy path on the left side of the ridge. Easy terrain then leads to the summit.

The summit panorama is amazing! From south to north you get to see a few of the Canadian Rockies' most beautiful glacier-fed lakes: Bow, Peyto, Mistaya and the Waterfowl. Of course, those lakes sit under or near the gorgeous mountains of the Wapta Icefield, including Crowfoot, Jimmy Simpson, Mistaya, Rhondda, Habel, Baker, Patterson, Howse and the striking Mount Chephren. Needless to say, Observation Peak to the south and Mount Weed to the north are very prominent. Many of the light-brown summits to the northeast are unnamed (except Conical Peak), but they certainly add to the variety of hues characteristic of the summit view.

Return the same way. If you scrambled up the rock on the north side of the drainage, if might be a little easier to stick closer to the drainage on the way down.

The remainder of the route from the first high point north of Silverhorn. **S**: summit; **MW**: Mount Weed; **MC**: Mount Chephren; **D**: descent route.

Extension to GR338361, 2813 m

For some added adventure, a side trip north to an intermediate high point between Silverhorn and Weed is a good way to spend an extra hour or two. The route is easy and interesting, although the summit view is not as good as that from Silverhorn.

The directions are simple. Follow the surprisingly colourful ridge north, dropping down to the left side of it occasionally, and then scramble up to the summit. It will take about 1.5 hours to get there. Views and scenery are very interesting along the way. It is possible to continue north and ascend Mount Weed, but this would make for an extremely long trip with considerable route-finding and elevation gain. Better to save it for a different day and follow Kane's route up Weed.

For the return trip, descend the summit block and then turn right, going down steep scree slopes. Unfortunately the scree-surfing here is not fantastic, but better terrain can be found to the left. A drainage soon forms. Much lower down you will want to be to the right (north) side of this drainage. Cliff bands that are not downclimbable have formed on the left side. Stay on the scree slopes above the drainage until it becomes obvious and easy to get back down into it. Follow this drainage down to where it intersects with the one you came up, and then return the way you came.

150. MOUNT NOYES 3084 m

(MAP 42, PAGE 471)
Rating moderate, with mild exposure
Round-trip time 7–9 hours
Elevation gain 1400 m
Maps 82 N/15 Mistaya Lake; Gem Trek Bow Lake and Saskatchewan Crossing

Mount Noyes is the quintessential "high-pressure system" scramble. In other words, don't even think about doing this trip unless you are all but guaranteed clear skies. To be unable to enjoy the amazing summit panorama would be most disappointing. An early-season ascent may require crampons and an ice axe. It's best to wait until mid-July when most of the snow is gone.

Drive north on Highway 93 North for about 53 km. Park on the east side of the road at a small drainage 800 m north of the Silverhorn campground (marked on a sign as "OVERFLOW CAMPING"). This drainage is about 12 km north of the turnoff to Bow Summit and Peyto Lake. Hike along the left side of the drainage, staying within earshot of the creek. As the grade becomes steeper, scenic waterfalls appear. Eventually you'll arrive at a steep rock band that blocks the way. Traverse left about 50 m alongside the band to an obvious weakness. Moderate scrambling takes you through the rock band. Finding this weakness on return can be problematic, so make good mental notes of your surroundings or mark with a GPS waypoint.

Continue up and to the right through easier outcrops of rock, working your way back towards the drainage. This is not necessary, but it will afford you the opportunity to take little detours to best view the waterfalls. The terrain near the edge is often a little easier to negotiate, too. Hopefully this will also serve to break up the tedium of 600-odd vertical metres of gain to the upper basin. Perhaps the most scenic section of the fall sits near the top of the slope. Here you are able to traverse to the right on easy slopes into the drainage. Take a few photos and then either continue up slopes on the right of the drainage or return to the left side of it. Both routes take you into a beautiful cirque as the creek takes a sharp right turn. Follow the creek southeast into the cirque and take a few minutes to contemplate the remaining 800 vertical metres. Also take note of the striking peak right in front of you to the northeast. An alternative descent

Left: Almost at the very scenic upper basin. The ascent route swings around to the right once you are there. **AD**: alternative descent route.
Below: The summit of Noyes comes into view.
LR: left-rising ramp; **S**: summit.

Above: The suggested route to the summit. Variations are possible. **S**: summit.
Below: The first part of the alternative descent route. Go to the Big Boulder (**BB**).

route exists alongside the upper rock band and down scree slopes. You may want to use this route on the way back.

At this point, the summit of Noyes is not visible. Hike southeast up the drainage. Quickly it swings around to the northeast, where the summit and route come into view.

A significant headwall is the first obstacle. Hike and boulder-hop up rubble slopes towards the headwall, looking for a left-rising ramp to the right of the waterfall. Someday the glacier that feeds this fall may disappear and there be will no water. Still, the ramp through the headwall will remain, a little to the right of centre. Make your way up the ramp. Use care, as the rock underfoot is loose and a few steps near the top may feel mildly exposed when the ground to the left suddenly disappears. Above the headwall, continue up scree slopes towards the summit.

From above the headwall, the easiest route gains the west ridge and then follows it to the summit. This way is best used on descent. A better option for ascent is to go up step-like terrain in the middle. Hike up scree to the base of low-angled rock steps. Pick your own line from here, but generally the more left you are the easier the ascent. Good moderate to difficult scrambling lies more to the right. When the rock steps end, trend left towards the west ridge to complete the ascent.

Unfortunately the terrain here deteriorates to rubble and scree. The first rock band appears intimidating, but there is a narrow yet easy weakness through it. Above that, it's just an annoying, steep scree slog to the summit.

The summit panorama is definitely the highlight of the trip. Immediately to the west lie the aesthetic forms of Howse Peak, White Pyramid and Mount Chephren. Mount Weed is immediately south, and to the north sits the northerly and slightly lower summit of Noyes, with the striking towers of massive Mount Murchison beyond. Peaks above 11,000 feet in your field of vision include Recondite, Willingdon, Hector, Temple and all five Lyells.

For descent, once below the aforementioned rock band below the summit, swing to the right to the west ridge and make an easy scree descent down the ridge. When it is easiest, go left and follow your ascent route down. Another option, before you leave, is a quick visit to the high point to the west – a 20-minute diversion that grants good views of the faces of south and north summits of Noyes. Simply follow the west ridge to the high point and then return the same way.

A more interesting descent route exists by staying high on the slopes. This route requires some elevation gain, and it is important to descend the correct slope around the west side of the peak. The variety of rock along the way is worth the price of a few additional metres. From the west ridge, descend into the bowl, but stay to the right side, aiming for a massive, square, solitary boulder at the northwest end of the headwall.

When you get to the boulder, start traversing around the peak above you, along its base. Cross several slopes before you must gain elevation up a steep slope. Hug the side of the peak here. The rock is solid with good holds, just in case the entire scree slope decides to slide with you on it. The top of the slope marks the start of the descent and is characterized by beautiful, solid, orange rock. The creek you came up now lies slightly to your left. Descend the orange rock for a few metres and then turn right, down scree of variable quality. When feasible, angle left down to the creek and back to your ascent route.

This strikingly orange rock is one of the many highlights of the alternative descent route. Mistaya Lake is far below. Aim for the creek (**C**).

151. "BUFFALO (BISON) PEAK" 2925 m

(MAP 43, PAGE 471)
Rating moderate/difficult via southwest face
Round-trip time 6–8 hours
Elevation gain 1340 m
Maps 82 N/15 Mistaya Lake; Gem Trek Bow Lake and Saskatchewan River Crossing

This is one mountain you are likely to have all to yourself. The ascent is interesting and challenging in regards to route-finding. A unique and quite remarkable summit view will be your reward. Yet another terrific Graeme Pole route, with some helpful changes from Vern Dewit and Wietse Bijlsma. Try from mid-July on.

Drive about 64 km north on Highway 93 North and park at a large pullout on the west side of the road some 6.4 km north of the Waterfowl Lakes Campground turnoff or 7.5 km south of the Mistaya Canyon parking lot. Although you can start the trip from where Bison Creek intersects the road, it is easier and shorter to simply cross the road and bushwhack northeastward to an unnamed creek about 20–30 minutes up. The bush is light and easy to negotiate.

To find the creek, trend more to the left as you gain elevation. Once in the creek, follow it upward until it forks around GR225484. Take the left fork (see left photo opposite). This fork of the creek is narrower and steeper and will actually require a little scrambling. When a steep wall of rock appears in front, scramble up to the left to reach the base of a complex array of rock bands that bars the way. This is where the going gets a little more intense.

There is a moderate scrambling route through the rock bands, but route-finding and going back and forth across the terrain is required. The track starts at the left side. Make GPS waypoints or build cairns to guide you for the return.

Above the rock bands (GR229487) the next section is clearly revealed (right photo opposite). Ascend the steep gully between the huge rock formations above. This gully is littered with loose debris, and knocking rocks down is a big concern. If by some very small chance there is a party above you, wait until they are all the way up. Once again

the easiest route requires only easy to moderate scrambling.

Above the gully the summit is 270 vertical metres and just a simple slog, with some minor rock bands near the top. The view is spectacular. To the immediate west sit Mount Sarbach, the double summit of Kaufmann Peaks, Epaulette Mountain and the magnificent forms of White Pyramid and Mount Chephren. Sarbach and Chephren are both fantastic Kane scrambles and not to be missed. The awesome towers that surround Buffalo Peak are mostly part of the Mount Murchison massif and many have specific but unofficial names. The exception is Totem Tower due east. Mounts Amery and Wilson are the glacier-topped peaks to the northwest.

Perhaps of equal interest is the view of the major lakes alongside the highway, dropping down like giant steps from Bow Lake at an elevation of 1920 m to the Waterfowl Lakes at 1660 m. The wickedly meandering Mistaya River is also particularly eye-catching.

Start by returning the same way, once again taking care to not dislodge rocks down the gully. Below the rock bands it is not necessary to descend back into the creek just yet. It is easier to stay up high on the north bank and go down through the trees. Once past the steeper terrain of the creek you should work your way back into the creek and then out the same way you came.

Wietse Bijlsma nears the fork in the creek. Photo: Vern Dewit

Wietse returns from the gully. Photo: Vern Dewit

One of many reasons to complete this ascent, the wildly impressive towers of the Mount Murchison massif are close at hand. Photo: Vern Dewit

THE VALLEY NORTH OF MOUNT SASKATCHEWAN

This is one of the more breathtaking valleys in the Canadian Rockies and contains several unnamed peaks, each providing phenomenal views in all directions. Having completed all as winter ascents (snowshoe/mountaineering), I decided to return when the snow was gone. I found the experience to be very different but equally enthralling. Big Bend Peak is a terrific introduction to the area, and the North Towers of Mount Saskatchewan are the crowning achievement.

One of the innumerable spectacular views from the valley, taken from the north ridge of the North Towers of Mount Saskatchewan.

152. "BIG BEND PEAK" 2814 m

(MAP 44, PAGE 471)
Rating easy via northeast ridge
Round-trip time 6–9 hours
Elevation gain 1110 m
Maps 82 C/03 Columbia Icefield; Gem Trek Columbia Icefield

Big Bend Peak looks easy and obvious from the Big Bend in Highway 93 North. While not difficult, there can be route-finding challenges and ascending the steep scree and rubble is not terribly aesthetic or fun. However, once you are on the ridge the views are amazing and they get better with each step up. Try from mid-July on.

On Highway 93 North, drive 34.5 km north of the Highway 11 turn-off (near Saskatchewan River Crossing) to the Big Bend in the road. This is a good place to stop and check out the route and snow conditions for Big Bend Peak. Turn around, drive about 1 km back along the highway and turn right, onto an unsigned and difficult to see gravel road that goes down to a bridge over the North Saskatchewan River in 100 m. Park there.

Cross the bridge and hike back along the deep canyon/river on an obvious trail. Follow the river almost until it disappears into the forest and then go left towards the trees, looking for the obvious trail going up and to the left. Ascend this to its high point in about 10–15 minutes (GR946794). If you start losing elevation you have gone too far. Turn left (southeast) and bushwhack up easy, then steeper slopes to a forested high point around GR950791. Animal trails help along the way.

Turn right (southwest) and bushwhack up additional easy slopes, then steeper ones again for about 1 km to treeline. Once you are out of the trees and on the wide northeast ridge, the route is obvious. Slog your way up the steep scree, scrambling

Big Bend Peak and some of the ascent route to the false summit as seen after crossing the river. **FS**: false summit. Photo: Matthew Clay

The beautiful ridge connecting the false summit and the true summit. The North Towers of Mount Saskatchewan are just left of centre. Photo: Matthew Clay

up or circumventing any minor rock bands along the way. The false summit sits around GR932780 and offers a wonderfully aesthetic view of the summit mass of Big Bend Peak.

All obstacles from here to the summit can be negotiated on the left side. The scrambling is never difficult and a decent trail is developing, mostly on the left side of the ridge. Highlights of the summit view include the southeast sides of mounts Athabasca and Andromeda, a little glimpse of the second-highest mountain in the Canadian Rockies, Mount Columbia, and of course the real giant in the area, Mount Saskatchewan. This is a good chance to also see "Mount Saskatchewan Junior" and the "North Towers of Mount Saskatchewan," other ascents described in this section.

Return the same way. It may be tempting to continue southwestward to Saskatchewan Junior, but avoiding the glacier between the two peaks can be tricky or requires a huge elevation loss. Best to save that one for another day and combine it with an ascent of the North Towers.

153. "MOUNT SASKATCHEWAN JUNIOR I" 2840 m

(MAP 44, PAGE 471)

Rating easy via the east ridge
Round-trip time 9–12 hours
Elevation gain 1140 m
Maps 82 C/03 Columbia Icefield; Gem Trek Columbia Icefield

If Big Bend Peak is elementary school, then consider Mount Saskatchewan Junior I to be junior/ senior high school (the North Towers are definitely university!). This trip is considerably longer than Big Bend, and although the scrambling (grovelling up steep scree) is about on the same level, route-finding and navigation can be a little more challenging. As you might expect, the summit view is magnificent. Try from mid-July on.

On Highway 93 North, drive 34.5 km north of the Highway 11 turn-off (near Saskatchewan River Crossing) to the Big Bend in the road. This is a good place to stop and check out the route and snow conditions for Big Bend Peak. If Big Bend is plastered in snow, so will be Mount Saskatchewan Junior. Turn around, drive about 1 km back along the highway and turn right, onto an unsigned and difficult to see gravel road that goes down to a bridge over the North Saskatchewan River in 100 m or so. Park there.

Cross the bridge and hike back along the deep canyon/river on an obvious trail. Follow the river almost until it disappears into the forest and then

Three potential routes to the summit are **MSJ**: Mount Saskatchewan Junior; **IH**: intermediate high point; **EE**: east end of ridge.

Above: The east ridge. **JI**: Mount Saskatchewan Junior I; **JII**: Junior II.
Below: Less than perfect weather, but what a view! **JI**: Mount Saskatchewan Junior I; **A**: Mount Amery;
MS: Mount Saskatchewan; **NT**: North Towers of Mount Saskatchewan; **L**: The Lyells.

go left towards the trees, looking for the obvious trail, going up and to the left. Ascend this trail to its high point in about 10–15 minutes (GR946794). If you start losing elevation you have gone too far. Turn left (south) and bushwhack up easy slopes, then steeper ones to a forested high point, around GR950791. Animal trails help along the way and so will making your own GPS track. It is easy to get disoriented on the way back.

Once you reach that high point continue going south, but now losing elevation, down into the valley below. Trend to the right as you descend. Eventually you'll arrive at the fast-flowing glacial stream that runs the length of the valley. Start hiking southwest along the west side of the stream. For the most part there is a trail. Several beautiful, water-carved canyons interrupt progress but are easily circumvented. Bushy sections are likewise generally easy to navigate as long as you don't stray too far from the stream.

Make your way about 3 km up the valley to where the trees disappear on both sides of the stream. There are many routes to the summit from here. The suggested way is to continue up the valley for 500 or so metres to GR939760 and then turn right (west), ascending rubbly slopes to gain the plateau above. After gaining a few hundred metres of elevation, the objective and all potential routes there will appear in front of you.

Gaining the east end of the ridge (GR922767) is the most scenic route but involves the most elevation gain. Sidesloping all the way to the col immediately east of the summit block is the shortest but most tedious. A good compromise is to aim for the intermediate high point ("IH" in the photo on page 441). A healthy side of scree bashing is on the menu regardless which entree you choose. At least the stellar views of massive Mount Saskatchewan are present to take your mind off the grind.

If you opted for the east end, once you get there simply follow the ridge west to the summit. Obstacles are minimal and easily circumvented, usually on the left side. For all routes the only challenge occurs near the summit, where the terrain steepens and a rock band appears. Either scramble directly up the band or go around it on the left side.

Enjoy the spectacular view of everything and then return the same way; or go northwest to Junior II (highly recommended); and/or head south to the North Towers of Mount Saskatchewan (also highly recommended).

Extension to Junior II

The nearby summit to the northwest is marginally higher and has a summit view that is different enough to warrant a quick visit. It's about 45 minutes round-trip, with 145 m of total elevation gain. The route is easy and obvious. Any obstacles can be circumvented on the left side.

This summit offers a more comprehensive vista of mighty Saskatchewan Glacier, with even mightier Mount Columbia at the end, a more "in-your-face" view of mounts Athabasca and Andromeda and a good look at the back side (north side) of The Lyells. The impressive glacier clinging to the northeast side of Junior I will also compete for attention. Return to Junior I when satiated, then decide whether you have enough time and energy to summit the North Towers of Mount Saskatchewan. If not, return the way you came.

154. "NORTH TOWERS OF MOUNT SASKATCHEWAN" 2970 m

(MAP 44, PAGE 471)
Rating moderate/difficult via the north ridge; the summit ridge is exposed
Round-trip time 11–14 hours
Elevation gain 1270 m
Maps 82 C/03 Columbia Icefield; Gem Trek Columbia Icefield

Although I somewhat regret giving this peak such a cumbersome name, I certainly don't have any misgivings about having made the long trek to the summit on two separate occasions. The view is about as good as anything you will ever experience and the journey there is fantastic. While just a hop, skip and a big jump from "Mount Saskatchewan Junior," completing the Tower makes for a long day. Bring lots of food, water and sunscreen. There are ways to avoid going up Saskatchewan Junior first, but those routes are more hassle than they're worth and you can inadvertently end up on the glacier even though the terrain looks to be only glacial moraine. Note that although the peak is comprised of multiple "Towers" it is only necessary to reach the highest one at the north end of the ridge. Try from mid-July on.

Follow the directions to Mount Saskatchewan Junior. The Tower and the route there are very obvious. Descend south to the Junior/Tower col and then ascend the north ridge of the first Tower. A black rock band is quickly reached and can be ascended via a steep but obvious weakness to the right. Continue up to the summit ridge, enjoying the ever-expanding view.

The 50 m summit ridge can be "a real bear," especially if snow-covered. Either scramble right along the ridgecrest or drop down a little to the right side and traverse below the ridge. Both routes will feel exposed. Thankfully the traverse is short and within minutes you will be standing on the small summit (GR912748), experiencing one of the premier views in the Canadian Rockies. Other than the stunning view of Mount Saskatchewan to the south, with the "other towers" in front, a number of impressive 11,000ers are beautifully visible. In case you are wondering about the very distinctive mountain immediately to the west, it has been very appropriately named "Mount Totally Awesome View" by Eric Coulthard.

Return the same way. Reascending Mount Saskatchewan Junior may not be particularly palatable at this point of an already long day, but it is still the easiest way to go. If you are intent on avoiding Junior, there is a shortcut down east-facing scree slopes as you approach Junior. If you are confident in your route-finding skills and prepared for descending and traversing steep scree and avoiding cliff bands and the glacier below, then go for it. It is also possible to sideslope Saskatchewan Junior and its east ridge in order to avoid unnecessary elevation gains, but this way can be tedious. Pick your poison! Regardless of your specific descent route, allow 4–6 hours from summit to car.

Above: Heading for the North Towers in early May. Note the avalanche debris at left and the fact that snowcover hides the exact location of the crevassed glacier. **S**: summit; **MS**: Mount Saskatchewan.
Below: From the summit, looking back along the ridge and the fantastic view to the north and northwest.

155. "BOUNDARY PEAK" 2870 m

(MAP 45, PAGE 471)
Rating easy via the northwest face
Round-trip time 4–6 hours
Elevation gain 880 m
Maps 82 C/03 Columbia Icefield; Gem Trek Columbia Icefield

No matter how many times you see it, the stunning view of Mount Athabasca from Highway 93 North leaves you mesmerized. An ascent of Boundary Peak is an opportunity to get up close and personal with the spectacular 11,000er. Most of the trip is steep hiking and there are plenty of trails to make the ascent easier. Try from mid-July and wait patiently for clear skies.

From Saskatchewan River Crossing, drive 52 km north on Highway 93 North to the Columbia Icefield. As you approach the Icefield Discovery Centre, turn left at the sign for Athabasca Glacier and then left again at the sign for Forefield Trail. Park here. Do not drive the road with the barricade across it, even if the barricade arm is up. Boundary Peak and much of the ascent route is clearly visible from the parking area (see photo opposite).

Hike alongside, but not on, the road (it would really ruin your day to get hit by one of the Snowcoach buses while tourists on the bus capture your messy demise on their iPhones!). There is also a trail that leaves the parking area, bypassing some of the roadside hiking. Hike almost all the way to the Snowcoach terminal and find the Boundary Peak trail (unsigned) by a small stump of wood.

Hike the trail, going east-southeast towards the objective. Higher up, a distinctive peak appears in front of you and to the right. Follow the trail to its base. From here you can ascend the peak or stay in the valley and go around it. Staying in the valley takes you to a scree trail that goes up to the col between the north and south (true) summits. Going up the distinctive peak takes you

more directly to the true summit. Take your pick. The distinctive peak route does expose you earlier to the awesome views of Mount Athabasca. Personally, I recommend going up this route and down the other.

For both routes, once you get to the ridge, turn right and scramble easily up to the summit, at GR867832. The summer view of Mount Athabasca reveals all the incredible details and intricacies of its formidable glacier that are usually covered up by a thick layer of snow in winter. Of course, there are other terrific sights to see, including many other 11,000ers; the Columbia Icefield; Mount Wilcox, Tangle Ridge, Sunwapta Peak and Nigel Peak (four great Kane scrambles); and pointy Hilda Peak immediately to the southeast.

Either return the way you came or continue north along the ridge and then go down via the trail from the col between the two summits. Going farther north up to the north summit and down the north ridge grants interesting views of Hilda Peak and the glacier on the northeast side of Athabasca. There is tons of room to explore here and routes back to the trail are numerous and obvious.

Above: Dinah Kruze returns from an ascent of the mountain. Much of the route is visible from the parking lot. **C**: col between the north and true summits and the route to get there; **D**: more direct route to the ridge; **S**: summit; **P**: distinctive peak; **R**: Snowcoach road; **A**: Mount Athabasca; **SI**: the well-known and popular Silverhorn route for climbing Athabasca. Photo: Bob Spirko
Below: Not a bad view for a couple hours of good exercise!

MAPS

Map 1

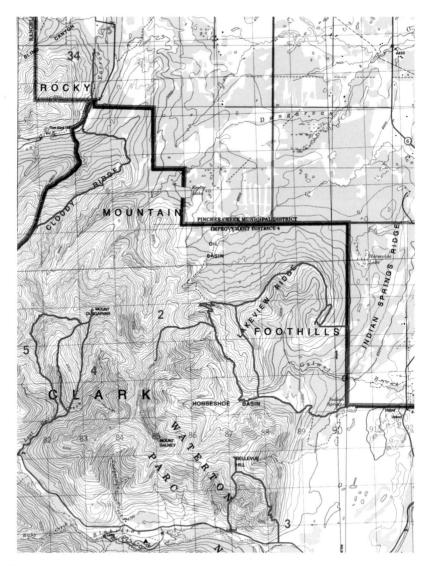

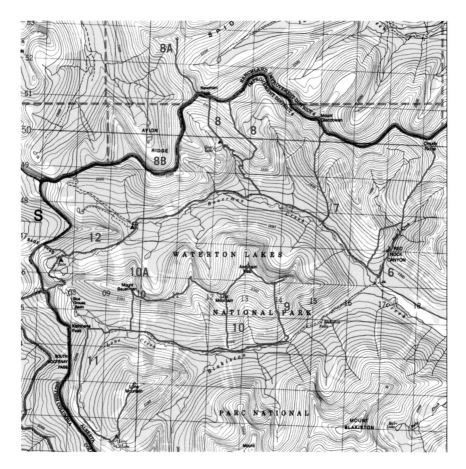

Map 2

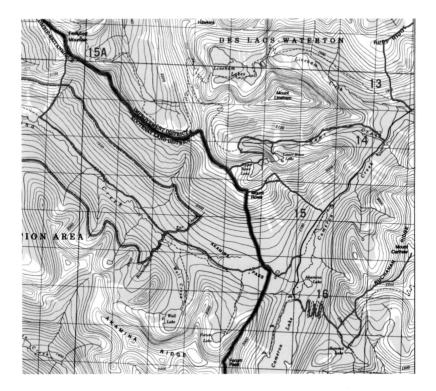

Map 3

Map 4

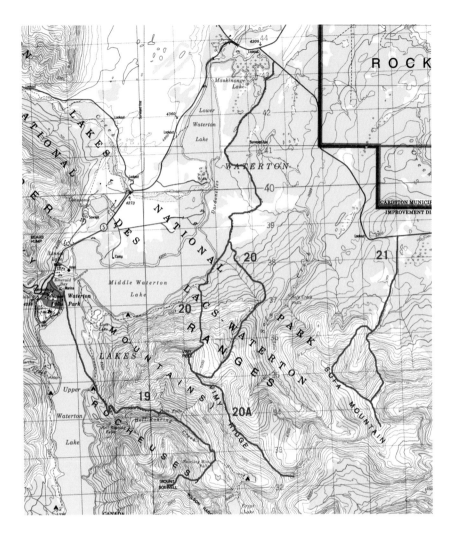

Map 5

Map 6

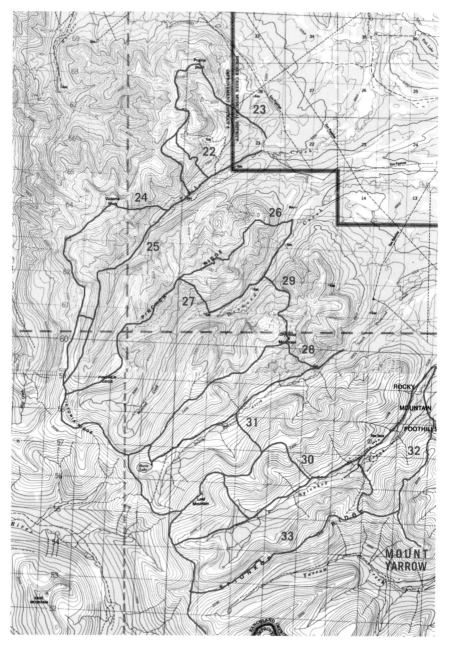

Map 7

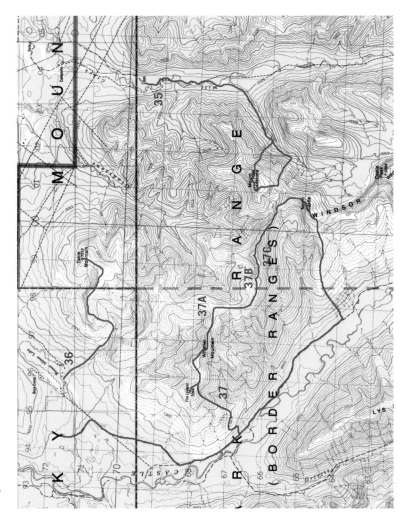

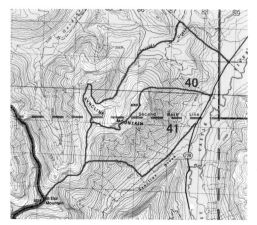

Map 9

Map 11

Map 8

Map 12

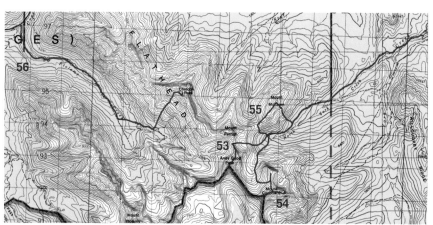

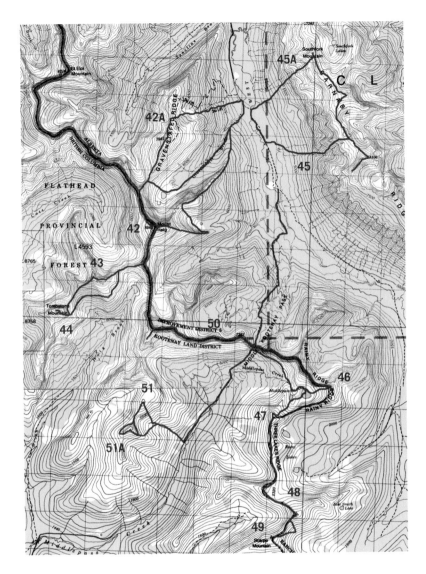

Map 10

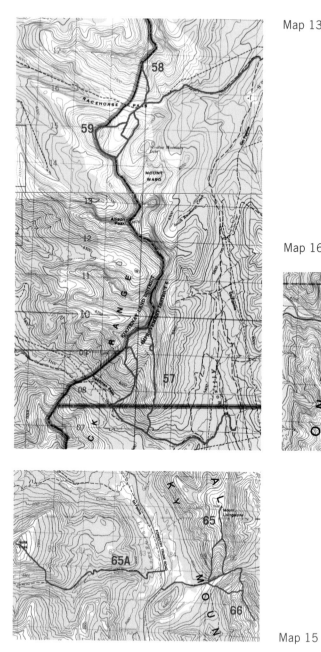

Map 13

Map 16

Map 15

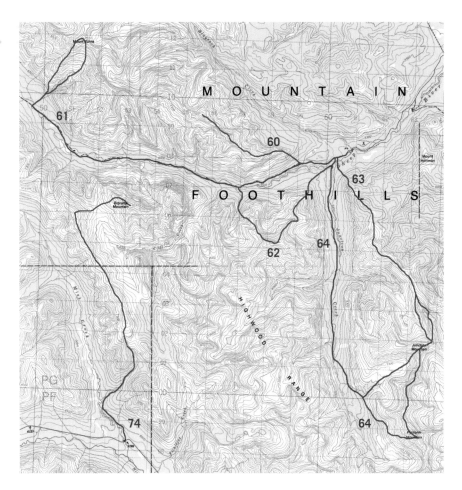

Map 14

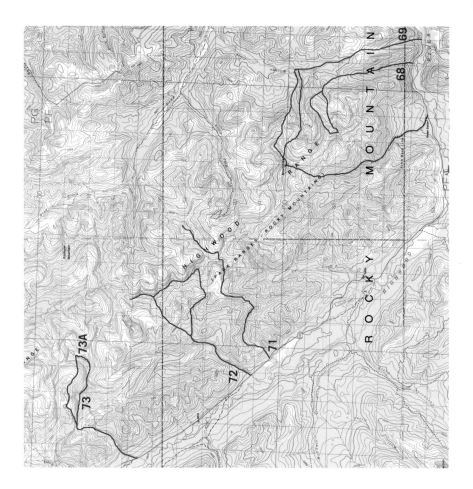

Map 17

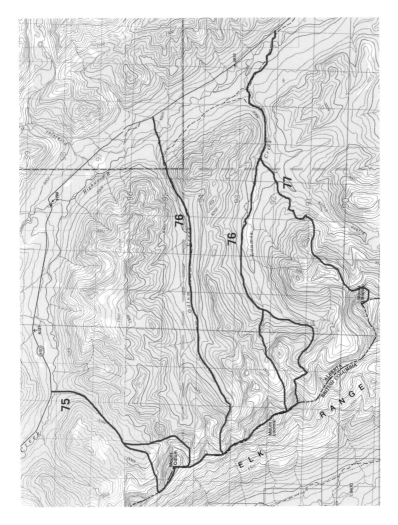

Map 18

Map 19

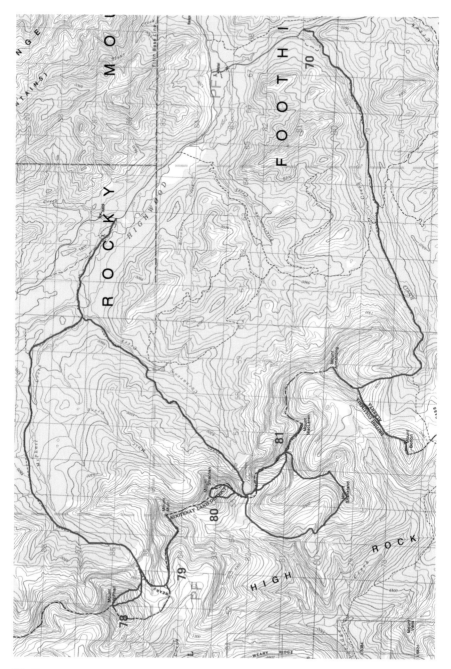

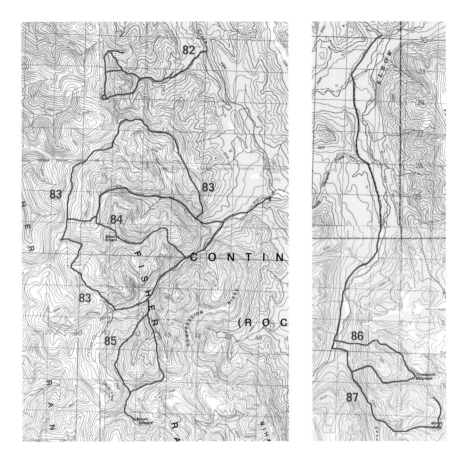

Map 20

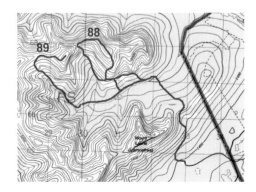

Map 21

Map 22

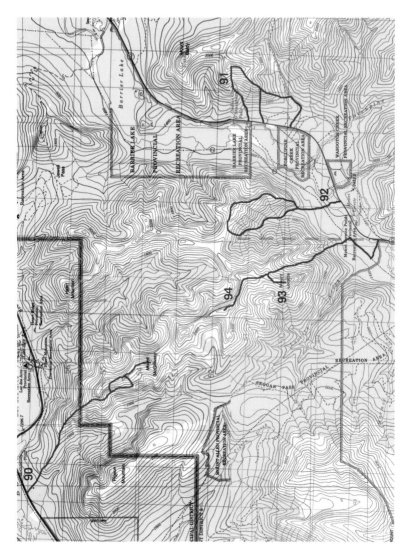

Map 23

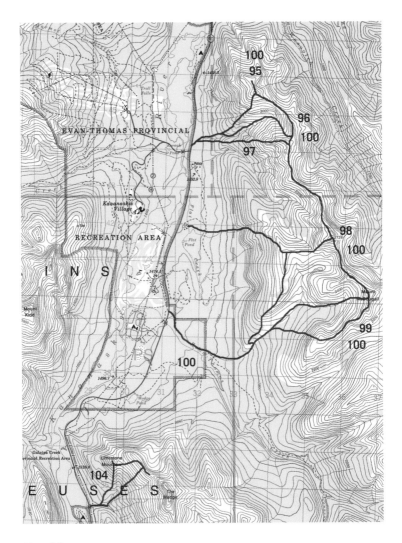

Map 24

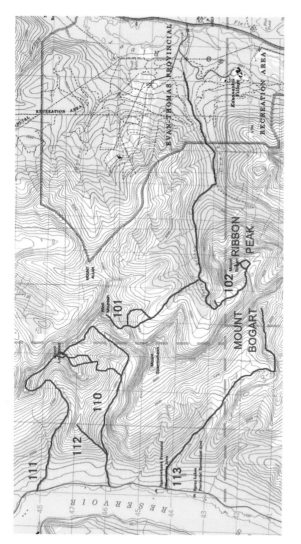

Map 25

Map 26

Map 26

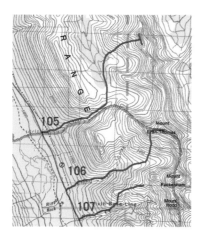

Map 27

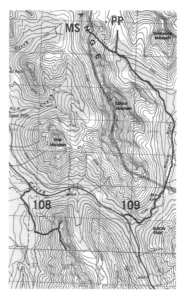

Map 28

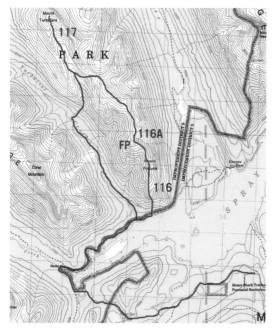

Map 29

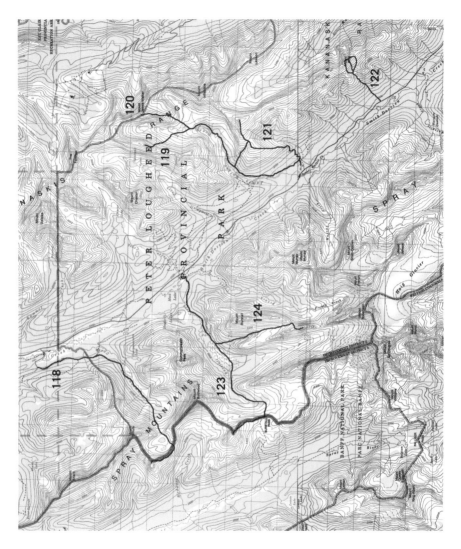

Map 30

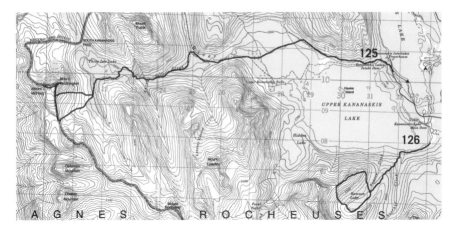

Map 31

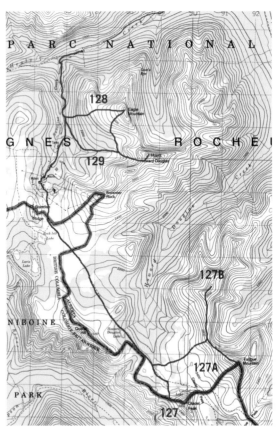

Map 32

Map 35

Map 36

Map 34

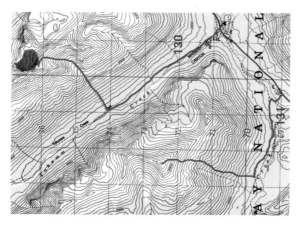

Map 33

Map 37

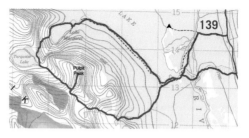

Map 38

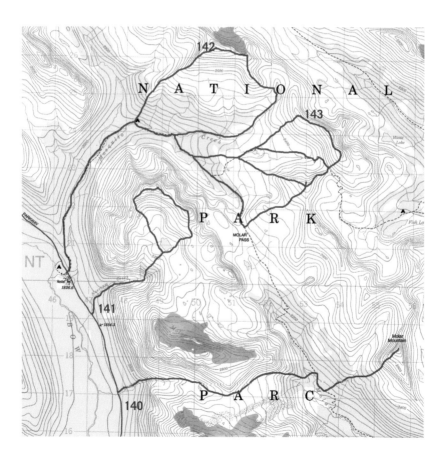

Map 39

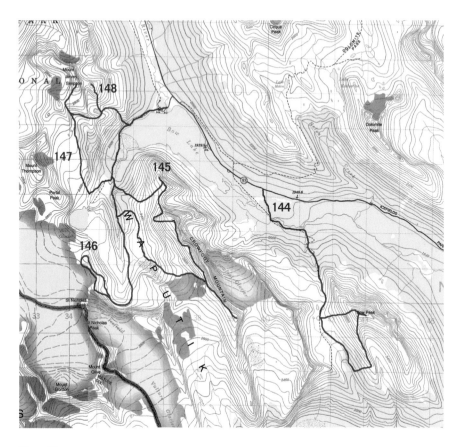

Map 40

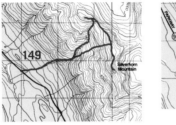

Map 41

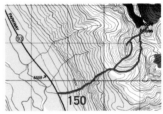

Map 42

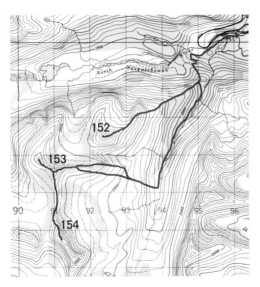

Map 44

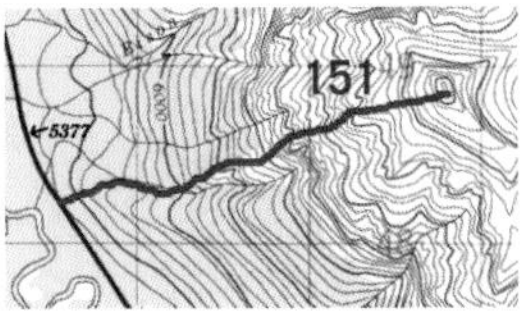

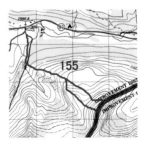

Map 43

Map 45

APPENDIXES

Picking a good objective for the day can present a challenge. On a clear and calm summer day pretty much anything is feasible. On such days perhaps a multi-peak trip is in order. When the hours of daylight are limited or snow and ice cover the mountains, however, you have to be a little more careful in your choice. Following are some suggestions for multi-peak days, good-weather days, short days, early/late season trips and larch-season trips. See also the section grouping peaks by degree of difficulty.

A. MULTI-PEAK DAY TRIPS

To get the most out of your hiking/scrambling day, the following are suggestions for combining trips in order to summit more than one mountain in a single trip. The list includes levels of difficulty, approximate round-trip times and total elevation gains. Note that the difficulty rating refers only to the scrambling; the sheer length of these trips makes them difficult in other ways as well, and they should only be undertaken by fit and competent parties. Four outstanding ridgewalks not outlined below are more thoroughly described in Ultimate High-Level Ridgewalks on page 127. Also, combinations for the Crowsnest area are described on page 177.

MULTI-PEAK COMBINATIONS			
Peaks	Rating	Duration	Gain
"Dundy," Dungarvan	difficult	9–11 hours	1400 m
Anderson, Lost, Bauerman	moderate to difficult	8–12 hours	1550 m
Newman Peak, Avion Ridge	easy	7–10 hours	1200 m
Newman Peak, Spionkop Ridge, Avion Ridge	easy	9–11 hours	1600 m
Rowe, Festubert	moderate	8.5–11 hours	1225 m
Vimy Peak, Vimy Ridge	easy to difficult	13–16 hours	1600 m
Victoria Peak, Victoria Ridge	moderate	10–14 hours	1400 m
Pincher Ridge (centre and south), Victoria Ridge	moderate	9–12 hours	1600 m
Whistler, "Frankie," "Larry," North Castle	moderate to difficult	9–12 hours	1350 m
Barnaby, Southfork	moderate	6–8 hours	1300 m
Haig, Gravenstafel	moderate	8–11 hours	1400 m
Haig, "Boot Hill," Tombstone	moderate	12–15 hours	2400 m
Three Lakes Ridge, Rainy Ridge	difficult	9–11 hours	1400 m
Three Lakes Ridge, "Jake Smith Peak," Scarpe	difficult	11–14 hours	2300 m
"Racehorse Peak," "Mount Racehorse"	moderate	7–10 hours	1450 m
Junction, Pyriform	moderate to difficult	12–14 hours	1500 m
McPhail, Muir	easy	11–14 hours	1800 m
Armstrong, Bolton	moderate	12–16 hours	1600 m

MULTI-PEAK COMBINATIONS			
Loomis, Odlum	moderate	13–16 hours	1400 m
MacLaren, Shankland	moderate	13–16 hours	1750 m
MacLaren, Strachan	easy	12–15 hours	1850 m
Lorette, "Skogan Peak"	moderate	9–12 hours	1400 m
McDougall, Old Baldy Mountain	difficult	11–14 hours	1500 m
"Wasootch Peak," "Kananaskis Peak"	difficult	8–10 hours	1200 m
"Wasootch Peak," "Kananaskis Peak," "Old Baldy Mountain," McDougall	difficult	11–14 hours	1700 m
GR338442, "Kananaskis Peak"	moderate	6–8 hours	900 m
"Mount Lillian," "Buller Creek Peak"	moderate to difficult	8–10 hours	1300 m
Fortune, "Fortulent," Turbulent	easy	11–14 hours	1800 m
Citadel, Fatigue, "Little Fatigue"	moderate	10–12 hours	1400 m
Eagle, Howard Douglas	moderate	7.5–10 hours	1700 m
Livingstone, Coffin	easy or difficult	6–8 hours	1300 m
Jimmy Simpson, "Jimmy Junior"	easy	8–11 hours	1500 m

B. GOOD-WEATHER DAYS

Of course, if the weather is good you have the pick of the litter, though you may want to go for the more scenic, challenging, long and visually rewarding trips. These are some of Mark's and my personal favourites that can definitely be more fully appreciated under clear skies. Given the amazing variety of colours in Waterton and the Castle, we have become partial to those areas when the weather is favourable. In this edition, trips along Highway 93 North have also joined those ranks.

- Mount Dungarvan
- Mount Glendowan
- Victoria Peak and Victoria Ridge
- Loaf Mountain (south side)
- Spionkop Traverse
- Drywood Mountain
- "Jake Smith Peak"
- Mount Strachan
- Mount McPhail
- "Skogan Peak"
- "Mount Lillian"
- Molar Mountain
- "Noseeum Peak"
- Mosquito Mountain

- "Molarstone Mountain"
- Bow Peak
- 'The Onion'
- Mount Jimmy Simpson
- "Jimmy Junior"
- Mount Noyes
- Yoho Peak
- "Big Bend Peak"
- "Mount Saskatchewan Junior"
- "The North Towers of Mount Saskatchewan"

C. SHORT DAYS

Given good conditions, these trips can generally be completed in under six hours round-trip. Bad weather and snow or ice could increase the time required.

- Bellevue Hill
- Ruby Ridge
- Mount Rowe
- "Carthew Minor"
- Prairie Bluff south ridge
- Table Mountain
- Hillcrest Mountain
- Thunder Mountain
- Mount Livingstone

- Coffin Mountain
- Mount Baldy west peak via west ridge
- Limestone Mountain
- "Wasootch Peak" north and south
- Mount Lorette
- "Packenham Junior"
- "Mount Roberta"
- "Rawson Lake Ridge"
- "Little Lougheed"
- Mount Kent
- "Little Temple"
- "Devil's Thumb"
- "Boundary Peak"

D. EARLY/LATE-SEASON TRIPS

These peaks may come into season earlier than most and/or may be possible very late in the season when others are snowbound. In fact, several days of warm chinook weather can make some of them feasible during any month of the year, provided their access roads are open. Of course, there are other contributing factors to consider: high water in rivers and streams, as well as unseen snow, ice and verglas higher on the peak.

- Lakeview Ridge
- Prairie Bluff (south ridge)
- Table Mountain
- Hillcrest Mountain
- Mount Howard
- Threepoint Mountain
- Mount Rose
- Holy Cross
- "Tiara Peak"
- Wendell Mountain
- Wendell Mountain east peak
- West Ridge of Mount Baldy
- "Mary Barclay Mountain"
- Mount Lorette
- Limestone Mountain
- "Wasootch Peak" north and south
- GR338442
- Old Baldy Mountain
- "Packenham Junior"
- "Mount Roberta" (late season only)
- "Little Lougheed"
- "Seven Peaks"
- Mount Bryant

E. LARCH-SEASON TRIPS

The last two weeks of September and the first week of October could possibly be the best times of the year to make trips to the Rockies. During that period, the needles on larch trees turn a vibrant yellow, often resulting in some of the most strikingly beautiful scenery and colours you will ever see in the mountains. With their already interesting and unique rock colours, areas of the southern Canadian Rockies can provide surreal vistas. Bluebird days are obviously preferred, yet one of my most memorable "larch" experiences occurred on a less than perfect October day on the centre peak of Pincher Ridge (see page 103). If you love these trees, try the following trips during larch season:

- Avion Ridge
- Mount Rowe via the Rowe Lakes
- Victoria Peak and Ridge
- Pincher Ridge (centre and south peaks primarily)
- Mount Roche (Spread Eagle Mountain)
- Lys Ridge
- Rainy Ridge (Middlepass Lakes)
- "Smutwood Peak"
- Wasatch Mountain
- "Devil's Thumb"

OTHER USEFUL GUIDEBOOKS

Daffern, Gillean. *Gillean Daffern's Kananaskis Country Trail Guide*. 4th ed., 5 vols. Calgary: RMB, 2010–2015.

Gadd, Ben. *Geology Road Tours*. Jasper, Alta.: Corax Press, 2008.

———. *Handbook of the Canadian Rockies*. Jasper, Alta.: Corax Press, 1995.

Jones, David P. *Rockies Central*. Vol. 2 (but first to be released) of projected 4-volume series *A Climber's Guide to the Rocky Mountains of Canada*. Squamish, BC: High Col, 2015.

Kane, Alan. *Scrambles in the Canadian Rockies*. 3rd ed. Calgary: RMB, 2016.

Kershaw, Robert. *Exploring the Castle*. Calgary: RMB, 2008.

Patton, Brian, and Bart Robinson. *Canadian Rockies Trail Guide*. Banff: Summerthought, 2011.

Potter, Mike. *Ridgewalks in the Canadian Rockies*. 2nd ed. Turner Valley, Alta.: Luminous Compositions, 2001.

INDEX OF PEAKS BY DEGREE OF DIFFICULTY

Note that some peaks appear in more than one list because of route variations that have different levels of difficulty.

Easy

Avion Ridge
Bauerman, Mount
Bellevue Hill
"Big Bend Peak"
"Boot Hill" (via Mt. Haig)
"Boundary Peak"
Bow Peak
Bryant, Mount
"Buller Creek Peak"
"Carthew Minor"
Citadel Peak
Coffin Mountain (via northwest ridge)
Coulthard, Mount (via northwest slopes)
Crowfoot Mountain (north peak)
"Deadman Peak"
"Devil's Thumb" (via south side)
Eagle Mountain
Fatigue Mountain
Festubert Mountain
"Fortulent Peak"
Fortune, Mount
"Frankie Peak"
GR338442
Gravenstafel Ridge
Hillcrest Mountain
Holy Cross Mountain (via east face)
Howard, Mount
Howard Douglas, Mount
Isola Peak
"Jake Smith Peak"
Jimmy Simpson, Mount
Kent Ridge (north summit)
Lakeview Ridge
"Little Temple"
Livingstone Mountain
Loaf Mountain (north side)
Loaf Mountain (south side)
Lone Mountain
Lost Mountain
Lougheed, Mount (direct)
MacLaren, Mount
McLaren, Mount (via southwest ridge)
McPhail, Mount (via southeast ridge)
"Middle Kootenay Mountain" (to false summit)

"Molarstone Mountain"
Mosquito Mountain
Muir, Mount
Old Baldy Mountain
Onion, The
"Packenham Junior"
Pincher Ridge centre and south
Prairie Bluff (south ridge)
"Racehorse, Mount" (via northeast face)
"Racehorse Peak"
"Rawson Lake Ridge"
"Roberta Peak"
"Rogan Peak"
Rose, Mount
Ruby Ridge
"Saskatchewan Junior I, Mount"
Seven Peaks
"Smutwood Peak"
Snow Peak
Spionkop Ridge
Spionkop Ridge traverse
Southfork Mountain
St. Eloi Mountain
Strachan, Mount
Syncline Mountain (first summit)
Table Mountain
Threepoint Mountain
Thunder Mountain
"Tiara Peak"
Turbulent, Mount
Victoria Ridge
Vimy Ridge
"Wasootch Peak"
Wendell Mountain East Peak (via south ridge)
Whistler Mountain
Yoho Peak

Moderate

Anderson Peak
Andy Good Peak
Armstrong, Mount
Barnaby Ridge
Bellevue Hill
Bishop, Mount
Bogart, Mount (via west ridge)
"Boot Hill"
Boswell, Mount
"Buffalo (Bison) Peak"
Burns, Mount (via southwest face)

Burns, Mount (east peak at GR555096)
Castle, North
"Carthew Minor"
"Chimper Peak"
Cloudy Ridge
"Cloudy Ridge Junior"
Crowfoot Mountain
"Deadman Peak"
Denny, Mount
Drywood Mountain (north side)
Drywood Mountain (south side)
"Dundy Peak"
Emerald Peak
"Frankie Peak"
Gibraltar Mountain
Gladstone, Mount
Glendowan, Mount
GR338442
Haig, Mount
Head, Mount (via southeast slopes)
"Headwall Peak" (via southeast face)
Holy Cross Mountain (via northeast ridge)
Howard Douglas, Mount
"Jake Smith Peak"
James Walker, Mount
"Jimmy Junior"
Junction Mountain
Kent, Mount
Kishinena Peak
"Krowicki Peak"/"Mount Miles"
Lakeview Ridge
"Larry Mountain"
"Lillian, Mount" (via Buller Pass)
"Lillian, Mount" (via Upper Galatea Lake)
Limestone Mountain
"Lineham Creek Peaks" (via northwest ridge to GR618951)
Lineham Ridge and GR593982
"Little Fatigue"
"Little Lougheed"
Loomis, Mount (from north)
Lorette, Mount
Lougheed, Mount (direct)
Lys Ridge (north ridge)
Lys Ridge (Ruby Lake)
"Mary Barclay's Mountain"
McDougall, Mount
McPhail, Mount (via south slopes)
"Middle Kootenay Mountain" (to true summit)
"Miles, Mount"/"Krowicki Peak"
Molar Mountain

"Molarstone Mountain"
Mosquito Mountain (via southwest slopes and for extension)
Newman Peak
"North Towers of Mount Saskatchewan"
"Noseeum Peak" (via southwest ridge)
Noyes, Mount
"Ochre Spring Peak"
Odlum, Mount
Old Baldy Mountain
Patterson's Peak
Pincher Ridge centre and south
Prairie Bluff (south face)
Pulpit Peak (via south slopes)
Pyriform Mountain
"Racehorse, Mount" (loop route)
"Racehorse Peak"
Rainy Ridge
Richards, Mount (north face)
Roche, Mount
Rowe, Mount
"Saskatchewan, Mount, North Towers"
Schlee, Mount
Shunga-la-she
Silverhorn Mountain
"Skogan Peak"
Sofa Mountain
Spionkop Ridge traverse
Syncline Mountain (second summit)
Threepoint Mountain
Three Lakes Ridge
Tombstone Mountain (from "Boot Hill")
"Top Hat"
Victoria Peak
Vimy Peak/Ridge
Wasatch Mountain
Wendell Mountain
Wind Mountain
Worthington, Mount

Difficult
Anderson Peak
Andy Good Peak
Baldy, Mount (west peak via west ridge)
Big Traverse, The ("Wasootch Peak" to Mount McDougall)
Bogart, Mount (via west ridge)
Bryant, Mount
"Buffalo (Bison) Peak"
Burns, Mount (via southwest face)
Burns, Mount (via east ridge at GR555096)

Chinook Peak
"Cloudy Ridge Junior"
Coffin Mountain (via north face)
Coulthard, Mount (via west ridge)
"Deadman Peak"
"Devil's Thumb" (via east ridge)
"Dundy Peak"
Dungarvan, Mount
Emerald Peak
Evan-Thomas, Mount
Head, Mount (via east ridge)
"Headwall Peak" (summit ridge)
"Jake Smith Peak"
"Kananaskis Peak"
"Krowicki Peak"
"Larry Mountain"
"Lillian, Mount" (via Buller Pass)
"Lillian, Mount" (via Upper Galatea Lake)
"Lineham Creek Peaks" (to GR628936)
Loomis, Mount (from south)
Lougheed, Mount (traverse)
McDougall, Mount
McGillivray, Mount

McLaren, Mount (via east face)
"Molarstone Mountain" (extension)
Mosquito Mountain (via southwest slopes and for extension)
"North Towers of Mount Saskatchewan"
"Noseeum Peak" (via southeast ridge)
Ogden, Mount
"Piggy Plus"
Pincher Ridge
Pulpit Peak (via lakes and west slopes)
"Rawson Lake Ridge" (to summit)
Ribbon Peak
Richards, Mount (north ridge)
Roche, Mount
"Saskatchewan, Mount, North Towers"
Scarpe Mountain
Seven Peaks
Shunga-la-she
Syncline Mountain (third summit)
"Tiara Peak"
Three Lakes Ridge
Wendell Mountain East Peak (via col, west ridge)

USEFUL CONTACTS

Park administrative offices
Kananaskis Country Office, Canmore
403-678-5508

Information centres
Waterton (mid-May to mid-October)
403-859-5133
Elbow Valley   403-949-4261
Bow Valley Provincial Park   403-673-3663
Kananaskis Village   403-591-7555
Barrier Lake Information Centre 403-673-3985
Kananaskis Lakes Visitor Centre 403-591-6322
Banff/Lake Louise Tourism   403-762-8421
Yoho National Park   250-343-6783

In an emergency
In an emergency, contact the Royal Canadian Mounted Police (RCMP) or the nearest ranger or warden office.

RCMP detachments
Crowsnest   403-562-2866
Waterton (May–October)   403-859-2244
Waterton (November–April)   403-627-4424
Kananaskis   403-591-7707
Canmore   403-678-5516
Banff   403-762-2228

Park ranger or warden emergency numbers
Waterton   403-859-2636
Kananaskis Country   403-591-7767

INDEX OF ALL PEAKS

The author enjoying a break while traversing from Victoria Peak to Victoria Ridge.

ABOUT THE AUTHOR

Andrew Nugara was born in Rugby, England, and moved to Canada in 1979. With his brother Mark, Andrew started to hike and scramble up mountains in 2001. Shortly after, the Nugara brothers began to pursue other forms of mountain recreation such as alpine climbing, technical climbing, ice climbing and snowshoeing. Scrambling, however, has remained the primary focus for the brothers. Since 2001 Andrew has completed over 750 mountain ascents.

Andrew earned degrees in classical guitar performance and education from the University of Calgary. He lives in Calgary, Alberta, and teaches high school physics and music.